Derivatives and the Transformation of Capitalism

This book discusses the astonishing rise of so-called *derivatives*, economic instruments related to different types of risks, and the changes this has imposed to the functioning of advanced capitalist economies.

The market for *derivatives* has grown exponentially since the 1980s, dwarfing today's traditional financial markets. The conventional view claims that *derivatives* perform a crucial function in corporate risk management, providing a hedge against undesirable movements in prices. Yet, most transactions considered to be part of *derivatives* are inherently speculative and significantly increase the levels of risks and occurrence of crises in an economy: for example, instruments known as CDS (credit default swaps) played an important role in the 2007–2008 subprime debacle. Thus, it is necessary to understand the role of these transactions in present-day advanced capitalist economies. Do they add more instability to the economy, including speculative and non-speculative activities, enhancing macroeconomic crises and contributing to destroying income, production, jobs and wealth? Do they provide effective hedging against measurable risks to the operation of capitalist firms, thus allowing corporations to engage in more transactions and expand capital accumulation domestically and internationally, in an environment characterised by increased volatility and uncertainty caused by *derivatives* themselves?

The book addresses these questions and many others, going beyond an emphasis on operational and technical aspects of contracts, and providing a historical, analytical and critical interpretation of the qualitative and quantitative workings of so-called *derivatives* markets and their role in the financial dynamics of modern advanced capitalist economies.

This book is vital reading for those interested in financial markets, risk management, financial history, speculation and instability, regulation and alternative economic theories.

Marcelo Milan holds B.A. and M.A. in economics, both from the University of Sao Paulo, Brazil. He obtained his Ph.D. in economics from the University of Massachusetts Amherst. He taught economics at the Universities of Rhode Island (South Kingston), Wisconsin (Parkside) and in the Department of Economics and International Relations at the Federal University of Rio Grande do Sul, Brazil, where he is an associate professor. He is currently a visiting scholar at the Federal University of ABC, Brazil. His research interests include macroeconomics, money, finance, radical political economics, international political economy, the Brazilian economy, and the cultural and creative economy.

Routledge Frontiers of Political Economy

Public Economics and Democracy
The Moral Foundations of Economic Governance
Shahzavar Karimzadi

Keynes and Macroeconomics
An Alternative Theory of Employment, Finance and Sustainability
Arne Heise

Corruption and the Sustainable Development Goals
Edited by Robert Gillanders and Chandan Kumar Jha

Bank Profitability and Interest Rates
An Endogenous Money Theory Perspective
Riccardo Zolea

Heterodox Economics and Social Policy
Reassessing Equality of Opportunity and Equality of Place
Edited by Camilo Andrés Guevara Castañeda

Welfare States After the Eurozone Crisis
An Evolutionary Economics Perspective
Cristina Soeiro Matos

Reimagining the Welfare State
Celia Lessa Kerstenetzky

***Derivatives* and the Transformation of Capitalism**
Marcelo Milan

For more information about this series, please visit: www.routledge.com/Routledge-Frontiers-of-Political-Economy/book-series/SE0345

Derivatives and the Transformation of Capitalism

Marcelo Milan

Routledge
Taylor & Francis Group
LONDON AND NEW YORK

First published 2026
by Routledge
4 Park Square, Milton Park, Abingdon, Oxon OX14 4RN

and by Routledge
605 Third Avenue, New York, NY 10158

Routledge is an imprint of the Taylor & Francis Group, an informa business

British Library Cataloguing-in-Publication Data
A catalogue record for this book is available from the British Library

ISBN: 978-0-367-68352-8 (hbk)
ISBN: 978-0-367-68353-5 (pbk)
ISBN: 978-1-003-13709-2 (ebk)

DOI: 10.4324/9781003137092

Typeset in Times New Roman
by Newgen Publishing UK

Contents

Figures

Tables

Acknowledgements

I would like to thank, first and foremost, the hard work of Andy Humphrey, Senior Editor for Economics at Routledge. He was very, very patient since we first met at the Eastern Economic Association gathering at the Washington Marriott Wardman Park in Washington, D.C., in early 2016 and started discussing the publication of this book. Andy never gave up on this project, even when I was very slow in responding to his kind reminders and encouragements. Yarisa Wahlang Kharbuli was equally and incredibly understanding and professional. Samuvel Sampath and the team at Newgen KnowledgeWorks provided a superb and diligent support. Many health issues involving me and my family, enlarged by the blissful arrival of my son Bernardo in 2019, along the way, prevented the delivery of the typed document on the original agreed date. Not to mention my continuous services in the university bureaucracy. To elongate the delay, during the finalisation of the manuscript phase, my city of Porto Alegre, was hit by the global climate crisis with a huge flood. Finally, I started a visiting position at the Federal University of ABC, in São Bernardo do Campo, state of São Paulo, after all that.

This book is a significantly changed offspring of my PhD dissertation in economics, defended 18 years ago at the University of Massachusetts Amherst. Despite the time distance, it is still a product of that period and of the then existing rich intellectual environment in the Pioneer Valley. It could not exist if the dissertation had not been written and defended. And she could not be defended without all the people hereby acknowledged. I hence would like to express my gratitude for the role of Bob Pollin as my PhD advisor, without implying him for any mistakes in the dissertation or in this book. His classes, ECON 711 – Money, Credit, and Financial Markets, and ECON 753 – Applied Econometrics, were inspiring sources for the dissertation, but only the former is reflected in this book. I was not a completely mature researcher at that time, but, during the summer of 2008, Bob and I had a very pleasant meeting at his vacation house in Rhode Island. It was possible to overcome most of the weaknesses of the research and to define the necessary strategy and effort for completing the manuscript. Bob and his sweetheart Sigried Pollin were always very courteous and gentle, making the life of a Brazilian student in the United States a lot easier.

Many other faculty members also were instrumental in moving me along the graduate program. The late Jim Crotty was specially inspiring. Being his teaching assistant for an undergraduate Macroeconomics class taught me important lessons, not necessarily, or not only, academic ones. His seminar on Financialisation in the fall of 2005 allowed me to think about *derivatives*. James Heintz was on my prospectus defence committee and was extremely helpful in providing a rigorous reading and discussions. Randall Dodd gave me important specific insights about *derivatives*. Michael Ash co-taught ECON 753 with Bob and gave me the tools for the quantitative part of the dissertation, not included in this work.

My cohort was probably one of the last to enjoy the vintage Radical Political Economics at Umass, learning in the classic Thompson Hall, before the department moved to Gordon Hall and then to Crotty Hall in Amherst. Having access to the wisdom of David Kotz, Carol Heim, Jerry Friedman, Peter Skott, Nancy Folbre, Jerry Epstein, Arslan Razmi, Samuel Bowles, Rick Wolff and Steve Resnick shaped the dissertation and this book in many different ways. Beyond the intellectual climate, other faculty and university employees provided all different types of support, like Carmen Deere and Rosa Ramos at Center for Latin American, Caribbean, and Latino Studies (CLACLS).

The student collectivity was something special and singular. It is impossible not to remember Merrilee Mardon and Chris Russell, who sheltered me and my wife in his own apartment in Easthampton during our first month in the Pioneer Valley. Bob Reinauer, Kristen Maeve, Ryan Isakson and 'Little' Katie are all examples of the best human beings America has gifted the world. The Economics Graduate Students Organization (EGSO) played an important role in providing engagement but also means to sustain a less arduous economic life in wealthy Massachusetts. My postgraduate colleagues at Umass Amherst contributed to format my thinking beyond what they might guess. Armagan Gezici took detailed notes during the qualification exam, understanding my nervousness. And next the complete team, with possibly some names gone missing: James Baird, Smita, Soon, Sungha, Jackie, Celeste, Fabian, Nuria, Luis, Marina, Martin, Hasan Comert, Hasan Tekguc, Sam Schenck, Amit, Evelyn, Bengi, Gul, Özgür, Arjun, Vamsi. Michael Carr, Ningyu Li, Cruz Bueno, Josh Mason, Alejandro 'the best New England speech' Reuss, Lynda, Matthew Riddle, Wei Zhang, Anna, Joe Rebello, Ellen, Nina, Harry Charalampos, Rajesh, Helen, Adam Hersh, Sue, Iren, Zhun Xu, Jared Ragusett and Elizabeth Ramey. Special thanks to Zeke Nims, my 'angel' for transportation issues. My good friends Wesley Pech and Andressa Pech made life more interesting in Western Massachusetts. Wesley and I wrote and published our first academic paper together, enticed by the postgraduate Macroeconomics class of Jim Crotty. In Brazil, my colleagues and students at the Federal Universities of Rio Grande do Sul and of ABC have animated my spirits to finish the book. My brother Marcelo de Carvalho has been a reliable support.

And finally, but not least, my wife Glaucie, who suffered with me the home-sickness and the hardship during that time, despite our families' gratefully acknowledged help during the summers, not to mention the challenges faced during our period at Wisconsin. She has provided a strong and enduring support (and being very patient).

General Introduction

This book is about the astonishing rise of contemporary financial instruments known as *derivatives*, here understood as a result of profound transformations in present-day capitalism, mainly the strengthening of financialisation (Steinherr, 2000; Mader et al., 2020). The so-called *derivatives*, a concept that includes forwards, futures, options, swaps and their combinations, have been a remarkable feature of financialised capitalism; a phase of this mode of production that has the valorisation and accumulation of finance capital as its driving force. They have acquired an enormous importance in terms of turnover and values transacted, dwarfing traditional financial markets by a wide margin. Up to the early 1970s, some of these tools were associated with various traditional types of risks that are an integral part of a typical capitalist economy, a monetary economy whose goal is to accumulate more money by means of production and circulation of commodities, whose prices, costs, financial conditions and location can change in unpredictable ways. But these old risks were magnified and new ones have been created by neo-liberalism and financialisation since the mid-1970s and 1980s, including risks generated by the development and use of the instruments themselves.

Only after this new socioeconomic and historical configuration started out, about four decades ago, a full spectrum of arrangements apparently geared to financial and economic risks management became available, mainly with the fast growth of a specific kind of contracts: swaps. They grew rapidly, encroaching also on millenary operations such as credit. Swaps particularly fit into financial transactions with net transfers of money as the outcome of the arrangement, although all types of *derivatives* have gradually introduced cash settlement as a central feature (Taylor, 2010). It would not make sense, except in orthodox economics models, characterised by barter, to swap corn, the favourite commodity in the *derivatives* textbook examples, for lumber, if they were actually delivered rather than replaced by cash settlements. Only macro-financial variables like interest and exchange rates, whose volatility has increased under neo-liberalism and financialisation, have quality gradients attached to capitalist inner trends that justify exchanging or swapping flows of money associated with particular circuits of valorisation and accumulation. Yet, this connection with risk management is only an appearance, since speculative or risk-taking behaviour epitomises the world of *derivatives*.

DOI: 10.4324/9781003137092-1

Considering the gigantic size of *derivatives* markets, as reported by the Bank for International Settlements (BIS, 2023 and 2024) – the notional value of outstanding over-the-counter (OTC) *derivatives* reached $715 trillion by the end of June 2023 and the exchange-traded open interest for the third quarter of 2024 reached more than $102 trillion, against the U.S. GDP of $29.2 trillion – if the risk management perception were correct, one would expect enormous amounts of income and wealth at risk, faced mainly by capitalist organisations, banks in particular. Thus, un-hedged transactions might be exposing massive amounts of stocks and flows to risks of monetary devaluation and losses. Thus, *derivatives* and the hedging they supposedly allow could avoid such problems. Yet, hedge might fail, as it is not fully effective due to so-called basis risk and may still not be, ex post, necessary for some organisations, as potentially negative developments do not materialise. And since the proportions between the value of *derivatives* contracts and the volume of transactions on the one hand and exposures to risks on the other do not match by a large amount, they have been compared instead to weapons of mass destruction and other blasting metaphors. The American International Group's (AIG) collapse caused by credit default swaps (CDS) during the 2007–2008 subprime crisis is a valid illustration (McDonald and Paulson, 2015).

This analogy highlights the other dimension of *derivatives* markets, a more relevant one, in fact. They enhance and boost the speculative nature of some financial activities, given their capacity to magnify movements in financial flows and stocks, increasing financial fragility and crises. Thus, *derivatives* are superimposed on an economy that is intrinsically unstable and has become even more crisis-prone, a tendency that has been somewhat temporarily contained by non-market stabilising forces. The menace of a major financial collapse, thus, is always present.

Yet, according to many *derivatives* advocates' beliefs, as discussed below, these instruments perform a crucial function of risk management, providing protection against undesirable movements in prices and values. Thus, it is necessary to understand the role of *derivatives* in contemporary capitalist economies, the United States in particular, characterised by enhanced fluctuations in interest rates, exchange rates, commodity prices, equity and securities prices, credit flows and the corresponding debts. Do *derivatives* add more instability to markets, speculative and non-speculative alike, enhancing macroeconomic crises and contributing to the net destruction of income, production, jobs and wealth? Or do they provide effective protection against measurable risks to the operation of capitalist firms and other organisations, allowing the former in particular to engage in more transactions and expand physical capital accumulation domestically and internationally, in an environment of increased volatility and uncertainty that is supposedly unrelated to *derivatives* themselves? This book addresses these and other questions, going beyond the usual emphasis on the operational aspects of *derivatives* and providing a historical, analytical and critical interpretation of the workings of *derivatives* markets and their role in the dynamics of contemporary, mostly advanced, financialised capitalist economies.

This book's main themes are, along with *derivatives*, their markets, features and evolution, also financial markets and risks, risk management, financial and economic history, speculation and instability or volatility, crises, regulation and alternative economic theories that provide analytical tools to make sense of all the previous topics intertwined. The goals are to understand, from a critical or radical political economics perspective, how *derivatives* are supposed to work, how they do really work, how they have evolved, why they have become quantitatively and qualitatively so important, what are the most important economic consequences of their usage, what is the role of regulation (or lack thereof) in the unfolding of these trends and to provide an alternative interpretation of the role of *derivatives* in a contemporary capitalist economy. These panoramic goals are what set this book apart from the existing conventional literature. Unlike most analytical books on *derivatives*, with a few exceptions, this one does not offer trading strategies or another instrument for the supposed corporate risk management toolkit but examines this activity in the light of an economic system that deliberately creates new risks and hasten existing ones at a high frequency. The proposed broader perspective in terms of history and unconventional theoretical approaches is missing in the literature, but it is nonetheless important to frame *derivatives* from many different angles, enriching our understanding of this phenomenon. By engaging in a critical reading of contemporary financialised capitalism and the *derivatives* markets, which is one the former's most important circuits, by bringing about their genesis, it highlights the importance of a wide heterodox perspective to understand how finance in general and *derivatives* in particular have transformed capitalism over time and were at the same time dialectically affected by it. To the best of our knowledge, no existing work has provided such temporal and intellectual scope in the discussion of *derivatives*. This book, as a consequence, is comprehensive rather than deep, since each chapter would make for a long book on its own (I hope Andy Humphrey at Routledge will skip this comment).

But why another book on *derivatives* now? Is it a necessity of the present time and economic conditions? There are no major crises in the making on the surface – so it seems, despite the fact that many times they cannot be predicted or hinted at, as pretty much everything else in the economy. The original PhD dissertation that is the starting point of this book was defended at UMass Amherst during the deepest of the so-called subprime mortgage crisis, with Lehman's collapse shattering the financial system and therefore the global economy. But when the research was being carried out, such a major crisis was off the radar, with a few heterodox exceptions. Yet, crises are a perennial and intrinsic feature of capitalism. So, any discussion of the sources of crises, be it structural, a trigger or a ferment should be of permanent interest to students, professionals and policymakers.

What has changed regarding this subject in terms of the dissertation version? First, the literature, as it is inevitable, kept growing faster than one could follow it up. Thus, a large volume of material has been published and many preliminary ideas had to be revaluated. The dissertation had a focus on institutional comparisons regarding the management of macro-financial, that is foreign exchange and interest rates, risks. It considered, at the macroeconomic level, the role of international arrangements, like fixed but adjustable exchange rates and capital controls under Bretton Woods, and national constraints on interest rates like Regulation Q and the

Glass–Steagall Act in the United States. At the microeconomic level, it considered Keynesian liquidity preference and accumulation of liquid assets at the firm level as a better answer to increased risks, comparing econometrically the portfolio of non-financial users and non-users of *derivatives*. But it assumed that the latter could somehow and imperfectly hedge macro-financial risks, an assumption that is challenged in this book.

Since the literature has grown so vast since the time the dissertation was defended, the selection of new books and articles for this book was *ad hoc*, although at the cost of, mainly regarding the introductory texts, being extremely repetitive. What were the general criteria? More recent works, books and articles published since then and newer editions of the books that were consulted for the original research. Of course, including books, chapters and articles that could not be read back then (I hope my former advisor Bob Pollin will skip this comment if he comes across this book). However, an attempt to fill the gap between the publication of the material I came across during my PhD research and the more recent works would still be laborious, as I have to face a quite long list. Should I consider the most read and cited instead? It is not trivial to assess the influence of a work, but it is important to engage with the most referenced works. And the two criteria are not necessarily consistent. Good older books tend to accumulate more readers over time, but technical books and documents do not attract wider audiences. The choice is therefore subjective. As a consequence, the methodology adopted in this book is more qualitative than quantitative, holistic more than focused, and I consulted a few representative works and critically evaluated them.

Most textbooks are apologetic or at least pretend to be neutral by focusing on definitions and technical developments, including back-office activities, like straight through processing or post-trade operations. We avoided such a route. Hence, issues such as binominal trees and other technical topics are not tackled in this book either. Although they provide, regarding the latter attributes, and with different emphases, relevant features of what has come to be known as *derivatives*, most of the time they never discuss critical issues or conventional questions from a fault-finding perspective.

Legitimate criticisms against *derivatives* are therefore considered by most of the advocates in books and articles as misguided or based on lack of understanding. After the subprime collapse, for example, this seems to have become more pronounced. The *derivatives* militants went on a fully defensive mode. On the other hand, treating the essential or even the more profound features of those instruments may not be enough, mainly if one considers the need of a critical, not exegetical, approach to provide a more comprehensive picture of the phenomenon under scrutiny. For instance, some books promise a 360-degree view of *derivatives*. Others claim to be all about *derivatives*. Yet, they rarely mention the historical developments of *derivatives*, not to mention their intellectual evolution, for example. Also, the order of the presentation could be a cause of further confusion. Sometimes, the focus is on the *derivatives* instruments. But there are discussions based on the so-called underlying that supposedly originates its *derivatives* as well. The approach adopted in this book uses a small sample of representative books to identify key points that are repeated in the literature and then presents the issues and also a critical evaluation of both the objective content or phenomenon and the treatment provided by the selected authors since these are clearly two separated things.

This book has three major claims. First, there is no such thing as *derivatives* from an ontological perspective. Individual economic arrangements were lumped together in a unifying concept despite relevant differences among them. It is an idea without a counterpart in the material or concrete world. It is perhaps a shortcut to avoid repeating the names of the basic individual arrangements (Forwards, Futures, Options and Swaps (FFOS)) when referring to plain vanilla contracts. If they were called FFOS, OFFS or FOFS, just like there are Credit Default Swaps (CDS), Asset-Backed Securities (ABS), Special Purpose Entities (SPE), Special Purpose Vehicles (SPV) and so on, it would make no difference for the transactions themselves. Swaps could be in a different position in the above acronyms like SOFF for stressing the idea that *derivatives* is a plural name, not a single entity or a building block in the real world. That is why they are always written using italics in this book. *Derivatives*, as a category, shown in Chapters 4 and 5, are recent, part of contemporary capitalism started in the 1970s. It is an example of an idealistic phenomenon brought about by the rise of financialised capitalism and neo-liberalism.

It contends in particular that contemporary *derivatives*, as a specific type of economic arrangement for profiting with different types of risks, do not exist as an ontological entity. Nor any other type of *derivative* for that matter. Despite the unifying attempt, there has always been, albeit usually downplayed, differences regarding the instruments denominated *derivatives*, and similarities with others that are not so considered, which places doubt on the term itself. In a nutshell, if considered rigorously, *derivatives* are far more comprehensive than forwards, futures, options and swaps, even in the financial realm alone. But all that can be derived from an already existing phenomenon is by definition a derivative, including shares, derived from the ownership over stocks that generate dividend flows. And thus *derivatives* as a jack-of-all-trade concept points to a substance that is not completely appropriate to deal with the specific nature of the contracts and transactions and may be wrong in some cases.

It is also important to emphasise the words contemporary, specific and economic in the first sentence of the previous paragraph. Contemporary *derivatives* are a concept, an intellectual creation of the 1980s. By convention, when capitalists or other agents enter into a specific sort of contract that shares some features, usually projecting future realisations for economic variables, they are labelled, for short, a *derivative*. This is due to the supposedly common attributes they share, not the specific cash flows arranged or designed by the contract. But conventions, by definition, are hard to change, due to vested interests, and mainly during the very period that necessitates them as an unquestionable idea that legitimises a business innovation and therefore a source of profits. So, a general, all-embracing term is used to refer to specific arrangements. Thus, *derivatives* as a concept should be always considered with great care.

Independently of its ontological existence, it is clear that there are specific economic arrangements that can be tied to existing risks in other settings, that is, to unpredictable changes in economic variables over time, creating new risks along the way of the linkage. And the assumption or pretending that they are a real or concrete phenomenon has mobilised researchers in several academic endeavours and also politicians, bureaucrats, capitalists with valorisation and accumulation strategies of all kinds, and mainly finance capital, into the realm of *derivatives*. Even if they do not exist as such, however, the impacts of the specific instruments over time have been real, mainly on stocks of wealth and flows of income and their distribution. By the same token, since they are monetary contracts, they can be collectively grasped monetarily by the sum of their values. Or even by the number of contracts, just like shares or bonds. This does not affect the argument that they mentally exist as a composite phenomenon built up by different concrete arrangements in the material world.

The second overarching argument is that *derivatives* are about finance, but financial *derivatives* is an over-reaching concept. It is related to financial institutions, products, markets and incomes. It is not a coincidence that commodity *derivatives*, the arrangements that deal with agricultural goods and extractive raw materials and that characterised modern capitalism until the 1970s, have been only a small fraction of total transactions. Santos (2008) informs that the volume of agricultural futures contract trades dropped below 50% of all trading in the early 1980s. By the middle of that decade, it had been reduced to less than one-fourth. More interesting, he shows, by that time the volume of futures contracts for the United States Treasury bonds alone exceeded negotiations in all agricultural commodities combined.

The third argument claims that the volatility, risks and crises associated with *derivatives* are derived from the second claim. Regulation has been, since the latest subprime mortgage crisis, able, so far, to avoid major collapses, but not smaller failures. And this cannot be properly addressed by an apologetic perspective. *Derivatives* can be better captured by heterodox views within economics, since they are equipped with a critical frame that allows looking behind the veil of finance and *derivatives* to see financialised capitalism and its inner workings.

A final warning to the reader is necessary. This is not a book about philosophy or law of *derivatives* despite the titles of some chapters. But the research has shown that it is necessary to move beyond economics and finance if a complete, albeit always provisory, understanding of *derivatives* and their financial logic is deeply sought after. Or even their fundamental laws. Or even better: their socioeconomic logic and genetic laws. Hence, the chapters can be read independently, but they are parts of an organic and integrated whole that converge to the need of a theoretical synthesis.

The book has ten chapters. In Chapter 1, the ontology of *derivatives* as such is put into perspective. Thus, the question of what they really are must be answered. This completely changes the meaning of their role within capitalism. Considering some important functions, they may not be needed for enlarged reproduction of capitalism in general, only for the specific needs of financial capital in particular circuits of valorisation and accumulation. The Chapter 2 completes the previous discussion, approaching the apparent or superficial functioning of *derivatives* markets in terms of prices, uses and relationship with risks. Chapter 3 argues that financialised capitalism needs risks and it cannot function without them, making *derivatives* needed on the surface, but it cannot also function properly with them both. It discusses the nature of risks, how they could be managed or not and the continuous fabrication of volatility in different markets, including those of *derivatives*. Chapter 4 approaches the recent evolution of *derivatives* markets as it reflects on the phenomenon of finance capital unleashed under neo-liberal and financialised capitalism, the increased risks and the markets related to them and their financial arrangements. Chapter 5 investigates the historical origins of *derivatives*, arguing that, contrary to stubborn beliefs, they never existed concretely, but are a mental creation to justify a specific configuration of capitalism, dominated by finance and the ensuing fabrication of risks. Chapter 6 tackles the intellectual reflections about *derivatives* and their functions over time and the historical origins of the idealistic concept of *derivatives*, not real-world transactions that are lumped together under this category. Chapter 7 provides some arguments in defence of *derivatives* and how they should be seen in the context of the need for managing risks for capital and other supposedly beneficial attributes. The next chapter (Chapter 8) highlights some arguments that have been mobilised against *derivatives*, to the extent that they facilitate speculation, frauds, instability and reinforce financialisation. Chapter 9 considers the context of the neo-liberal deregulation of finance in general at the same time that there are some attempts at regulating *derivatives*, mainly after significant financial collapses. It brings forth some specific regulations that have been implemented in the United States over the past decades, in a dynamic setting typical of a spiral. The final chapter (Chapter 10) attempts to build a radical political economics of *derivatives* by means of a heterodox synthesis of Marxism and post-Keynesianism. The conclusion laces all these points together.

References

Bank for International Settlements (BIS). Data Portal 2024. Available at: https://data.bis.org Retrieved December 2024.

Bank for International Settlements (BIS). OTC Derivatives Statistics at End-June 2023 (2023). Available at: www.bis.org/publ/otc_hy2311.pdf Retrieved October 2023.

Mader, Philip, Daniel Mertens,and Natasha van der Zwan (eds.) *The Routledge International Handbook of Financialization*. London/New York: Routledge, 2020.

McDonald, Robert, and Anna Paulson. "AIG in Hindsight." *Journal of Economic Perspectives* 29, no. 2 (2015): 81–106.

Santos, Joseph. "A History of Futures Trading in the United States." *EH.Net Encyclopedia*, 2008. Available at https://eh.net/encyclopedia/a-history-of-futures-trading-in-the-united-states/ Retrieved April 2024.

Steinherr, Alfred. *Derivatives – The Wild Beast of Finance: A Path to Effective Globalisation?* New York: Wiley, 2000.

Taylor, Francesca. *Mastering Derivatives Markets*. 2nd ed. London: FT/Prentice Hall, 2010.

1 The Ontology of *Derivatives*

What Are They? What Are They Not?

> Here, the good writer uses the word *derivative* in the same way that Hegel uses *being*: as the ultimate abstraction from which all categories are derived. Of course, he is no Hegel. So where Hegel begins, he stops, not realizing that if light is a derivative and humans are also derivatives – we are 'derived' from star dust – and a forward currency is also a derivative, then derivatives have no distinguishing characteristics except *being*. As such, the proper place for discussing them would be a meeting of philosophy enthusiasts and not the *American Banker*, certainly not in a book on finance.
>
> Saber (1999b, p. 4, italics in the original)

Introduction

This chapter has two goals. It first aims at presenting and then critically discussing the standard definitions of *derivatives*, that is, what *derivatives* are and what they do and then what they are not. The approach for achieving this end is rather simple. It starts with standard definitions of *derivatives* offered in the literature regarding basic or plain vanilla instruments, known as futures, forwards, options and swaps, and also a few wrong comparisons. And then shows their shortcomings, that is, the insufficiency of the portrayals because the instruments are very specific. At the end of the chapter, an attempt at definition is provided for these arrangements alone, keeping in mind that it would be impossible to suggest a definition comprehensive enough to be able to encompass all existing features, including those of instruments no longer in use or even exotic ones, as opposed to plain vanilla, for instance. This discussion must be seen as an initial evidence that *derivatives* as such do not exist.

Thus, the chapter is a first step in building the central argument that the concept of *derivatives* is inadequate, arguing that they are an idea without a corresponding concrete phenomenon, and then evaluating, in the following chapters, the fundamental rationale behind them. The different types of *derivatives* and an overview of their basic uses are discussed. In order to highlight the ontology of *derivatives*, they are contrasted with other types of financial instruments to evaluate their supposed singularity and to highlight the inherent difficulty in defining them as a collective entity. Other concepts necessary to understand the attributed functions performed

DOI: 10.4324/9781003137092-2

by different *derivatives* are provided in Chapter 2, which is a complement to this one. This functional problematisation is necessary to answer the question of why *derivatives* might be needed by capital, but without qualifying which specific type of *derivative*. In a nutshell, they are a consequence of general financial changes in the advanced capitalist economies since the collapse of Bretton Woods arrangements and the financial deregulation that followed neo-liberalism, with the rise of finance capital (Palley, 2013).

The chapter is organised as follows. It briefly presents the standard definitions and then moves to additional aspects, returning to the basic approaches from an enriched discussion, to evaluate them, qualifying and criticising as a way to show the shortcomings of the concepts presented. Of course, such complex phenomena cannot be explained in this way, in a single chapter. Anyway, this method is employed throughout this book. When new dimensions of *derivatives* are added, the initial criticisms gain depth and scope. This means that the work design is linear, but with expected loops. The discussions are logically weaved together by the main interpretation advanced, with a proposed interpretative construction resembling a spiral.

Therefore, the standard textbook definitions are the starting point, just to be qualified as the presentation follows. It needs definitions as entry points, but most conventional accounts are incomplete or, to use Lynch's (2011) words, under-inclusive, and the associated discussion may sound as incomplete as the idea, demanding complements and explanations that cannot be developed at that point, since other necessary ideas are still not available. It may cause, as a consequence, a long loop, with a first view requiring developments that can only be offered with additional elements that, by their turn, can be only understood by appealing to third degree elements, and the picture is less incomplete only at the designed end of the limits planned for the book, after many movements back and forth. The method is imposed by the very complex nature of the phenomenon. Also, *derivatives* may be over-inclusive, but at the cost of including non-*derivatives* in the package (Lynch, 2011). For instance, these typical definitions in the usual textbook are presented assuming that the subject and its parts are already known. That is, to follow Saber (1999b), *derivatives* are not derived but primary beings.

This requires organising the presentation in a non-linear way since it is necessary to define and explain the concepts before they are analytically deployed and then introduce other aspects and return to the initial concepts. Yet, the additional attributes or components, which cannot be introduced all lumped together, are somehow related and complement the meaning. They are reciprocal. And this reciprocity is at the kernel of the question. Financialised capitalism enhances risks and supplies instruments considered appropriate to respond to this situation, but those instruments tools or arrangements may create more potentially harmful risks. That is, the instruments cannot be left hanging in the air, without the financialised risks that require them and the additional financial risks created by them. A subject needs its predicate. But both are historically distinct, and their chronological convergence does not follow a linear path.

The chapter is organised as follows. In the next section, standard definitions are presented and criticised. Then, a few suspicious comparisons between *derivatives* and other instruments are discussed. The third section introduces the question regarding the contrast between general terms and specific arrangements. The fourth section brings forth issues related to risks. The final section sums it up.

What Are *Derivatives*? Standard Definitions and Their Critical Appraisal

The majority of the definitions of *derivatives* falls in one out of two possible classifications. The most fashionable ones start with their value or price and argue that it is derived from some other variable, usually an asset, that surprisingly is not also a liability, called the underlying, or its corresponding flows, which entails a hierarchical and necessary relationship or subordinate position of the derived contract in terms of the primitive. One is 'above' or 'over', protecting against the risks in the value of the asset or corresponding flows 'below' or 'under'. The underlying usually appears as a qualifier of the contract: interest rate *derivatives* or credit *derivatives* for example. *Derivatives* are thus, in these definitions, financial instruments whose value is derived from the value of an underlying asset or corresponding flow.

The second standard classification emphasises all possible remaining attributes, but without rejecting the first definition. Thus, these definitions highlight their supposed function or functions: avoiding the risks of losses impinging on the asset or corresponding flow by transferring or shifting them to counterparts, in smaller amounts, but who are nonetheless willing to accept the risk of loss because there is also a chance of gains. Some accounts are more comprehensive, or what Lynch (2011) calls over-inclusive, and others are succinct or under-inclusive. They can add their accounting status such as on or off-balance sheet, their nature as financial contracts, their markets in exchanges or traded over the counter (OTC) and so on. Each one has its own developments and is outstretched to new concepts. Perhaps the differences between both definitions are not only a matter of emphasis but can be explained by the existence of a complex set of phenomena and aspects that admits multiple treatments or also that they try to define specific arrangements with an inappropriate, all-embracing concept. The result is disappointing in terms of obtaining a clear definition.

The essential mechanics is always the same, however: *derivatives* are about time. They involve a contract, usually having at least a financial institution involved, a period of time that is the core of the contract, an economic reference named underlying providing parameters for the price of the contract, a measure of this reference's attribute to be gauged against a benchmark and whose expected difference is supposedly to be transferred or shifted, to the extent that there is a variation, also called risk, in the quantity of money, and when the maturity or end time comes, a winner and a loser and therefore a transfer of cash representing a distribution of income caused by changes in the value of the reference and therefore in the *derivatives* contract. Different arrangements are characterised by how future losers will lose, and how different types of noises and twists, many times simply shenanigans, in the period are added to reference in the case of exotic, as opposed to plain vanilla, contracts.

These issues are complex. Just to avoid accumulating more and more aspects without definitions, *derivatives* are thus named because they would not exist without the reference, that is, they supposedly can never be stand-alone, independent arrangements for the financial system as a whole. But it seems that this is only valid, at most, for a specific historical configuration. The setting of the reference or underlying in terms of assets or liabilities, events, indices and so on is irrelevant for most of contemporary *derivatives*, since it is possible to have a *derivative* on another *derivative*, like swaptions, swaps of options or options on futures, for example. Would these contracts be squared *derivatives*? And even plain vanilla contracts have gained an autonomy and could exist with only a vague reference to the underlying, based on any type of variation, including changes in non-financial or even non-economic parameters. For instance, a stock price does not depend univocally on expected profits, but also on the anticipation of buying and selling behaviour of other speculators, if one accepts Keynes' beauty contest, regardless of their motivation, such as believing in a greater fool, in the big foot, in perfect competition or even in future profits affected by sunspots, for example.

Most of the time the reference is only a unit of monetary account or notional value, since it is not actually transferred or cannot be transferred, as only monetary payments are made, that is, only a fraction of the liquid part of wealth is transferred. Thus, many *derivatives* do not have an underlying accounting entry point, like the weather, electricity, carbon emissions and so on. The completed transactions have a winner and a loser in terms of variations of sums of money owed regarding cash settlements. So, money is always the real reason behind all transactions and the true universal reference or underlying. All capitalist transactions have money as the underlying and are therefore *derivatives*.

Hence, since money is the starting and ending point, it has to be added to the discussion of *derivatives* up front. In Marxist parlance, the circuit of M increasing to M′ using *derivatives* as conduits abbreviates the time of expected valorisation and realisation of profits, fictitious or real. Otherwise, why not include, for example, indexed contracts as *derivatives*? If someone has a cost of living adjustment (COLA) clause in a specific contract, the monetary adjustments change with inflation, which represents a risk just like an increase in floating interest rates for a debtor, but the index-adjusted contract it is not, for some reason, considered a *derivative*. GDP is also a composite monetary measure of different goods and services that can be added together because of their monetary values. The aggregate value of GDP is derived from the value of many goods and services, but it is not a *derivative*. That is, *derivatives* share a spurious similarity with other economic transactions, because things happen over time. There is a before and there is an after.

As an example of a quite large literature using the first definition, in the third edition of his textbook, Hull (1997, p.1, italics in the original) defines: "A *derivative* (or *derivative security*) is a financial instrument whose value depends on the values of other, more basic underlying variables" and, in line with a fundamental argument for this book regarding financialised capitalism, "Very often the variables underlying derivatives are the prices of traded securities. (…). However (…) derivatives can be contingent on almost any variable, from the price of hogs to the amount of snow falling at a certain ski resort." Similar definitions can be found in numerous *derivatives* textbooks and books (Chance, 2008; Jarrow and Chatterjea, 2019; Jarrow and Turnbull, 2000; Kolb and Overdahl, 2009; Poitras, 2002; Somanathan et al., 2017; Stulz, 2003; Whaley, 2007).

Considering Hull's definition, it is important to emphasise that *derivatives* are not necessarily 'financial' in the sense of financing something, since that action may have happened before they are contracted and is already reflected in the underlying. Regarding the nature of the arrangement, therefore, it does not need to be financial, since no purchase has to be financed, although options have premiums and futures have margin deposits. The nature of the underlying is clearly not financial by definition. Otherwise, how to classify hogs and snow falling? For instance, the IMF (2009, pp. 94–95) explicitly puts the types of underlying in terms of real or financial. They are economic arrangements and thus they may involve financial variables, and under financialised capitalism, the finance-related is the type of contract that really matters. But it is wider than finance.

What is financial in financial *derivatives* then? Would it be the nature of the most important institutions developing, offering and transacting such contracts? Or the classification of the services and products that characterise such transactions? Would it be the cash nexus that is the real goal of *derivatives*, that is, the centrality of money as part of financial markets more broadly, epitomised in the cash settlement of contracts? Indeed, what gives them a financial complexion is mainly the fact that financial firms dominate the industry.

The problem with the adjective 'financial' can be illustrated with an example. Assume that a corn producer, the hero of most *derivatives* textbooks, sells corn to a food processing company. They enter a formal contract or an informal deal today, for the producer to effectively deliver corn to the buyer in three months at a fixed price. Is this arrangement a financial one? There is no finance, in the sense of anticipating liquidity or purchasing power, involved, although formal promises can be negotiated in secondary markets. Is the commodity (corn) produced an asset? To the producer, yes. When it is harvested and stored, but with a variable value without the deal. A reproducible or fungible asset, but not a financial one. For the buyer, it initially implies a cost to transfer the ownership of a real asset. When it is manufactured, it becomes a work-in-progress, an economic, but not financial, asset. And there is the cost of maintenance of an asset, since it must be stored, in the case of corn purchased, given a use value to the fixed asset used to store corn. So, no financial transactions are directly involved.

This spurious association is derived from the financialised nature of contemporary capitalism, when even commodities such as corn are financialised. But it is not about time and the time value of money in terms of interest rates, since these are older than *derivatives*. The paradox is evident. If we consider the title of Kolb (1992), it is about financial *derivatives*. And then applying the definition employed by Hull (1997), we can call a financial *derivative* a financial financial instrument. Meaningless, to the extent that *derivatives* are financial instruments for supposed financial risk management. There are other examples about the underlying. Should indices primarily not related to financial activity like snowfall, rainfall or changes in the weather in general be considered financial? Have carbon or environmental events a financial nature? The Dodd–Frank Act of 2010, discussed in detail in Chapter 9 of this book, has in Section 750 a provision to study carbon spot and *derivatives* markets and energy and environment in Section 751. Dowd (2002, p. 2) also mentions catastrophe, electricity and weather as underlying. If agricultural markets were efficient, environmental events, or at least their probability distribution, had to be fully anticipated and reflected in the price of commodities, given that they would affect production conditions and costs. Since they are not, other instruments must be searched for. *Derivatives* provide an apparent solution to the impact of nature on agricultural prices. Spot markets cannot anticipate the future and *derivatives* assume that role. What does it all have to do with finance? Nothing.

In the non-financial sector, non-financial assets generate income flows by means of production of goods and services when it is sold during circulation. Production is priced and then sold; that is, exchanged for money. For producers, prices may be low enough to generate losses or reduced profits. If production is sold overseas, there is another source of losses brought about by erratic exchange rates. The same producer may need imported goods or even fixed assets, like machines. In this case, there is the chance that imported costs increase when priced in the foreign currency. Firms will probably stop importing if costs are so high that markups are not enough to provide profitable sales. They could suffer losses for a short period. Or lower profits. Foreign exchange and commodity *derivatives* could offset these negative changes. But more likely, they could regulate the distribution of income flows between different capitals, as argued below. The point is that *derivatives* do not have to be financial by definition.

The issue about economic transactions in general is also related to this historical interpretation of the phenomenon under investigation, as explained in Chapter 5. *Derivatives* are usually qualified in terms of a supposed perennial financial nature of economic activity. This is because they were created and are traded by financial institutions, are normally produced and offered by them, and therefore are dominated by transactions with economic goals, which is not enough to turn all contracts into financial ones, however. In the particular case of options, and again it is necessary to introduce new concepts before they are explained, the idea that there are real options as well (Dixit and Piyndyick, 1993) could provide a stronger argument in favour of the adjective 'financial' to differentiate *derivatives*. But it cannot. Options do not need financial as a qualifier.

In this book, *derivatives* are related to activities, institutions and variables that are connected specifically to financing, like equity, interest rates and credit and to international monetary and financial flows that affect exchange rates and therefore the calculations of nominal incomes and wealth priced using different currencies. But commodities also have become increasingly financialised. As embedded references in contracts that are part of the *derivatives* sub-system of the financial system, they all represent the characteristics of financialised capitalism where finance sets the tune and non-financial institutions are obliged to adjust.[1]

This explanation is needed because there are *derivatives* not related to financial variables, but to commodities that are older than capitalism, related to money and commerce. Therefore, *derivatives* cannot be defined as financial instruments in this sense. That is, embracing commodities and other variables like the weather, even though they are negotiated by financial institutions and may involve financial variables. Financialisation is the reason why commodity futures exchanges should be considered as belonging to the *derivatives* sub-system of the financial system specifically today, but extrapolating and maintaining references to the economic system at large to which they belonged under modern capitalism as real values and not only as non-traded references for cash calculations.[2]

In the 11th edition of his book, Hull (2021, p. 1) wisely decided not to define *derivatives*. He just stated that "A derivative involves two parties agreeing to a future tranasaction (sic)." This is also wrong, of course. It is a description of the number of parties in a transaction and what the transaction is about regarding time. Yet, although the initial transaction may involve only two parties, the necessity of additional hedging or taking speculative positions may bring more parties to the business along the circuit, based on the same initial underlying value, developing a chain of derived transactions. That is why the notional value used as references to *derivatives* is so large, as is shown in Chapter 4. Every time a new deal is struck, the notional value is duplicated.

Of course, if the original transaction includes, for example, a bank loan, the lending bank may not be involved in a *derivative* deal. But are not banks supposed to be financial supermarkets? Is this example representative? Is this an exception? It is hard to tell. But it is clear that *derivatives* are sold by financial companies that cannot passively be exposed to risks, assuming instead the position or risk of their clients, and must aim at gains or avoiding losses. Thus, an initial swap to shed risks of a loan can be complemented by many others. The point is that these negotiations are not always necessary. Also, the agreement is in itself a transaction. A present one, signed today. Not an agreement that will happen in the future. There are two different acts in *derivatives* transactions as in many other economic deals: contracting and settlement, with a variable but usually short time interval between them. Anyway, the definition or description is wide enough to encompass all activities happening over a period. Merchants engage in agreements like that all the time. And these negotiations are not *derivatives*. Of course, many merchant activities are inverted, time-wise. With commercial credit, delivery happens first, with payment happening later.

Also, the IMF (2009, p. 94) states that

> A fixed-price contract for goods and services is not a financial derivative unless the contract is standardized so that the market risk therein can be traded in financial markets in its own right. For example, an option to purchase an aircraft from the manufacturer is not classified as a financial derivative.

By the same token, the fund warns that, "Timing delays that arise in the normal course of business and may entail exposure to price movements do not give rise to financial *derivatives*. Timing delays include normal settlement periods for spot transactions in financial markets" (IMF, 2009, p.4). If there is a shortage in a specific market for example, smartphones, costumers might be willing to pay and receive in the future. They do not need to arrange for payment later in order to match delivery time. The buyer and the seller agree to a future delivery. But it is not a *derivative*. And they should not be considered as such. That is, not all transactions involving a future delivery is a *derivative* despite many attempts to force such identity, mainly in pseudo-historical accounts as discussed in Chapter 5. Other than that, Hull (2021) sticks to the same old definition, emphasising the value of the underlying.

Another introductory book, seemingly based on a practitioner experience more than academic research, is Taylor (2010). Taylor (2010, p. 2) defines *derivatives* using the second approach, but sticking to the financial nature: "Derivatives are financial tools that are used to manage risk or to take risk." The same criticism regarding the use of the adjective financial applies here. It is worth noticing that managing risks is opposed to taking risks in her definition. But an antonym to 'taking' could be 'avoiding'. Risk management cannot be about managing risks that have not been taken yet. This would be risk prevention. The definition assumes that risks were involuntarily taken, that is, there is a passive exposure. This seems to be reasonable in the context of financialised capitalism, when all capitalists may be initially subjected to instability created by a minor group of financial capitalists. Her second definition is longer and elaborates on the first approach (Taylor, 2010, p. 3). Now, a *derivative* instrument is one whose performance depends on, or is derived from, the evolution of the price of an underlying asset. She emphasises that the underlying asset does not need to be negotiated and the majority of deals are cash settled. Finally, she makes reference to options, explaining that a premium may be paid.[3] Again, a specific type of contract is highlighted as feature of a general category, but the specificity makes the latter innocuous.

Yet, the underlying should not necessarily be an asset. It depends on the perspective of the respective agent. This confusion between stocks and flows appears again in her treatment of the underlying in terms of five primary 'asset' classes: Interest rates, foreign exchange, equity, commodities and credit. The assets related to interest rates, however, are actually bonds, bills, consoles, outright loans and so on. On the other hand, according to the double entry bookkeeping, these assets are also liabilities for some agents. Das (2006), for example, shows a debt in Rupiah swapped into Dollar. The original debt is the underlying, and of course, it cannot be an asset for the debtor. If a firm has a debt with a floating interest rate, it could enter into a *derivative* contract to hedge against interest rate risk using the debt value as the reference notional value. And the value of the *derivative* would then change with interest rates, not with the book value of the debt. On the same thread, as mentioned, *derivatives* may be the underlying of other *derivatives*. Again, if they are an underlying or a principal, this might be a source of a spurious similarity. If on the other hand *derivatives* are not, but tend to be, considered more and more on the balance sheet stock, as a consequence, they cannot be a flow. But they regulate flows, which affect at least one stock when they are settled: cash or liquid assets. The principal is not traded but used as reference upon which the value of *derivatives* or whatever is called is based.

The source of this confusion is old. In reviewing Axel Leijonhufvud's *Information and Coordination – Essays in Macroeconomic*, Joan Robinson (1982) mentions an informal conversation with Richard Khan, famous for discovering the employment multiplier, and the great Polish political economist Michal Kalecki. According to Robinson (p. 295), Kalecki claimed: "I have found out what economics is; it is the science of confusing stocks with flows." This problem seems more general than what is seen in economics. In the *derivatives* literature, it is pervasive. In order to be straight: Assets may generate flows of income[4] and the liabilities used to finance asset acquisitions generate flows of expenditures. This connects static balance sheets or stocks with dynamic income and expenditure statements of flows. An exposure to risks produced by markets occurs when the composition and type of the former generates fluctuations not only in their values, but it is reflected in the ensuing chained changes in the latter. Of course, this can only happen in a capitalist economy.

Continuing with the search for a precise definition, it is important to see what institutions use. The IMF supposedly has to set rigorous standards for the statistical measurement and recording of international transactions. It started dealing with *derivatives* measurement only by the end of the 1990s, suggesting that they might not be worth measuring before (Heath, 1998). In the latest version of the Balance of Payments Manual, BPM6, it has fully developed a method for standardising the accounting of *derivatives* (Valdivia-Velarde, 2012). However, the accounting rules lump financial *derivatives* and employee stock options together, since the latter are considered financial assets. Nonetheless, since *derivatives* are part of the United States' financial hegemony in the global capitalism, in coordination with Europe and Japan, the balance of payments and international investment position manual is an important source to grasp the relevant definitions (National Research Council, 1995). Notwithstanding these features, the definitions in the manual are sometimes clearer, despite sharing the same problems identified above. IMF (2009, p. 93, italics in the original):

> A financial derivative contract is a financial instrument that is linked to another specific financial instrument or indicator or commodity and through which specific financial risks (such as interest rate risk, foreign exchange risk, equity and commodity price risks, credit risk, and so on) can be traded in their own right in financial markets.

The advantage of this definition is that the word 'instrument' is more generic than assets or liabilities as it represents both. And the link with the reference provides a looser connection, better than 'underlying'. The nature of the link may cause the idea of *derivation* to become irrelevant. It thus enlarges the underlying, but without treating them as such, at least explicitly in the definition.[5] It also includes risk and risk trading. The weaknesses are that it makes no mention to time and reinforces the idea of an exclusive financial transaction that captures, partially, only recent developments and misses history by conflating commodities with finance – commodity price risk is a financial risk – without reference to financialisation (see Bertilorenzi, 2022). For the question of assets and liabilities, it is much clearer. IMF (2009, p. 47): "In some cases, a clear distinction between assets and liabilities may not be feasible (such as for financial *derivatives* in the form of forward contracts, which could change between assets and liabilities)."

The Government Accountability Office (GAO) is not exempt, even though its managing director is also a very brilliant and talented professional, Lawrance J. Evans Jr.. The GAO defines *derivatives* using both approaches mentioned above:

> Derivatives are financial products that enable risk to be shifted from one entity to another. The value of the derivative is based on an underlying reference rate, index, or asset, such as stocks, bonds, commodities, interest rates, foreign currency exchange rates, and various market indexes.
>
> (GAO, 1998, p. 118)

It shows the same problem as Taylor (2010), IMF (2009) and Hull (1997) regarding the adjective 'financial'. And GAO could not resist the temptation of the underlying either. In this definition, everything that shifts risk is a *derivative*. Stocks are *derivatives* just like insurance policies.

So, practitioners, scholars, international and national institutions all cannot escape the trap of defining what cannot be defined. A more general definition is necessarily meaningless, encompassing the different instruments, different natures (financial or not) and so on. A synthesis of what has been presented and criticised so far combines the value of *derivatives*, their performance, the association with risks and, although not sufficiently emphasised, the fundamental time dimension. Thus, according to Lynch (2011), it should be considered under-inclusive. The restricted reference or underlying includes only real commodities, financial instruments (not assets or liabilities) and credit. Indices and non-economic events complete the picture.

A final issue with the definition of *derivatives* based on price of contracts reflecting prices of references is a paradox. *Derivatives* can be traded bilaterally in OTC markets or in exchanges. The ones traded on exchanges are marked to irrational market, that is, their values are continuously adjusted to the price of the reference. Continuous market disequilibrium is partially absorbed by changes in cash positions in margin deposits in the case of exchanges (clearing). They supposedly minimise the impact of the market volatility on key economic variables that affect income and expenditure flows for companies with exposures to changes in markets, that is, all organisations without fixed-price contracts, and not using *derivatives* for hedging. It is ironic in this case that the same volatile markets that are the raison d'être of *derivatives* are used as benchmark to adjust *derivatives*' positions and value them daily in the case of exchanges with centralised clearing house and margin accounts. And there is also the other way round: the price discovery performed by *derivatives* markets, which requires variations in speculative settings.

Is Everything a *Derivative?* Undue Comparisons

Saber (1999b) argues that the complexity of *derivatives* makes it difficult to define and explain them. As a consequence, theorists and practitioners appeal to analogies based on religion, the military and biology.[6] The military metaphors highlight the systemic risks associated with *derivatives*. The mega speculator Warren Buffett once famously remarked that *derivatives* were like weapons of mass destruction. Although his company, Berkshire Hathaway, uses *derivatives* in its portfolio, his claim is supported by other writers, like Das (2006), who has guns in the title of his book. The latter, however, argues that this role is not frequent. Of course, this must be the case, otherwise the financial system – and the global economy – would be destroyed by now. Steinherr (2000, p. xiii) equally affirms that "People have also become more aware that *derivatives* can be market-destabilising and are a permanent gunpowder barrel." Many texts on *derivatives* have a lethal explosive device in the subtitle. Along the same lines, Saber (1999a) mentions Roger Altman, investment banker and former member of the U.S. Treasury, that finance in general, not *derivatives*, was a nuclear weapon. This means that *derivatives* are anti-matter bombs.

On the economic realm, *derivatives* have been compared to many different types of assets. Saber (1999a, p. 4) quotes a hyperbole by a banker, for whom "Virtually all financial assets are *derivatives* of some sort", including stocks. But are stocks really similar to put options, that is, the right to sell if profits are not high enough? If this is the case, why stocks have not been included in the standard lists of *derivatives* products? And why, in the spurious economic history of *derivatives*, stocks do not appear? Henwood (1998) equally and surprisingly treats *derivatives* like other financial instruments, such as stocks, bonds and currencies, in a context of financial innovation.[7] He clings to the definition in terms of securities whose prices derive from the prices of other securities or things, and classifies them in terms of standardised, in the case of futures and options, and custom-made in the case of swaps, collars, swaptions and so on. However, he misses forwards and considers as instruments the combinations of original securities in the case of swaps of options or collars.

Scholes (1998), famous for developing a formula for pricing options discussed in Chapter 6 of this book, similarly defends that most financial instruments are *derivatives* in a form or another. He affirms that it is difficult to define *derivatives* in a dynamic environment and that the traditional definition relating the prices of two arrangements is comprehensive enough to encompass the existing instruments and also futures instruments. Weber (2009, p. 433) equally argues that the fast changes caused by new *derivatives* products has made definitions rapidly obsolete. However, most, if not all, new or recent *derivatives* products are similar to gambling schemes and do not fit into standard definitions. The false cognates continue in the case of debt. Thus, Scholes (1998, p. 146) states that "corporate debt and equity contracts are *derivatives* to the underlying investment". But are *derivatives* debt? The IMF clarifies (2009, p. 85–86): "Financial derivatives, both forwards and options, are distinguished from debt instruments because no principal amount is advanced that is required to be repaid, and no interest accrues on any financial *derivative* instrument." Unquestionable!

The word insurance is also widely employed for spurious comparisons in the *derivatives* literature. It is presented as a synonymous for protection when *derivatives* are used to hedge. For example, Miller (1997) associates futures and options traded on exchanges with insurance markets. How insurance contracts can be used for speculating or arbitrage defies logic, though. Insurance is just a small spending today to avoid a bigger spending in the future if a negative event is realised, with the difference paid collectively. The social nature of insurance requires some socialisation of losses. Yet, just like insurance does not always eliminate completely the impacts of realised damages as abstract risk becomes concrete losses, hedging using *derivatives* may also allow some residual risks and realised losses. The IMF (2009, p. 94) is very clear about the difference, correcting once more the mistakes of Chicago economics:

> Insurance and standardized guarantees are not financial derivatives. Insurance involves the collection of funds from policyholders to meet future claims arising from the occurrence of events specified in insurance policies. That is, insurance and standardized guarantees are used to manage event risk primarily by the pooling, not the trading, of risk.

Where does come the supposed similarity from? Insurance, debt and stocks are all in what is called FIRE or finance, insurance and real estate, whose growth reflects contemporary financialised capitalism and creates the illusion of an unicity of very different instruments.

The comparisons do not stop here. Hull (1997) mentions that *derivatives* are also known as contingent claims. But the contingent nature of *derivatives* claims is rejected, again, by the IMF (2009, p. 94), although they mistakenly adhere to the financial nature of the arrangements: "The following types of financial arrangements are not financial *derivatives*: (…) Contingent assets and liabilities, such as one-off guarantees and letters of credit, are not financial assets." And IMF (2009, p. 82): "Although the value of future payments arising from (…) financial derivatives (...) is uncertain, they are recognized as financial assets rather than as contingent assets. In these cases, the liability exists, but the amounts payable depend on subsequent events." So, today, at least according to the IMF, they cannot be considered completely contingent. It is a matter of accounting rules.

The confusion reaches a paradox in the Dodd–Frank Act of 2010, discussed in more detail in Chapter 9, with one specific arrangement, swaps, being identified with many others. It states that

> the term 'swap' means any agreement, contract, or transaction – (i) that is a put, call, cap, floor, collar, or similar *option* of any kind that is for the purchase or sale, or based on the value, of 1 or more interest or other rates, currencies,

> *commodities*, securities, instruments of indebtedness, indices, quantitative measures, or other financial or economic interests or *property of any kind*.
> (US Congress, 2010, p. 291, italics added)

So, basically everything is no longer a *derivative*, but a swap. Offering a different view, Weber (2009) stresses that an important feature of *derivatives* is that there is a risk of default. So, following Swan (2000), he defines *derivatives* as a promise that bears a risk of default.[8] A loan would be a *derivative* in this definition. However, exchange-traded *derivatives* do not have, most of the time, a risk of default, since the counterparty is the clearing house. Also, a groom may promise a big family to a bride, but he might fail to deliver. So, there is a promise and a risk of default. Yet, this is not a *derivative*.

What is missing in most of these accounts is a profound treatment of the time dimension of *derivatives*. The instruments under this category are non-exclusive anticipations of rightly or wrongly projected futures. Moriarty et al. (1981, p. 61) states it in an explicit way regarding one of the functions of *derivatives*: "Hedging – i.e., taking a position in a derivative market that represents a substitute for a transaction to be made at a later date – can be accomplished with either futures or options." Saber (1999a, p. 70) is very clear about that: "Time is the medium through which the risk – and everything else – materializes."[9] Considering the attributed functions of *derivatives*, he distinguishes between hedge and arbitrage in terms of time: hedge must follow a relatively longer sequence, whereas arbitrage is almost simultaneous, but in constant movement searching for anomalies, which, by the way, requires a sequential strategy that is passive regarding the active changes in prices, to which they can contribute in a reciprocal manner.[10] Saber (1999a) equally claims that arbitrageurs cannot always wait for anomalies to disappear rapidly after their very action in these markets and suffer heavy losses. The old adage is still valid: markets in general, and financial markets in particular, can stay irrational longer than the speculators that make them up can stay solvent.

Regarding time, the source of uncertainty and risks, at maturity the settlement happens, usually by cash, not delivery of the underlying. This is the case for futures, forwards and options. On the other hand, some options and swaps allow multiple settlements for long credit contracts with interest rates reset at fixed intervals, which must be converted into a guaranteed single long-term interest rate transaction, or contracts that need to be rolled over (Taylor, 2010). There are *derivatives* contracts for 75 years.[11] So, *derivatives* are hard to define, and this is because ontologically they do not exist as such. The necessity of having a supposedly firmer ground on an association with really existing but specific economic arrangements and contracting is proof of that.

Specific Types of Arrangements, Not *Derivatives*: An Ontological Primer

Taylor (2010) lists only three 'techniques' or arrangements for dealing with risks: futures, options and swaps. Despite the fact that futures started with commodities, Kolb (1992) conflates financial *derivatives* with futures, options, and swaps that take a financial instrument as the underlying. It excludes forwards, just like Das (2006) and, sometimes, the IMF (2009). There is no consensus regarding the way to approach the individual arrangements that are collectively designed as *derivatives*. On the other hand, following the methodology presented at the beginning of this chapter, it is necessary to consider the ways that economic and financial needs of capital have been addressed by the specific arrangements, considering only the plain vanilla types or basic contracts, unlike complex or exotic instruments. Again, products like synthetic options are not discussed. They are simply an even more geared position in the underlying. Saber (1999a) shows that they are not equivalent to options. Hybrids or combinations are not considered in this book. For example, a swap of options is a swaption. Why any capitalist needing hedge against risks would enter into a swaption transaction? Regardless of these speculative instruments, the plain vanilla are worth comparing, showing their uniqueness and the inexistence of *derivatives as a unifying category*.

Considering the first analysed plain vanilla contract, futures, they are traded only on exchanges. It is a contract to buy or sell something in a future date at a known price. The futures exchanges standardise the transactions in terms of quality requirements, when necessary, and time for delivery, which fixes the duration of the contracts. Of course, this makes sense only for commodities with variable quality. Hull (1997) points also to delivery date, with only the month being fixed, and the seller choosing the day and local. More important for the development of the central argument of this work, the quantities of the underlying are also fixed per contract. The exchanges assume the counterparty risk and require margins accounts with balances managed by commission merchants to minimise losses.

Exchange-traded *derivatives* represent therefore multilateral or open trading with many centralised features. There is a centralised or mutualised physical space or centralised trading system in electronic platforms. There are centralised legal arrangements and self-imposed rules. There are centralised settlement and offsetting or clearing of contracts. There is centralised gathering and disclosure of information about negotiated prices. There is a centralised transactions tracking. There is a centralised margins management system. That is, the exchanges avoid totally decentralised bilateral private arrangements typical of OTC transactions. It represents a distrust in purely private property exchange to make sure that it is really a transaction about tangible money or a reliable equivalent of solvent counterparts.

Therefore, exchanges provide specific characteristics to the arrangements traded in there. In particular, Taylor (2010) explains how the clearing house eliminates the credit or counterparty risks, making Weber's (2009) and Swan's (2000) definition inapplicable, and margin requirements keeps its own credit risk at low, but not irrelevant, levels. Initial margins are deposits kept at the clearing house by both parties, based on an estimate of volatility such that it is enough to cover eventual losses and prevent agents from accumulating larger losses. Market volatility is reflected in the adjustments of margin deposits. The deposits are thus adjusted daily according to market conditions, causing the margin to vary in line with volatility. When they are favourable, that is, prices increase for sellers or fall for buyers, the deposit of sellers increases by the profit earned by the same amount that the deposit of buyers decrease. And when they are unfavourable for sellers, the deposit is debited by the loss or through margin calls. That is, if the initial margin is depleted by accumulating and lasting losses, there is additional funding required by the clearing house. If the margin deposit is not replenished, the clearing house may close out the uncovered positions. Thus, if no additional funding is provided, the initial margin is lost. It is a kind of stop loss. The opposite happens for buyers. If wealth positions in futures and in the underlying spot market are perfectly hedged, the losses in *derivatives* markets are compensated in the spot market and vice-versa. In addition, it is collectively possible to net off transactions by means of the clearing house, reducing the amounts to be adjusted in the marked account. Yet, as Taylor (2010) correctly reminds, Barings Bank failed despite all these safety schemes. Of course, a sudden, large loss caused by extremely leveraged positions could make the initial or adjusted margin irrelevant.[12] And more recently, as argued in Chapter 8, many exchanges have been put into a fragile position by large losses.

So, futures allow an increased gearing due to the reduced initial monetary amount necessary to transact, a feature that is shared by other arrangements in this financial sub-system. Moreover, it is clear that the initial margin requirements set by exchanges represent a transfer, albeit temporary, of liquid balance sheet items. The futures transaction in itself is conceived as off-balance sheet, but regardless of how it is accounted for it has repercussions on the balance sheet, upfront and when the deal is finally unwound and settled, with significant implications for gearing and crisis (Breuer, 2002). The off-balance sheet feature of futures and other *derivatives*, although the tendency is to move to balance sheet, as the IMF (2009) explains, creates accounting and financial assessment problems, allowing a different type of gearing and fragility.

But on economic grounds, on balance sheet is considered by the advocates of *derivatives* more expensive. Is it actually? It is not clear. A capitalist could borrow long-term funds at very low, fixed interest rates. Long-term contracting between buyers and sellers or borrowers and lenders would perform the same hedging role, and possibly cheaper. Regarding specifically interest-rate contracts, one could point to the LIBOR (London Interbank Offered Rate) fix, done when this interest rate existed. Given that markets are usually unstable, and that financial markets are always very unstable, interest rates can change between different financial circuits and over time. Since marking interest rates to markets could make it difficult and costly to devise longer-term plans, an answer is fixing interest rates, like the LIBOR fix (Taylor, 2010). But the fix is for intra-day deals only. For day-to-day deals, it can change.

Also, currency contracts depend on the existence of floating exchange rates. Under fixed exchange rates, it was unnecessary to hedge. Monetary unions pose different types of problems for capitalists, but the exchange rate risk disappear.[13] In general, there are price stabilisation mechanisms that obviates the need of hedging by new instruments. Hilferding (1981) mentions the role of monopolies as price stabilisation devices in the long run, making price fluctuations, and therefore risk, speculation and futures markets irrelevant. However, Sotiropoulos (2012) argues that international competition may create room for specific arrangements. But this is valid for commodities in general. For financial markets, stability in the price of assets and liabilities is unprofitable.

Actually, this point is not sufficiently discussed in the literature. And data about the proportions or market share of short run versus long run contracts with fixed prices are not available, since the latter helps to eliminate the problem of rolling over or transacting frequently. Taylor (2010) points to the existence of 75-year interest rate *derivatives* contracts. It is not clear which type of capitalist financial need would require three-fourths of a century to hedge, not to mention the business demographics and mortality rates among firms that may be such that most firms will not last more than 70 years.

This specific type of gearing using futures, since there are margin deposits, but also options, for which there are premiums, both with immediate balance sheet effects, suggests that they might not be enough to avoid huge future balance sheet losses. In other words, how can one explain the very known disasters discussed in Chapter 8 of this book, that is, wiping out balance sheet values? Thus, income losses can be larger than the stocks accounted in the books and off the books. In the case of shares, portfolio theory claims that diversification can minimise loses when the stock market goes down. So, a diversified portfolio of shares is partially hedged, although individual stocks are very probably not. Is it possible to know which ones? How to further manage an already diversified portfolio using futures or options? By buying contracts on indices like S&P 500 or FTSE 100?

In order to resume the specific differences between arrangements, forwards contracts usually do not receive a lot of attention because they are considered similar to futures as both involve future delivery. Yet, forwards are traded OTC, that is, in private, bilateral transactions without the same structural support of exchanges. "The over-the-counter market involves parties negotiating directly with one another, rather than on a public exchange" (IMF, 2009, p. 82). There is no clearing house and therefore no imposed margins requirements. There is delivery in the definitions, but not in the real outcome, since cash settlement is the norm and the goal (Hull, 1997; Taylor, 2010).

For the initial agreement, the value of the forward is null for both parties, that is, unconditional initial zero value for both parties. It is neutral at this point. But as the price of the reference or underlying changes, the value of the forward changes accordingly, assuming they do not perform price discovery functions. This is achieved as risk exposures of equal or symmetrical current market values are exchanged. Thus, the level of the fixed strike price guarantees, at the beginning, the zero value of the contract. But over the course of the period between the initial agreement and the maturity date, forward and strike prices will differ, creating a zero-sum game, no longer a zero value for the forward contract, as time evolves and the spot price of the underlying changes. Thus, one party will lose money and the other will gain, but during the lifetime of the contract, these positions can change and even alternate, as unrealised or paper profits or losses before maturity. If they have perfectly matched positions in the underlying market, the outcomes will be reversed, restoring the zero-sum game nature at the delivery date in one market and the opposite in the other. The transaction can be reversed at any point, by just taking a contrary position. Since it is OTC, there is always counterparty or credit risk. As a consequence, the collateral value of a forward contract is less than the collateral value of a futures contract. This is enough to show that they are different arrangements, sharing some superficial similarities only.

To continue with the difference among arrangements that invalidate the idea of *derivatives*, only options are traded both on exchanges, and in this case, they are called listed options, and on OTC markets, creating a layer of difference between and within instruments. The exchange-traded contracts do not follow the same rules as the futures. Anyway, exchanges bring more liquidity whereas OTC deals offer specific contracts designed according to the particular needs of different pieces of capital. It cannot be liquid by definition, as a consequence. Actually, the singular nature would make them illiquid like any other fixed asset despite the fact that they are plain vanilla instruments (Taylor, 2010). By the same token, credit risk is greater in OTC markets, since it can be considered less important in exchanges with the clearing system assuming the counterparty role when the original player defaults.

Another difference is that the buyer and the seller of an option have contrasting perspectives, providing additional elements of differentiation. A call is a right to buy a quantity of the underlying at a given price and a put is a right to sell the underlying at a given price. That is, to the buyer of an option it grants the right, but not the obligation, to buy or sell, receive or pay, a standard quantity at a given maximum date at a known price. This right must be purchased by disbursing a premium upfront to the seller or writer of the option. The latter has no option at all and must abide by the terms of the contract, although they might default in OTC markets. Using Weber (2009)'s and Swan (2000)'s definition, an OTC option is a *derivative*, but an exchange-traded one is not.

Saber (1999b) shows that there is an asymmetry in options. The right configures an option only to the buyer. The seller has no option, only obligations. An option, as the name itself suggests, should be an alternative, but it is so to the buyer only. It is however a non-binding choice. Yet, all instruments may be reverted close to maturity by an inverse operation. A contract long, for example, may be reverted by a contract short in the same instruments. The operations cancel out and the fair value is used to settle any difference. Nonetheless, a callable bond is not an option. Hirsa and Neftci (2014) also mention a cancellable swap. It remains the question of whether or not this offsetting mechanisms are costlier than option premiums plus any interest income foregone depending on the time horizon of the contract, considering also the transaction costs.

Equally important is the fact that an option is not transferable and cannot be resold in a secondary market. But, as mentioned, it can be returned to the issuing bank for the fair value at that time. Taylor (2010) claims that there is no basis risk for options, an important aspect of the efficiency in managing risks. Unlike futures or forwards, when hedge means buying market protection from the market disorder itself, options are deliberate choices of not completely isolating wealth and income from market instability in order to speculate by gaining from favourable movements in prices, and at the same time limiting losses in case of unfavourable movements in prices over and above the premium paid. The premium value is calculated based on five aspects, discussed below. The complexity involved obliged the literature to acknowledge that there are options-like *derivatives* and forwards-like *derivatives* (IMF, 2009; Saber, 2017). The ontology begins to demand credible answers and classifications.

At the cost of being repetitive, financial instruments are not the only 'underlying' possible to link with an option. Regarding the other features, the future date is the expiry date. The right may be exercised or not at that date. Exercise represents a metamorphosis, just like money turn itself into physical commodities and capital in the latter's circuit. Not exercising the right represents a cost to the buyer but a positive net revenue in the form of a premium for the writer or seller. There are many different types of options, making it a very specific type of arrangement. An American option allows the buyer to exercise the right on any business day, on both countries in the case of currency options, before the expiry. European options have less flexibility and can be exercised only at the expiry date but can be sold back to the writer at any time by its fair value. Taylor (2010) also mentions Bermudan option, with selected expiry dates, an instrument intermediary between American and European in terms of flexibility. Finally, Asian options consider the exercise based on the average price over a period.

These features of options can be discussed considering the time-varying necessities of finance capital. If the circuit of money capital, from initial money expended to profits earned, that is, additional money, is relatively stable and constant, then the time intervals between purchases and sales and the prices negotiated will be relatively well known. Thus, an European option would be adequate. This seems reasonable for very short periods of the calendar time. The American option is the quintessential representation of finance capital mobilised for speculation. Rather than reducing uncertainty, it adds doubts to agents. What defines the time of exercise are not the needs of reproduction of real capital, but the speculative gains of finance capital. It is the realm of money generating more money at the quickest possible time. Bermudan could also represent a valid instrument for risk management considering possible irregularities in the circuit of capital. It depends on the periodicity of the exercise dates. Asian options have a built-in smoothing provision, which may provide useful hedging tools in very volatile markets, but without reducing uncertainty. A future study may shed light on the relative share of each type of option in the option circuit.

The guaranteed future price of an option is named strike price, which may not be the same as the future spot price, which cannot be known today. The current market price, for the date when the option is transacted, provides another important parameter, along with other benchmarks. The present value of the difference between the strike price and the current market price, current forward prices or any other options' benchmark, named 'intrinsic value', can be considered a proxy for capitalists' expectations regarding the likely changes in prices or values in the near future. On the other hand, if the premium is compared to intrinsic value, the difference is the time value of the option.[14] Adding time value and intrinsic value gives the fair value, which, in theory, must be equal to the premium.

Considering only the relationship between strike price and current, in the case of American option, or forward in the case of European option, spot price as the benchmark, there are three possible situations for each right transacted: if the current or forward spot price, which includes the underlying price plus the cost of carrying it, is above the strike price, a call option is out of the money and the premium is considered low. If both prices are equal, the call option is at the money. If the current spot or forward price is below the strike price, then a call option is in the money and the premium is considered more expensive. That is, if the intrinsic value is large, then the option is in the money. Conversely, if the current or forward spot price is above the strike price, a put option is in the money. If both prices are equal, the put option is at the money, like before. If the current or forward spot price is below the strike price, then a put option is out of the money. The results are inverted if the price is a rate. It is worth observing that the use of different prepositions is a market convention to adjust the option premium, along with the time to expiry or maturity. Since options, just like other *derivatives,* involve time as they project a future value, that may be far off the real future value when it materialises, the relevant parameter for the buyer is the future spot price at maturity, or future spot prices at exercise dates in the case of American options.

An option therefore has a conversion provision. It is a choice to convert a bought right into more cash or forfeit the premium, but it is not a security option to buy or sell with a premium attached. One specific type of option, albeit one with a longer maturity, is a warrant. This instrument is issued by corporations and has as the underlying a given quantity of new bonds or equities, diluting the existing ownership structure when exercised by the buyer (IMF, 2009; Bernstein, 2005). A similar arrangement is a convertible bond, a security that can be turned into a given quantity of stocks at maturity. But in the particular case of options, since the premium is only a fraction of the face value of the underlying, gearing is a built-in feature, just like in futures. Yet, uncertainty about the future does not turn options into contingent claims. The class of assets with contingent claim features are broader than free-standing options.

The conversion features are choices to transform one class of assets or liabilities into another, not to buy or sell, that is, to transform something into cash or the inverse. In Marxist parlance, the former is an option to change the form of capital, not to change capital into money or into a commodity. The latter is an option to transform cash into assets or commodities or vice-versa. An option, understood as the broad existence of alternatives, financial, economic, social, cultural or otherwise, does not boil down to option as a narrow *derivative* security. A worker exercising her right to quit a job, or exit, to borrow Albert Hirschman's known expression, is exercising an option given to her since she signed a labour contract. This is what characterises capitalism as an 'employer of choice' option in general for the worker. Or a career choice option, since bonded labour is now formally understood not to be a regular part of this economic system.

Another issue related to options is the volatility. Volatility of the price of the underlying is taken into account when the option's premium is priced in a linear fashion. Thus, the higher the volatility, the higher the premium – such that it is possible to calculate the implied volatility from historical records of quoted premiums. Yet, the relationship between the volatility and the price of the underlying is non-linear. Volatility is equivalent to the standard deviation of the returns of an underlying asset. If prices and, when relevant, cost of carry are equally volatile, then the return is also volatile. But if they are not, returns and prices bear different types of risks. However, volatility could be related to any quantifiable attribute of a stock or flow, not only its return, like liquidity, turnover, share of portfolios and so on.

Dowd (2002) includes the mean-variance as a framework to measure financial risks, for example. And then he adds the value at risk (VaR)[15] technique and the expected tail loss (ETL) as two other possibilities regarding risk measurement. He also discusses an important source of risk, underrated by the literature: the models themselves. Whatever the definition might be, if volatility is relevant, then all different types of *derivatives*, not only options, supposedly exist to deal with it. Volatility, therefore, makes *derivatives* valuable to the writers or sellers, to speculators, and usually they are the same organisation, and to those who believe they can minimise the negative consequences of risks. It should influence the price of all *derivatives*. But since the elements that are subsumed under this category are very different, they will have different pricing methods.

In the particular case of currency options, it is even more important to differentiate between hedging, on the one hand, and speculation or arbitrage, on the other, that is, between the typical functions expected from these arrangements. The former requires paying the premium in one currency for purchasing the right to buy or sell another currency that is necessary to carry out regular business operations. There is an unavoidable exposure to exchange rate fluctuations whose effects must be offset or hedged. Hedging requires that the profit in realising the right granted by the option compensates the loss in the underlying currency market in the case of call. For a put, a loss in exercising the option compensates a profit in the underlying currency market. Speculation, however, allows paying the premium in a currency and buying or selling in the same currency for gambling, with cash settlement based on the changes in the exchange rate. The exposure is planned and willingly taken. It may involve rapid transactions in spot exchange rates to change currencies if the right is exercised, but the same currency is at the start and at the end of the process. There are no required future payments in the foreign currency.

In most textbooks, the discussions about options present a profit and loss profile. Profit or loss depends on whether the agent is a writer or seller short on the option or buyer long in the option, but the profiles are symmetrical. Just like Saber (1999b), Taylor (2010) explains that there is actually an asymmetry of risk. Option has a potential limited loss, or the premium paid, and large potential, but not unlimited, as claimed, gain for the buyer. The loss potential should also include any funding and holding costs. That is, a fixed expense and potential unlimited gain, hence. For the seller, there is a limited potential gain given by the premium and a large potential loss. Of course, in the case of the option buyer, the payoff is hyperbolic and the gains cannot be unlimited. Saber (1999b) demolishes the standard option pricing techniques to show that this is indeed the point.

Yet, it would be a task left to empirical research to discover what was the largest option gain ever paid. But it depends on the price of the underlying and, despite the fact that volatility is the norm, it is unlikely that price movements, at least in deep and thick markets, would be extremely large for almost all relevant transactions. For example, considering the downside, equity shares cannot fall by a large amount, since in most stock exchanges there are circuit breakers just to prevent that from happening, although it is set off for an index, not individual stocks. Thus, equity puts cannot generate unlimited gains to their buyers. On the other hand, although stock prices can be affected by herd behaviour, and runs can cause wild increases, there is always an upper limit. Empirical research can offer an answer to the highest daily price increase ever faced by a single stock. For instance, in October 28, 2008, the stocks of Volkswagen AG increased from €211 on Friday, October 24, to €1,005. And this hike was caused by an attempt of acquisition of 75% of the company by Porsche, using options negotiated with Maple Bank to buy the VW stock (Allen et al., 2021). The record was set on February 8, 2011, when stocks of Gateway Industries, a small cap, increased by 30,000% (Schaeffer, 2011). However, this is because the starting price was very low, and in absolute terms, this increase would not represent a substantial amount of money. Finally, it remains the question about why would a financial capitalist sell a call option if, on average, prices had a very high rate of change. Black swans are not the norm.

Finally, regarding real swaps, not the all-embracing view of Dodd–Frank, in this kind of contract the counterparties exchange cash flows based on specific arrangements on an agreed notional value that may not be linked to underlying. The instruments are complex, and, like futures, forward-like, since the contractual terms are mandatory. However, according to the IMF (2009), credit default swaps are not forward-like, but option-like, since premiums are charged to transfer credit risks. As mentioned before, the IMF (2009) and many authors, like Saber (2017), assume only two basic types of *derivatives*: options- and forwards-like, including futures and swaps, but not forwards, since the latter are considered a narrower term in financial markets that excludes swaps. Swaps can be understood as a sequence of forward rate agreement (FRAs; see below), but with a single fixed interest rate for the entire length of the contract (Taylor, 2010).

Hull (1997) mentions other types of non-standard *derivatives*, like the bonds issued by Standard Oil in 1986, with no interest or coupon payment. The yield at maturity would consist of a fixed sum – which could be considered a fixed interest after all – plus a variable amount based on the excess price of oil at maturity over a fixed price. This hybridisation is at the core of development of contemporary *derivatives* under financialised capitalism. Another non-standard *derivative* is the index currency option notes (ICON) sold by Bankers Trust in 1985, a bond whose return depends on foreign exchange rates, and range forward contracts or flexible forwards. Das (2006) mentions swap arrears reset, with the interest rate set according to the then LIBOR at the end of a period, not before. How do these specific contracts allow hedging? They do not. Although it is mentioned but not proved that some are popular in specific markets, it is clear that these combinations cannot be used for hedging purposes. This is a strong indication that speculation and gambling are immersed in the very core of what is called *derivatives*. Nonetheless, the point is that specific arrangements are sometimes so unique and particular that it is hard to consider the reason to put them under the same definition or class of instruments.

Bringing Some Risky Elements of Capital to Specific Arrangements: A Brief Excursion

As it was mentioned before, from a methodological standpoint, it is inevitable to bring the specific types of arrangements onto a discussion of the underlying, since they are intertwined and the risk that justify the existence of the instrument is related to the reference. If one points to financial futures traded on exchanges, it takes the general for the particular, like a synecdoche. Financial futures encompass a large amount of financial variables employed as reference for *derivatives* arrangements, but not only, since it started with commodities, not finance. How does it allow hedging for specific circuits of capital? It depends. Considering interest rates, what *derivatives* should accomplish to manage their risk is to provide compensating changes in interest income, so that changes in interest rates attached to liabilities would not bring about gains or losses. It is also possible to fix the future interest rate. But on which financial reference? Would the value of the underlying affect the magnitude of the interest rate agreed upon or are they independent? The latter seems to be the case. Finally, swaps in OTC, the most important arrangement today in terms of values, allow the direct exchange of interest payments, using as reference a sum of money. It is therefore important to stress the function of instruments, determined by capital needs, not generic markets where they are traded. Again, the mentioned swap arrears reset (Das, 2006), with the interest rate set according to the then LIBOR at the end of a period, not before, is supposed to hedge interest rate risks? Of course, it is not.

In the case of interest rate futures, the standardised contracts create difficulties for long-term debt or loans, since they are mostly short-term contracts, requiring a rolling over for longer future underlying needs. Forward rate agreements (FRAs) are thus introduced. They are financial futures with a different presentation. A strip of FRAs for a sequence of short-term credit transactions is also possible, but it has the disadvantage of bringing uncertainty about the future short-term rates, since they may reset at very different levels for each transaction. FRAs in OTC markets are a similar alternative.

Interest rate options are also available to interest-bearing capital. Options on short-term interest rates, for example, with a single period or a strip with a series of sequential periods. Actually, it is an option to pay or receive a value based on a fixed interest rate and a fixed notional amount, expressed in a given currency, equivalent to an amount of cash borrowed or deposited in that currency for a period of time. It is also cash settled, considering the difference between the strike interest rate and a benchmark. And then there is a plethora of instruments specific for subcircuits of money and financial capital in terms of values and time. Just to mention two, caps are a sequence of individual borrowing interest rate call options to cover borrowing exposures with multiple settlements. Each option has a specific and known period of time, with the cap being rolled over or reset at the individual shorter maturity, but they are part of the same long-run contract, with a single strike or exercise rate on a notional value and premium, a flat basis charged upfront for the entire period. Since premiums depend on the maturity of the contracts, the maturities will run from two to five years. Caps provide a ceiling to the interest rate expense or a maximum funding cost wherein the seller will reimburse any cost in excess. It appears like a useful tool for industrial and commercial capital in need of funding. Floors, on the other hand, are identical to caps, but the sequence of put options are for exposures in interest-bearing deposits, lending or investments, providing a lower limit to interest income, being useful for finance capital and its fractions, like banking capital (Taylor, 2010).

What about the movements of capital beyond national borders? Foreign currency is an asset for the holder and a liability to the central bank issuing it. And its price in terms of the domestic currency can cause capital gains and losses when exchange rates change. Prospective capitalists with future payments in a currency they do not receive regularly, or the ones with revenues in foreign markets can try to fix the exchange rate today using similar alternatives to interest rates, that is, futures, forwards, options and swaps. A third reference, equity, is perhaps the most troubling and difficult issue in this discussion. From the perspective of a corporation, equity is net wealth, not an asset. It brings expenses, like dividends and interest paid to stockholders. For stockholders, it is therefore an asset. Dividend and interest are the corresponding income if one ignores speculative capital gains. So, profits are distributed to stockholders. But *derivatives* cannot hedge the value of the stock forever or at least for the existence of the corporation if it lasts many decades. They can prevent the effects of falling stock prices up to a point in time. From them on, volatility will bring uncertainty. But it cannot protect dividends for the long run, since they depend on real, not financial or paper, short-term profits under financialised capitalism. Perhaps other *derivatives* can prevent lower profits, by preventing higher interest payments, more expensive foreign currency purchases, higher commodity costs and so on. But again, the alternatives do not match the lifespan of a capitalist firm and its continuous flows of cash. Another issue related to stock options is the employee, actually executive, compensation packages. As mentioned before, the IMF (2009) treats executive compensation with options part of the financial *derivatives* measurement. But this is not related to risk management whatsoever.

Moving on, unlike the previous references, most commodities should not be seen as a financial asset. They are the outcome of a production process and therefore are related to a flow, with risks of prices movements for capitalist farms or even sole proprietors. Only when they are sold or stored, they are real assets. But the price determines their value, which can change, mainly with financialised speculation. Of course, mined gold and other rare metals could be considered an asset, with an existing stock and increases and decreases in the volume and price overtime. Finally, credit is not an asset, but an economic relationship, based on trust, since credit originates in the Latin word *credere*, to trust. Credit is a temporary transfer of funds with the commitment of reverting the transfer in the future, plus interest income. Therefore, transfer of stocks generating flows of amortisation and interest. The loan is an asset for the lender. The corresponding debt is a liability for the borrower. So, to the extent that interest rate *derivatives* are related to flows of interest income, credit *derivatives* are related to stocks.

Finishing this chapter, it is important to notice that most examples in the literature assume a once-for-all *derivative* transaction. It is common, in the discussions, to assume that the transaction is one made only once and presented in the singular, like a currency depreciation, an interest rate hike, a drop in a commodity price and so on. This assumes that volatility happens only once and then prices stabilise. But if prices are continuously volatile and change a lot, then hedging must be permanent.[16] And for some institutions, it is indeed a continuous or recurrent necessity, best exemplified by options caps and floors. And for such a long period, they need also a structured team to manage the positions and 'portfolio', increasing the costs of hedging. In this case, are *derivatives* still worth? They deal with the consequences, not the fundamental causes of financialised capitalism and the manufacturing of risks. So, what *derivatives* are not? *Derivatives.*

Summing Up

It is clear that there are many different aspects related to different necessities of capital regarding financial and non-financial aspects of the valorisation and accumulation process that occurs through historical time and therefore is plagued by risks and uncertainty. Specific arrangements have been devised to cope with the specific ways that these risks affect the process of production and circulation of capital. Yet, since capitalism is all about money and more money after some preferably short time, it seems that a general concept like *derivatives* could not capture all the varied situations and the supposed solutions derived. The fact that this chapter had to appeal to many aspects and concepts without a prior definition illustrates the problem. Thus, the idea of *derivatives* eliminates all those differences, with the need of appealing to spurious comparisons. It is not *derivatives* that need a definition. It is the current phase of financialised capitalism that creates the need of a synthesis. It might be something like this: financialised capitalism increases financial risks, and consequently economic risks, and finds in specific arrangements, not generic *derivatives*, devised to cope with them in the different circuits of capital, an important source of accumulation and valorisation, self-reinforcing its intrinsic trend, as explained below.

The specific arrangements and the specific types of phenomena that they connect with point to the fact that *derivatives* ontologically do not exist and the idealistic perspective attempts to overcome this barrier by associating them with other arrangements or even pulling together completely different types of contracts designed to cope with specific risks. The specific arrangements resumed in terms of money circulation is not enough to set them apart of other repositories of capitalist wealth. How to provide a synthesis for four basic or plain vanilla different instruments? It must seek the common feature that justifies putting different things together under the same umbrella, but these are not specific enough to avoid including other instruments. In this regard, *derivatives*, more than a financial market convention, is a fiction. They are needed by finance capital to redistribute income from other fractions of capital and, as a consequence, from labour and the state.

Derivatives do not exist ontologically. They are but an imaginary ensemble of flexible and specialised arrangements with a time dimension that supposedly thwart the market mechanism related to the supposed efficiency of price flexibility, and provide, sometimes, known parameters to capitalist short-run calculations. These arrangements simply create negotiable ownership of the money flows associated with non-negotiable, in those markets at least, pieces of wealth when monetary values, rates, indices or events change, bringing risk to capital. But with the caveat that change is not exogenous, but caused with the contribution of the arrangements themselves under financialised capitalism.

Notes

1 Taylor (2010, p. 27) highlights a pivotal issue in an indirect way, arguing that, although banks in particular are used to marking to market, this procedure is not very familiar for utilities and corporations, mainly the ones that traditionally did not have to, but have now been obliged by changes in rules like IAS 39 and SFAS 133. That is, non-financial firms are not used to short-run financial fluctuations, but must learn to cope with them by force of norms under the new economic logic of financialised capitalism. And managing risks in accordance to financially induced accounting regulation brings forth the mandatory costs associated with this function, as discussed later.

2 This justifies the old, before financialisation, institutional separation of the Commodity Futures Trading Commission (CFTC) and the Securities and Exchange Commissions (SEC) in the United States, for example. See Chapter 9 for a discussion of this split.

3 Taylor oddly writes that (2010, p. 3, italics added) "Assets will include *interest rates*, share (or stock) *prices*, currency *rates*, oil, gas and metal *prices* and even credit and credit *risk*." She uses the term assets too broadly here. Of course, rates are not assets, but financial or monetary ratios that, applied to stocks, generate flows. For debtors, the interest rate is part of a financial cost (expense). Prices are not assets either, but monetary values used to measure, for instance, tradeable assets, liabilities or net worth. Credit is a relationship. A loan is an asset to a lender, but a liability to a borrower. This type of confusion is pervasive in the financial literature. And again she uses (Taylor, 2010) the second approach to define *derivatives*, mentioning off-balance sheet instruments, financial products, risk management instruments and financial engineering – all meaning much the same thing. These are all now collectively covered by the expression *derivative*. Naturally, a loan commitment is off-balance sheet but not a *derivative*. There are many financial products that are not *derivatives* (saving accounts, for example). There are on-balance sheet risk management instruments that are not *derivatives* (cash or long-term assets or liabilities with fixed rates, for instance). Financial engineering can be carried out without any *derivative* transaction whatsoever.

4 Of course, cash is an asset that does not generate a flow of interest income. A shut-off industrial plant neither.

5 However, this term is used in many parts of the document.

6 There are all sorts of analogies. Stulz (2003; 2005) uses a chemical one, for example.

7 See also Steinherr (2000) and Scholes (1998) for stressing the financial innovation dimension of *derivatives*.

8 Saber (1999b) argues that the right of default is a feature of options.

9 On the other hand, he ignores time when discussing the example of Chicago Mercantile Exchange (CME) or Merc. He quotes a work by Robert Tamarkin on the beginnings of exchange operations in eggs and butter at the end of the nineteenth century in the United States. At that epoch, speculators or gamblers in his words would compensate bad years with profitable ones, even though butter and eggs are highly perishable, that is, their life-span is short, which means that compensation was in cash. So, the time horizon would be measured in years, which is at odds with Saber's claim that speculative capital seeks to bring, by means of arbitrage, the time interval between buying and selling to as close as possible to zero, that is, immediate.

10 Another issue that this approach raises is related to the suggested synchronisation of markets by the action of arbitrageurs. If markets are functioning more or less at the same time, this would make them more predictable, since a deviation in one of them would cause speculative capital to exploit the difference, restoring the previous situation. But if this is indeed the case, the role of hedge and therefore of *derivatives* for this specific purpose is questionable.

11 It is necessary to obtain additional evidence about turnover and number of long-term contracts negotiated in this case to assess their appeal in a financialised economy in which the relevant time horizon for valorisation is short. As argued before, there are long-term credit contracts with fixed interest rates. It is not reasonable to enter long-term *derivatives* contracts, built from a sequence of shorter-term contracts, to fix rates for longer periods when they are already available under other instruments, lest the interest and other costs are significantly lower. Chapter 5 shows that, in the case of exchange-traded instruments, long-term contracts are only a small fraction of the total.

12 Saber (1999a) discusses the role of gearing, combined with basis risk, in bringing systemic risk about. This means that individual risk management can cause an aggregate financial and economic turmoil, even though *derivatives* advocates deny that (Scholes, 1996).

13 The possible existence of net positions on intra-Euro zone foreign exchange *derivatives* transactions among European dealers would offer further evidence that these contracts are speculative tools more than hedging ones. Empirical evidence is necessary for further investigating this possibility.

14 The option writer charges a premium above the intrinsic value, since she has to manage the associated time value, that is, a risk premium, and take into account the volatility of the underlying, the time interval, the cost of carry and so on (Taylor, 2010, p. 61). Could these costs be compressed to such extent that option is really one of the cheapest methods of risk management?

15 VaR is the "(…) maximum likely loss over some target period – the most we expect to lose over that period, at a specified probability level." And ETL is "(…) the loss we can expect to make if we get a loss in excess of VaR." (Dowd, 2002, pp. xi–xii)

16 Koppenhaver (2009, p. 4–6) presents four graphs that makes clear the volatility in different markets like foreign exchange, oil, bond and credit. Saber (1999a, p. 119) would call it 'zigzagging'.

References

Allen, Franklin, Marlene D. Haas, Eric Nowak, and Angel Tengulov. "Market Efficiency and Limits to Arbitrage: Evidence from the Volkswagen Short Squeeze." *Journal of Financial Economics* 142, no. 1 (2021): 166–194.

Bernstein, Peter. *Capital Ideas: The Improbable Origins of Modern Wall Street.* New York: Wiley, 2005.

Bertilorenzi, Marco. "Futures of Europe: The City of London's Commodity Exchanges, the European Economic Community, and the Global Regulation of Futures Trading (1960s–1980s)". *Enterprise & Society* 24, no.3 (2022): 731–758.

Breuer, Peter. "Measuring Off-Balance-Sheet Leverage." *Journal of Banking & Finance* 26, (2002): 223–242.

Chance, Don. *Essays in Derivatives: Risk-Transfer Tools and Topics Made Easy*. 2nd ed. Hoboken: Wiley, 2008.

Das, Satyajit. *Traders, Guns and Money: Knowns and Unknowns in the Dazzling World of Derivatives*. London: FT Press/Prentice Hall, 2006.

Dixit, Avinash K., and Robert S. Pindyck. *Investment Under Uncertainty*. Princeton: Princeton University Press, 1993.

Dowd, Kevin. *Measuring Market Risk*. Chichester/West Sussex: Wiley, 2002.

Government Accountability Office (GAO) *Risk-Based Capital: Regulatory and Industry Approaches to Capital and Risk*, GAO/GGD-98-153, July, 1998.

Heath, Robert. "The Statistical Measurement of Financial Derivatives." Working Paper of the International Monetary Fund, *WP/98/24*, Washington, DC: IMF, 1998.

Henwood, Doug. *Wall Street: How it Works and for Whom?* London: Verso, 1998.

Hilferding, Rudolf. *Finance Capital: A Study in the Latest Phase of Capitalist Development.* London: Routledge and Kegan Paul, 1981.

Hirsa, Ali; Salih N. Neftci. *An Introduction to the Mathematics of Financial Derivatives*. Waltham: Academic Press/Elsevier, 2014.

Hull, John. *Options, Futures, and Other Derivatives*. 3rd ed. Upper Saddle River: Prentice Hall, 1997.

Hull, John. *Options, Futures, and Other Derivatives*. 11th ed. London: Pearson, 2021.

International Monetary Fund (IMF). *Balance of Payments and International Investment Position Manual*. Washington, DC: IMF, 2009.

Jarrow, Robert A., and Arkadev Chatterjea. *An Introduction to Derivative Securities, Financial Markets, and Risk Management*. 2nd ed. New Jersey: World Scientific, 2019.

Jarrow, Robert A., and Stuart M. Turnbull. *Derivatives Securities*. 2nd ed. Cincinnati: South-Western College Publishing, 2000.

Kolb, Robert W. *The Financial Derivatives Reader*. Miami: Kolb Publishing Company, 1992.

Kolb, Robert W., and James A. Overdahl (eds.) *Financial Derivatives: Pricing and Risk Management*. New York: Wiley, 2009.

Koppenhaver, Gary. "Derivative Instruments: Forwards, Futures, Options, Swaps, and Structured Products." In: Robert W. Kolb and James A. Overdahl (eds.) *Financial Derivatives: Pricing and Risk Management*. New York: Wiley, 2009.

Lynch, Timothy E. "Derivatives: A Twenty-First Century Understanding." *Loyola University Chicago Law Journal* 43, no. 1 (2011): 1–51.

Miller, Merton. *Merton Miller on Derivatives.* New York: Wiley, 1997.

Moriarty, Eugene, Susan Phillips, and Paula Tosini. "A Comparison of Options and Futures in the Management of Portfolio Risk." *Financial Analysts Journal* 37, no. 1 (1981): 61–67.

National Research Council. *Following the Money: U.S. Finance in the World Economy.* Washington, DC: The National Academies Press, 1995.

Palley, Thomas. *Financialization. The Economics of Finance Capital Domination.* New York/London: Palgrave MacMillan, 2013.

Poitras, Geoffrey. *Risk Management, Speculation and Derivative Securities.* New York: Academic Press, 2002.

Robinson, Joan. "Shedding Darkness." *Cambridge Journal of Economics* 6, no. 3 (1982): 295–296.

Saber, Nasser. "The Challenges of Regulation of Derivatives." In: Raphaël Douady, Clément Goulet, and Pierre-Charles Pradier (eds.) *Financial Regulation in the EU: From Resilience to Growth.* Cham: Palgrave MacMillan/Springer International Publishing, 2017.

Saber, Nasser. *Speculative Capital & Derivatives: The Nature of Risk in Capital Markets.* Vol. 2. London: Financial Times/Prentice Hall, 1999b.

Saber, Nasser. *Speculative Capital: The Invisible Hand of Global Finance.* Vol. 1. London: Financial Times/Prentice Hall, 1999a.

Schaefer, Steve. "CKX Founder Sillerman Gives Penny Stock Monumental Pop." *Forbes Magazine*, February 08, 2011. Available at: www.forbes.com/sites/steveschaefer/2011/02/08/ckx-founder-sillerman-gives-penny-stock-monumental-pop/ Access December 2024.

Scholes, Myron. "Derivatives in a Dynamic Environment." *The American Economic Review* 88, no. 3 (1998): 350–370.

Scholes, Myron. "Global Financial Markets, Derivative Securities, and Systemic Risks." *Journal of Risk and Uncertainty* 12, (1996): 271–286.

Somanathan, T. V., Venkatramanan A. Nageswaran, and Harsh Gupta. *Derivatives*, 2nd ed. Cambridge: Cambridge University Press, 2017.

Sotiropoulos, Dimitris P. "Hilferding on Derivatives." *The European Journal of the History of Economic Thought* 22, no. 1 (2012): 77–96.

Steinherr, Alfred. *Derivatives – The Wild Beast of Finance: A Path to Effective Globalisation?* New York: Wiley, 2000.

Stulz, René M. "Demystifying Financial Derivatives." *The Milken Institute Review,* third quarter (2005): 20–31.

Stulz, René M. *Risk Management and Derivatives.* Mason, OH: South-Western/Cengage Learning, 2003.

Swan, Edward. *Building the Global Market: A 4000 Year History of Derivatives.* The Hague: Kluwer Law International, 2000.

Taylor, Francesca. *Mastering Derivatives Markets.* 2nd ed. London: FT/Prentice Hall, 2010.

United States of America Congress (US Congress). *Dodd-Frank Wall Street Reform and Consumer Protection Act*, January 5, 2010. Available at: www.cftc.gov/sites/default/files/idc/groups/public/@swaps/documents/file/hr4173_enrolledbill.pdf Accessed June 2024.

Valdivia-Velarde, Eduardo. "The Treatment of Financial Derivatives in BPM6." *IFC Bulletin* 35, (2012): 31–43.

Weber, Ernst J. "A Short History of Derivative Security Markets." In: Hafner Wolfgang and Heinz Zimmermann (eds.) *Vinzenz Bronzin's Option Pricing Models.* Berlin/Heidelberg: Springer-Verlag, 2009: 431–466.

Whaley, Robert E. *Derivatives: Markets, Valuation, and Risk Management.* New York: Wiley, 2007.

2 The General Appearance of Specific Circuits of Capital

The Institutions, Prices and Risks behind Arrangements in the *Derivatives* Sub-System

Introduction

The previous chapter introduced the specific arrangements developed before, but mainly the ones created or transformed under financialised capitalism. This chapter presents the institutional settings behind the format of a typical contract, as in the case of exchange-traded instruments, in contrast to bilateral agreement in the OTC markets. Some details associated with the prices dealt with by *derivatives* are equally and briefly brought forth. It also briefly highlights how the most simple or plain vanilla types of *derivatives* markets work, and selects a more complex financial instrument, exchange-traded funds (ETFs), to resume the discussion started in Chapter 1 and highlight their exotic and mainly different nature, which points to the impossibility of lodging them under the same general umbrella just because there is an underlying, since the underlying in this particular case is a *derivative*. The real need is not to manage risks, but to profit from the continuous fabrication of risks.

Thus, the specialised functions and workings point to the necessity of understanding the nature of risk under capitalism in general and under financialised capitalism in particular, just to go beyond the appearance and show the true needs of finance capital. In appearance, the specific arrangements that are lumped together under the label of *derivatives* are related to risks in general. But from a capitalist perspective, risks are very specific, related to the unique circuits of each individual capital, in specific places, times and relationship with other capitals. As a consequence, the arrangements must be specific. This specificity is related to types of contracts, institutional environment, regulation, price formation and so on. In order to gain wide circulation, they are produced, sold and institutionally backed by specific financial organisations interlinked with different circuits. They engage different types of concrete labour and functions in the circuits of capital. Their workings are therefore specific, and this specificity is given by particular forms and needs of specialised capitals.

Before the discussion about the specialised nature of the arrangements known collectively as *derivatives* and some particular institutions starts, a caveat is necessary. This discussion about the institutions and organisations behind the functioning of particular *derivatives* markets, and the appearance that they bear a primary relationship with risks, has a focus on advanced capitalist economies,

DOI: 10.4324/9781003137092-3

mainly the United States and Europe, that dominates financial markets in general and *derivatives* markets in particular, as the empirical evidence overwhelmingly demonstrates in Chapter 4. Of course, although capitalism tends to homogenise practices and circuits of capital in different spaces of accumulation, they may work differently in underdeveloped countries.[1] But the differences are likely to be more institutional and quantitative than functional.

For instance, *derivatives* markets points towards the pre-determination of prices and quantities of underlying to avoid risks as the surface of the phenomenon. Yet, since it is a feature of financialised capitalism, it must go beyond generic markets or circulation, because it must include, on the one hand, regulations by both governments and the industry itself, which is country-specific, the former discussed in Chapter 9, and internal accumulation and cash flow management strategies of capitalist firms, mainly financial firms, on the other. The latter tends to be homogenised by capitalist competition to the extent that financial regulation has not been completely removed. These aspects form an international *derivatives* sub-system or structure, chaining different national spaces, and therefore markets as trade mechanisms are only part of a more complex whole geared towards valorisation and accumulation of finance capital. But, since markets do not work in a vacuum, except in most microeconomics textbooks, it is necessary to show what are the institutions necessary for them to circulate and trade values, capitals and commodities.

Specific Arrangements and their Functions: Singular Institutional Dynamics and Industry Interests

In the previous chapter, specific arrangements like exchange-traded futures and options were considered for some specific needs of capital, that is, to replace intrinsic market uncertainty enhanced by financialised capitalism with a contract fixing prices and quantities or giving an option to trade or not depending upon price differences. But what are the exchanges for trading futures and options contracts all about? Exchanges are a specific institutional arrangement to allow the trade of specific economic, not only financial, values, that is, they are organised capitalist enterprises that provide infrastructure, physical or electronic, and rules for trading, and they also must perform many other functions. The main exchanges that for many time operated in the United States, and many of them were created before contemporary financialised capitalism, are, for example, the Chicago Board of Trade (CBoT), Chicago Board Options Exchange (CBOE), Chicago Mercantile Exchange (Merc or CME), Minneapolis Grain Exchange, Coffee, Sugar and Cocoa Exchange in New York, fused with New York Cotton Exchange (NYCE) in 2004 to form New York Board of Trade (NYBoT), Commodities Exchange (COMEX), a division of the NY Mercantile Exchange (NYMEX), New York Futures Exchange (NYFE), North American Derivatives Exchange (NADEX), Financial Exchange, also a division of the NYMEX, OneChicago, and Kansas City Board of Trade. In Europe, the most important bourses are Euronext, European Exchange (Eurex), London International Financial Futures Exchange (LIFFE), acquired by Euronext in 2001, one year after the latter was formed by the fusion of three European bourses, and thus creating Euronext.liffe. In 2007 NYSE purchased Euronext, forming NYSE Euronext. And in 2013, the NYSE Euronext was acquired by Intercontinental Exchange (ICE), now ICE Futures Europe, which bought NYBoT in 2004. Other important commodity exchanges are the London Metal Exchange and International Petroleum Exchange, also a subsidiary of ICE Futures.

Several aspects must be stressed in the above list. First, there is usually a reference to space, with a city, dominated by Chicago and New York in the United States, or London and the continent in the case of Europe. If at the beginning of some of those institutions the unconnected physical places imposed the necessity of trading in locus, with the communications and technological innovations it became possible to just send orders from anywhere. So, it gets increasingly international, although this tends to receive more emphasis in Europe, for obvious reasons. The circuits in the sub-system were gradually expanded territorially, from local to regional to national and international. Second, there is sometimes a reference to the specific or concrete use values in the form of commodities. The reference to finance is rare, because the logic of specific arrangements like futures and options that were introduced to support the needs of commodity-capital predates the rise of financialised capitalism. Third, sometimes, the specific type of arrangement is emphasised, suggesting some specialisation. Equally important, the appeal to circulation is clear in the very concept of exchange or trade, pointing to exchange values. Only one has *derivatives* in the name, but it was created in 2004 as HedgeStreet and then was inaugurated with the new name in 2009.

However, a more important issue is to place the exchange in the context of capital overall needs of accumulation, concentration and centralisation. As mentioned in the previous chapter, exchanges are institutions for centralising negotiations and information. But centralisation and concentration go beyond the convergence of regional or territorial businesses and reach the functional dimension. As it is clear from the previous paragraphs, many mergers and acquisitions have taken place in the past few years, illustrating the concentration and centralisation phenomena typical of capitalism. In Europe, this process, at least when it comes to financial exchanges, was noticed in the late 1990s (Williamson, 1997, Geranio 2016).[2] In the United States, it is a continuous trend (Francis et al., 2009, Geranio 2016). This issue is addressed again in Chapter 3, but to discuss the mergers and acquisitions of exchanges would require an entire chapter.

Regarding the specific needs of capital attended by individual exchanges, consider that industrial capital accumulated in agriculture faces risks regarding the price and volume of commodities produced and sold. It may need hedge. In the case of hedging with futures and options, exchanges represent the social cost of managing those specific risks. It could also hedge risks associated with the first phases of its circuit, including interest rate, exchange rate and energy. In the case of speculation, they represent the primary social costs associated with net transfers of wealth and, when speculation causes crises, the additional social costs associated with the interruption of the circulation and reproduction of parts of capital. But the relevant issue is that the large initial number of exchanges, before concentration and centralisation, points to the needs of different capitals when they assume the form of specific commodities, with different reproduction processes and circuits. But are there ways to consider the needs of capital as a whole, as self-expanding value, not in the form of commodities with use values?

Collective capital is about power and politics. And since politics cannot be separated from finance and the economy, there are also industry associations that are part of *derivatives* sub-system, geared to channel income and wealth to the sector, with a different layer of intra-capitalist conflicts, that is, beyond distribution of surplus value by changes in prices. Thus, the same question regarding differentiation and specificity applies here. Lobbying is not about general capitalist interests, but specific ones. The associations present an evolution that reflects the transformations of advanced capitalist spaces, circuits, agents and accumulation and valorisation strategies that are also seen in the exchange industry (Geranio, 2016). Despite the apparent change from particular to universal institutions, representing different spaces and circuits, they remain specialised, linked to specific products and particular circuits. For instance, in the United States, just to highlight a few ones, there is the Futures Industry Association (FIA), emphasising in the title a single arrangement. On its webpage,[3] it explains the historical changes faced by the organisation, moving from commodities exchanges to futures in general and also options and, considered something apart, *derivatives*, without escaping the process of centralisation:

> FIA was founded in 1955 in New York as the Association of Commodity Exchange Firms. (...) In 1973, the New York association expanded to include Chicago FCMs [Futures Commission Merchants]. In 1978 it was renamed the Futures Industry Association and moved to Washington. (…) In January 2016 the merger of FIA, FIA Europe and FIA Asia into a single organization took effect. The merged organization serves both the global and regional needs of the futures, options and centrally cleared derivatives markets.

That is, the institutional reorganisation of the *derivatives* sub-system is continuously occurring, both at the state and the capitalist interest levels, national and international. Since they were created in the 1970s, *derivatives* did not exist even as a category, since they never existed as a phenomenon. That is why some of them keep the 'futures' in the name, even though they deal with the other specific types of what is referred to as *derivatives* transactions, such as options. It is not surprising that it started out as a commodity in general association and merged regional territorial capitalist interests with national politics. And then expanded to encompass international capitalist interests of the futures circuits of the global sub-system.

Another contemporary institution attached originally to futures and authorised by the state, that is, the CFTC, is the NFA (National Futures Association)[4]:

> In 1974, Congress established the Commodity Futures Trading Commission (CFTC). The same legislation that established the CFTC also authorized the creation of registered futures associations, giving the industry the opportunity to

> create a self-regulatory organization. NFA's formal designation as a "registered futures association" was granted by the CFTC on September 22, 1981. NFA began its regulatory operations in 1982.

It is interesting to see that, despite the fact that *derivatives* are considered very ancient, as discussed in Chapter 5, not only exchanges were being created in Europe in the late 1970s, but futures associations were still being created in the 1980s, under the auspices of financialised capitalism. On the other hand, the members of the NFA, as part of the *derivatives* market participants in general (Chui, 2012), show the specialised nature of the arrangements involving commodities and other instruments, considering both the reference or underlying and contract type. Many of the occupations that represent concrete labour described below are defined by the Title VII of Dodd–Frank Act and some of them were already regulated by the CFTC under the Futures Trading Act. These include commodity pool operators or managed money traders; commodity trading advisors; futures commission merchants, who trade on behalf of non-members of exchanges; forex dealer members; introducing brokers; associated persons; and swap dealers. Thus, it is clear the emphasis on commodities, foreign exchange, futures and swaps. The labour functions include operators, advisors, merchants, brokers and dealers. The Dodd–Frank Act emphasises other agents, such as floor brokers and floor traders.

A third institutional organisation is even more significant to an understanding of the *derivatives* sub-system, moving beyond exchange-traded arrangements. The International Swaps Dealers Association (ISDA) was created, not surprisingly, in 1985 for standardising the interest rate swap transactions in OTC markets, suggesting once more that *derivatives* as a concept is an invention of the 1980s. In the Nasdaq glossary, the original title appears.[5] It was specialised in the new arrangements that could not be part of the *derivatives* before, for the very reason that *derivatives* today include swap as the single most important specific arrangement. And it organises only a single function or concrete labour, that of the dealers. The association switched its name to International Swaps and Derivatives Association (ISDA), in 1994. Notwithstanding the more all-inclusive title, both in terms of instruments, as it moves beyond swaps, and of agents as it goes beyond dealers, and the maintenance of the abbreviation, it raises the doubt about the separation of swaps from all other *derivatives*, suggesting that swaps are not *derivatives*. Indeed, as concrete and specifically financial arrangements, they are not, but neither are the other instruments lumped together. Finally, the globalisation of capital requires that the specific circuits of finance capital assume an international dimension, and thus the associations that promote the specific interests of the sub-system must reflect that. More important, the interests of this specific circuit of the sub-system were not represented by the other two institutions, suggesting once more that they are singular.

The Dodd–Frank Act of 2010 prohibits any futures associations or national securities association to issue rules, regulations or orders. This jeopardises the idea of self-regulation that is one of the justifications for the associations. However, as Charles (2012) shows, there are master plans issued by the ISDA to homogenise transactions and mainly behaviours, which are at striking contrast with deep meaning of OTC settings, and under Dodd–Frank Master Agreements are also considered part of 'swaps' regulated by the Act.

The Circulation of Finance Capital and Its Needs: Pricing, Functioning and Usages of *Derivatives*

The *derivatives* sub-system has economic and political institutions to back the circulation and valorisation of fractions of finance capital. The former creates the environment for money to valorise as capital. But valorisation requires, at the surface, that an initial quantity of money turns into a larger one. This depends on prices and quantities. A large part of the literature concerned with *derivatives* deals with the pricing of those instruments, since risks can be traded only if there are prices to measure the amount of money to be transferred between parts. Since *derivatives* are related to the future time, their price is related to the unknown forward or spot price of the underlying in the future. This is the guesstimated benchmark, not the current or present spot price, though. If the price equals the benchmark, then the *derivatives* is being priced at its fair value (Taylor, 2010). In this case, the price of *derivatives* contracts is about speculation on changes in other prices, rates or conditions such as credit and defaults. Prices of commodities as inputs, prices of money in terms of time or interest rates, prices of money in terms of different monetary spaces or exchange rates, price of financial wealth such as stocks, bonds, stock market indices and so on. These prices are therefore related to flows of income and expenditures and stocks.

There is another aspect that is the time, not only as it relates to interest rate changes, but the fundamental measure of liquid wealth that connects the present and the future. What is the relevant horizon? For industrial capitalists who want to build long-lasting firms, production and sales must be continuous. And prices will have to be considered according to overlapping or sequential schedule sales. Even though it could be thought that the longer the horizon, the higher the degree of uncertainty, this depends on the specific dynamics of markets. For many fractions of finance capital, it is impossible to anticipate even intra-day prices. Since the accumulation of industrial capital happens slowly over time, this means that a non-financial company will have to hedge all the time if it does not have enough market power or constitute a monopoly in Hilferding's (1985) account. Hedging under unstable capitalist economies must be in this case a recurrent activity. If the cost of hedging is less than the expected loss or reduction in income, it would not be a problem to sustain a permanent succession of hedging transactions. But expected losses and income reductions are associated with volatile prices. This is also true for finance capital, of course. So, Taylor (2010, p. 89) laments, regarding futures, that, despite the fact that they offer finance capital excellent hedging and trading opportunities, most firms do not have the resources, that is, time and money, necessary to manage a portfolio of futures contracts. This is not about futures alone, for sure. Yet, it is clear that banks, financial institutions and large multinational firms with profit-driven treasury departments create volatility that requires hedging for all other less powerful capitalist units. It would not be unfortunate if smaller non-financial firms could find other hedging mechanisms or avoid some of the above risks created by finance capital.

That is, if prices and rates were, not completely, but reasonably stable, *derivatives* would not be necessary. Capitalist uncertainty also relates to lack of knowledge about when prices will be less volatile or when they will be more volatile and therefore when *derivatives* can be advantageously employed for hedging. Taylor (2010, p.24) exemplifies with a banking example for a prospective debtor willing to borrow, not now but three months later, because this is the need imposed by the working of the circuit wherein it operates. She remarks that since financial markets change continuously, the bank cannot guarantee the rate three months in advance. The only possibility is for the bank to assume the interest rate risk. She adds that with complex *derivatives*, it is not always possible to have quoted prices and therefore it is impossible to mark them to market prices. The fundamental uncertainty kicks back even stronger.

In discussing specific arrangements, their prices and their functions, it is important to distinguish between the central elements of the appearance of the circuits: spot markets, with known prices for present payment and instantaneous delivery, and markets where all these references are projected into the future, with known future contracted or quoted prices, no matter how frequently they change, a situation that cannot be applied to spot prices that will be formed in the future, for partially present or deferred payment and promised notional delivery that almost never occurs, since money, not commodities, is the goal. A margin deposit may be needed in the case of futures markets to balance the value of the contract, as mentioned. Options require a premium upfront. There is a time relationship between futures or forward prices and spot prices, depending on their evolution and the dynamics of both markets. It may be in a contango, with future prices above spot markets, or undergoing a backwardation, with future prices below spot prices (Kawai, 1987). It is impossible to know which trend will prevail in the future.

It is valid to state that spot prices are not manna from heaven. They are formed under conditions of uncertainty, since they are always future prices when regarded from the history or past periods. The present as history, as Marxist thinker Paul Sweezy would have it. Anyway, they are variable, but today at least the quotes for future or average or median expected prices are known with certainty and must be enforced by the state regulating contracts and the exchanges. *Derivatives* do not consider long-run trends or tendencies in prices, however. Finance is always geared to the shortest run. Moreover, as stated, price volatility is not constant. And, according to the Prebish–Singer hypothesis, commodity prices have a falling trend along modern history of international trade (Arezki et al., 2014). Buyers of commodities would profit more over time compared to the past. The authors demonstrate that volatility is time-varying and has increased recently. So, in the long run, speculators would rather short commodity *derivatives* if they were not focused exclusively on short-run gains. But who would long them in this case? Thus, what matters for finance and speculation is the short run movements in prices, regardless of their longer term trends. Even long-run falling prices can increase for shorter intervals. *Derivatives* represent short-termism. Thus, given durable stocks of wealth, it is not possible to calculate with accuracy their current value based on volatile market prices, both regarding the future cash flows and the future interest rates used to bring them to present values.

The above suggests that there are many prices involved in the *derivatives* subsystem, depending on the specific arrangements, not to mention the price of the *derivative* contracts themselves. There are references to forward prices, strike prices, future spot prices and so on. As discussed in the previous chapter, the traditional definition of *derivatives* emphasises this value relationship between two economic variables due to volatility that brings risks to capital valorisation and accumulation. Actually, this relationship involves three prices. Prices at two different periods of time: spot prices and future spot prices, but whose terminology changes with the instrument, being strike price for options and forward price for forwards, for example. But time-wise, they represent the same projection of capitalist ignorance. And then there are contracted future prices in *derivatives* arrangements, which may or may not turn out to be equal to the spot price in the future. Since future spot prices cannot be known before the future, other prices are offered as substitutes with a higher degree of certainty or lower degree of uncertainty, since there is basis risk, as discussed below. Except for future spot prices, which cannot be knowable except when they will be formed in a different period, all other prices are known in their averages, which can be more or less reliable depending upon volatility. This is a simple way to price risk, and lull capitalists' disquietude about the future value of their money, but, of course, it cannot eliminate uncertainty.

Regarding the pricing of futures specifically, Taylor (2010, p.78) affirms that it follows an auction that is competitive and are quoted on an index basis in terms of spreads between bids and offers. The prices must cover the related costs. There is an initial margin deposit requested in the form of a collateral, to cope with changes in the value of the underlying, and its level is adjusted by the exchange's clearing house according to market conditions, that is, generalised volatility, as captured by the standard portfolio analysis of risk (SPAN).[6] The collateral is returned with interest when the position is closed. The positions are marked-to-market daily, generating variation in the initial margin according to profits and losses. A sequence of short-term credit arrangements known as strips can be used. Margin calls are deployed to avoid a lack of funds. Therefore, the settlement is incremental, not once-for-all. This reduces the counterparty risk. As a consequence, institutional arrangements shape the way specific transactions are conducted, such that the required shorter and gradual amounts avoid substantial and sudden losses and gains. Transfers of wealth in the form of cash are gradual. But for hedgers, the price of future delivery of notional quantities is known. For forwards, there is no price or cost to start the transaction, but there might be costs to manage a portfolio with many positions, as mentioned before.

Derivatives prices have, sometimes, a complex determination, that goes against the risk management as it adds different sources of uncertainty. Considering only plain vanilla *derivatives*, options have the more complex pricing mechanism. Roughly, it involves (i) the underlying price or current spot price benchmark. The lower this price is compared to the strike price, the higher the premium for calls. It also includes (ii) the strike price, and the difference between the strike price and the spot is the intrinsic value. The (iii) maturity is part of the formula, such that the longer the maturity, the costlier the premium. The fourth element is the expected market volatility, having a positive correlation with the premium as well. And (v) whether the option is a call or a put. This is because the relationship between strike price and underlying price is inverted depending on the option type.

Considering the volatility, it is not clear why buyers would exercise the option more frequently when the market for the underlying is more volatile. Volatility would cause the benchmark price to be sometimes above, sometimes equal to and sometimes below the strike price. The existence of put–call parity supposedly prevents arbitrage. Any difference between the price of these two options on some underlying is the present value of the interest paid on a safe sum of money over the same time period. If the difference exceeds or is below the cumulative interest, then arbitrage takes place. Haug (2009) mentions older texts about equity options assuming that, despite a larger number of transactions in calls due to a propensity to expect higher stock prices, it would be possible for converters to transform an option into another one rather than exercising it. This behaviour is likely to induce capitalists to buy options, creating a floor to the price or premium paid, not necessarily to exercise them at maturity.[7] Summing it up, the issuer of the option estimates the likelihood of the buyer exercising the right, and adjusting the premium to this probability.

Cash settlement occurs by means of a reversed contract, that is, a long turns into a short or vice-versa, with the corresponding transaction cost, and the monetary difference, ultimate goal of the transaction, paid in cash to replace physical delivery. It is not about production and circulation of commodities, even when they serve as a reference for negotiating the contract. In the case of futures, Santos (2008, electronic source) informs that approximately 99% of all contracts are settled prior to maturity. Thus, the standardised time of contract is a maximum period for the valorisation of money capital. This means that the contracts for future delivery are transacted with dates not based on production and circulation by means of delivery in major physical markets, although they may have, in the case of agricultural commodities, some connection with harvest periods, just to pretend they are not about money only. It is about speculation on commodity prices.

Santos (2008) explains that the majority of contracts are therefore offset and that even outright delivery is really about a title of ownership. He also quotes another study claiming that more than 90% of transactions recorded in the industry did not involve delivery. Of course, commodities are produced, negotiated and delivered in industrial and commercial circuits of capital. Yet, *derivatives* markets are not, or may not be, the best venue to accomplish that last function. But by offsetting contracts, producers can hedge without any relationship with the amount produced, opening up room for speculative positions. And standardised volumes in contracts cannot fully anticipated the amounts produced or sold that must be hedged against market follies. That is, the *derivatives* standardised contracts traded on exchanges can be designed for quantities that differ from real production, being only notional quantities. The standardisation in exchanges explains the explosive growth of OTC deals, since the needs of capital are specific.

Cash settlement or, according to Taylor (2010), contracts for differences (CFD), is therefore a necessity of financialised capitalism, since neither commodity nor capital need to be transferred in totality in a situation of risk and uncertainty about future spot prices. She equally claims that speculators prefer cash settlement and hedgers prefer physical delivery. And she guestimates, without explicit supporting evidence, but aligned with Santos (2008), that only between 1% and 2% of contracts go for delivery in the case of futures. So, *derivatives* are about cash and changes in cash based on a random parameter or underlying, in the sense of not being deterministic or necessary. Future prices formed in exchanges are necessary in general, given intrinsic capitalist uncertainty about the future, but which specific price is irrelevant when speculation is the main activity in this sub-system, along as it is different, be it in the future, be it in the contract.

In this regard, the different types of capitalist users connect with the purposes of using *derivatives*. Banks can hedge, speculate, engage in arbitrage or all of these three. Taylor (2010) assumes that large, mainly non-financial corporations, prefer to hedge or mitigate risks, whereas banks are willing to take on risks and speculate. As a general assumption, it seems valid. However, there is room for different capitals within the same industry and even corporation. As Saber (1999) argues, the treasury departments in large non-financial corporations may more likely than not to be interested in speculating, at least for some periods, since they are, under 'speculative capital' imposition, required to generate profits, not only protecting the existing net income flows.[8] And bank managers may be obliged to hedge some of their operations with other financial institutions. Also, to the extent that banks engage with other banks, they can perform the role of either hedgers, arbitrageurs or speculators. More important, banks are not only users. They are market makers in *derivatives*. Saber (1999) and Steinherr (2000) argue that U.S. money centre banks are the more important players in *derivatives* markets. This is proved empirically in Chapter 4.

Beyond the Risk Management Usages and Functions of *Derivatives*: Finance Capital and Fabricated Volatility

So far, it may not have been clear why *derivatives* belong to circuits of capital pursing profits, and of financial capital in particular. This is easy to show, though. Governments usually do not need *derivatives* for their administrative functions, since the latter are arrangements associated with money-making goals by large for-profit financial institutions. Orange county in California, in the United States, being an exception, as discussed in Chapter 8. The same is true for government-sponsored enterprises. Workers usually do not need them either, even when they have floating interest rate debts or consume imported goods. At least for hedging purposes, even though they face major economic risks to their income such as unemployment or lack of safety on the job, wage and benefit cuts in real terms, having to default on their debts, mortgage interest hikes, and so on. Of course, better paid workers, mainly those working in the financial industry, can speculate with *derivatives*. And employee compensation schemes utilise options, as discussed in the previous chapter. If *derivatives* are effective in managing risks, why not expand *derivatives* and include price indices like the CPI, then? They would provide hedge to workers if Cost of Living Adjustment (COLA) clauses in labour contracts were not available. Or even the Producer Price Index (PPI) for producers? If stock market indices can be used to facilitate speculation, why not indices that are related to prices of the labour force and other productive inputs and also output? Because *derivatives* are about finance and finance capital in contemporary financialised capitalism (Palley, 2013).

As mentioned before, there are two positions in *derivatives* markets: short or sale and long or purchase, and the traditional classification of *derivatives* users places them as hedgers, traders and arbitrageurs. Again, it is inevitable that these functions appeared without explanation before. Hedgers seek to transfer risks to avoid losing money, usually assuming long positions. Speculators need risks to earn money, and so do agents engaged in arbitrage, with the distinction that the latter does not involve risks, but it does not need protection either. They can either short or long, or both, in different markets. Taylor (2010), on the other hand, confuses the type of users with their nature. For example, she mentions private clients – but would hedgers, traders and arbitrageurs be government agents otherwise? – and even volume of sales, that is, retail market – but hedgers can only insure their exposures in wholesale markets then? Basically, private means that it is not a market exclusive for corporations and that individuals may buy and sell. Retail markets is a more complex arrangement named 'arcade', with companies providing space, technology and capital to individuals.

Thus, hedgers seek insurance against unfavourable market movements or fixed rates. Traders make the market – price and then sell or short the contracts – and hedge or not their positions. So, they may also be hedgers and assume long positions. Arbitrageurs in the *derivatives* sub-system exploit price differential between *derivatives* markets and the cash markets for the underlying. It is important to draw attention to the vanishing of speculators in Taylor's account. Speculation becomes subsumed under traders and private clients and probably under retail as well. Hull (1997) provides a straightforward and complete classification, considering hedgers, speculators and arbitrageurs. Kuserk (2009), in turn, discusses only speculation and hedging.

Saber (1999) provides a deep discussion of arbitrage by speculative capital, a user type rarely emphasised in the literature. Of course, his stress on speculative capital suggests that speculation is central in his approach. To be precise, he claims that the activity of 'buying low and selling high' should not be considered arbitrage, but old-fashioned commerce. He rejects the conventional definition of arbitrage as the activity of locking in riskless profits associated with a simultaneous price differential between two markets or assets, since basis risk cannot be eliminated. Arbitrage, in his view, is carried out by speculative capital through a learning process associated with sequential speculation, to reduce the time between buying and selling. This is necessary to earn risk-free profits, as risks are strongly related to time intervals. As a consequence, he conflates arbitrage and speculation, to the extent that the former is carried out by speculative capital.

However, for him, arbitrage seems to be a sequential activity by herds of capital. Finance capital seeks opportunities in markets with price differentials. And then, it profits from these differentials until they disappear. Arbitrage restores temporarily the 'equilibrium' in a subset of markets and them move to a different market that is 'out of equilibrium', assuming that it has no impact on these states or situations, that is, equilibrium and disequilibrium simply appear out of nowhere. George Soros, the celebrated speculator, in a famous testimony given to the U.S. House Committee on Banking, Finance and Urban Affairs in 1994, in the context of a review of *derivatives* usage in the financial system, remarks that (U.S. House of Representatives, 1994, p. 37):

> I must state at the outset that I am in fundamental disagreement with the prevailing wisdom. The generally accepted theory is that financial markets tend toward equilibrium and, on the whole, discount the future correctly. I operate using a different theory, according to which financial markets can't possibly discount the future correctly because they don't merely discount the future; they help to shape it. In certain circumstances, financial markets can affect the so-called fundamentals which they are supposed to reflect. When that happens, markets enter into a state of dynamic disequilibrium and behave quite differently from what would be considered normal by the theory of efficient markets. Such boom–bust sequences don't arise very often, but when they do they can be very disruptive, exactly because they affect the fundamentals of the economy (...)

So, it is possible to argue that equilibrium is an irrelevant concept to understand how the economy and finance work (Kaldor, 1972). This is because speculation destabilise it (Kaldor, 1939). And more so under conditions of financialised capitalism. If speculative capital indeed contributes to eliminating the price differential and profit opportunities, it would commit suicide. So, it has to create another price differential when it moves to another market or even in the same market, mainly with herd behaviour and bandwagon as smaller capitals follow bigger capitals, like those accumulated by Soros and its fund.

Saber (1999) rejects this phenomenon, but it seems quite real and relevant to understand the dynamic of speculation. If prices change when speculative capital buys assets, the same must happen when they revert the transaction and sell to fly away. Thus, it seems more likely that arbitrage and speculation occur simultaneously in many different markets, since financialisation creates a large number of financial assets/liabilities, and with a corresponding large number of markets. Finance capital competes with other types of capitals for profits, and it competes with different fractions of finance capital originating from different spaces or circuits and even different firms, including large non-financial firms. And the final result is permanent state of volatility, there being no equilibrium. As Soros affirms (U.S. House of Representatives, 1994): "As long as price changes are continuous, no great harm is done except perhaps higher volatility which in turn increases the demand for derivative instruments." *Derivatives* have grown so fast because of the volatility they help to create.

The typical users of *derivatives* are varied, but concentrated in large economic units with market clout, like corporations, multilateral financial institutions, government agencies dealing with finance, wealthy individuals, and mainly banks and other financial institutions. Although small units can take part in the market, they are not the most important players, even in the financial sector, as discussed in Chapter 4. Another research would be necessary to discuss all the participants in *derivatives* markets, their functions, roles, sizes and performance (Chui, 2012). But the major financial institutions are very active and dominant. So, the market is about the needs of profits of finance capital and the risks it creates by its movements in different circuits.

Anyway, there are many sources of confusion related to *derivatives* and their uses. Take hedging, for example. Hedge funds are one of the largest buyers of *derivatives* from banks. But the long positions do not mean they hedge. So, the name is a misnomer. The testimony of Soros is useful again (U.S. House of Representatives, 1994, p.38):

> Generally, hedge funds don't act as issuers or writers of derivative instruments. They are more likely to be customers. Therefore, they constitute less of a risk to the system than the dynamic hedgers at the derivatives desks of financial intermediaries. So please don't confuse dynamic hedging with hedge funds. They have nothing in common except the word 'hedge'.

They have much more in common than Soros acknowledges, however. For example, profiting from speculation that is far away from hedging. Hedge funds and *derivatives* are an intrinsic part of speculative capital (Saber, 1999) or financialised capitalism. Yet, writers of *derivatives* could be hedged. And customers usually speculate with them in geared positions. Long or short is a matter of positioning regarding future spot prices. As a consequence, Soros is wrong, since large-scale speculation has always a systemic potential. The hedge fund LTCM collapsed using *derivatives* only four years after his testimony. Lleo and Ziemba (2014) discuss how to lose money using *derivatives* in the hedge funds industry.

Another example of very specific arrangements created by the needs of finance capital and that derive their value from an underlying but are not considered *derivatives*, although, like hedge funds, are huge users of *derivatives*, are exchange-traded funds (ETFs). There are many different types of these speculative repositories, such as leveraged, inverse and synthetic funds. They use *derivatives* for replication, that is, trying to achieve the net income of an underlying index, without owning the assets. They are therefore all synthetic, and traded not only on exchanges, as the name suggests, but also OTC (Saber, 2017). For instance, equity ETFs are composed of underlying shares to track an equity index. Yet, they are not *derivatives*. There are futures and options on ETFs, and they may have important consequences for the spot markets, that is, the underlying, mainly commodities. Some ETFs own physical assets. So, commodity *derivatives* are impacted by ETFs using commodity *derivatives* as the underlying. Thus, there is a double layer, at least. In the case of equity ETFs, there is a stock market index, a fund containing equities whose price depend on them, but nonetheless not accounted as *derivative*, or an equity derivative. This is quintessentially financialised capitalism built upon fictitious capital, duplicating values that must self-expand.

Is there any singularity related to *derivatives* in this regard? Are there functions that can be performed only by *derivatives*? Considering the capitalist ethos, it can be rephrased as 'are there functions that can be performed only by *derivatives* at the lowest possible monetary transfer'? At first, this question makes sense only in terms of hedging. Speculation can be carried out using a large number of tools. For example, a corn farm. If only physical activity is considered, no *derivatives* are unconditionally needed. Only for crop insurance, that is, protecting against falls in the price of corn. And then an important thing stressed by the literature surfaces: hedging may be unnecessary, since the corn price could go up. For the farm in the example, if the price rises, there are larger profits. But, if prices drop, hedging using *derivatives* may be useful. Maybe. Available contracts in exchanges can provide futures contracts at prices higher than expected future spot prices, but nonetheless still below costs of production, leading to losses, albeit smaller. Of course, hedging would be, in this case, merely a partial compensation. Under financialised capitalism, however, commodities are assets, and price volatility for capitalist producers is caused by the needs of finance.

Speculation, in turn, depends on entering a contract that allows gains or losses. There must be a counterparty. If the counterparty is willing to speculate, both of them must have divergent views about the future spot price. If the counterparty does not want to speculate, it must find another party willing to enter the opposite side of the bet. Yet, in order to hedge, the counterparty uses the underlying value as the reference. Thus, the same underlying can have its value multiplied as many times as a new transaction is needed to hedge. This explains why the notional value or nominal principal amount of *derivatives* contracts is so large as shown in Chapter 4.

In this case, hedgers or intermediaries could easily find a counterparty to trade risks. Yet, speculators would have to deal with other speculators or arbitrageurs in this market short of hedgers. Individually, it does not make any difference. All capitalist players can have their needs fulfilled. On the other hand, in the aggregate, there are potential problems, since gains are not balanced by losses. Whereas hedgers have a potential zero income position in the transaction, excluding the costs of hedging and margin deposits, speculators and arbitrageurs could suffer losses intrinsic to the deal. By definition, there are many risks unhedged for capital. If speculators losing money are geared, this means that a systemic impact could also be the result of unhedged bets. It spills over to other markets and instruments, mainly cash and short-term securities and credit. Systemic risks are inevitable with *derivatives*.

As a matter of fact, even hedgers may not be completed protected against losses. Basis or price risk, that is, the settlement price may be 'unusual' (Das, 2006). Hedgers may also buy protection for more than the value exposed. Finance, however, has the power to fix the contract parameters. Would people transact under such conditions? According to Das (2006), yes, since they are enticed or lured to. As long as the difference is not too large, this has no potential systemic or financial impact, as long as it does not spill into the real economy.

As mentioned, the literature has developed a consensus: *derivatives* may not be needed. For hedgers, prices may not move in the undesired direction. For arbitrageurs, there is a more interesting issue: if technology and low-cost information allows prices to converge among many global markets, are there remaining riskless opportunities for profit? Why would *derivatives* markets be different? It seems that arbitrage would persist only in less thick and deep markets, as in underdeveloped economies. And finally, for speculators, *derivatives* markets are only another source of potential bets. It is necessary therefore to compare volatility in different markets across the economies. One could guess that the more volatility there is in a market, the more speculators will be attracted to it. Even if *derivatives* did not exist, speculation would still exist. When existing speculative instruments are exhausted, finance capital concocts others, such as *derivatives* and ETFs.

If *derivatives* are not truly necessary for hedging, what else can be done to cope with an uncertain future in volatile markets brought about by financialised capitalism that creates ceaseless movements for calculating the valorisation of capital? Haug (2009) remarks that volatility is stochastic and not amenable to forecasting. This converges to Keynesian–Knightian fundamental uncertainty. As mentioned before, an alternative is bilateral negotiations of price and quantities. If there are not many buyers, this makes sense. On the other hand, for many buyers, it may be costly. Another alternative is to smooth out the impact on accounts of price and output fluctuations, by keeping a liquid reserve fund from previous profits (Milan, 2014). The third alternative is to diversify the commodity output, if natural conditions allow it, but specialisation goes against. The fourth alternative, to avoid extending the list any further, is to enter a long-term contract with an average price that is fixed. From a financial perspective, it would not be very different. So, *derivatives* are not intrinsically necessary for capital to manage different sources of risk, but they are necessary for the needs of finance capital once the economy is financialised. Connecting with the role of exchanges, Miller (1997, p. 4) suggests that *derivatives* with financial underlying are a response to volatility, but also to the decline of traditional *derivatives* in agricultural commodities and the necessity of portfolio diversification by financial corporations. He claims that CBOT and CME started developing options on common stocks along with interest and foreign exchange rates products and were compelled to diversify in view of the stagnation in their traditional agricultural markets. It is not about freedom of innovation, but about capitalist competition for profits.

How can these aspects be placed in a critical position? Financialised capitalism needs flexible arrangements to facilitate the passage of M to M′, such that the same contract can be used to arbitrate, to speculate and to hedge, depending on the specific needs of specific forms of capital at specific times. These functions are somehow intertwined. Considering hedging and speculating, for example, hedging means incurring a smaller cost to avoid a bigger loss and speculating means betting on a change that is expected to generate a gain, although there is a risk of a loss that cannot be avoided. The specific arrangements are, in this sense, contradictory, just like finance capital that gives rise to them or transforms them.

Besides, as already mentioned, it is possible to use some of the arrangements for executive compensation packages, with employee stock options. Are capitalist firms buying options to pay executives with them to hedge against what risks? Ineffectual managers, including failure to hedge against financial and economic risks? Are corporations speculating, hedging or engaging in arbitrage? None. *Derivatives* can be used as a part of the pay of executives without any relationship with hedging or speculation, since under financialised capitalism they are profitable. Executives are the only non-business agents, except for central banks and government agencies, that have economic access to *derivatives*. This is partially a reaction the principal–agent problems associated with the division between ownership of the means of production and the control over them. Stock options, in theory, would align the interests of managers and shareholders. However, historically this has caused corporations to buy back their stocks, boosting the prices up and promoting handsome rewards to executives regardless of firm's real performance. This issue is discussed in Chapter 7. But it adds to the failures of *derivatives*.

Summing Up

This chapter kept the overall emphasis on the specificity of arrangements that are wrongly called *derivatives*. It considered first the existence of exchanges, specialised institutions wherein the first arrangements were traded and today reflects the impact of financialisation. It also considered other institutions that promote the interests of the capitalists circulating in the circuits of the *derivatives* financial sub-system. Next, the chapter dealt with the operations of *derivatives*, considering all the prices that matter for the sub-system and typical uses that show an asymmetry, with the prevalence of speculation. Finally, the chapter discussed the issue of risks and how they, albeit real, are fabricated and *derivatives* are a false solution to a problem that exists only because of the volatility created by finance capital.

Notes

1 The IFC Bulletin 35 (BIS, 2012) is the outcome of a workshop on Data Requirements for Monitoring Derivative Transactions, which took place at the People's Bank of China (PBoC) training centre in Zhengzhou in 2010. The publication has chapters on advanced capitalist countries like France and Japan, but also on underdeveloped capitalist countries like Chile. There is a chapter on China, but the socioeconomic system in China is hard to define (Schweickart, 2015). If China has a capitalist system, then it is still not completely advanced. If China follows a market socialism, the presence of *derivatives* suggests that it is more market and financialisation than socialism.

2 Williamson (1997, pp. 406 and 411) highlights another feature that is fundamental to this book: "Financial derivative exchanges, being much younger (the first European derivative exchanges – the London Traded Options Market and the Amsterdam European Options Exchange – were established in 1978) (…)" And "They [mergers] have been facilitated

by (...) greater understanding of derivative markets by stock market participants (…).” *Derivatives* are a creature of contemporary capitalism and finance capital.

3 Available at: www.fia.org/fia/about-fia Retrieved December 2023.

4 Available at: www.nfa.futures.org/about/index.html Retrieved December 2023.

5 Available at: www.nasdaq.com/glossary/i/international-swap-dealers-association Retrieved December 2023. See also Charles (2012).

6 Dowd (2002) explains that SPAN was developed by the CME and takes into account 14 scenarios in which volatility can change, both up and down, and futures price can stay constant or assume one out of three movements in either direction. It additionally considers two extreme movements in both directions. Each one of these settings has a price identified by a theoretical model. The gauge of risk is the maximum loss incurred, with full loss for all scenarios except the two extreme ones, in which the loss is limited to 35%. Exchanges here attempt to satisfies the needs of capital, but why only 14 scenarios and not 15 or 13?

7 In reality, the volatility is not known but implied. Taylor (2010) mentions that there are exchange-traded options on interest rate futures. Since the price of these options is known, it is easy to calculate backwards the implied volatility.

8 In the Ph.D. dissertation that gave birth to this book, it is argued that, for non-financial corporations in the United States since the 1990s, holding liquid assets like cash and cash equivalents seemed the option for managing macro-financial risks like interest rates and foreign exchange rates. If this is the case, both Saber and Taylor’s accounts must be challenged. To the extent that non-financial firms hedged their risks, it was not by means of *derivatives*. And if they were taking on positions, it was not by the treasury department, since their cash holdings had had an important cushion in protecting the flows. If they were speculating with *derivatives*, their positions were small compared to liquid assets. Of course, comparing on balance sheet variables with off-balance sheet positions is tricky. But there is an important literature showing that firms do not hedge with *derivatives* (Guay and Kothari 2003; McPhail et al. 2024; Minton et al. 2009).

References

Arezki, Rabah, Kaddour Hadri, Prakash Loungani, and Yao Rao. “Testing the Prebisch–Singer Hypothesis since 1650: Evidence from Panel Techniques that Allow for Multiple Breaks.” *Journal of International Money and Finance* 42, (2014): 208–223.

Bank for International Settlements (BIS). “Data Requirements for Monitoring Derivative Transactions”, Irving Fisher Committee on Central Bank Statistics. *IFC Bulletin* 35, (2012): 1–116.

Charles, GuyLane. “The ISDA Master Agreement – Part I: Architecture, Risks and Compliance.” *Practical Compliance & Risk Management for the Securities Industry*, (January/February, 2012): 25–32.

Chui, Michael. “Derivatives Markets, Products and Participants: An Overview.” *IFC Bulletin* no. 35 (2012): 3–11.

Das, Satyajit. *Traders, Guns and Money: Knowns and Unknowns in the Dazzling World of Derivatives*. London: FT Press/Prentice Hall, 2006.

Dowd, Kevin. *Measuring Market Risk*. Chichester/West Sussex: Wiley, 2002.

Francis, Jack C., Arie Harel, and Giora Harpaz. “Exchange Mergers and Electronic Trading.” *The Journal of Trading*, 4, no. 1 (Winter 2009): 35–43.

Geranio, Manuela. *Evolution of the Exchange Industry: From Dealers' Clubs to Multinational Companies*. Cham, Switzerland: Springer Nature, 2016.

Guay, Wayne, and S. P. Kothari. "How Much Do Firms Hedge with Derivatives?" *Journal of Financial Economics* 70, no. 3 (2003): 423–461.

Haug, Espen G. "The History of Option Pricing and Hedging." In:Wolfgang Hafner and Heinz Zimmermann (eds.) *Vinzenz Bronzin's Option Pricing Models*. Berlin/Heidelberg: Springer-Verlag, 2009: 471–486.

Hilferding, Rudolf. *Finance Capital: A Study in the Latest Phase of Capitalist Development*. London: Routledge/Kegan Paul, 1985.

Hull, John. *Options, Futures, and Other Derivatives*. 3rd ed. Upper Saddle River, NJ: Prentice Hall, 1997.

Kaldor, Nicholas. "The Irrelevance of Equilibrium Economics." *The Economic Journal* 82, no. 328 (1972): 1237–1255.

Kaldor, Nicholas. "Speculation and Economic Stability." *The Review of Economic Studies* 7, no. 1 (1939): 1–27.

Kawai, Masahiro. "Backwardation." In: John Eatwell, Murray Milgate, and Peter Newman (eds.) *The New Palgrave: A Dictionary of Economics*. London/Basingstoke: The Macmillan Press Limited, 1987.

Kuserk, Greg. "Speculation and Hedging." In: Robert W. Kolb, and James A.Overdahl (eds.) *Financial Derivatives: Pricing and Risk Management*. New York: Wiley, 2009.

Lleo, Sebastien, and William Ziemba. "How to Lose Money in Derivatives: Examples from Hedge Funds and Bank Trading Departments." *The London School of Economics and Political Science, Systemic Risk Centre, Special Paper no. 2*, 2014.

McPhail, Lihong, Philipp Schnabl, and Bruce Tuckman. "Do Banks Hedge Using Interest Rate Swaps?" CFTC, Office of the Chief Economist, Staff Papers and Reports, Number 2019-011, 2024.

Milan, Marcelo. "Macrofinancial Risks and Liquidity Preference." *International Journal of Political Economy* 43, no. 1 (2014): 43–64.

Miller, Merton. *Merton Miller on Derivatives*. New York: Wiley, 1997.

Minton, Bernadette A., René M. Stulz, and Rohan Williamson. "How Much Do Banks Use Credit Derivatives to Hedge Loans?" *Journal of Financial Services Research* 35, (2009):1–31.

Palley, Thomas. *Financialization. The Economics of Finance Capital Domination*. New York/London: Palgrave MacMillan, 2013.

Saber, Nasser. The Challenges of Regulation of Derivatives. In: Raphaël Douady, Clément Goulet; Pierre-Charles Pradier (eds.) *Financial Regulation in the EU: From Resilience to Growth*. **Cham: Palgrave MacMillan/Springer International Publishing,** 2017.

Saber, Nasser. *Speculative Capital: The Invisible Hand of Global Finance*. Vol. 1. London: Financial Times/Prentice Hall, 1999.

Santos, Joseph. "A History of Futures Trading in the United States." *EH.Net Encyclopedia*, 2008. Available at https://eh.net/encyclopedia/a-history-of-futures-trading-in-the-united-states/ Retrieved April 2024.

Schweickart, David. "China: Socialist or Capitalist?" *Perspectives on Global Development and Technology* 14, no. 1-2 (2015): 13–25.

Steinherr, Alfred. *Derivatives – The Wild Beast of Finance: A Path to Effective Globalisation?* New York: Wiley, 2000.

Taylor, Francesca. *Mastering Derivatives Markets*. 2nd ed. London: FT/Prentice Hall, 2010.

United States House of Representatives (U.S. House of Representatives). *Hearing before the Committee on Banking, Finance and Urban Affairs. Risks that Hedge Funds Pose to the Banking System*. Washington DC: U.S. Government Printing Office, 1994.

Williamson, Claire. "Rationalisation of European Equity and Derivative Exchanges." *Bank of England Quarterly Bulletin*, 37, no. 4 (November 1997): 406–412.

3 The Second Layer of the Surface

The Nature of Risks Under Financialised Capitalism and the Real Functions of *Derivatives*

Introduction

Chapter 2 briefly discussed the generic issues of risk, since this is the apparent justification for the existence of arrangements known as *derivatives*. This chapter is mainly about a more detailed discussion of different types of risks, as a way to complement and deepen the discussion in the previous chapters, providing developments that are necessary to understand some of the issues just introduced and assumed provisorily to be known. It discusses the potential hedging activities based on specific arrangements, like futures and options, showing to what extent *derivatives* might differ from other risk management techniques and therefore whether they are needed at all, mainly for small capitalists. It shows how *derivatives* are used to speculate and engage in arbitrage but performing other functions that adds complexity to the arrangements. Yet they are hardly effective hedging instruments, since *derivatives* are an important source of many other types of risks, including basis risk. The chapter also stresses an important feature of *derivatives*: their potential for gearing the returns and losses of transactions, creating potential systemic risks. *Derivatives* are, in this regard, about big finance capital.

Identifying the Risks of Capital in Movement

The literature points to a long list of different risks when *derivatives* are discussed. To mention just a couple, Taylor (2010), without a firm basis on the extant literature, divides risks broadly into financial and operational. Market risk is subsumed under financial risk, since she classifies the latter into market, including interest rate, foreign exchange rate and commodity, credit or counterparty and liquidity risks. Operational risk includes operating risks proper, including those related to human resources – errors, lack of adequate cover for staff, insufficient people, inappropriate training and management, fraud or money laundering and business discontinuity – and systems and operations risk, encompassing reliability and performance of systems, including warehousing trade information, and integrity of data. So far, more than dozen different risks. *Derivatives* cannot hedge all of them. Dowd (2002), on the other hand, stresses only market risks, but adding equity risk

DOI: 10.4324/9781003137092-4

to the previous list, and therefore excluding internal risks. As mentioned before, he also provides operational gauges for financial volatility: value at risk (VaR) and estimated tail loss (ETL) as effective measures.

These classification schemes seem to ignore the nature of the phenomena. Perhaps it is a slippage, possibly meaning by risks those that financial institutions are typically exposed to in their intra-industrial contracts or dealings with non-financial firms. From a financialised capitalist economy perspective, it makes perfect sense. The non-financial phenomena tend to be seen or naturalised as financial.[1] As noticed, they include commodity price risk, an economic phenomenon from modern capitalism, as a financial rather than an economic aspect, even though it is valid only under financialised capitalism, when all economic processes are understood as having an inner financial function. This is a financial fetishism. Just like before financialisation there was a commodity fetishism, under financialised capitalism finance rules the social imaginary (Appadurai, 2015). Martin (2002) points to the financialisation of daily life.

Let's consider the issue of a pure market risk. Interest rates for example, to the extent that they have a term structure or yield curve, are somehow related to overnight rates that are influenced by central banks. If the latter were also independent from financial institutions, and not only from democratic needs, interest rate risk could not be attributed only to market conditions and therefore should not be subsumed under market risk, even the market for overnight banking reserves. Also, longer interest rates may be locked-in in this maturity profile by issuers, even when short-term rates fluctuate, or expectations of future short-term interest rates change.[2] These movements modify the present market value of wealth, like bonds and notes, but for older transactions, before the change in interest rates, it is only a change in the entries of accounting books.

One thing that must be further inquired is the relationship between interest rate volatility, the pattern of the volatility over the period considered,[3] the ensuing macro-financial risks, the wealth and incomes at risk, and the specific arrangements developed to cope with it. If financial institutions that sell *derivatives* contracts to deal with increased risks also contribute to this volatility, fabricating risks as argued in Chapter 2, an effect called treadmill by LiPuma and Lee (2004, p.38) then *derivatives* are just a source of revenue in terms of related fees for providing a medicine sold to fight a disease caused by the very infectious agents. LiPuma and Lee (2004) point to "(…) self-generating and self-perpetuating circularity (...)".

Taylor (2010) further divides liquidity risks into cash flow risk when there is insufficient cash to fulfil obligations, funding risk when there are inadequate external resources, and market liquidity risk in the case of an inability to buy or sell. However, liquidity risks are general and should not be attributed to financial dealings alone. As Keynes (1936) explained, most tangible assets are by nature illiquid. Also, the amount of credit is related to stocks when there is repayment or amortisation of principal and interest is related to flows, with additional payments and revenues to the principal. The estimated credit risk is an information that influences the credit lines offered by banks and lenders and is related to stocks alone. Credit lines are not credit risk per se. Moreover, credit lines are off-balance sheet when they are available but not accessed by borrowers. There is a strong interaction between credit risk and interest rate risk.

Stretching the already long list, Taylor (2010) also refers to concentration risk associated with credit lines offered to a few borrowers. She raises two interesting points regarding the market concentration in the banking sector. First, with bankruptcies, on the one hand, and mergers and acquisitions, on the other, it might well be the case that there are necessarily fewer institutions to trade to, transact with or borrow from. This means that the net margins tend to be larger, and, if Hilferding's (1985) view on monopolies and oligopolies is right, this fact in itself would have the ability to smooth out interest rates, making interest rate *derivatives* potentially less useful for hedging, but not necessarily so for geared speculation. Second, capacity utilisation is also a concern from the borrower's perspective. With just a few large institutions available, globalisation of capital notwithstanding, firms that need to diversify the circuits of capital face an important problem. Credit rationing may come about not due to issues with information about debtors' ability to pay back due to asymmetric information, but to lack of economies of scale to gather, organise and process information. What Taylor (2010) calls concentration risk is actually the credit risk associated with concentrating loans on a few large borrowers. An example from the subprime crisis may be useful, with the large amount of speculative sales of credit default swaps (CDS) to agents without exposure to non-performing loans. If buyers of CDS do not own a debt, that is, they do not have an exposure to failure of debt repayment, they are speculating. AIG went bankrupt for this very reason.

Following with the plethora of risks, Taylor (2010) presents settlement risk similarly to counterparty risk, not related to credit transactions, but to foreign exchange markets. These markets are located in different time zones, with little room for simultaneous settlements, implying the existence of time lags. This is a risk derived from the astronomical properties of the planet and imposed to always-expanding capitalism. There are also independent clearance arrangements in terms of intra-day and final settlement.[4] Taylor (2010) mentions that the continuous linked settlement (CLS) – actually a bank – was created to provide global settlement services for foreign exchange transactions using payments versus payments (PvP) systems.[5]

This type of risk was first identified, or at least popularised, during the West German Bankhaus Herstatt's collapse in the 1970s, caused by speculation with the U.S. dollar.[6] Capitalists had paid the equivalent of $200 million in Deutsche Marks, but the bank did not transfer the dollars, interrupting multilateral payment and net settlement systems on both sides of the Atlantic. Despite the fact that this kind of risk is not frequently discussed, the exposure here may be sizeable. In the year 2000, the daily average value of transactions in Switzerland's SIC reached above 43% of GDP (Galati, 2002). The systemic risks are unequivocal, given the international and interconnected nature of the market and the rapid growing volume of trading, concentrated in a few large banks. Magdoff and Sweezy (1987) had already pointed to the system-wide implications of settlement and operational, mainly computer-related, risks.

Other initiatives have been taken to prevent systemic risks originated in settlement failures, showing that *derivatives* are very partial means to avoid all the different types of risks that endogenously plague capitalist economies. For instance, the Bank for International Settlements (BIS) created the Basel Committee on Banking Supervision to prevent clearance issues (Schenk, 2014). Additional measures were adopted by individual banks, the banking industry and central banks. One measure was the creation of the gross real time settlement (GRTS) for intra-day settlement, replacing the deferred net settlement (DNS), shortening the individual exposures and extending the operating hours,[7] thereby time and risk.

Another step taken was to reduce gross settlement flows by focusing on netting. However, Galati (2002) explains that settlement risk was reduced, but not eliminated. And then the CLS bank international was created by large international banks, known as G20,[8] to improve the settlement system. The PvP and the positive overall account balance rule[9] strongly reduce the credit risk component of settlement risk. Only in extreme circumstances a default could not be covered by the haircuts applied, triggering a loss-sharing scheme among the other members, in a rare situation of not socialising losses with the taxpayers. Regarding the liquidity risks, the CLS bank can have insufficient specific currencies, requiring facilities with other players. For example, it may need to swap currencies. Yet, the risk is not eliminated, since the facilities are finite and provided by institutions that are also settlement members. On the other hand, the bank fosters an in/out swap among members to minimise currency shortfalls, although these deals are settled in the traditional way. This management of liquidity risk imposes a heavy technical burden on the system, creating operational risks and biasing it towards the wealthier institutions.

Just like the intertwined relationship between credit risk and interest risk, Galati (2002) explains that settlement risk involves both credit risk in the case of insolvency by a counterparty and liquidity risk in the case of incomplete payment or deferred payment, arguing that the latter is caused by operational risk. This is because, unlike *derivatives*, the full notional value must be transferred in foreign exchange markets. Of course, settlement risk is not only about *derivatives*, since the Herstatt bank went bankrupt due to foreign exchange speculation and its forward transactions were not initially affected. On exchanges, the settlement risk would be associated with failures of the exchange themselves. It could be a problem in OTC transactions as well.

Finally, Taylor (2010) mentions exoteric risks, including alpha or the excess return in the capital asset pricing model[10] – and therefore additional risks according to the model itself, basis risk or convergence, when there is a mismatch in terms of maturity or structure – basically contango or backwardation and black swan or risk of being unprepared to a situation because it is deemed rare – similar to the examples quoted and analysed by Dowd (2002). Saber (1999a) and Das (2006) argue that basis risk is central to understand *derivatives* failures and systemic risks, as discussed in Chapter 8.

The myriad of risks associated with *derivatives* cannot be fully discussed in a single chapter. And since there are so many different types of risks, the chance of not being comprehensive about them is substantial. For example, there is another important risk, never mentioned by the literature, at least the conventional, pro-business one, that is the dishonesty risk, one that is never considered along market, counterparty, liquidity, operational, systemic and so on. Das (2006) provides many examples. He shows how many deals are made in the *derivatives* industry, being more than exceptions. First, clients of financial institutions dealing with these arrangements must be dumb. Financial institutions will lure them by offering an instrument with small profits at the beginning and bigger losses at the end, usually by lying that there are no specific risks.

Partnoy (2009) calls the dishonesty risk of *derivatives* a deceit. It is a cause of many losses on the non-financial or small capitalist side discussed in Chapter 8. There are many other works showing the same pattern, but without linking it to a specific risk. For example, the LIBOR fix mentioned in Chapter 1 was calculated by an association of British banks, assuming that the information provided represents the truth. Yet, a major scandal erupted when banks were caught informing fraudulent numbers to the association (Vaughan and Finch 2017). This component of interest rate risk necessitates criminal investigations to be found. The LIBOR rate was extinct on June 30, 2023. The industry associations discussed in the previous chapter were supposed to prevent that from happening. Market transactions alone cannot avoid dishonesty. Regulation could also intervene. But this is a promise always made and almost never effective, as discussed in Chapter 9. New shenanigans are concocted all the time.

The most important risk under financialised capitalism, however, is financial risk, the one associated with financial flows and stocks that feed systemic risks. Anyway, the significant amount and types of risks discussed above boil down to a straight question: is it actually possible to effectively reduce or, better yet, efficiently redistribute risks with *derivatives* without adding new ones to the sub-system and then to the entire system? It is clear that there are other means to manage those risks without creating new ones. And even with the arrangements the tools are specialised. It is therefore hard to identify an ontological totality that justifies the term. Again, commodity prices are not and do not represent a financial variable, but an economic one. *Derivatives* is a mental exercise. Fitting the parts together into a framework that does not exist in the real world, only in the mind of scholars and of practitioners, although for the latter the name is irrelevant, as long as the thing is profitable. As discussed below, Dowd (2002) mentions still other risks associated with *derivatives* positions, not the underlying. The risks are estimated by so called Greeks like delta, gamma, rho, vega, theta and so on. Hedge may not only be unnecessary, but also risky. He quotes statements of risk managers about how useless *derivatives* may be when changes are large enough.

The Nature of Risks Under Capitalism and Financialised Capitalism

The discussion about the nature of risk and its measurement requires different forms of treatment. First, it seems that risk is not an abstract concept and thus requires social and historical qualifiers. Standing alone it may be irrelevant. Second, there are different levels of risks under capitalism, at the capitalist unit, at the industry, at the marketplace at wide, and finally at the system, incorporating all the previous dimensions and the non-economic aspects, such as politics. This is because there are generic risks in different societies. Slavery has political risks, for example, as in the social revolt of Spartacus, with economic repercussions in the form of an insufficient flow of enslaved people or insufficient tributes from colonies. Feudalism has also different risks related to agriculture and nature, but that cannot be commodified. If it were a full market economy with well-developed monetary arrangements, commodity *derivatives* could play a role, as they had done so under modern capitalism, although for different uses.

But the centrality of money in capitalism makes the nature of risk straightforward, and its measurement, if not easier, at least less complex. Risk is somehow related to a change over time in a quantity of money earned or paid. It could thus be possible to consider unemployment and wage loss risks for workers. But this is related to the situation were money wages drop or cease for a period. Hence the need of unemployment insurance, not *derivatives*. The governments promise to pay the future wages if a worker is fired, such that they are hedged for a short period. Is it a futures or a cash-settled call option and triggered by a change in the underlying like the expected corporate profits? The same is true for the risk of disease, with welfare providing some social insurance.

Commodification of risks and financialisation of the capital valorisation process is what sets financialised capitalism apart. Risks are no longer permanently attached attributes of assets or liabilities but can be shifted to specific arrangements for a while. They are unbundled and traded separately, but never losing the reference to money. This configuration fabricates risks and puts agents in situations in which risks cannot be ignored. Which agents are in a position to buy risks then? Speculators or arbitrageurs as expressions of money capital in the circuit M–M′. Who is in a position to sell risks? Hedgers as expression of all different types and circuits of capital, including money capital, that may have the valorisation of capital jeopardised by the movements of finance capital.

As further evidence of pervasive financial risks imposed by financialisation, with the proliferation of volatility in economic activity, caused by finance's uncontrolled growth in its permanent portfolio changes, the *derivatives* sub-system has also caused a growth in 'risk institutes', 'institutes for risk management', 'global risk institutes' and so on, as private consulting and training organisations or as research bodies at universities and colleges mainly connect to business departments and programmes. This suggests that enhanced risks in general and financial risks in particular have been turned into relevant socioeconomic aspects that must be examined. This could also justify the use of *derivatives*, including the fact that they may contribute to boost risks on a net basis, adding more than mitigating. If this is the case, it is important to further discuss the major risks faced by capitalist firms.

First, is market risk an accurate term or is it market-caused risk a better one? Unregulated markets create by definition different types of risks, although regulated markets are not exempt, as shown in Chapter 9. Those are unpredictable changes in market prices and/or in market quantities. Market changes represent the trigger that sets risks off. Hedge is a supposed solution to neutralise the effects of market activity on the value of capitalist firms' flows and stocks, creating an artificial projected market into the future. Of course, the phenomenon is much more complex, because models of pure or perfectly competitive markets, where all agents are price takers, are a hallucination. Even in imperfectly competitive markets, firms are price setters. And in the typical orthodox textbook models, price changes cause substitution and adjustments in quantities, not hedge. Thus, market structure matters for understanding the source of market risks.[11] And private firms are not the only ones able to fix and therefore change the prices that are a fundamental component of risks. Governments can also have an impact on different prices and costs. Indirect taxes affect prices. Rules affect quantities and prices. As mentioned, interest rates, mainly short-term rates, can be influenced by central banks.[12] The same holds true for foreign exchange rates, including monetary unions that eliminate the volatility problem. Oil prices in international commodity markets depend on political institutions like the Organisation of the Petroleum Exporting Countries (OPEC). Legal notices about non-payment trigger the credit default swaps.[13] It is a complex interaction of units of a sub-system and the entire economic system as resulting from individual units and individual behaviour being shaped by the rest of the system.

Moreover, macro-financial risks after neo-liberalism and globalisation of capitalism are such that there are continuous interaction of interest and foreign exchange. Actually, since money is the interlinking objective, all these risks interact with one or more of the others. It would be possible to classify them in terms of independent or dependent, but these attributes are not immutable. For example, credit risk and liquidity risk play a role in settlement risk. Operational risk can cause credit risk. Credit risk is the only risk considering volumes, not prices. Credit risk is actually creditor risk, since at first default would affect lenders more than borrowers. Saber (1999b) argues that the static credit risk is a poor measure of counterpart risk, and the dynamic credit exposure is more important to assess it. That is why, in his evaluation, credit ratings cannot predict major financial dislocations. The OCC in the United States shares the same view regarding the uncertainty of counterpart risk (2024, pp. 3–4):

> Because the credit exposure is a function of movements in market factors, banks do not know, and can only estimate, how much the value of the derivative contract might be at various points in the future. The credit exposure is bilateral in most derivative transactions, such as swaps (which make up the bulk of bank derivative contracts). Each party to the contract may (and, if the contract has a long enough tenor, probably will) have a credit exposure to the other party at various times during the contract's life. With a funded traditional loan, the amount at risk is the amount advanced to the borrower. The credit risk is unilateral as the bank faces the credit exposure of the borrower. Measuring credit exposure in derivative contracts involves identifying those contracts on which a bank would lose value if the counterparty to a contract defaulted. The total of all contracts with positive value (i.e., derivative receivables) to the bank is

> the gross positive fair value (GPFV) and represents an initial measurement of credit exposure. The total of all contracts with negative value (i.e., derivative payables) to the bank is the gross negative fair value (GNFV) and represents a measurement of the exposure the bank poses to its counterparties.

All these risks affect capitalist units in different ways, depending on the length of the circuit where capital circulates and accumulation strategies are devised in a context of fierce intra-capitalist conflicts over surplus value. This issue can be seen from the perspective of the capitalist units in their attempts to manage risks and also from a systemic perspective where systemic risks cannot be managed.

Risks from the Point of View of Capitalist Units: Apparently Manageable

The nature of risks discussed above under financialised capitalism can be divided into internal to the capitalist units, stemming from their valorisation and accumulation strategies, and external to them when finance capital in its aggregate or collective strategies of valorisation and accumulation cause systemic crises. And since risks are complex phenomena, it seems inappropriate to sum up some of the risks below as market risks. *Derivatives* are a market for risk but also a risk for individual financial and non-financial firms, industries and markets. So, specific arrangements provide different ways to cope with risks. Thus, according to the IMF (2009, pp. 93–94, all italics added):

> The *risk embodied in a financial derivative contract* can be traded either by trading the contract itself, *as is possible with options*, or by creating a new contract embodying risk characteristics that match, in a countervailing manner, those of the existing contract. The latter practice, which is termed offsetability, *occurs in forward markets*. Offsetability means that it is often possible to eliminate the *risk associated with a derivative* by creating a new but 'reverse' contract having characteristics that *countervail the risk underlying the first derivative.* Buying the new derivative is the functional equivalent of selling the first derivative because the result is the elimination of the underlying financial risk. The ability to countervail the underlying risk in the market is therefore considered the equivalent of tradability in demonstrating value. The outlay that would be required to replace the existing derivative contract represents its value; actual offsetting is not required.

What is the meaning of trading commodified risks from an individual capitalist firm? Trading a contract that has a single price and the emphasis is placed upon this variable. The fact that the underlying is not transferred does not mean that only the risk reflecting changes in prices is being bought or sold. With delivery, the value of the contract includes a given quantity and the price is per unit. Since the value of the underlying is included, how to sort out the intrinsic value of the underlying and value of risk of price changes? This leads to a second question: What is the meaning of embodying risk in a contract? Since at maturity the final outcome is still uncertain, that is, an adverse market condition is avoided, but a favourable one is equally averted, except for options, then it is not risk that is being traded, but a given certainty level.

However, even in the case of call options, there is still a risk of losing the premium per contract, and for larger values, the losses can be significant. It is intrinsic and cannot be traded away. Only the risk of losing more than the equivalent to the premium paid is potentially avoided. But there is range of prices, albeit small, for which the call option is out of the money at maturity (see Chapter 1). It is not necessary to invoke the issue of uncertainty. The risk simply does not disappear and it is only apparently manageable. If it does not go away, then it is not completely traded. Is it possible to isolate and price the risk under such typical circumstances? It does not seem plausible. What about foreign exchange risk, that is already a price, of money in terms of foreign money? It is related to exchange rate volatility, causing uncertainty about the value of capital and commodities when they move internationally. The same is true for interest rate risk, already a price, of money in terms of time and availability, with future expenses or incomes unknown.

Focusing on the latter, Taylor (2010) considers that interest risk is not neutral, but something negative, representing increased costs of funding[14] for individual borrowers like governments or firms or lower revenues for financial firms, lenders and rentiers. Here there is scope for a natural hedge, that is, a hedge in spot markets, without *derivatives*, considering the intra-capitalist distributive conflict. It is unlikely that small depositors would mind hedging an expected reduction in interest earnings, as Taylor herself acknowledges, justifying it in terms of the scale involved.[15] The author argues that the choice of the *derivative* type depends on the maturity of the underlying. Futures and forward best fit short-term exposures, whereas long-term risks require multiple settlements and instruments like options and swaps, including contracts cleared by centralised exchange-like organisations in the latter case, but noticing that they can also be used for dealing with shorter term risks.[16] Actually, the longer-dated instruments are built from shorter-dated contracts linked together (Taylor 2010). Evidence in the next chapter suggests that the most important arrangements are interest rate swaps for shorter terms since they are speculative vehicles.

Yet, the amount of value exposed to interest rate risk seems to make an important difference, highlighting the fact the *derivatives* is mainly a large finance capital business, that is, a large financial corporate business. More important, hedging in particular seems to be disposable when rentier's interests (no pun intended) are subdued. Considering forwards (forward rate agreements (FRA)), for instance, Taylor (2010, p. 99) contends that when interest rates are low, the compensating values associated with FRAs are also small. But it nonetheless demands time and effort from managers to protect against the impact of a few basis points if the firm decides to hedge. This means that risks are not worth hedging. It is expensive for the small capitalist. This is also valid for options (Taylor, 2010, p. 107).

Moreover, it seems that, for smaller capitalists, banks would credit ration them and the risk is about quantities, not rates. They would not have the underlying credit in the first place, and thus the interest rate and its risks would be immaterial.

And, to the extent that there would be a credit line arranged, the interest rate would be higher than for larger firms, but still probably not worthy of a hedge using *derivatives*. It is possible to identify alternatives here as well. The IMF (2009, p. 91, italics in the original) mentions the existence of standardised guarantees:

> *Standardized guarantees are defined as those that are not provided by means of a financial derivative (such as credit default swaps), but for which the probability of default can be well established.* These guarantees cover similar types of credit risk for a large number of cases. Examples include guarantees issued by governments on export credit or student loans.

Capital must reach an accumulated critical mass to use *derivatives* for hedging or speculating with interest rates. This adds a new thread to the fabric of *derivatives*. Usually, the discussion revolves around volatility or risks, that is, changes in the levels of prices and rates and in credit conditions. But now, it seems that the response to the variance depends also on the very levels of the variables. From a capitalist perspective, it is reasonable, since *derivatives* are not cost-free arrangements, even for forward contracts that have zero value when the counterparties initiate the deal, and to the extent that they do not remove completely the risks for many reasons discussed along this book. Saber (1999b), however, argues that *derivatives* costs are low, considering that its system is necessary. Yet, there are intermediary or transaction costs, given the intra-capitalist conflict: brokerage fees, for example. Moreover, anticipating the issue of basis risk, the offered hedge is imperfect. As Taylor (2010) argues, the standardised contracts in exchanges, for example, will rarely match the specific needs of hedgers, and they may be obliged to cross-hedge. This explains the growth of OTC markets over exchanges. And, contrary to Saber's argument, most non-financial firms will not have the economic capacity to continuously run and manage a portfolio of *derivatives* for the period with volatility, that is, eternally as long as the firm does not shut down. In the end, interest rate *derivatives* are transacted mainly by banks, other financial institutions and large non-financial firms based on the needs of finance capital and its fractions.

In a rentier-dominated socioeconomic configurations, with characteristic higher than historically average interest rates, *derivatives* then may be, at least for the capitalists with economic power, a feasible arrangement to prevent or minimise additional financial costs associated with still higher interest rates. To the extent that for speculators, the level is irrelevant as long as it changes and create profit opportunities, a harmful environment could develop, with rentiers absorbing higher flows of interest revenue at the expense of debtors, and big speculators pushing for increased volatility to absorb higher flows of capital gains and profits in *derivatives* markets.

As interest rates are expected to change, because they cannot be stable or constant, then if firms do not need to borrow, the fluctuation is immaterial. But if some firms anticipate borrowing in the near future, they may consider the possible movements in the future rates of interest. If they are expected to fall, the firms just wait and borrow, saving money. But if the rates are believed to rise, implying higher future costs reflecting intra-capitalist distributive conflicts, the firms may be willing to consider possible defences. They may look at current quotes of future interest rates for the dates when the money will be needed. If the future interest rate quoted is lower than the one expected to prevail in the money market, then it may be to the advantage of a financialised firm to short futures contracts on interest rates.

This still raises doubts about the capacity of every single or individual unit of finance capital as a corporate or enterprise entity, and then its internal strategies and departments or divisions, at every point in time, to be able to evaluate the risk factors of every transaction made or to be made. The reason is that, more than being firm-specific, risk is also transaction-specific and time-varying. Actually, as Dowd (2002) remarks this type of risk evaluation is unpractical and unlikely mainly if compared to VaR, in itself another attempt at controlling the future. What these capitalist organisations should do is to project or map a few basic positions linearly onto benchmark or underlying risk factors. This is known, he adds, as mapping or synthetic substitution of real positions by representative or proxy core instruments in terms of representatives of capitalist stocks and flows, such as equity, fixed-income, foreign exchange that is non-interest bearing, spot and forward, and commodities. What is important for the purposes of this chapter, is how *derivatives* are considered in this mapping of risk factors.

The core instruments mentioned by Dowd (2002) are equity indices in each of the core currencies, combinations of cash flows of a limited number of fixed-income securities of specific maturities in a given currency, relevant amounts of core currencies and fixed-income positions in specific foreign exchange currencies and selected exchange-traded commodities futures. Basically, assets and wealth from the perspective of the circuits of international capital. The utilisation of two types of *derivatives* variables for a core of four instruments, among a vast universe of potential candidates, show that they are indeed an integral part of the high echelons of the financial world. Next, he discusses the construction of the basic building blocks of the mapping exercise, considering the decomposition of the core instruments into primitive ones. In the case of *derivatives*, the basic or primitive instruments are futures or forwards. It is newsworthy that the VaR estimated can only be an approximation, since the maintenance costs of collateral or margin requirements depends on volatile interest rates. Also, forwards, unlike futures, that can be reverted by an opposing transaction, have a thin secondary market and are illiquid. This points to the issue of futures costs and liquidity risk of forwards. Risks come into full circle, with reciprocal feedback mechanisms where a given initial amount of money-capital that seeks valorisation stumbles upon significant risks of devalorisation or losses that demands the creation of a new financial industry, only because other capitals cannot complete their metamorphosis back into money for lack of cash.

Another issue raised by the exposition of Dowd (2002) is the fact that the complex positions can be mapped once the building blocks are available and can work as synthetic equivalents. What are the instruments? The examples provided are FRAs, vanilla interest rate swaps, structured notes, foreign exchange forwards and commodity, equity and foreign exchange swaps. The kernel of the matter is that *derivatives* represent complex positions. Hence, they have features that put their risk management prowess into doubt. For instance, the author states about options, in particular, that despite the Greeks, their returns are not a linear function of underlying risk factors because, it seems, risks are continuously created. He argues that, even if the mappings are initially sound, the synthetic mapping of positions in options can be quickly dismantled by market changes. The example given is a gamma-approximation, which reaches very high values when an at the money option is expiring and it is irrelevant.[17] The solution is to update the mapping continuously to the market volatility in a dynamic way (Dowd, 2002, p. 56)

If monetary values are only notional references because interest rates in themselves have no meaning without a corresponding interest payment based on a value, then they are not a *derivative* since the on-balance sheet value is not related to the *derivative*. In the end, it is all about money. Interest rates do not exist without money and time. But for the speculative purposes that characterises most of contemporary finance, the important thing is the accrual of money that is sought after in a short interval. The increase or decrease in money in itself is a rate of change, which under capitalist conditions is a profit or loss, or an income or an expense. So, the notional values are concocted to bringing money into the equation when there is none involved in terms of circulation or transfer of property, only in terms of an amount owned outside the *derivative* market that has to increase, or at least avoid decreasing due to market volatility.

Considering other types of risks faced by capitalist units, commodity price risk can be better understood by means of an example. Oil is the most important commodity for the world capitalist economy. So, changing prices would represent a major economic risk regarding production and inflation. But oil contracts do not represent the single most important reference for transactions in the *derivatives* sub-system. So, why did volatile oil prices not assume a major stance in *derivatives* markets? Because there is a limit to financialisation of commodities when this aggravates the intra-capitalist distributive conflict. And oil is also about politics among states. More important, *derivatives* are about finance, and there are financial instruments more adequate to faster valorisation.

The same seems to be valid for equity price risk that affects the portfolio of money manager capitals as another view of the firm challenges under external risks. Saber (1999a, p. 219) quotes an article from the *Wall Street Journal* reporting the losses of a hedge fund manager who claims that his organisation business is to buy a large number of the best stocks and short a large number of the worst stocks. The executive complains that the difficulties start when the improbable happens and there is a reversal in the performance of stocks. He contradictorily affirms that the improbable happens frequently, mainly in international markets. If it is frequent, why complain? Why not hedge the portfolio with equity *derivatives*? Dowd (2002, p. 7) also quotes Robert Gumerlock's remarks about the effectiveness of certain corporate strategies related to risk. The specific arrangement are options. Gumerlock affirms that when O'Connor[18] was established in London during the Big Bang,[19] he developed an option risk control system with all the measures known as

Greeks – deltas, gammas, rhos, thetas, vegas and so on. He added also higher order measures of risk, highlighting the intricacies of volatility under financialised capitalism. But all that turned out to be useless during the 1987 stock market crash in the United States. Despite all their shortcomings, Saber (2017) claims that *derivatives* are necessary. He must have added: they are needed by capital, mainly finance capital.

Exogenous Risks to the Capitalist Units: Or Why Disasters Cannot be Hedged after They Happen

As mentioned, an important issue pointing to the possibility that *derivatives* may not be needed is the existence of pervasive mismatched positions. Why there is normally no perfect match? Capital has two needs, one general and one specific. The general need is to accumulate through profits. The specific need is to devise different schemes or circuits to obtain these profits. Those circuits have specific economic and financial arrangements in terms of transactions involved, time necessary to complete it, length of each stage and of the circuit as a whole, interconnections with other capitals and circuits and so on. And also the corresponding legal, social, cultural and political arrangements. Class conflicts interfere with both needs. First between capital and labour. And also within and between capitals. It is this particular need and its variable arrangements that make it difficult to find perfect matches. The consequence is basis risk.

Das (2006) shows how basis risk was employed to deceive and rip off potential hedgers by a financial institution he worked for. Indeed, Saber (1999a, p. 204) claims that this basis risk or the risk of change in the difference of two variables, caused by asymmetric movements of the initially matched positions, is well known by financial market practitioners, but not by non-financial firms. He adds that in efficient markets there should be not basis risk. Moreover, the value of *derivatives* is based on the assumption of no basis risk. Santos (2008) argues that basis risk is the difference between the future price and the spot price of an underlying and that hedgers indeed shift price risk in exchange for basis risk, considered by the financial 'community' to be lower than the former and therefore more acceptable[20]. This reinforces the view that risks cannot be eliminated in capitalism, only transformed.

Saber (1999a) complements that the basis risk is not related to the direction of change, but the change in the basis that was initially employed as reference for the contracts. And also that basis risk exists due to the interaction of many variables with qualitative features that are seldom quantifiable. Hull (1997) adds that imperfect substitutes that constitute capitalist wealth cause basis risk. Moriarty et al. (1981) explain the difference in terms of the attributes in futures and the underlying markets. They argue that in futures exchanges the assets are standardised and the underlying markets assets can be heterogeneous, creating price differences or basis risk. But in OTC markets, this imperfection should not be a problem since contracts are customised.

Therefore, it is now clear that the risks associated with every specific arrangement must be included in the list of risks, even though they are supposed to manage specific risks associated with the projected exposures of underlying variables in the future. And here the complex nature of *derivatives* becomes clear, bringing uncertainty back to the calculations. According to Dowd (2002, p. 7), the risks of *derivatives* positions can be estimated by the Greeks. The basic ones are delta, or the change in the *derivative* price for a given change in the underlying price; gamma, or the change in delta for a given change in the price of the underlying; rho is the change in the price of the *derivative* in response to the change in the risk-free interest rate, theta is the change in the price of the *derivative* when time changes; and vega is the change in the price when volatility changes.

This way of gauging risks is further evidence that the traditional concept of *derivatives* discussed in Chapter 1 is wrong. There are *derivatives* of higher degree. *Derivatives* of *derivatives*. The issue is not only the underlying, since there are markets for *derivatives* and their price can change for many reasons other than the underlying. And the price of the underlying can change because of *derivatives* markets. Consider delta. There must be a change in the price of the underlying for *derivatives* to exist. Since price changes are frequent, the initial price when the *derivative* contract is signed is likely to change, affecting its price in turn. Consider now rho. Changes in interest rates can affect the price of all *derivatives* contracts, including those not related to credit or interest rates themselves. This is because *derivatives* are a mechanism for transferring money. Theta shows again that the risks in *derivatives* are inevitable and they are short-term instruments. And volatility in the price of the underlying is what justifies *derivatives*. If volatility changes, it is another illustration that *derivatives* are not about risk management of the underlying. Indeed, Taleb (1997), looking at options, argues that there is transmission of instability from *derivatives* markets to spot markets when financial capitalists engage in dynamic hedging.

Dowd (2002) explains that the Greek variables themselves are volatile. All that suggests a significant amount of money, effort, knowledge, abilities and so on associated with managing the risks of *derivatives* alone, that is, ignoring the underlying who is supposedly the main source of concern regarding risks. He remarks that Greeks and hedge positions can work well only under two circumstances: the changes in risk factors are small and the hedged positions are revised frequently. Major changes and crises make them irrelevant. The loss in the underlying is not covered by the gain in *derivatives*.

These personal and subjective assessments of *derivatives* when they are most needed are relevant. Dowd (2002, p. 7) continues by quoting a risk manager, according to whom gamma in option desks are designed for small changes in the price of the underlying. If a desk has a zero gamma[21] but the market change is large, like the stock market crash of 1987, the strategy does not work and the capitalist unit suffers heavy losses. And stress tests with many standard deviations are not enough either. Dowd (2002) remarks that dynamic hedge and portfolio insurance may be an illusion, when large, unpredicted market changes, coupled with the ensuing liquidity risk, happens and large losses follow. Thus, this boils down to a chain of risks, starting with the underlying price and then with the price of its supposedly limited loss options and next the change in price of its options and then the change in the change.[22] Volatility is pervasive and enhanced under financialised capitalism, with multiple, iterative and layered risks.[23]

In the conventional accounts of *derivatives*, it is assumed that they are neutral instruments, albeit with imperfect hedging properties. Yet, it remains the question of the active role *derivatives* may play in the onset of financial and or economic disturbances that cannot be 'managed' at the individual level. It is a logical question. First, if *derivatives* are supposed to hedge positions by transferring risks of underlying, capitalists may be tempted to take on riskier positions in terms of distribution of capital to different valorisation projects. But if the positions are not, without a conscientious knowledge on the part of capitalists and their managers, fully or mostly hedged, then the losses are inevitable when markets change the conditions of circulation and unpredicted and therefore unhedged risks are realised. So, the problem is indirectly caused by *derivatives*. Second, what happens to risk transfers? If risk buyers are concentrated, that is, risks are bought by a handful of banks and financial institutions, in a chain of interlocked balance sheets and off-balance sheets claims, shifting them creates systemic risks. Third, firms taking geared positions are not necessarily protected, since residual risks persist. Hence, *derivatives* create diverse types of risks and cause losses both in *derivatives* positions and in the underlying markets. More than that, they amplify risks. Although the orthodox view assumes a stabilising role for speculation, in the works of Friedman (1969) for example, speculation can be very destabilising, mainly when geared. There are several examples of this provided in Chapter 8. For instance, herd behaviour is an outstanding feature of behavioural finance that provides an example of destabilising forces associated with speculation.

A final important risk that is external or effectively non-manageable to *derivatives* agents and non-users alike is the systemic risk. In his summary account of systemic risk, Saber (1999a) argues that it is the result of two forces. The first is gearing, offered by credit institutions, and the second is the basis risk discussed above, since initially matched assets and liabilities do not eliminate market and credit risks. The threat of systemic risk, understood as a chain reaction of defaults and bankruptcies linkages, is the tendency of speculative capital, the total sum of capital earmarked for speculation, to self-destruct in its movements. In the case of *derivatives*, Saber states that gearing is attached to the structure of the contracts, there being no voluntary choice about it. All *derivatives* parties are geared, willingly or not. If credit capital is added, the mass of capital directly and indirectly creating potential systemic risk is astonishing.

The system subject to risk is made up of a process of circulation of speculative capital and markets of variable size that form the course of its movement. That is, there is a web or network of markets linked by speculative capital. This includes local markets as segments of global markets. Systemic risk is indeed global under financialised capitalism (LiPuma and Lee, 2004). Steinherr (2000) retorts to a reaction to the original edition of his book that it overemphasises systemic risks and underestimates the ability of large banks in managing risks. He contends at the time that the recent risk management technology made explicit its failures when most needed (Steinherr, 2000). Yet, he proceeds to praise and worship *derivatives* as astounding financial innovations.

Thus, considering the risks discussed, and the failures to hedge them, the analysis suggests that *derivatives*, as risk management tools, are not truly needed. So, they must perform a different role. But this role can only be ascertained by looking at the specific arrangements. Which type of capitalism needs capitalists voluntarily taking risks, besides the mythical and rhetorical figure of the free entrepreneur? Contemporary, financialised capitalism. But of course, there are widespread conflicts, and not all capitalists need or long for risks. As Saber (1999a) argues, speculative capital, the dominant form of capital today in his view, is contested by other forms of capital, like industrial, commercial and credit. Financialised capitalism breeds what Marthinsen (2018) correctly names risk takers, with important consequences. However, in his view, it is not only the way *derivatives* are used but mainly how they are abused. But when they are correctly used, the problems are also present. Although risk shifting implies risk taking, there is no need of natural hedge. It is possible to take risk without a counterparty shifting or transferring and thus hedging. Saber (1999a) lists many such cases: Glaxo, Metallgesellschaft, Sony, Lufthansa, Procter & Gamble, Bankers Trust and so on. And, as Partnoy (2009) has it, the greed is infectious and contaminates even governments, with the now famous case of Orange County, California. The local government used (or abused) *derivatives* to arbitrage the long and the short sides of the Treasury yield curve and went bankrupt. Some of these cases are discussed in Chapter 8.

This issue converges to the treadmill effect proposed by LiPuma and Lee (2004). Financial markets indeed create risks that they are supposed to help hedge. Financial markets are intrinsically unstable and volatile. To protect against the consequences of this instability, instruments are mobilised by the very institutions responsible for the problem. If it were not a problem, *derivatives* would have to find another justification. This is clearly wasteful. But in a capitalist economy, social waste is private innovation, albeit in a different format. And also fees, profits and unproductive employment. So, volatility and risks are not exogenous to the system. They are created, consciously or not, by the very agents that make up the market. And market structure plays a role, since big financial firms can move the markets.

Most of the exegetical *derivatives* literature assumes that the two markets, for *derivatives* and for the underlying are independent in terms of flows and transactions. For an example of this presupposition, Brennan (1979, p. 53, italics added) assumes that "A contingent claim [the original term for *derivative* – see Chapter 6] is an asset whose payoff depends upon the value of another 'underlying' asset, the value of which is *exogenously determined*." Yet, this operational autonomy is by no means true (Taleb, 1997). The two markets are cash-connected in different ways, not to mention the jack of all trades, expectations. When industrial capitalists start their circuit of capital valorisation, decades ago they indeed could not consider *derivatives*, or at least they did not have or did not need to, since the circuit was structured along the lines of modern capitalism, before financialisation transformed *derivatives*. This is the case even though the necessary passage of time, and the connection between the past, the present and the futures, is embedded in the path of capital, with many risks along the trajectory. For commercial capital back then, and financial capital yesterday and today, though, this is not true, since *derivatives* are a potential hedging but also a profitable product.

That is, the different types of risks have always been present in the different circuits, starting with interest rates or exchange rate for the money borrowed nationally or internationally to start the circuit. Equity may represent a risk in the case of takeovers, but there is no point for non-financial firms to hedge against falling stock prices.[24] And then the risk of commodities' prices that are part of the circulating capital,[25] including exchange rate risks for imports. And the level of sales themselves (*salto mortale* of Marx), with foreign exchange risk in the case of exports. For banks and other financial institutions, credit risk. But if prices in the *derivatives* markets are discovered and informed to spot markets, then the argument vanishes. If *derivatives* markets generate volatility and uncertainty, affecting decisions in the spot markets, the argument fades away. If positions in the *derivatives* markets require simultaneous transactions in the underlying markets, the assumption is wrong. The only evident economic justification for *derivatives* is that they provide huge profits to behemoth finance capital.

Summing Up

Contemporary financialised capitalism produces many different risks on a large scale, but also transforms old-fashioned risks. And financial institutions responsible for this feature by means of speculation are also in a position to offer specific arrangements to supposedly cope with those risks, but without assurance that they will be properly handled or necessary. Finance capital separates risks from the wealth and capital that generate them in its movements within circuits of valorisation and accumulation. Wealth is only a reference that is not negotiated in the markets for risk. The traditional risks usually discussed are interest rate risk, exchange rate risk, commodity price risk, equity risk and credit risk. All of them are derived from the different and specific circuits of capital as they involve relationships with other capitals and only indirectly with labour, to the extent that if affects the costs of inputs. Other risks, some of them being pre-capitalist, just highlight the fact that risks must be commoditised to be a source of profits in this new phase or stage of capitalism. Exotic or exoteric risks captured by the Greeks just represent an additional layer of fictitious valorisation of capitals, since these risks are not associated with the typical functions and circuits of industrial and commercial capital. Even money capital does not incur, voluntarily, such types of risks. Only when it enters the new circuits opened up by finance capital.

Some of these risks are considered manageable from the perspective of capitalist units in their search for profits. This explains the risk management approach to *derivatives*. But there are risks that do not pertain to capital as a unit in search for valorisation, but capital as a collective value seeking redistribution of surplus. And the perception that some risks are easily manageable can cause more risks to be taken, increasing the fragility of the system. But it may be necessarily to continuously manage them, what creates a flow of income and payments to the financial system to which the *derivatives* sub-system pertains. If they are not managed on a continuous basis, the losses are likely to occur in the spot markets, given pervasive risks created by different types of large capital. And some risks are simply not manageable at the capitalist unit level. And other are not even mentioned, like dishonesty risk. They require collective attempts, and there is no guarantee that they will not bring losses to the level of collapse and crises. But then the system of *derivatives* engulfs capital and mainly capital that matters for accumulation and growth in a net that risk management and speculation are all interwoven, with a system at risk.

Notes

1 Saber (1999a, p. 19) captures this financial illusionism or fetishism by resorting to the concept of speculative capital. For him, this capital is so ubiquitous in modern finance that its existence, like the air or gravity, is assumed to be the natural order of things. And again (Saber, 1999a, p. 177), he adds that the expansion of speculative capital appears to be part of the natural state of affairs such that everything must be measured against it. Martin (2007, p.3) equally identifies "(…) the powers of finance, not simply as a form of capital but as a set of protocols for organizing daily life." Bryan and Rafferty (2006), on the other hand, defend exactly the significant transformation of capitalism by *derivatives* in their ability to measure every single quantifiable attribute of assets, every bit of capital.

2 It would be necessary to consider, of course, the duration, or the sensitivity of asset yields to changes in interest rates (Dempsey, 2021). And also the convexity, the change in the duration when interest rates change, of the corresponding interest-bearing assets. Convexity is an indirect measure of interest rate risk. And duration is about the effective time necessary to cash the interest payments. Risk and time are associated, again.

3 Volatility means that the price of a variable has an unstable pattern over time. But, as mentioned before, the volatility itself may also be unstable, what in econometrics is related to heteroscedasticity. This means that volatility, in terms of highs and lows, can increase, decrease or stay within the same amplitude. But it may keep the same amplitude at a high level for the period of time relevant for the capitalists exposed to it. If volatility is a proxy for risk, then this unstable volatility pattern would be additional evidence that uncertainty is what matters for relevant capitalist decision-making, not risks.

4 This would make what Saber (1999a) calls speculative capital's instantaneous arbitrage operationally very difficult.

5 PvP or DvP (Delivery vs Payment) requires that the two legs of a deal be settled simultaneously, making impossible to finalise the transaction if one of them is not carried through.

6 Galati (2002) mentions other similar cases that occurred in the 1990s, like those of Drexel Burnham Lambert Group, Bank of Credit and Commerce International (BCCI) and Baring Brothers.

7 Saber (1999a) argues that the function of real-time quotation systems is to eliminate the spatial distances between markets.

8 Not to be confused with the Group of 20 Countries (G-20).

9 Members are not allowed to present intra-day overdrafts, with CLS applying the difference between the market value of the currency and the value of the collateral or haircut when computing the balances and also imposing short position limits on negative balances for each currency.

10 Saber (1999a) provides a devastating critique of this model, mainly regarding the possibility of measuring a market return.

11 The empirical *derivatives* surveys of FIA, called market structure, may cause significant misunderstandings in this case. See www.fia.org/fia/articles/fia-releases-report-derivatives-industry-trends Access on January, 2025.

12 Vrolijk (1997) shows that even with *derivatives*, the monetary policy transmission mechanisms were not affected in the United Kingdom. This conclusion has far reaching consequences regarding *derivatives*. If *derivatives* do not make a difference after changes in interest rates, there is, they do not affect interest flows, credit decisions, balance sheets and exchange rates, then *derivatives* are useless as hedging mechanisms.

13 Yet, it is hard to see how credit default swaps were legally triggered against AIG during the subprime collapse, since they had no borrowings outstanding related to these instruments. And CDS buyers like hedge funds did not have necessarily any loan outstanding related to mortgages. See Jacque (2015).

14 In some Post Keynesian approaches there is a difference between finance and funding of investment, the former being the initial or short-run provision of funds, usually by means of bank credit, and the latter being the long-run provision of purchasing power to match the maturity of the assets acquired and liabilities, usually by the channeling the new savings to capital markets. See Davidson (1986). In this book they are considered synonymous.

15 Actually, in the case of futures, the value of a single standardised contract transacted in exchanges can be higher than the equity or assets of many small companies or depositors. Although this means that they would not have sufficient exposure to transact in *derivatives* markets, it would still be a fair game if they were speculating, but probably not with a fair outcome. There are exceptions, however. Saber (1999a) emphasises that, during the 1987 stock market crash in the United States, the market makers at Nasdaq, in collusion, refused to take small orders. Then the system for executing small orders became mandatory, showing all bid-ask quotes and trades of all dealers. Out of line prices allowed large spreads and opportunities for arbitrage by retail traders.

16 See Sears (2024) for a more recent troublesome development in the length of options.

17 A delta for at the money options is robust, that is, it does not depend on the volatility, that is unknown. For out of the money delta is not robust because it is sensitive to volatility.

18 O'Connor & Associates was an option trading boutique based in Chicago, acquired in 1992 by the Swiss Bank Corporation. The latter merged with UBS in 1998 (Lovell, 2015).

19 Big Bang was the sweeping neo-liberal deregulation of finance in the United Kingdom in the 1980s (Copley, 2022).

20 Saber (1999a) provides an illustration for futures contracts. In this case, basis = spot price – forward price. For the underlying the spot price (known today) is S_0 and the price at time T (future, unknown today) is S_T. Without hedge, the risk is S_T - S_0. By hedging, the spot price (also known today) is F_0, the future contracted prices (and therefore known today) is F_T, with the risk being transformed to $(S_T - S_0) - (F_T - F_0)$, that can be rearranged to $(S_T - F_T) - (S_0 - F_0)$. The latter term is the current basis and is known. The basis risk at time T and therefore unknown is the first term. Marthinsen (2018) shows that if markets conditions indicate a backwardation, the basis is positive. Under contango, the basis becomes negative.

21 Zero gamma means that the option risk metric gamma, the rate of change in the option risk metric delta, when the underlying asset's price changes by 1%, is equal to zero. Of course, mathematically this means that delta is constant, an unrealistic assumption for a capitalist economy. By its turn, delta measures how much an option's premium changes

when the underlying asset's price changes by 1%, that is, the volatility in the price of the option. Thus, hedging options positions by having gamma as a reference means adjusting the portfolio to keep delta constant. This requires continuously or dynamic trading matched long, with positive Gamma, and short, with negative gamma options such that there is, apparently, full compensation. The result should be a net gamma close to zero or gamma-neutral (Natenberg, 2015).

22 Natenberg (2015) mentions the existence of color, the rate of change in gamma over time, and zomma. The infinite is the limit for financialised capitalism.

23 Bryan and Rafferty (2006) remarks that this feature is at odds with orthodox approaches to economics that are based on the idea of equilibrium prices. Of course, volatility could only mean that equilibrium prices are continuously changing, like a moving target. And this means, paraphrasing Kaldor (1972), that equilibrium in itself, and its economics, are irrelevant.

24 Of course, for financial and financialised firms with portfolios of shares this risk is real.

25 The risk of wage hikes or strikes has been dealt with historically by several means, mainly police repression or relocation of plants.

References

Appadurai, Arjun. *Banking on Words: The Failure of Language in the Age of Derivative Finance*. Chicago: University of Chicago Press, 2015.

Brennan, Michael J. "The Pricing of Contingent Claims in Discrete Time Models." *The Journal of Finance* 34, no. 1 (1979): 53–68.

Bryan, Dick, and Michael Rafferty. *Capitalism with Derivatives: A Political Economy of Financial Derivatives, Capital and Class*. New York: Palgrave Macmillan, 2006.

Copley, Jack. *Governing Financialization: The Tangled Politics of Financial Liberalization in Britain*. Oxford: Oxford University Press, 2022.

Das, Satyajit. *Traders, Guns and Money: Knowns and Unknowns in the Dazzling World of Derivatives*. London: FT Press/Prentice Hall, 2006.

Davidson, Paul. "Finance, Funding, Saving, and Investment." *Journal of Post Keynesian Economics* IX, no. 1 (1986):101–110.

Dempsey, Michael. *Financial Risk Management and Derivative Instruments*. London/New York: Routledge, 2021.

Dowd, Kevin. *Measuring Market Risk*. Chichester/West Sussex: Wiley, 2002.

Friedman, Milton. "In Defense of Destabilizing Speculation." In: Milton Friedman (ed.) *The Optimum Quantity of Money and Other Essays*. Chicago: Aldine, 1969.

Galati, Gabriele. "Settlement Risk in Foreign Exchange Markets and CLS Bank." *BIS Quarterly Review*, (December 2002): 55–65.

Hilferding, Rudolf. *Finance Capital: A Study in the Latest Phase of Capitalist Development*. London: Routledge/Kegan Paul, 1985.

Hull, John. *Options, Futures, and Other Derivatives*. 3rd ed. Upper Saddle River: Prentice Hall, 1997.

International Monetary Fund (IMF). *Balance of Payments and International Investment Position Manual*. Washington, DC.: IMF, 2009.

Jacque, Laurent. *Global Derivative Debacles: From Theory to Malpractice*. Singapore: World Scientific Publishing, 2015.

Kaldor, Nicholas. "The Irrelevance of Equilibrium Economics." *The Economic Journal* 82, no. 328 (1972): 1237–1255.

Keynes, John M. *The General Theory of Employment, Interest and Money*. London: Macmillan, 1936.

LiPuma, Edward, and Benjamin Lee. *Financial Derivatives and the Globalisation of Risk*. Durham: Duke University Press, 2004.

Lovell, Hamlin. "UBS O'Connor." Profile, *the Hedge Fund Journal*, no. 101 2015.

Magdoff, Harry, and Paul Sweezy. *Estagnation and Financial Explosion*. New York: Monthly Review Press, 1987.

Marthinsen, John E. *Risk Takers: Uses and Abuses of Financial Derivatives*. 3rd ed. Berlin: De|G Press, 2018.

Martin, Randy. *An Empire of Indifference: American War and the Financial Logic of Risk Management*. Durham: Duke University Press, 2007.

Martin, Randy. *Financialization of Daily Life*. Philadelphia, Temple University Press, 2002.

Moriarty, Eugene, Susan Phillips, and Paula Tosini. "A Comparison of Options and Futures in the Management of Portfolio Risk." *Financial Analysts Journal* 37, no. 1 (1981): 61–67.

Natenberg, Sheldon. *Option Volatility and Pricing*. 2nd ed. New York: McGraw Hill Education, 2015.

Partnoy, Frank. *Infectious Greed: How Deceit and Risk Corrupted the Financial Markets*. Revised edition. New York: Public Affairs, 2009.

Saber, Nasser. "The Challenges of Regulation of Derivatives." In: Raphaël Douady, Clément Goulet, and Pierre-Charles Pradier (eds.) *Financial Regulation in the EU: From Resilience to Growth*. Cham: Palgrave Macmillan/Springer International Publishing, 2017.

Saber, Nasser. S*peculative Capital & Derivatives: The Nature of Risk in Capital Markets*. Vol. 2. London: Financial Times/Prentice Hall, 1999b.

Saber, Nasser. *Speculative Capital: The Invisible Hand of Global Finance*. Vol. 1. London: Financial Times/Prentice Hall, 1999a.

Santos, Joseph. "A History of Futures Trading in the United States." EH.Net Encyclopedia, 2008. Available at https://eh.net/encyclopedia/a-history-of-futures-trading-in-the-united-states/ Retrieved April 2024.

Schenk, Catherine R. "Summer in the City: Banking Failures of 1974 and the Development of International Banking Supervision." *English Historical Review* CXXIX, no. 540 (2014): 1129–1156.

Sears, Steven M. "The Latest Options Craze Resembles Past Manias. That's Not a Good Thing." *Barrons*, March 20, 2024. Available at: www.barrons.com/articles/options-craze-past-manias-stock-trouble-bb109fb5 Retrieved May 2024.

Steinherr, Alfred. *Derivatives – The Wild Beast of Finance: A Path to Effective Globalisation?* New York: Wiley, 2000.

Taleb, Nassim N. *Dynamic Hedging: Managing Vanilla and Exotic Options*. New York: Wiley, 1997.

Taylor, Francesca. *Mastering Derivatives Markets*. 2nd ed. London: FT/Prentice Hall, 2010.

Vaughan, Liam and Gavin Finch. *The Fix: How Bankers Lied, Cheated and Colluded to Rig the World's Most Important Number*. London: Wiley/Bloomberg Press, 2017.

Vrolijk, Conrad. "Derivatives Effect on Monetary Policy Transmission." *IMF Working Paper* 97/121, 1997.

4 The True Short of It, or Finance Capital Unleashed

The Recent Evolution of *Derivatives* Markets

Introduction

This chapter has a quantitative bent. It presents the recent evolution of *derivatives* transactions to highlight the size of their markets in terms of notional, market or fair values, open interest and turnover, and also the most important types of references and of arrangements, and the most relevant users or agents, at the sectoral level and at the spatial location of circuits. The phenomenal quantitative growth observed is usually associated with overall changes in the way that non-financial and financial institutions operate in an environment of increased risks caused by finance capital movements in adjusting the composition of its wealth and also by the negotiations involving the very arrangements lumped together under the label of *derivatives*.

These instruments are treated in the literature as financial innovations having an enormous disruptive capacity or, in the words of Schumpeter, a potential for creative destruction. So, growth reflects effectively performed hedging functions in a world of exogenous risks. But it could be only a substantial shift in the circuits of finance capital, unleashed by financialisation and neo-liberalism. Thus, the huge volume of *derivatives* is not proportional to the amount of values at risk and growth might not be explained by efficiency or effectiveness in protecting wealth and incomes from uncontrolled financial institutions, but the very functioning of these transactions.

Given the complexity of the sub-system, it is impossible to analyse all the data produced about presumed *derivatives* today in a single chapter. They would require another book, with one database explored in detail per chapter. The account below is therefore only a summary of the phenomenon represented by the astounding growth of finance capital and its *derivatives* fractions under contemporary capitalism, focusing on only two sources.

The chapter is organised as follows. In the next section, a general and brief discussion about the challenges of measuring *derivatives*, the ontological non-entity, is offered. Then a quantitative overview of international circuits of *derivatives* is provided, with a focus on the Bank for International Settlements (BIS) database. Thereafter, data for the United States, the most important space for the *derivatives* sub-system, is presented, using the OCC figures for commercial banks. Other databases are briefly mentioned next. Before summing up the chapter, a

DOI: 10.4324/9781003137092-5

short reflection about the growth of instruments lumped together as *derivatives* is carried out.

The Challenge of Measuring What Does not Exist

As argued in Chapter 1, *derivatives* do not exist ontologically. So, they cannot be measured as such. But is there any evidence that this is the case? Yes. Even today information about *derivatives* is still a source of trouble for government and international statistical offices, accounting boards and financial and non-financial institutions, to mention a few. For example, Poitras (2016, p. 371) remarks that the concept of free-standing *derivatives* introduced by SFAS 133 poses significant challenges to accounting at the capitalist unit level. It is worth underlining, according to him, that the accounting profession has dedicated, for decades, efforts to develop a set of standards that avoid discretionary accounts.

An example may be helpful to illustrate. In the case of exchange-traded contracts, the clearing house may balance positions daily to minimise cash-settlement transfers. How are all these offset positions accounted and recorded for statistical purposes in monthly or quarterly figures? Are all gross contracts over the entire period measured, or only the net positions at the closing period, the last day of the month or quarter? The fifth edition of the IMF manual requires that net cash settlement payments must be reported as financial transactions and not investment income flows.[1] It dodges the fundamental questions about time since balance sheet items take a longer timer to be publicised.

By the same token, Weber (2009) notes that *derivatives* are not included in national economic statistics. They are beyond official data. The IMF (2000) informs that the evolving *derivatives* markets spurred requests from national statisticians about their measurement, that is, they had no clue about the proper gauge of *derivatives*. Since the IMF had no answer either, despite the fact that the contemporary arrangements were growing since the 1970s and 1980s, an informal group on the measurement of financial *derivatives* was created: the IMF Committee on Balance of Payments Statistics (Heath, 1998). The conclusion reached and recommended was that financial *derivatives* must be accounted for as assets, separating them from the underlying transactions or other financial assets that may be using them as hedge. That is, *derivatives* should be considered on the balance of payments and also on national accounting systems that deal with wealth and stocks. As a consequence, some OTC instruments started being recorded, and interest rate swaps and FRA were considered financial assets, not contingent claims. Of course, in this case, assets could generate net out-payments. Uncertainty cannot be eliminated by arbitrarily measuring what cannot be measured.

There are other initiatives to fill this impossible gap. For example, the UK Office for National Statistics (ONS, 2019) was still developing a methodology for including *derivatives* and employee stock options in the flows of funds accounts matrices later in 2019 (ONS, 2019), some three centuries after modern arrangements were developed. Notwithstanding the difficulties, conventions allowed some imperfect measurement to be made. Today, there are data about different circuits of the so-called *derivatives* sub-system. The most important data sources about *derivatives* are the BIS and FIA for the world economy, and OCC and CFTC for the United States. Some of these institutions have supervisory mandates, and therefore need accurate information (BIS, 2012; Hollanders, 2012). However, they cannot gather information about what does not exist. They can only collect data about specific arrangements and, since they are measured in monetary units, collapse them all under a concept of *derivatives*, that is as discretionary as the statements that accountants have been trying to avoid mismeasurement for decades.

The Sub-system Circuits from an International Perspective: The BIS Database

The BIS has developed a robust, albeit incomplete and imperfect, framework for monitoring and measuring what they think to be *derivatives* market activity (BIS, 2012; Hollanders, 2012; von Kleist, 2012). It has three surveys. In the triennial review, dealers from more than 50 jurisdictions provide data. The statistics are then aggregated as coming from single countries, rather than displayed at the individual dealer level. As expected, the reporting universe for the turnover part of the investigation, conducted on a sales desk location basis, is made up of large commercial banks, investment banks and securities or reporting dealers. Specific fractions of finance capital basically. Central banks are not part of the survey, although they are important non-profit users, since they co-manage the monetary and financial systems with private institutions. The survey has 12 tables, being six for spot foreign exchange turnover, not *derivatives*, and another six for OTC interest rate *derivatives* turnover (BIS, 2024). The triennial survey is not analysed in this book.

For the exchange-traded instruments survey, the numbers are compiled from undisclosed commercial data sources, covering over 50 organised exchanges. The bank converts the number of contracts, not published, into notional amounts using information about contract sizes. In a major gap about the dynamics of contemporary finance capital, the BIS does not collect statistics for exchange-traded equity, commodity, credit *derivatives* indices and non-standard underlying references like inflation, weather or energy contracts (BIS, 2024). Thus, the exchange-traded BIS data do not have information about commodities arrangements, albeit exchanges were for a long time the traditional institutional setting for this type of transaction, the birth of modern *derivatives*. Of course, agriculture became less and less important as manufacturing and later services assumed greater weight as concrete forms of commodities and bearers of value as reflected in income and wealth. The commodities' market values represent financialised transactions today, belonging to circuits of finance capital, not the hedging necessities of farming. Credit or longer term loans used to have some importance, but, after the 2007–2008 collapse, they lost relevance. Thus, the representatives of the antediluvian forms of capital experimented a significative decline as financialisation advanced and found more appropriate vessels in the fluctuations of interest and foreign exchange rates, rather than in staple prices and creditworthiness of borrowers.

The database has four tables with numbers for interest rate and foreign exchange circuits, for both futures and options, separated by location of exchange and by currency. It has different levels of details. For example, at level 4, it is possible to divide interest rate trades into short- and long-run contracts, although sometimes the numbers do not add up. Considering the frequency of data, there are quarterly figures for open interest since 1993. There are also monthly data for daily average turnover since 1993 and annual since 1976, after the beginning of contemporary capitalism (BIS, 2024). Before, it seems, they were not quantitatively important to the point of reporting. For the analysis, a few points in time were selected. For daily turnover, the beginning of the series, the neo-liberal 1980s, the roaring 1990s, the period before the housing bubble collapse and today. For open interest, given the shorter series, it highlights the early roaring 1990s, the period before the peak of the housing bubble, the years after the crash in the United States, but during the Euro crisis, the year before the start of the COVID-19 pandemics and today. Table 4.1 shows the daily average turnover for each year.[2] Turnover has continuously increased over time.

It is striking that neither foreign exchange arrangements nor options were reported before 1986, more than a decade after the end of Bretton Woods and an enhanced volatility. Asia-Pacific was more important than Europe for futures in the 1980s. Does this mean that, as the circuit of industrial capital was enlarged, by segmented production chains outside the North Atlantic, and accumulation and valorisation also shifted to Asia, hedging with *derivatives* followed suit? Or it is just a temporary reconfiguration of finance capital worldwide? Anyway, Asia lost importance in terms of turnover in the following years, whereas the U.S. finance capital recovered its previous supremacy after the 1990s and sustained its hegemony, as capitals located in Europe, not necessarily European, could not compete.

In the first ten years with data, there was an explosive growth, as identified by Magdoff and Sweezy (1987). Futures remained dominant despite a slight declining trend until 2006, with an apparent recovery by 2024. For this type of arrangement and measure of market activity, foreign exchange is not relevant, probably because spot markets are more significant. Given that turnover is a gauge of short-term capital movements, finance capitalists do not seem to rotate their capitals with exchange-traded foreign exchange futures. Or with options, which grew slightly until a peak in 2006 just to decline again in relative terms. Interest rates are by far the most important reference for speculation on bourses, mainly short-term contracts, as it has to be. Finance capital seeks rapid profits. Summing up, regarding turnover, exchange-trade reported *derivatives* are about short-term interest rate futures with dealers located mostly in the United States and Europe.

Regarding open interest in *derivatives* exchanges shown in Table 4.2, in the first quarter of 1993, futures dominated this sub-system, and interest rate instruments dominated both the futures and the option circuits. The aggregate performance over time displays a rapid growth until 2010, slow changes up to 2019 and then decline in the most recent period. Are *derivatives* losing importance as a financial subsystem? The fall is explained by the decreasing value of open interest for options. Unlike the picture for turnover data, considering open interest, these arrangements

Table 4.1 Daily average turnover of selected exchange-traded *derivatives* (in billions of U.S. unadjusted dollars), selected years

Instrument/reference	*1976*	*1986*	*1996*	*2006*	*2024*
Futures	1 (100%)	120 (86.3%)	1,072 (85.8%)	4,694 (72.6%)	10,513 (82.2%)
Interest rate	1 (100%)	114 (95%)	1,061 (98.9%)	4,627 (98.6%)	10,357 (98.5%)
Short-term	-	64	857	4,005	9,082
Long-term	-	51	204	622	1,275
Foreign exchange	0	6 (5%)	11 (1.1%)	66 (1.4%)	156 (1.5%)
North America	1 (100%)	83 (69.2%)	468 (43.7%)	2,706 (57.6%)	7,156 (68%)
Europe	0	9 (7.5%)	350 (32.6%)	1,681 (35.8%)	2,970 (28.3%)
Rest of the World	0	28 (23.3%)	254 (23.7%)	306 (6.5%)	388 (3.7%)
Options	0	19 (13.7%)	177 (14.2%)	1,775 (27.4%)	2,275 (17,8%)
Interest rate	0	16 (84.2%)	172 (97.2%)	1,771 (99.8%)	2,262 (99.4%)
Short-term	-	8	135	1,687	2,110
Long-term	-	8	37	84	152
Foreign exchange	0	2 (10.5%)	5 (2.8%)	5 (0.2%)	13 (0.5%)
North America	0	18 (94.7%)	112 (63.3%)	1,301 (73.3%)	1,663 (73.1%)
Europe		1 (5.3%)	50 (28.2)	447 (25.2%)	576 (25.3%)
Rest of the World	0	0	15 (8.4%)	27 (1.5%)	36 (1.6%)
Total	1 (100%)	139 (100%)	1,249 (100%)	6,469 (100%)	12,788 (100%)

Source: Elaborated by the author using BIS exchange-traded *derivatives* statistics, table D1.

Table 4.2 Quarterly value of open interest of exchange-traded *derivatives* contracts (notional principal in billions of U.S. unadjusted dollars), first quarter of selected years

Instrument/reference	*1993.Q1*	*2003.Q1*	*2010.Q1*	*2019.Q1*	*2024.Q1*
Futures	4,989 (67.2%)	11,119 (38.6%)	23,771 (31.6%)	37,753 (35.6%)	39,315 (42.1%)
Interest rate	4,955 (99.3%)	11,047 (99.4%)	23,593 (99.3%)	37,496 (99.4%)	38,992 (99.2%)
Short-term	4,632	10,510	22,327	34,568	35,583
Long-term	323	537	1,266	2,928	3,410
Foreign exchange	34 (0.7%)	72 (0.6%)	178 (0.7%)	257 (0.6%)	323 (0.8%)
North America	2,484 (49.8%)	6,357 (57.2%)	12,401 (52.2%)	25,072 (66.4%)	28,833 (73.3%)
Europe	1,115 (22.3%)	3,652 (32.8%)	8,141 (34.2%)	9,358 (24.8%)	7,843 (19.9%)
Rest of the world	1,390 (27.9%)	1,110 (10%)	3,229 (13.6%)	3,324 (8.8%)	2,639 (6.8%)
Options	2,437 (32.8%)	17,652 (61.4%)	51,557 (68.4%)	68,283 (64.4%)	54,117 (57.9%)
Interest rate	2,361 (96.9%)	17,622 (99.8%)	51,351 (99.6%)	68,141 (99.8%)	53,969 (99.7%)
Short-term	2,132	17,111	50,872	67,008	53,331
Long-term	229	511	479	1,133	639
Foreign exchange	76 (3.1%)	30 (0.2%)	206 (0.4%)	142 (0.2%)	148 (0.3%)
North America	1,688 (69.3%)	9,096 (51.5%)	22,687 (44%)	53,320 (78.1%)	35,202 (65%)
Europe	579 (23.8%)	8,513 (48.2%)	27,807 (53.9%)	14,372 (21%)	17,438 (32.2%)
Rest of the World	169 (6.9%)	43 (0.3%)	1,063 (2.1%)	591 (0.9%)	1,478 (2.8%)
Total	7,426 (100%)	28,771 (100%)	75,328 (100%)	106,036 (100%)	93,432 (100%)

Source: Elaborated by the author using BIS exchange-traded *derivatives* statistics, table D1.

became relatively more important sometime by the end of the twentieth century or beginning of the new millennium. Futures maintained a positive growth over the period, albeit less rapid in the more recent years. The United States had a decline in its share of futures after the subprime crash but recovered its hegemony afterwards. In options, there was a declining trend until 2010, but a rapid recovery in the more recent period. Europe grew in the vacuum but seems to be losing ground again. These two capitalist spaces dominate the *derivatives* sub-system.

Considering the references, interest rate deals can be seen as a synonymous of *derivatives* for the open interest of exchange-traded instruments also. Foreign exchange is negligible. Again, if only the aggregate numbers are considered, and that is actually what the acceptance of the world *derivatives* would entail, the quantitative, beyond the qualitative, differences are missed. The circuit of exchange-traded contracts are basically about short-term interest rate contracts, no longer the commodities that started it all many decades ago, options more than futures today, mainly in the North Atlantic.

The BIS (2024) affirms that the OTC statistics, the third survey, capture the outstanding positions of *derivatives* dealers, mainly banks in 12 jurisdictions (Australia, Canada, France, Germany, Italy, Japan, the Netherlands, Spain, Sweden, Switzerland, the UK and the United States). Dealers report on a consolidated basis, including the positions of their foreign affiliates, and excluding intra-group positions. The statistics are collected and reported to the BIS at a country, rather than individual dealer, level, just like the numbers at exchanges. This is not ideal, of course, as is seen in the next section, since *derivatives* are about banks.

This database is more comprehensive. It has 11 tables, five of them about CDS (after 2004). There are two tables for separating foreign exchange, interest and equity, on the one hand, and commodity and CDS, on the other. For a global view, that is the only systematic information about the circuit of commodity *derivatives*. There are three tables for financials, one being for the maturity. The frequency is semi-annual and the data start in 1998. Although it is a quarter of century past the birth of contemporary capitalism, only recent information is available. OTC transactions are older than that, of course.

There are many levels of disaggregation. The tables have 14 choices between instrument data, including detailed deals like options sold or bought, currencies for both legs of the transactions, counterparty sector and country, rating, risk category, underlying risk sector and maturities. Herfindahl concentration measures and credit exposures are provided as well. The values include notional amounts outstanding (NAO) or the total book value of all open contracts, and gross market value (GMV), the value of all contracts at the current market prices. This reduces the number of data points for the purposes of this chapter. So, it shows the end of the roaring 1990s, the start of the sub-prime bubble collapse and today. Given the fragmented information, conclusions are harder to come by without a comprehensive synthesis that this chapter cannot deliver. What is the best representative picture of this circuit of finance capital? How does it complement the analysis on exchanges?

It is interesting to notice that, comparing exchange-traded and OTC instruments, there are different economic measures in the same unit of money for arrangements that are part of the same ideal concept, for example, open interest and notional amounts outstanding, gross market and fair values, all associated with different *loci* of negotiations. This would be another source of doubt about the existence of *derivatives*.

Considering the five basic references in Tables 4.3 and 4.4, it is clear that the references credit, equity and commodities are not very important in relative terms, which could justify the BIS cuts for the exchange survey. In world OTC circuits as a whole, commodities *derivatives* are irrelevant, despite the fact that gold has become more important. Considering the types, options are less relevant. Of course, agriculture became less and less important as manufacturing and later services assumed greater importance. Poitras (2016) mentions the growth of equity *derivatives* markets, but today they are irrelevant when it comes to the need of measuring flows and stocks in the *derivatives* sub-system, even in absolute terms. Regarding the types of arrangements, options lost ground to forwards and swaps, although they remain somewhat important for the smaller equity and commodities subcircuits. Swaps are the single most important type of arrangement in general OTC subcircuits, mainly for interest rate and foreign exchange. Thus, hedging and speculation based on foreign currencies are important in OTC markets, but not on exchanges. Also, comparing gross market values and notional amounts outstanding, the former are only a minor fraction of the latter. But there is no information about some specific types of arrangements. This means that OTC circuits are similar to what Fernand Braudel calls the anti-market. Without public market prices, it is not possible to calculate values. Unlike exchange-based data, for the OTC circuits, the locations of the transactions were not considered in this discussion and the position of U.S.-based finance capitals is not approached. But it is not far fetched to assume that the United States is the single most important space for capitalist organisations dealing with these OTC arrangements as well.

Non-financial firms are not important players, in relative terms, in OTC circuits. Even for originating the loan that serves as the reference for CDS. They are not hedging or speculating with *derivatives*. Also, regarding the credit circuit, given the average maturity of the underlying loans, the *derivatives* have relatively longer times to expire. And, although the credibility of credit rating agencies should be considered with caution, the share of CDS with better risk profiles has gradually increased. The circuit is dominated by dealers and other financial institutions, as expected.

Unlike the exchange circuits, foreign exchange values kept growing over time, and the crisis was not sufficient to revert the trend, although it may have moderated the exponential growth. Interest rate values have stagnated when compared to the crisis years, with oscillations after the peak in 2013. That is, it is hovering around high values. But it represents 80% of the notional values of contracts with financial references or macro-financial prices. Hence, based on BIS incomplete data, OTC circuits are about finance capital. In particular, short-term interest rate and

Table 4.3 Semi-annual accumulated value of OTC *derivatives* contracts with financial references (unadjusted US$ billion). Selected years

Selected measures	*1998.S2*		*2007.S2*		*2024.S2*	
	NAO	*GMV*	*NAO*	*GMV*	*NAO*	*GMV*
Foreign Exchange	**21,713 (27%)**	**1,012 (31.5%)**	**66,575 (11.4%)**	**2,187 (14%)**	**130,093 (18.6%)**	**4,874 (27.7%)**
Outright forwards and forex swaps	14,858 (68.4%)	656 (64.8%)	35,195 (52.9%)	925 (42.3%)	72,827 (56%)	2,557 (52.5%)
Currency swaps	2,672 (12.3%)	230 (22.7%)	16,445 (24.7%)	885 (40.5%)	38,071 (29.3%)	1,993 (40.9%)
Options	4,159 (19.2%)	126 (12.5%)	14,892 (22.4%)	378 (17.3%)	19,171 (14.7%)	324 (6.6%)
Reporting dealers	8,879 (40.9%)	429 (42.4%)	25,089 (37.7%)	735 (33.6%)	45,487 (35%)	1,629 (33.4%)
Non-financial	4,078 (18.8%)	200 (19.8%)	13,044 (19.6%)	502 (22.9%)	16,769 (12.9%)	812 (16.7%)
Maturity: up to 1 year	18,898 (87%)	-	48,254 (72.5%)	-	101,077 (77.7%)	-
Currency: dollar	19,152 (88.2%)	905 (89.4%)	55,334 (83.1%)	1,828(83.6%)	114,295 (87.9%)	4,238 (86.9%)
Interest rate	**56,395 (70.3%)**	**1,897 (59.1%)**	**432,404 (73.8%)**	**8,125 (51.9%)**	**548,341 (78.4%)**	**11,547 (65.6%)**
FRA	7,375 (13.1%)	62 (3.3%)	29,827 (6.9%)	187 (2.3%)	55,105 (10%)	367 (3.2%)
Swaps	40,246 (71.4%)	1,657 (87.3%)	340,666 (78.8%)	6,890 (84.8%)	446,875 (81.5%)	10,581 (91.6%)
Options	8,743 (15.5%)	179 (9.4%)	61,911 (14.3%)	1,048 (12.9%)	46,156 (8.4%)	600 (5.2%)
Reporting dealers	28,015 (49.7%)	871 (45.9%)	173,703 (40.2%)	3,181 (39.2%)	28,384 (5.2%)	725 (6.3%)
Non-financial	6,603 (11.7%)	272 (14.3%)	48,974 (11.3%)	768 (9.5%)	16,041 (2.9%)	642 (5.6%)
Maturity: up to 1 year	21,226 (37.6%)	-	143,059 (33%)	-	233,782 (42.6%)	-
Currency: dollar	15,026 (26.6%)	412 (21.7%)	140,636 (32.5%)	3,370 (41.5%)	167,021 (30.4%)	3,498 (30.3%)
Equity	**1,563 (1.95%)**	**248 (7.7%)**	**9,541 (1.6%)**	**1,280 (8.2%)**	**8,901 (1.3%)**	**662 (3.8%)**
Forwards and swaps	175 (11.2%)	49 (19.8%)	2,461 (25.8%)	270 (21.1%)	4,674 (52.5%)	280 (1.6%)
Options	1,388 (88.8%)	199 (80.2%)	7,079 (74.2%)	1,010 (78.9%)	4,226 (47.5%)	382 (57.7%)
Reporting dealers	445 (28.5%)	77 (31%)	3,321 (34.8%)	441 (34.4%)	1,247 (14%)	72 (10.9%)
Non-financial	503 (32.2%)	61 (24.6%)	1,244 (13%)	206 (16.1%)	1,153 (12.9%)	156 (23.6%)
Maturity: up to 1 year	855 (54.7%)	-	5,128 (53.7%)	-	5,802 (65.2%)	-
All contracts (*)	**80,277**	**3,209 (4.0%)**	**585,926**	**15,653 (2.7%)**	**699,476**	**17,615 (2.5%)**

Source: Elaborated by the author using the BIS database, table D5.1. Totals do not always sum up to 100% due to incomplete information or rounding off.

(*) Summing up the values of all three types of contracts reported does not equal the reported value for all contracts for both NAO and GMV. There are some unexplained missing values.

Table 4.4 Semi-annual accumulated value of OTC commodity and credit (antediluvian) *derivatives* contracts (in unadjusted US$ billion). Selected years

Selected measures	*2004.S2 (*)*		*2009.S2*		*2024.S2*	
	NAO	*GMV*	*NAO*	*GMV*	*NAO*	*GMV*
Commodities (**)	**1,542 (11.5%)**	**186 (32.3%)**	**3,762 (8.1%)**	**589 (23.2%)**	**2,408 (19.8%)**	**257 (48.4%)**
Gold	418 (27.1%)	35 (18.8%)	1,167 (31%)	68 (11.5%)	1,025 (42.6%)	43 (16.7%)
Other commodities	1,067 (69,2%)	147 (79%)	2,480 (65,9%)	505 (85,7%)	1,280 (53,2%)	206 (80,2%)
Forwards and swaps	769 (49.9%)	-	2,594 (69%)	-	1,824 (75.7%)	-
Options	774 (50.1%)	-	1,169 (31%)	-	583 (24.3%)	-
Credit Derivatives	**11,653 (86.8%)**	**308 (53.6%)**	**42,816 (91.7%)**	**1,943 (76.6%)**	**9,229 (76%)**	**213 (40.1%)**
Credit default swaps (***)	6,396 (54.9%)	134 (43.5%)	35,783 (83.6%)	1,936 (99.6%)	9,045 (98%)	182 (85.4%)
Single-name instruments	5,117 (80%)	112 (83.6%)	22,945 (64.1%)	1,314 (67.9%)	3,886 (43%)	81 (44.5%)
Reporting dealers	2,752 (43%)	49 (36.6%)	19,520 (54.6%)	915 (47.3%)	921 (10.2%)	24 (13.2%)
Other financial	3,121 (48.8%)	73 (54.5%)	14,646 (40.9%)	792 (40.1%)	8,047 (89%)	154 (84.6%)
Non-financial	523 (8.2%)	12 (8.9%)	1,617 (4.5%)	97 (5%)	76 (0.8%)	4 (2.2%)
Investment grade	2,423 (37.9%)	-	16,692 (46.6%)	-	4,565 (50.5%)	-
Maturity up to 1 year	491 (7.7%)	-	3,432 (9.6%)	-	1,210 (13.4%)	-

(Continued)

Table 4.4 (Continued)

Selected measures	*2004.S2 (*)*		*2009.S2*		*2024.S2*	
	NAO	*GMV*	*NAO*	*GMV*	*NAO*	*GMV*
Non-financial firms (obligor of underlying)	1,289 (20.2%)	-	3,399 (9.5%)	-	2,457 (27.2%)	-
Home country	-	-	-	-	2,886 (31.9%)	-
Abroad: United States	-	-	-	-	2,560 (28.3%)	-
Other derivatives	**224 (1.7%)**	**81 (14.1%)**	**93 (0.2%)**	**3 (0.2%)**	**505 (4.2%)**	**61 (11.5%)**
Total	**13,419**	**575 (4.3%)**	**46,671**	**2,535 (5.4%)**	**12,142**	**531 (4.4%)**

Source: elaborated by the author using the BIS database, table D5.2. Totals not always do sum up to 100% due to incomplete information or rounding off.

(*) Although the BIS has OTC commodity *derivatives* data harking back to 1998, for credit *derivatives* the bank has data starting in 2004. This year was adopted here for commodities as well.

(**) The structure of the data presentation has three entries: gold, other metals and other commodity.

(***)Composition is for credit default swaps, a fraction of credit *derivatives*, which also include total return swaps, credit options and collateralised debt obligations. But there is no information about these other contracts. The structure of the data presentation is the following. Instruments are divided into single-name (single entity) and multi-name (like a portfolio or basket of credits, including tranches) or index. Counterparty has reporting dealers, six other financial institutions: central counterparties, banks and securities firms, insurance firms, SPVs (special purpose vehicles), SPCs (special purpose companies), SPEs (special purpose entities), hedge funds and other financial customers and non-financial customers. Rating categories include investment grade, non-investment grade and non-rated. Maturity has up to 1 year, between 1 and 5 years and over 5 years. Sector is not the same as counterparties, but economic sector of the obligor of the underlying reference obligation, and have sovereigns, financial firms, non-financial firms, securitised products and multiple sectors. Finally, the location of the counterparty has home country and abroad, the latter including the United States, European developed countries, Japan, other Asian countries, Latin America and all other countries. Data by economic sector and rating are incomplete (do not add up to the total). Gross market value is not always available, since OTC markets involve tailored contracts without a market and therefore without a public price. The BIS requests best effort estimates, but this may only entail LIBOR-type dishonesty risks. The table has also other *derivatives*, that cannot be decomposed into plain vanilla instruments, and gross credit exposure.

foreign exchange swaps, with capital circulating in international circuits with its movements happening over shorter periods of time.

Commercial Banks in U.S. *Derivatives* Circuits: The Data from the Office of the Comptroller of the Currency

A very important source of detailed, bank-level data on *derivatives* in the United States, usually neglected, is the Office of the Comptroller of the Currency (OCC, 2025). It has so far published 118 very useful quarterly reports on bank trading and *derivatives* activities in the United States, starting in 1995, but with digital reports available only for the period starting in the first quarter of 1996, in this latter case without tables and graphs on the document retrievable on the OCC webpage. These documents rely primarily on information obtained from the Call Reports, formally Consolidated Reports of Condition and Income, filed by all insured commercial banks and trust companies.[3]

There was a change in the presentation of the reports during the third quarter of 1998 and then again on the first quarter of 2006. The first reports had a general section about notional values, shares of OTC and exchange transactions, maturities and the number of banks holding *derivatives*, including concentration. They had also a section about risks of *derivatives*, mainly credit exposures, including *derivatives* for trading that is the majority for larger banks, and for risk management. It adds a new measure to analytical tool – the fair value of contracts. More important, the OCC provides information about revenues generated by *derivatives*. And a section about mortgage securities and structured notes. Data disclosure is not homogeneous, however. To address this issue, spreadsheets are available from the fourth quarter of 1998 on.

The newest reports are about ten times longer, mainly due to the figures. They have a section on market risks, and discuss centrally cleared *derivatives*, an imposition of the legislation (see Chapter 9). The wealth of detailed information include also bird-eye data about counterparty credit risks, broken down by underlying, distribution of net current credit exposures by counterpart, for which corporations are the more important group, followed by other banks – hedge funds, surprisingly, are not important – the relationship between the fair value of collateral to credit exposure, the asset composition of collateral, VaR and the rating of credit *derivatives*. It is interesting to notice that many banks associated with *derivatives* failures are not part of the top 25 ones in the more recent report.

The report for the first quarter of 1996, amidst the roaring 1990s, as well as the latest one for the second quarter of 2025, support many of the claims made in this book, as discussed later. For 1996, in terms of the figures, and considering initially the number of institutions and the stocks, the notional value in the portfolio of the 549 commercial banks holding *derivatives* was $17.9 trillion, against an annual GDP of $8 trillion. Current GDP is the basic measure from which risks associated with new flows are derived, mainly investment and foreign trade. The remaining sources of risks are related to stocks of wealth, mainly financial wealth. In 1996, the net worth of all sectors in the United States, including the public sector and millions of poor households, amounted to $37.6 trillion, probably including *derivatives*.[4] Regarding the references, about $11.8 trillion (66% of the total) in notional value was related to interest rate contracts, $5.6 trillion (32% of the total) to foreign exchange contracts and only $0.38 trillion (2%) to equity and commodities. This is similar to the BIS figures for the past decades for the world market, in which the United States is the hegemonic nation.

The distribution of maturities is also skewed. Short-term contracts with remaining maturity of less than one year had a notional value of $8.8 trillion. Contracts with remaining maturities between one and five years, $3.9 trillion. And long-term contracts $0.99 trillion. Concerning the venue of the transactions, 87% of the notional amounts were traded in OTC circuits. The report states that the composition of contract types remained relatively unchanged since 1991. It is a remarkable stability for contemporary capitalism. In terms of concentration, the OCC report claims that *derivatives* continued to be concentrated, with the C_9 reaching 94% and the C_{25} responding for 97% of the total notional value.[5]

Another interesting finding of the report concerns the purposes of using *derivatives*. For the first quarter of 1996, the banks with the 25 largest *derivatives* portfolios held almost 94% of their contracts for trading. And this represented almost 92% of all notional values. Smaller banks, on the contrary, held 74% of their *derivatives* as end-users, for risk management or at least not for trading purposes. The portfolios built for trading purposes were balanced in terms of gross positive and negative fair values. The sums maintained for risk management had a slightly larger positive fair value. Considering risks, in the first quarter of 1996, the total credit exposure of banks was equal to $234 billion. Although this sum is adjusted to bilateral netting arrangements and represented only 1.3% of the total notional value, it corresponded to 234% of the risk-based capital of the top nine banks. This is the relevant issue concerning systemic risks. Despite that, credit losses were immaterial in that period.

Since notional values are only references on money stocks for calculating net payment flows, they have informational content about *derivatives* activity levels and possibly trends, but are not completely reliable information about the credit risk exposure of these instruments. The OCC report stressed the potential of bilateral netting arrangements, not captured by aggregate notional amounts, to reduce credit exposures. This impacts on the risk-adjusted levels of capital of each bank dealing with *derivatives*. At the same time, the gross fair value data do not reckon the cash positions in trading portfolios. They may also be misleading, to the extent that the values are reported on a legal entity basis and do not reflect the portfolios of affiliates. And when they do, a double-counting of bank and non-bank affiliate positions may distort the numbers.

Last but not least, considering flows, unfortunately there is no data about profits, only gross revenues. But this represents an enormous advantage when compared to the BIS data. In 1996, banks trading *derivatives* realised approximately $1.9 billion in revenues from cash and off-balance sheet *derivative* contracts. And the gross revenue for all banks with *derivatives* was $75 billion. The top nine banks accounted for 86% of these trading incomes. It is worth noticing that, for the second quarter report of 1996, one-third of the *derivatives* trading revenues, or $634 million, was attributable to Morgan Guaranty Trust alone. Out of the total trading revenues, $1.2 billion was derived from interest rate contracts, $628 million from foreign exchange instruments and $191 million from equity and commodities. Again, interest rate contracts are the single most important dimension of this sub-system. And *derivatives* are about a few big finance capital organisations earning huge profits.

Has the picture depicted above changed in the almost three decades between 1996 and 2023? It is important emphasising that, as mentioned, the recent reports available on the OCC webpage (OCC, 2025) changed a lot in terms of presentation and contents, having much more data and information today. According to its report about the fourth quarter of 2023, there was a total of 1,185 insured U.S. national and state commercial banks and savings associations with trading and *derivatives* activities. The terminology changed, so it is not possible to evaluate if there are more commercial banks reporting, along with trust companies and savings associations.[6] The issue of comparison over time is further complicated by the presence, in the more recent reports, of the consolidated bank holding company (BHC) information.[7] Also, institutions with less than $5 billion in assets may fill in a different form, with less detailed *derivatives* activities required. It is impossible to have a complete view of the sub-system.

Regarding stocks, the notional value reached $192.5 trillion in 2023, increasing by a factor of almost 11 since 1996, against an annual GDP of $27.4 trillion, increasing by a factor of 3.4 since 1996[8]. The total net worth was close to $156.3 trillion (see footnote 4), increasing by a factor of 4.2. The total assets of all banks with *derivatives* was equal to $21 trillion. The four largest commercial banks or C_4 accounted for 87.4% of the total banking industry notional amounts, that is held by only 25 banks.[9] Regarding the underlying, about $136 trillion (70.6% of the total) in notional value was related to interest rate contracts, $45 trillion (23.4% of the total) to foreign exchange contracts, $5.7 trillion to equity (3%), $3.7 trillion to credit *derivatives* (1.9%),[10] with credit default swaps representing 85% of this notional value, and $1.5 trillion (0.6 %) to commodity and other. Not a significant change over time and compared to the BIS for the long haul. This sub-system of finance capital seems remarkably stable in its long-run structure.

The more recent reports also inform data on the contract type. For the fourth quarter of 2023, swaps represented 61% of the total notional amount of the banks, options 21%, futures and forwards 16.5% and credit *derivatives* only 1.9%. There were 113 banks that net sold credit protection, that is, assumed credit risk in the notional amount of $1.7 trillion and 90 banks that purchased credit protection (net value), that is, hedged credit risk, for a total of $2 trillion. Taking the maturities of interest rates and foreign exchange deals[11] into account, short-term contracts with remaining maturity of less than one year had a notional value of $87.6 trillion. Contracts with remaining maturities between one and five years, $29.6 trillion. And longer term contracts $21.8 trillion. It is about money changes in the short run, again.

In the same report, the OCC affirms that the notional amounts outstanding of banks' *derivatives* had declined since 2014 due to so-called trade compression efforts. This measure aggregates a large number of similar swap contracts into fewer trades, removing economic redundancy in a *derivative* book and reducing operational risks. The report also shows the share of *derivatives* contracts that are centrally cleared, a legal imposition (see Chapter 9). Overall, only 34% of the contracts were centrally cleared in the fourth quarter of 2023. For interest rate contracts, about 45% were cleared in a central counterparty. For credit contracts, only 28%. For equity, 24%. Only 3% of foreign exchange contracts were centrally cleared. This means that the regulatory efforts of Dodd–Frank had no significant impact on the *derivatives* sub-system.

As mentioned, there is no data on *derivatives* profits on the OCC reports. And since this is the only publicly available database with bank-level information, it would make sense to include more data on *derivatives*-related performance. As a consequence, only trading revenue is displayed regarding monetary flows. The trading revenue related to cash and *derivatives* of commercial banks and savings associations totalled $11.6 billion in the last quarter of 2023 alone. Considering bank holding companies, the number jumps to $32 billion, and equity *derivatives* are as important as interest rate instruments in this total. Part of the difference is due to contributions of investment banks to the bank holding companies' sum. The trading revenue for the four[12] largest banks were the following in the period: JP Morgan Chase with $5.6 billion, Citibank National with $1.6 billion, Goldman Sachs with $1.3 billion and Bank of America with $1.2 billion. The big four accounts for almost 84% of the net trading revenue of all commercial banks with *derivatives*. It is a big bank game.

How important *derivatives* trading income were for thegross income of the OCC reporting banks in the last quarter of 2023, since there are no data for profits? For the period since 2015, the report shows a relatively stable contribution of trading revenue to gross income for the top four banks, with a slight increase in the past few years. For the last quarter of 2023, and considering net income or earnings rather than gross income, for Goldman Sachs,[13] cash and *derivatives* trading revenue represented, 65% of net earnings. Of course, *derivatives* trading implies operational costs. And the overall efficiency ratio for Goldman Sachs for the entire year was almost 75%, that is, non-interest income represented three-fourths of revenue. The bank had relevant overhead inefficiencies in that year and, assuming that it was similar for all departments or divisions, the net trading revenue for *derivatives* represents a smaller contribution than the one suggested above. But it seems, nonetheless, substantial. It is not about hedging, again.

For JP Morgan Chase,[14] cash and *derivatives* trading income represented 60% of net income, and the overhead ratio was 63%. The trade income was greater than the net income of all bank divisions that include consumer and community banking, corporate and investment bank, commercial banking, asset and wealth management and corporate. For Citibank National, there was a net loss of $1.8 billion in the last quarter of 2023.[15] Thus, without *derivatives* trading, the net loss would almost double. Operational costs would be lower as well. Finally, for Bank of America,[16] cash and off-balance sheet positions represented only 39% of net income for the period. The efficiency ratio was 81% for the quarter but 67% for the year. It is clear that *derivatives* trading revenue represents a significant amount for the largest banks with *derivatives* positions. It is not about risk management and hedging. It is about financial profits.

Taking risks into account, the net current aggregate credit exposure was 'only' $240 billion[17] due to legally enforceable netting agreement,[18] and 65% of that potential credit risk was concentrated on the four largest banks. This is systemic risk in potential. For Goldman Sach, the one with the highest ratios, the credit exposure of *derivatives* alone was 142% of the risk-based capital. For the top four together, the ratio is very different, but they all show a downward trend since 2017 (Figure 11 of the report on page 34). The portfolios held for trading purposes continued relatively balanced in terms of gross positive and negative fair values, with a positive excess. For the four largest banks, 98.5% of the contracts were held for trading and marked to market. For all other banks with *derivatives*, the number drops to 87.4%. It is not about hedging. Nor small banks.

Besides the comparison between two points in time, the reports have figures that show the evolution of some of the above metrics over longer periods of time, but covering only years in the new millennium. Figure 4.1 shows that, in terms of notional values, *derivatives* in the new millennium are dominated in the U.S. banking system by trading, not using for hedging. End-users are irrelevant. And credit *derivatives* are irrelevant, although this is not a user, but a product or contract type. Speculative capital operating in *derivatives* circuits shows a rapid growth until 2011 and slight decline until 2017. It presents an oscillating recovery since them.

It is important to realise that the trend is not about the entire *derivatives* subsystem, but only the most important fraction of financial capitals in the United States operating in it. If one considers the flow of funds accounts of the Federal Reserve Board, it is possible to identify at least 22 apparently different generic types of money and finance-related institutions that make up the finance capital system.[19] And there are non-financial institutions, mainly corporations, involved with *derivatives*, although it is clear that their share is small based on the BIS database. But is not likely that they hedge using *derivatives*.

Considering depository institutions, there is a remarkable concentration of notional values and therefore trading income and credit exposure in four institutions, some of them also being investment or wholesale banking institutions. Figure 4.2, for the fourth quarter of each year and a shorter period, shows that there is a concentration of type of products or contracts in swaps, with options, futures, and forwards representing much smaller circuits. Credit *derivatives* are irrelevant. Figure 4.3, for the same time period, shows a concentration of underlying in interest rates, followed by foreign exchange. Commodities almost disappeared under contemporary financial capitalism, despite the fact that these contracts are financialised. Equities are equally irrelevant. Stock portfolios are not hedged with *derivatives*. Credit *derivatives* have become very small.

Regarding net current credit exposure for a longer period of annual data (Figure 4.4), it increased briskly with the housing bubble and fell rapidly, but not to

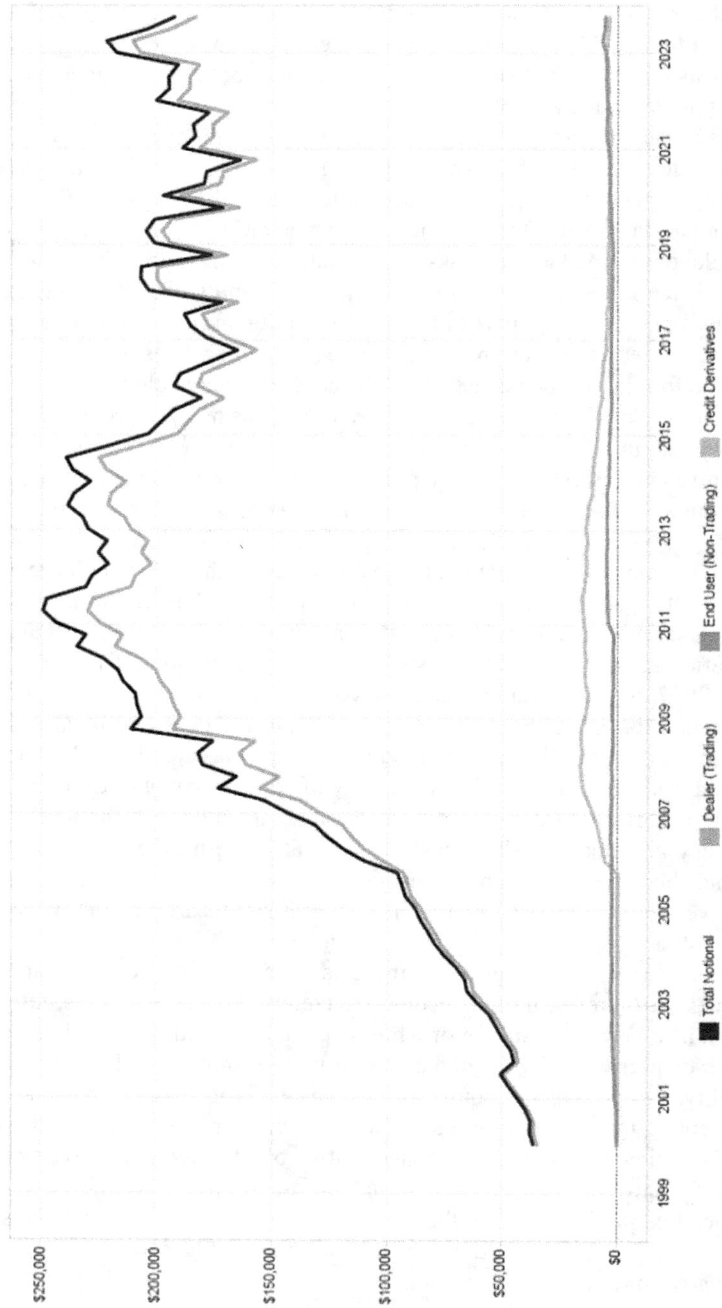

Figure 4.1 Derivatives notional amounts (in US$ billion) by user type.

Source: Office of the Comptroller of the Currency (OCC).

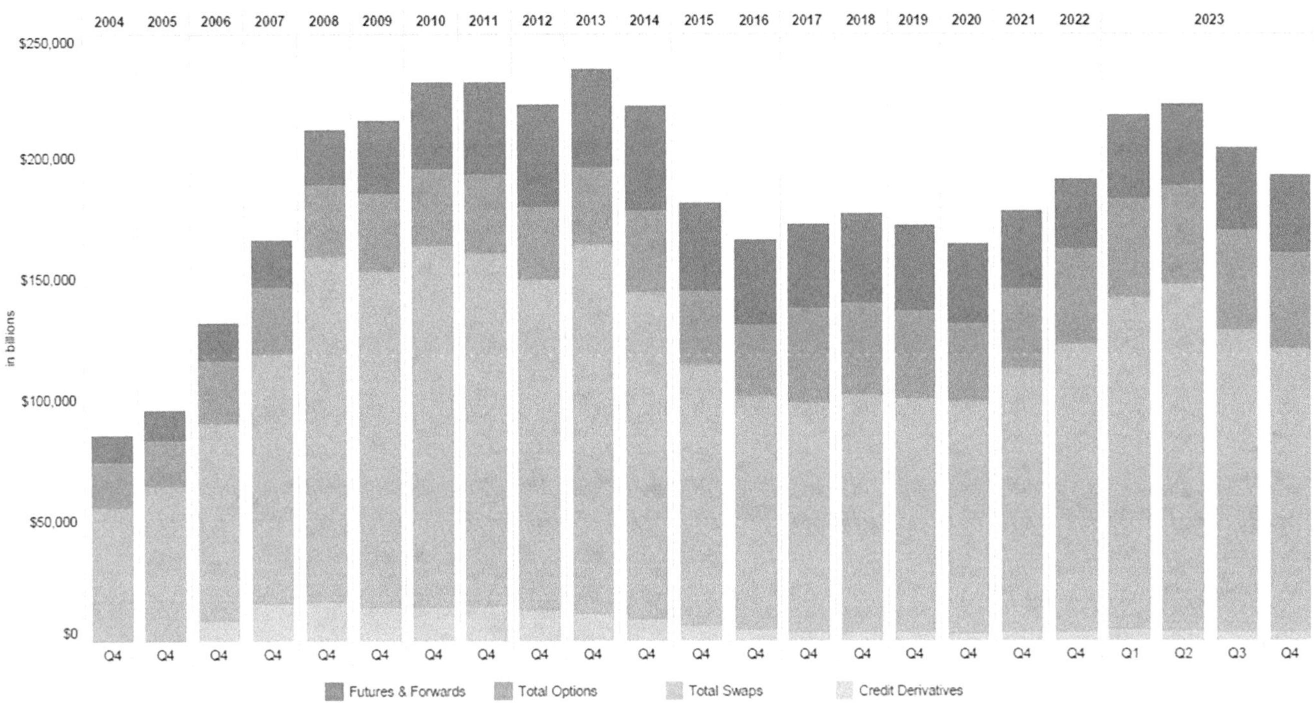

Figure 4.2 Derivatives notional amounts (in US$ billion) by product type.

Source: Office of the Comptroller of the Currency (OCC).

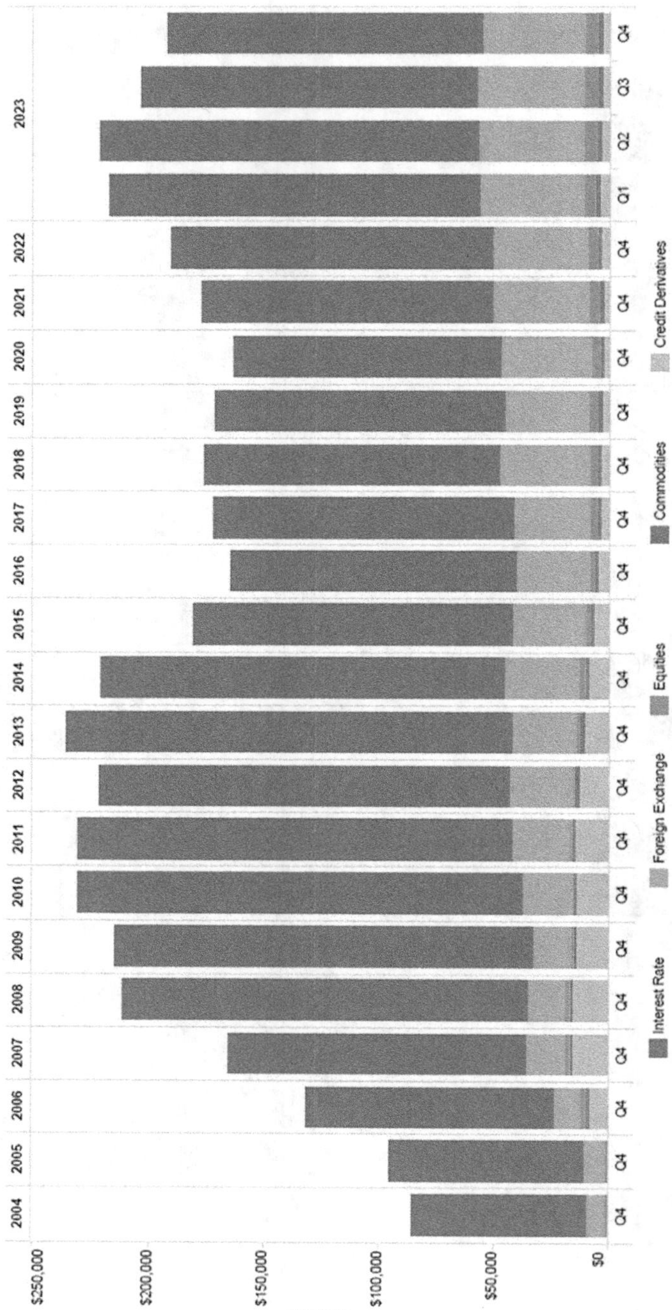

Figure 4.3 Derivatives notional amounts (in US$ billion) by contract type.

Source: Office of the Comptroller of the Currency (OCC).

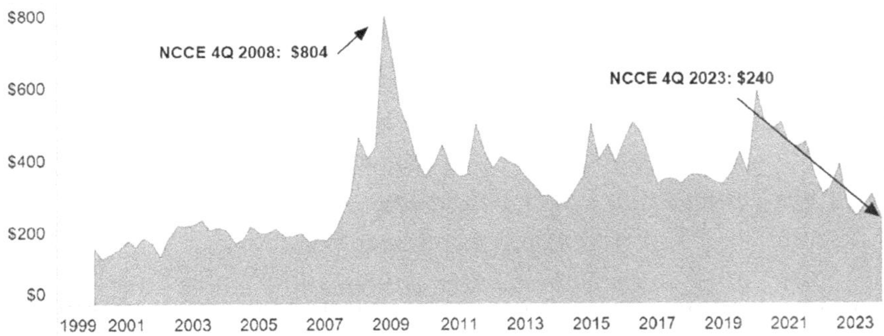

Figure 4.4 Derivatives net current credit exposure (NCCE) (in US$ billion).

Source: Office of the Comptroller of the Currency (OCC).

the previous average levels. And then oscillated for about 10 years, with a growth tendency, and has since them declined, but it is still very large in absolute and in relative terms, taking into account that it is concentrated in four large banks. As discussed before, netting explains the reduction.

Figure 4.5 shows that trading revenues fluctuate, given the numbers for the last quarter and a much shorter interval, but with a visible growing trend. Here the distribution is not so asymmetric in terms of the references. Commodities and mainly equities represent an important share of revenues. Credit is still less important. And interest rates have recently contributed less to revenues when compared to foreign exchange. So, the size of the specific circuit is not always correlated with earnings. Smaller notional amounts can still provide substantial earnings if the underlying faces volatility. The numbers are larger for banking holding companies, as the OCC report shows.

The contribution of foreign exchange to trading revenue is understandable when one observes the maturity of the *derivatives* contracts, for a longer series, in Figure 4.6. Foreign exchange arrangements are mostly short run. Interest rate contracts, on the other hand, have a larger share for longer maturities. Short-run contracts have also a higher value for equity and other commodity (not gold) contracts (Figure 4.7). So, it is very unlikely that hedging needs are so focused on short periods, unless financialisation is pervasive and valorisation must be quick. This phenomenon is more compatible with short run speculative positions. Hedging of long-term stocks and flows would require a continuous chain of short-term hedging operations, which would bring costs and risks up, but that is exactly what the arrangements should supposedly avoid.

Finally, Figure 4.8 shows that, despite the rapid falling volumes of credit *derivatives*, investment grade contracts for a composition dominated by intermediate maturities is still prevalent.

Figure 4.5 Cash and *derivatives* quarterly trading revenue (in US$ million) of banks, by contract type and total.

Source: Office of the Comptroller of the Currency (OCC).

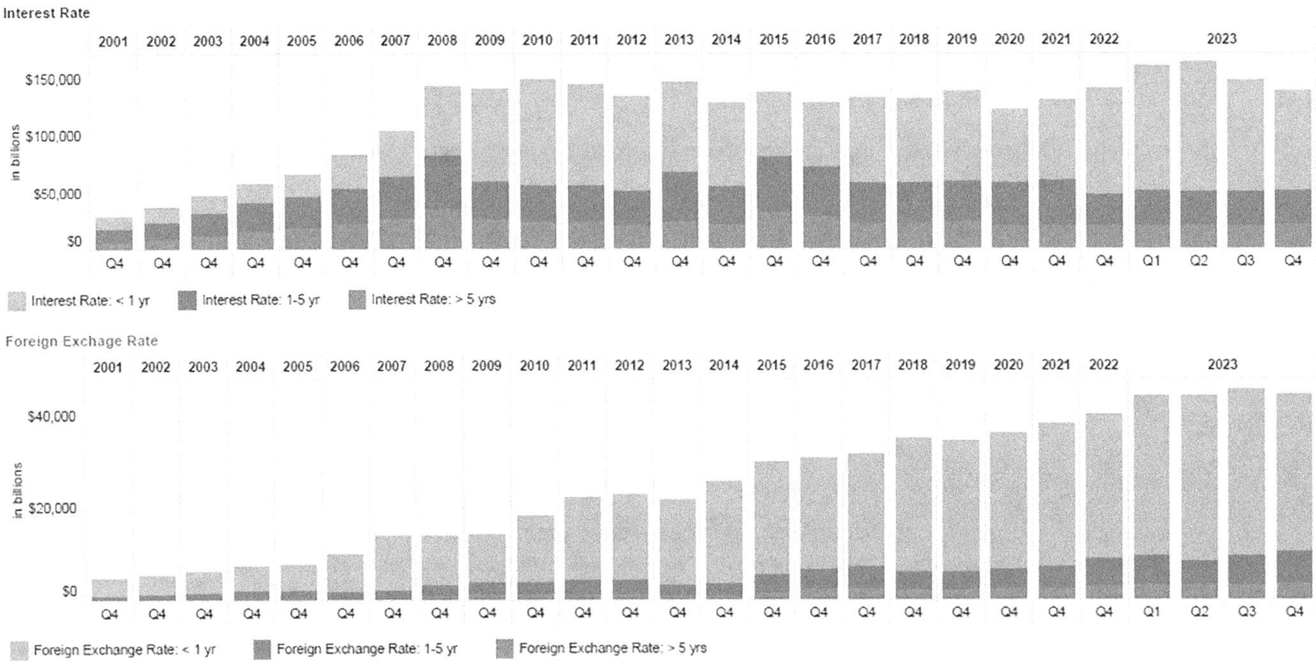

Figure 4.6 Derivatives notional amounts (in US$ billion) of interest rate and foreign exchange rate contracts by maturity.

Source: Office of the Comptroller of the Currency (OCC).

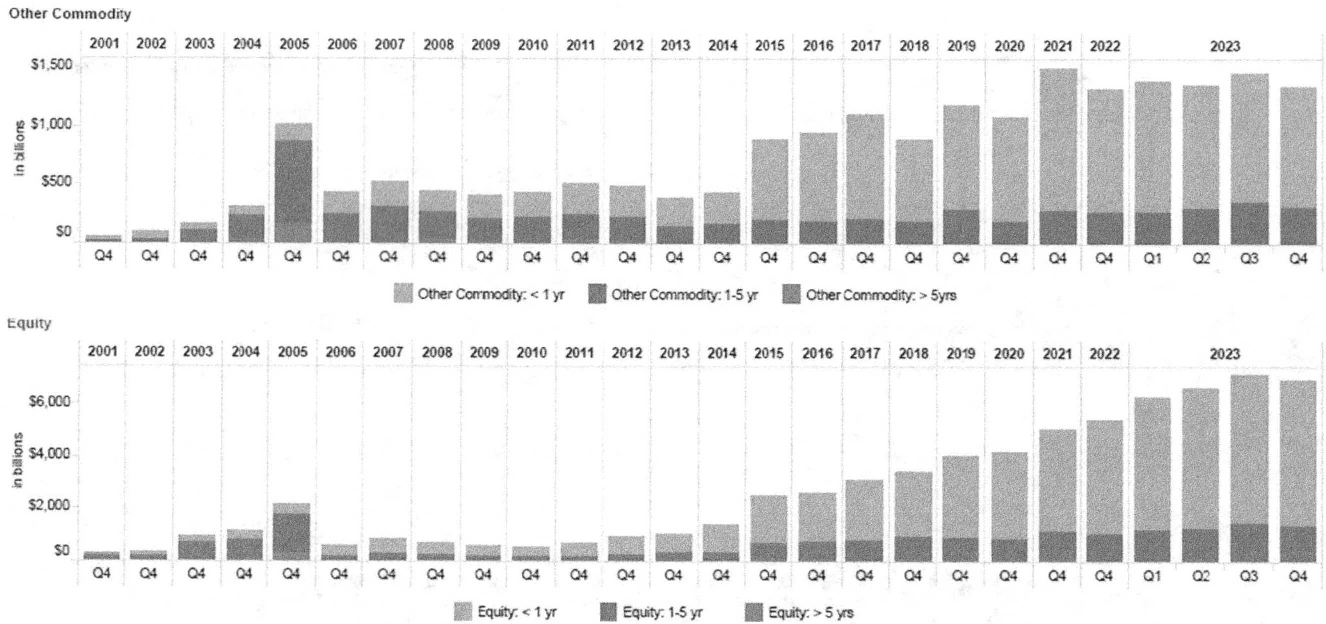

Figure 4.7 Derivatives notional amounts (in US$ billion) of other commodity and equity contracts by maturity.

Source: Office of the Comptroller of the Currency (OCC).

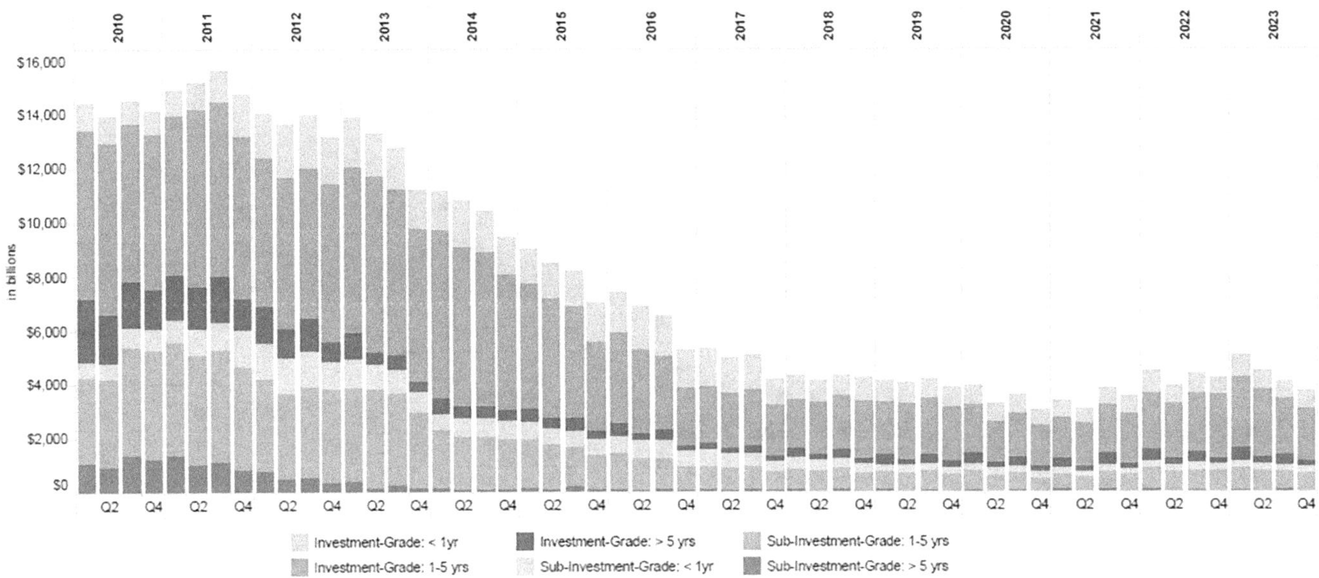

Figure 4.8 Notional amounts (in US$ billion) of credit *derivatives* contracts by credit quality and maturity

Source: Office of the Comptroller of the Currency (OCC).

The OCC numbers do not show a picture noticeably different from the BIS figures. *Derivatives* are used by a small number of big banks for trading. End-users are not important. Interest rate swaps are the most important arrangements, with a predominance of short-term instruments. Futures, forwards and options have a secondary importance. Foreign exchange is not irrelevant, but equity, commodities and credit have been losing importance in terms of notional values but generate a significant share of trading revenues for the large banks, which depends on *derivatives* to earn money.

Other Sources of *Derivatives* Data: The Circuits Have Many Dimensions

Just to provide a non-exhaustive view of other sources of data about *derivatives*, this section briefly discusses some of the available ones.

CFTC and the Bird-Eye View of the Exchange-Traded Circuit

The CFTC database is another important source of detailed information with minutia mainly about the exchange circuits. The commission gathers data from market participants under its supervision. It is possible to access numbers about the commitments of traders, including legacy, supplemental, disaggregated and traders in financial futures, bank participation reports, cotton on-call, that is, data for a specific commodity, financial data for futures commission merchants (FCMs), net position changes for large trader and trading account, staff reports, weekly swaps reports with aggregate data and figures by asset class, including gross notional amounts, dollar values and ticket volume – in terms of both cleared status and participation type and cleared margin reports.

A worth reading material is the research from the CFTC's Office of the Chief Economist. For example, a recent research concludes that banks do not hedge the risk of their long-term assets, like loans and securities, using interest rate swaps (McPhail et al. 2024).[20] A convergent result was found out by Minton et al. (2009) for credit *derivatives*.[21] Contemporary *derivatives* were not introduced to help organisations to hedge risks, but to allow banks to make enormous profits creating the risks that is the justification for selling the profitable instruments.

FIA and the Tracking of **Derivatives**

Besides the market structure already mentioned, the FIA (see Chapter 2) developed three tracking bases.[22] It has an ETD or exchange-traded *derivatives* tracker, a CCP or central clearing counterparty tracker and a FCM tracker. The ETD provides monthly information about volumes, not available in other bases, and open interest of futures and options in exchanges worldwide, with breaks for year, region and exchange. It is possible to see numbers for specific references like agriculture and energy. According to the association "The CCP Tracker is designed to provide greater transparency into the amount of risk in the global clearing system and the financial resources available to protect the system from losses." It offers quarterly data on financial resources through margins and defaults, potential loss exposures and concentration risks. One of the advantages identified in the exchange-traded *derivatives* circuit is the absence of credit or counterparty risk. However, this work of the FIA points to the existence of risks in this realm. Finally, the FCM tracker organises CFTC monthly data about customer segregated funds held by FCMs and the number of FCMs.

Compustat and the Non-financial Users of derivatives

Compustat Financials, compiled by Standard and Poor's, offers financial statements and market data for more than 80,000 active and inactive publicly traded companies, including, among others, income statements, balance sheets and cash flows.[23] That is an important source for micro-data about capitalist units and groups, mainly non-financial ones.

Growth of Specific Arrangements: Particular Conduits for the General Search for Speculative Profits

The appearance of contemporary economic phenomena such as the rapid expansion of specific arrangements of finance capital can cause a strong impression when their aggregate size, and sums of money can always be added up, is compared to traditional capitalist wealth, mainly capital in different forms, such as stock market capitalisation or the value of outstanding debt securities or loans, and incomes in the form of profits and interest, as reflected in GDP. Actually, this should raise the suspicion that the phenomenon is not only about hedging, unless *derivatives* are extremely inefficient by necessitating to establish a long chain of interconnected balance sheets and incomes and expenses to fulfil their roles. By measuring the overall sum of money circulating and accumulating in the so-called *derivatives* sub-system over time, it shows the most important part of the financial system today. By the same token, the values circulating and accumulating are much above the exposed values and surplus produced in the non-financial sector, what is incompatible with efficient hedging. More important, the *derivatives* sub-system is formed by a complex web of capitals and institutions, as captured by the databases discussed above.

Alternatively to hedging functions, Saber (1999) claims that the rapid growth of *derivatives* can be explained by the flexibility they offer for speculative capital to arbitrage many different markets. But why are *derivatives* more flexible than other liquid forms of capitalist wealth, like money itself? Moreover, the data show a market or industry concentrated in the United States and in the dollar. Why would this single space, even as headquarter for capitals operating in many nations, and this specific currency, provide most of the needed flexibility for speculative capital? So, it seems that it is not about flexibility, although this is important when associated with universal forms of value. *Derivatives* as a financial capital sub-system are about power, the power of finance capital, intertwined with other capitals increasingly dominated by the logic of the former that characterise the financialised contemporary capitalism, to open new circuits of valorisation and accumulation, and reshape older ones.

Another piece of anecdotal evidence that the recent growth of *derivatives* is fuelled mostly by short-run speculation is provided by the account in Sears (2024). He mentions that, back in 2004, option markets were in the throes of a speculative mania. The reason was that the quantity of shares that were potentially controlled by options had exceeded the number of shares traded. Despite the fact that Sears assumes that stock markets have an equilibrium, the point is that, if option buyers wanted to, they could not exercise their rights. And the problem could not be addressed by new issues over time. He argues that the maturities of most of the options traded were short-dated, ranging from a day (0DTE or zero-day-to-expire) for market indices to five days for mostly technology stocks, and this innovations allows excessive inexpensive and therefore geared gambling on short-term stock prices and indices.[24] Of course, this is what short-sellers do all the time.

This anomaly, in his view, is deemed unusual by most agents, albeit it has been happening with alarming frequency for a very long time. His historical examples come from the stock market frenzy in bucket shops right before the Great Depression of the twentieth century. Yet, speculation has been a companion to contemporary *derivatives* since their inception, and even for modern *derivatives*. Speculators keep trying to find easy ways of making a quick profit. The data about maturities presented in this chapter capture this inner trend. And options are indeed the most important instrument for equity-linked references. However, today, after 20 years, they are not, by far, the most important arrangement in the *derivatives* sub-system. If speculation in a relatively minor circuit is so frightening, it is not hard to realise the threats in the major interest rate swaps circuit dominated by a few large banks.

The real issue not grasped by Sears is that neither options nor any other arrangement for that matter are about delivery of the reference value or wealth in specific forms. They are about searching for increased sums of money over shorter periods of time. 0DTE are just about that.

Summing Up

The point raised by Sears (2024) is that high-frequency statistics about specific arrangements are necessary if a proper measurement is sought after. *Derivatives*, as quintessential representation of contemporary financialised capitalism, must be seen as enabling short-term transactions. Thus, annual or semi-annual data such as the ones presented in this chapter may not capture or even synthesise the circuits in the *derivatives* sub-system. Monthly data cannot do it either, however. Given this caveat, the BIS and the OCC data show that *derivatives* is a misguided term. That is why it has been so hard to measure this ideal concept. It does not matter if one gauges the specific circuits for the arrangements in terms of turnover, value of open interest, notional amounts, gross market value or fair value. What is called *derivatives* as an aggregate term is mostly short-term interest rate swaps, traded mostly by U.S. banks in OTC markets. Foreign exchange contracts come next.

Equity, commodities and credit *derivatives* are irrelevant in terms of notional and gross market values, although, in the United States, they are important sources of earnings for banks. This is because interest rate swaps are the concrete result of finance capital unleashed. Its growth is the growth of financialisation, although some of the circuits are shrinking. It is not about risk management or hedging. Non-financial capitalists are not important agents in the circuits of the sub-system, even though uncontrolled finance fabricates all different types of risks for flows and stocks of wealth. In this regard, the high level of net credit exposures in the U.S. banks and the reduced volume of centrally cleared contracts point to the failure of regulation and the building up of systemic risks. Is another crash necessary to eliminate the excess finance capital created by neo-liberal financialisation?

Notes

1 The fund explains in the sixth edition of the manual (IMF, 2009, p. 94) that, at the settlement date, any unpaid overdue amount must be reclassified as accounts receivable/ payable, since the buckshee value is fixed, and therefore the claim becomes a debt. A stock on balance sheets.

2 Of course, the apparently low number for 1976 does not mean that there were no futures and options trades outside North America's exchanges, meaning probably the United States, given that Canada and Mexico have likely been very small markets for *derivatives*. It could be a question of reporting to the BIS. It remains the question of whether commodities contracts, unreported, were more important than short-term interest rate contracts at that time in the passage from modern to contemporary capitalism.

3 A call report is a regulatory, standardised formulary filed by banks with the Federal Financial Institutions Examination Council (FFIEC). At first reading, following a chronological order, since there is no methodological disclosure about the nature of banks in the OCC quarterly reports, it is not clear if the reports survey all commercial banks operating in the United States, regardless of their nationality, or only commercial banks headquartered in the United States, regardless of their desks locations. On the first page of the third quarter report of 2006, it is explained: "(…) there are a number of other providers of *derivatives* products, such as investment banks and foreign banks, whose activity is not reflected in the data in this report." So, this database is also incomplete.

4 Although, as this chapter argues, estimating the value of *derivatives* is tricky. The best source of more recent data about net worth is the Federal Reserve Board and its financial accounts of the United States, available at: www.federalreserve.gov/releases/z1/default.htm Retrieved on December 2023.

5 In the industrial organisation literature, there are many indices to measure the concentration in specific markets, like the Herfindahl index mentioned in the section about the BIS database. The C_n measure is known as n-firm concentration ratio, capturing the total sum or combined market share (or any other performance) of the n largest firms (Marfels, 1971). Regardless of how the market concentration is gauged, it is important to notice that the OCC data for concentration include spot foreign exchange transactions. Since the values and volumes traded on this market is immense, it may bias the ratio.

6 Until 2006, the OCC reports referred to commercial banks only. From 2006 on, some reports refer to banks without adjectives, sometimes to insured commercial banks. The new description, including savings institutions, appeared for the first time in the first

quarter of 2012. The newest ones refer to trust companies. The document splits the number of reporting institutions into insured commercial banks and savings associations. Out of the 1,291 institutions filling in at that time, 192 were savings associations. Yet, since the system is concentrated in a small group of banks, it does not seem to make a noticeable difference. Anyway, the period 1990–2011 is not totally comparable to the period 2012–2023 in terms of the number of financial institutions holding *derivatives* positions.

7 Bank holding companies do not have to fill the call report, only the consolidated financial statements for holding companies.

8 It is assumed that inflation would not affect the nominal value of GDP or net worth on the one hand and the nominal value of notional amounts on the other by a remarkably different rate. According to the Federal Reserve Bank of Minneapolis (www.minneapolisfed.org/about-us/monetary-policy/inflation-calculator/consumer-price-index-1913-), the CPI-U was equal to 156.9 in 1996 and reached 304.7 in 2023, increasing by a factor of 1.94. So, using the CPI-U as the price index, there was a moderate real GDP and real net worth growth and extremely rapid real notional value growth of *derivatives*. It confirms that finance capital, part of net worth, was unleashed by neo-liberalism.

9 That is, $C_{25} = 100\%$.

10 Despite being introduced in 1993, credit *derivatives* appeared for the first time in the OCC reports in the document for the first quarter of 1997, earlier than in the BIS database. The notional value at that time was $19 billion. But Hull (1997) does not mention them either. In his chapter about credit risk, the central issue is the pricing of *derivatives* when risk of default is not negligible. And this risk is not managed, but reflected in regulatory capital levels. In the more recent edition, there is a full chapter about credit *derivatives* (Hull, 2021).

11 A similar pattern of distribution is clear for all other underlyings.

12 Up to a certain point in time, HSBC was part of the top banks, consisting of five and not four institutions. Anyway, it was mentioned that international banks were not considered in the reports.

13 The bank's earning results are available at www.goldmansachs.com/media-relations/press-releases/current/pdfs/2023-q4-results.pdf Retrieved January 2024.

14 The quarterly earnings of J.P. Morgan Chase for the fourth quarter of 2023 is available at: www.jpmorganchase.com/content/dam/jpmc/jpmorgan-chase-and-co/investor-relations/documents/quarterly-earnings/2023/4th-quarter/30e66a2f-5f41-4616-b831-fee985b61b8a.pdf Retrieved January 2024

15 The full report of earnings for Citigroup, for the fourth quarter of 2023, is available at: www.citigroup.com/global/news/press-release/2024/fourth-quarter-full-year-2023-results-key-metrics Retrieved January 2024.

16 The earnings of the fourth quarter of 2023 for the Bank of America is available at: https://d1io3yog0oux5.cloudfront.net/_42418afb69fb5be995d2fece075e25b7/bankofamerica/db/806/9995/earnings_release/The+Press+Release_4Q23_ADA.pdf Retrieved January 2024.

17 To put this number into perspective, Lowenstein (2010) shows that, by the end of 2005, AIG had guaranteed more than 400 of the riskiest CDOs and had an exposure close to $80 billion, although he does not qualify the nature of that vulnerability as gross or net.

18 Between 2007 and 2023, the amount of gross credit exposure eliminated through bilateral netting was never lower than 78% of the total. Most of the time it was above 85%, according to the OCC final report of 2023.

19 They are Monetary Authority, Private Depository Institutions, U.S.-Chartered Depository Institutions, Foreign Banking Offices in U.S., Banks in U.S.-Affiliated Areas, Credit

Unions, Property-Casualty Insurance Companies, Life Insurance Companies, Private Pension Funds, Government Employee Retirement Funds, Money Market Funds, Mutual Funds, Closed-End Funds, Exchange-Traded Funds, Government-Sponsored Enterprises, Agency- and GSE-Backed Mortgage Pools, Issuers of Asset-Backed Securities (ABS), Finance Companies, Mortgage Real Estate Investment Trusts (REITs), Security Brokers and Dealers, Holding Companies and Other Financial Business. It is not clear whether or not they are individually as important and insured banks in the *derivatives* sub-system. See endnote 4 for the source.

20 They use regulatory data from the largest 250 U.S. banks. The reason for using such a large sample, the desired statistical properties of the estimations aside, is not clear, given that the *derivatives* are highly concentrated in the four largest banks, and the universe of banks dealing with *derivatives* is less than 30, as discussed in the previous section. Anyway, the authors find that the average bank has a large gross notional amount of *derivatives* equal to $434 billion. Taking into account the offsetting positions, they found that the average bank has no significant net interest rate risk from swaps, with a minimum impact, on equity, of the variation in swap values after a 100-basis point increase in interest rates (this is the delta discussed in Chapter 3). As a consequence, banks' swap positions are not economically significant for hedging the interest rate risk of banking system's assets. Of course, another conclusion to be drawn is that banks are trading swaps to profit and speculate.

21 They examine the use of credit *derivatives* by large 23 U.S. bank holding companies with assets above $1 billion for the period 1999 to 2005, that is, just after the instruments were introduced. They report that in 2005 the gross notional amount of credit *derivatives* exceeded the amount of loans on their books. Thus, the net positions are held for dealer activities (trading), not hedging of loans, as they represent only 2% of their lending. They try to explain this surprising result, for those assuming that *derivatives* make banks sounder, in terms of asymmetrical information and accounting difficulties. A more interesting conclusion is that, since credit *derivatives* are just a small fraction of total *derivatives* notional amounts, and banks are the single most important dealers, hedging is completely irrelevant in the *derivatives* circuits.

22 The tracking databases assembled and kept by the FIA are available at: www.fia.org/fia/data-resources?utm_source=FIAWeb&utm_medium=Top Accessed January 2025.

23 In the Ph.D. dissertation that inspired this book, the econometric studies were carried out using this database. It provides firm-level data about, among others, non-financial users of *derivatives*.

24 As mentioned in Chapter 2, the premium of an option depends on five determinants, the maturity is one of them.

References

Bank for International Settlements (BIS). "Data Portal." 2024. Available at: https://data.bis.org Retrieved on December, 2024.

Bank for International Settlements (BIS). "Data Requirements for Monitoring Derivative Transactions", Irving Fisher Committee on Central Bank Statistics *IFC Bulletin* 35, (2012): 1–116.

Heath, Robert. *The Statistical Measurement of Financial Derivatives*. Working Paper of the International Monetary Fund, WP/98/24, Washington, DC: IMF, 1998.

Hollanders, Marc. "The Role of Oversight in Collecting Derivatives Data." BIS *IFC Bulletin* 35, (2012): 70–79.

Hull, John. *Options, Futures, and Other Derivatives*. 3rd ed. Upper Saddle River: Prentice Hall, 1997.

Hull, John. *Options, Futures, and Other Derivatives*. 11th ed.. London: Pearson, 2021.

International Monetary Fund (IMF). *Balance of Payments and International Investment Position Manual*. Washington, DC: IMF, 2009.

International Monetary Fund (IMF). *Financial Derivatives, a Supplement to Fifth Edition (1993) of the Balance of Payments Manual*. Washington, DC: IMF, 2000.

Lowenstein, Roger. *The End of Wall Street*. New York: The Penguin Press, 2010.

Magdoff, Harry, and Paul Sweezy. *Estagnation and Financial Explosion*. New York: Monthly Review Press, 1987.

Marfels, Christian. "A Guide to the Literature on the Measurement of Industrial Concentration in the Post-War Period." *Zeitschrift für Nationalökonomie* 31, (1971): 483–506.

McPhail, Lihong, Philipp Schnabl, and Bruce Tuckman. "Do Banks Hedge Using Interest Rate Swaps?" *CFTC, Office of the Chief Economist*, Staff Papers and Reports, Number 2019-011, 2024.

Minton, Bernadette A., René M. Stulz, and Rohan Williamson. "How Much Do Banks Use Credit Derivatives to Hedge Loans?" *Journal of Financial Services Research* 35, (2009): 1–31.

Office of the Comptroller of the Currency (OCC). "Quarterly Report on Bank Trading and Derivatives Activities." 2025. Available at: www.occ.gov/publications-and-resources/publications/quarterly-report-on-bank-trading-and-derivatives-activities/index-quarterly-report-on-bank-trading-and-derivatives-activities.html Retrieved on June, 2025.

Office of National Statistics (ONS). "Financial Derivatives and Employee Stock Option Statistics in the UK Flow of Funds Accounts Matrices." 2019. Available at: www.ons.gov.uk/economy/nationalaccounts/uksectoraccounts/methodologies/financialderivativesandemployeestockoptionstatisticsintheukflowoffundsaccountsmatrices Retrieved June 2022.

Poitras, Geoffrey. *Equity Capital: From Ancient Partnerships to Modern Exchange Traded Funds*. New York: Routledge, 2016.

Saber, Nasser. *Speculative Capital: The Invisible Hand of Global Finance*. Vol. 1. London: Financial Times/Prentice Hall, 1999.

Sears, Steven M. "The Latest Options Craze Resembles Past Manias. That's Not a Good Thing." *Barrons*, March 20, 2024. Available at: www.barrons.com/articles/options-craze-past-manias-stock-trouble-bb109fb5 Retrieved on May, 2024.

Von Kleist, Karsten. "The BIS Framework for Monitoring Financial Derivatives." BIS *IFC Bulletin*, no. 35 (2012): 43–53.

Weber, Ernst J. "A Short History of Derivative Security Markets." In: Wolfgang Hafner and Heinz Zimmermann (eds.) *Vinzenz Bronzin's Option Pricing Models*. Berlin/Heidelberg: Springer-Verlag, 2009: 431–466.

5 The False Long of It

Economic and Financial History, Phases of Capitalism and the Pseudo-Genesis of *Derivatives*

Introduction

This chapter presents a critical discussion about the historical origins of instruments claimed to be evidence of a long or eternal existence of *derivatives* and the evolution of real arrangements similar or analogous to the ones cobbled together as *derivatives*. It evaluates both direct and indirect evidence based on studies, interpretations and first-hand experiences, and researchers of economic, not only financial, *derivatives* history. It is argued that the relevant historical demarcation for understanding the origins of specific arrangements, not *derivatives*, is the birth of and transition to capitalism and the economic transformations these movements brought about by their own particular accumulation and valorisation needs.

For designing a historiographical investigation of *derivatives* that is compatible with the hypothesis that they have not existed ontologically, it is hereby suggested that four conditions must be satisfied for a valid interpretation of the historical studies or accounts of arrangements and rejection of the supposed eternal existence of *derivatives*:

(i) It is necessary and sufficient to prove the existence of all four plain-vanilla, specialised arrangements, that are really or supposedly identical or very similar to present-day instruments, in the pre-capitalist period. That is, to discover the thing-in-itself, with documented existence in archival history provided by the literature or perhaps archaeology.
(ii) It is necessary and sufficient to show that the three basic functions performed by such existing arrangements justify the identity or similarity, by homology or analogy, although they may have had different names in history. The functions depend on the specialised uses given by at least partially differentiated economic users in their transactions.
(iii) It is necessary and sufficient to identify the existence of institutions or rules needed for the arrangements to perform their functions, that is, to identify the existence of other required complementary components of a *derivatives* sub-system.
(iv) It is necessary and sufficient to provide information about the socioeconomic significance and regularity of the *derivatives* transactions, the economic size

DOI: 10.4324/9781003137092-6

> of the sub-system, however measured, to the size of other sub-systems or the economic system itself. If it is not economically relevant, it is not part of the functioning and logic of the system, it cannot be compared to contemporary instruments, given the magnitudes discussed in the previous chapter.

And there is a fifth one: the necessity of identifying ideas about the existence of arrangements, their functions and functioning, supporting institutions and also their importance, that reinforce these concrete features in the realm of thought. This is the subject of next chapter. Of course, it is not always possible to separate the evidence for satisfying the four conditions independently, since they are interconnected, but the first one is the most important and requires a longer discussion. If it is not satisfied, any attempt at validating the other four does not make sense. Yet, this chapter debunks the thesis of eternal *derivatives* by arguing that all conditions cannot be satisfied neither conjointly nor independently.

Condition (i): *Derivatives* or Specific Arrangements? The Economic and Financial Record

Is there any documented historical evidence about the existence of *derivatives* before the transition or birth of capitalism from the fifteenth century on? Or what can be found instead are specific arrangements with variable degrees of similitude, real or imagined, to the modern and contemporary ones, but scattered over time and space? In order to answer this question, it is necessary to consult scholarly historiographical works of economic and financial historians, both general and specialised, since *derivatives* have been treated, erroneously as argued in Chapters 1 and 2, as exclusively financial instruments. Historiography discovers dates and documented sources. Since contemporary history may provide indirect hints, the views of practitioners may also be helpful to deny the long existence of instruments.

An empirical examination of the historical facts necessary to satisfy the first condition suggests that the arrangements, apart from the issue of similarity, were not all created at the same time or within close periods in history; if nothing else, because they were not supposed to form an ensemble that was superimposed afterwards, in an example of a fallacy of *nunc pro tunc*. This is another evidence that *derivatives* ontologically do not exist and could never exist. But then it is necessary to investigate the staggered appearance of potentially similar arrangements. This boils down to the historical question about which one came out first. Were look-alike of forwards or options the first historical arrangements of what would come to be known as *derivatives* in the future, as suggested by many sources discussed below? Of course, since futures require exchanges and swaps are contemporary innovations, they cannot be candidates, rejecting condition (i). But the historical interest in the other two arrangements remains.

One should bear in mind that most texts on the history of what came to be viewed as *derivatives* focus on western accounts and studies or, at most, the Middle East, about Mesopotamia, Egypt and Byzantium. Only a few on Japan or India.

Geography is indissociable of capital (Harvey, 2001) and thus of history. A chronological examination can be pursued as follows. Considering both the primary historiographical literature and the secondary one, at first, the inquiry must hark back to the ancient and medieval pre-capitalist economies to show the myth about the future delivery of commodities as protoforms of *derivatives* that demonstrate their eternal existence. It then jumps to the Low Countries in the seventeenth century, where arrangements supposed to be similar to modern financial instruments under the label of *derivatives* were transacted at the birth of capitalism, after major institutional changes (condition (iii)). Next, it brings forward the appearance of specific arrangements for commodities in the nineteenth century, when the rapid changes in capitalist agriculture created risks for farmers and buyers of staples but mainly for merchants. Finally, it points to the rapid rise of financial *derivatives* after the fall of Bretton Woods in the 1970s, when finance changed and brought transformations to contemporary capitalist accumulation and valorisation by recreating old risks and enhancing financial risks typical of financialisation and the landmark introduction of swaps.

Ancient and Medieval or Pre-capitalist Economies

With a few exceptions, like Chance (1995), many studies do not provide an explicit *derivatives* chronology. Thus, Taylor (2010) states that *derivatives* is a new name for a set of older instruments. But she does not explain how much older. Saber (1999b) equally remarks that *derivative* products are very old. But his measure of time is in centuries, not millennia. Similarly, Cox and Rubinstein (1985, p. vii) affirms, without historical backing and precise measurement of time, that options have been traded for centuries. Elongating the origin, and attempting an escape route with an appeal to likeness, Schinasi et al. (2000, p. 62) claim that "*derivatives* or financial contracts with derivative-like features seem to have existed throughout recorded financial history". Indefinite, nonetheless.

Providing specific periods, Weber (2009) argues that *derivatives* securities existed since 4,000 BCE with the start of commerce of pre-capitalist Mesopotamia, and later in the pre-capitalist Roman and Byzantine empires, in the form of future delivery of commodities, or forwards. In Athens and Egypt, which preserved contracts in the form of papyri under the aegis of Greece, contracts for future delivery of commodities have also been found. He claims that *derivatives* continued later on, that is, already under capitalism in Western Europe, in the form of future delivery of securities. Swan (2000), approaching the issue from a legal perspective, after providing different definitions, considers *derivatives* to be promises with the option of default. He also goes back as far as 4,000 years ago to show a timeline of *derivatives*.

The evidence for Mesopotamia is based on surviving clay tablets of the Code of Hammurabi in 1,750 BCE. It shows delivery of future goods with a loan. Other examples include 30 pieces of wood for future delivery in the nineteenth century BCE, a silver loan to finance a trade mission coupled with a forward sale of sesame seeds and slave trade with an option to deliver currency rather than slaves. Swan

(2000) identifies barley to be returned. However, this is a commodity loan or short selling.

Other accounts date *derivatives*, actually options, back to the Code of Hammurabi in 1,750 BCE, with the law allowing farmers to default on their rents if the harvest could not earn enough grain. For instance, Kummer and Pauletto (2012, p. 1) refers to the famous transcription of a clay tablet that preserved the Code:

> If any one owe a debt for a loan, and a storm prostrates the grain, or the harvest fail, or the grain does not grow for lack of water; in that year he need not give his creditor any grain, he washes his debt-tablet in water and pays no rent for the year.

Of course, this is not an OTC put option in the modern sense of the word, that is, a voluntary choice not to deliver grain at maturity because the spot price is above the strike price. The near impossibility of paying the rent due to lost expected income, regardless of will, is ignored.

The ruling is a writing-off clause for a borrower. The authors translate the literal code into *derivatives* lingo. But the necessity of translation itself is a rhetorical device that creates the interpretation of similarity or homology when it is, perhaps, merely a formal one, with a completely different economic substance. *Nunc pro tunc*. The debt-tablet is not an option tradeable in a specialised market at intrinsic value or reverted by a new contract, shifting risks to the temple with the grain as the underlying. It is about flows of real income between creditor and debtor, not movements in grain prices or interest rates.

It seems even more prosaic. The Code provides in this case a public insurance for farmers, a political ruling allowing borrowers to default if they do not have the expected income, which motivated the loan, to service their debts. Santos (2008) mentions 'semantic ambiguities' between arrangements known as 'to arrive', forwards and futures. This term is equally useful to describe the usage of contemporary experiences to validate past situations with words deemed universal fixes, when they may make no sense to describe a phenomenon in archaic or ancient societies, like 'futures' in the nineteenth-century United States, because for humankind, so far, the future has always arrived.

Beyond the forced interpretation of archaeological documents, a widely used 'proof' that *derivatives* always existed is anecdotal and only half thousand years BCE. The passage in Aristotle's *Politics* reporting the endeavours of Greek philosopher Thales of Miletus is considered factual evidence. So, during the winter, Greek gambler Thales supposedly hired, paying in advance what would be equivalent, therefore, to a premium, the right to use all olive oil presses in Miletus and Chios during the harvest of olives six months ahead. Olive oil producers would have to bow to his monopolistic power after the harvest. This is time again, causing confusion in the minds of eternal *derivatives* advocates. This anecdote is hence presented as an early example of *derivatives* (actually option) usage (Poitras, 2009b; Steinherr, 2000). Bernstein (2005, p. 327) cites Thales' 'options' as financial devices deploying a principle of universal application. So, for him options are the universal financial arrangement. *Derivatives* are eternal.

In a different version, Somanathan et al. (2017, p. 11) mentions the capacity of Thales the Greek astrologer to read the starts – which seems more effective than professional economic forecasting – to predict a large olive harvest nine, not six, months ahead. He then secretly went to every single farmer and bought the right of first refusal on all future olives at a known price. That is, he purchased a call option at a very low premium. As his forecast turned out to be correct, he purchased the entire crop, stored it and could use his monopoly power in the olive market to scalp the buyers. But as there were *derivatives*, why olive farmers or olive oil producers did not use them to hedge against the unfavourable prices of the huge harvests? Was Thales the Greek a Schumpeterian entrepreneur?

Just like the history of the Dojima rice market discussed below, the existence of two conflicting versions about Thales' abilities to anticipate an unknown market, assuming there was one, an anecdote about renting the machines or fixed capital since capitalism is eternal and another about the raw material or circulating capital raises suspicion. Yet, there is a formal similitude but a completely different ontological difference. Bad harvests could affect the physical availability of olives and therefore the use of presses, but this is hardly comparable to national banks outside the United States bidding for futures contracts of dollars when they are not directly involved in international financial transactions, as pointed by Saber (1999b). Thales himself was not an olive farmer or oil producer and thus the hedging function (condition ii) could not be satisfied. Also, it is not clear whether or not Thales had the obligation to use all the presses he hired, even if the harvest were not plentiful. Or the obligation to buy the olives in the other scenario. The homology or analogy is false.

The spurious *nunc pro tunc* comparisons are very creative. Even the Christian Bible serves as anecdotal evidence. Poitras (2009b) mentions a passage in Genesis 29: to identify in the offer of Laban to Jacob, 1,700 years BCE, another arrangement analogous to an option or forward. Laban offered Jacob to marry his younger daughter Rachel, in a few years. The future, of course. But, in return, Jacob had to work seven years for Laban. Poitras argues that the problem with these habits was the failure to deliver, or default. It could only be an option, hence. Laban's promise was non-binding, since after seven years of hard work by Jacob, he reneged and 'delivered' the eldest daughter, Leah, asking for seven more years of hard work for his 'slave' to marry Rachel.

Yet, Poitras acknowledges that Hebrew customs allowed this type of labour for marriage agreement. But he then reneges; it could not be an option indeed, despite the fact that polygamy permitted Jacob to marry both sisters. It certainly was a forward. The strike price to marry is the amount of unpaid hard work. Swapping labour for sex is also out of question. Why, at any rate, is this customary agreement compared to a *derivative* contract or transaction? Or even a simile? It is not even analogous. This mistake has been reproduced over time (Bernstein, 2005, Chance 1995 and 2008[1]). It is pervasive financial bias creating a naturalised financialised history.

In the Far East, Somanathan et al. (2017, p. 9) claim that there are documents proving the existence of forward trade in India at least since 2,000 BCE. And they argue, supposedly a forward market was systematic in the fairs of France and England in the twelfth century. Regarding options trading, Somanathan et al. (2017, p. 11) also state that it existed in India before the introduction of exchange-traded equity options in 2,000 ACE. Without dating the transactions, it mentions the Marwaris' indigenous commodity options known as *satta*, with calls (*teji*) and puts (*mandi*). The premium was known as *nazrana*. Ancient Hindus were proto-capitalists in disguise.

Moving along the timeline, Kummer and Pauletto (2012) also mentions the *commandas* in tenth-century Italian city-states. But these were actually commercial partnership in transport similar to capital advanced in return for commodities. Since there was no instantaneous shipping, the delivery could only happen in the future, assuming the ship returned. There is time and risk, but not *derivatives*. Hull (2021) claims, without any evidence of exchanges existence or historical research, that futures can be traced back to the Middle Ages and that, contrary to the literature, options are more recent, with their origins in Europe and the United States in the eighteenth century.

Swan (2000) argues that *derivatives* usage survived in the Middle Ages in monasteries with the support of Catholic Church, based on the Canon Law influenced by the Roman law. But it is not clear why would monks use *derivatives*, even though they could not enter a swap transaction. In the Roman law, after second century ACE, there were two types of merchant, not *derivatives*, contracts: *vendito re speratae*, which could be nullified if the seller did not have the goods at the delivery date, and *vendito spei*, which was supposedly similar to a forward contract, but the conditions for similarity beyond rhetoric is not clear (Weber, 2009).

Nevertheless, Gelderblom and Jonker (2005) points to the fact that, under Roman law, a forward could be considered as taking chances or waging a bet. It could not withstand the moral restrictions but in the underground. It has always been about speculation only (condition ii not satisfied). Weber (2009) also rejects Swan's interpretation, given that *derivatives* on securities were reborn in the protestant Low Countries only in the sixteenth century, not in Catholic Italy. Anyway, the privity of contracts implied that they could not be transferred or sold, which invalidates any comparison with contemporary contracts.[2] He argues that this feature held back the appearance of *derivatives* securities markets until centuries later in that territory. But, if this is the case, why this development did not take place in Mesopotamia or Egypt, where such restraints did not exist, and had longer trade histories? Was it because of costs of default? Anyway, during the Renaissance, and the transition to capitalism, security markets were finally developed, first dealing with Monti shares in the Italian city-states and then with bills of exchange. But clearly not *derivatives*.

Weber (2009) seems to emphasise the existence of private, OTC deals or the non-existence of records as evidence of lack of historical evidence about the existence *derivatives* instead. But in this case how could one possibly know that there were OTC trades if they were private and not recorded? More important, any remaining vestige of a transaction settled over a period of time can be considered actually a *derivative*? In case the answer is in the affirmative, is it a stand-alone? Or is it just a contract with an arrangement similar to the ones existing today? Was it widely used (condition iv) for hedge, arbitrage or speculation (condition ii)? Also, according to him, many contracts have no value when they are set up. Thus, why would someone record a zero value, asks Weber (2009). It is easy: just type or write zero in the books. Anyway, for him, the lack of records of dealings prevents a comprehensive history of *derivatives*.

So, historical research and commentaries and anecdotes suggest a confusion between commerce taking place over time and *derivatives* in the ancient and middle-age economies, given that the trade instruments did not have a formal derived arrangement, that is, a tradeable security. On the other hand, there are similar arrangements to *derivatives* in the transition and the birth of capitalism, mainly forwards and options. Swaps are completely missing from the research or comments on both time periods and condition (i) cannot be fulfilled.

Transitions to Modern and Contemporary Capitalism

The development of arrangements typical of capitalism is more recent. As seen, it is possible to identify in the literature suggestions of *derivative*-like transactions, excluding swaps, during the Renaissance in what would come to be Italy and the Low Countries, mainly in Antwerp and Amsterdam during the sixteenth century. But in Japan, arrangements like futures were also traded during that time in the Dojima exchange, intertwining conditions i and iii. Saber (1999b) points to futures in Amsterdam in the seventeenth century and options in feudal Japan, although the existence of this latter specific arrangement at this time and place is not backed by the literature. As mentioned, he explains that the form of *derivatives* is not new. The novelty, for him, is the speculative drive behind them, stronger than the forces of peasants in Japan or merchants in Low Countries. Actually, futures were developed by merchants rather than farmers in Japan. And speculation has been around for many centuries as well and cannot be set apart from *derivatives*. It is the scale that changed since the 1970s. And speculation could not become a driving force without the transformations capitalism underwent since then, with the financialisation.

Poitras (2009a) argues that *derivatives* securities markets were first developed in Antwerp in the sixteenth century, when forward contracts became transferable. He discusses the history of option contracts as well, differentiating between contracts with option features and free standing or pure security option contracts. This distinction is very important. Contracts with option features are not a *derivative*. The similarity with options is an imposed one. Regarding the feature of contracts that are similar to option, it is important to note a few issues. First, when Poitras (2009b, p. 488) informs that a twelfth-century Venetian debt instrument known as *prestiti* had a call provision allowing for the original sum to be repaid at par, conditional on financial situation, it is not an option per se. It is, again, a government loan condition. Without cash or liquid assets, it is not possible to pay the principal even if the debtor wanted to. By the same token, when the author explains that the arrangements for future sales had a clause permitting to refuse delivery in case of poor quality compared to the original sample, it does not seem to be a good analogy either. It is a commercial right or a condition on the delivered good, not the transaction per se and therefore certainly not an option. The same condition remains valid for the vast majority of goods and services today, under consumer protection acts.

Regarding free-standing option contracts, Poitras (2009b, p. 491) defends that they developed during the seventeenth century due to securitisation and speculation providing liquidity. This, on the other hand, became possible when commerce got concentrated in the urban centres that replaced previous medieval market fairs like Champagne, where clearing methods were developed in Bruges and Antwerp for commodities. And in Lyons clearing methods were developed for bills. Weber (2009) stresses that the settlement of contracts with cash could have happened also in Bruges from the twelfth to the fifteenth centuries, but it happened on a large scale, without explaining what large scale means, only in Antwerp. Indeed, for *derivatives,* just like capitalism, cash is king. This is an anticipation of features that could happen only in the 1980s in the United States, for example. Poitras (2009b) shows that sea trade in commodities was so large that transactions with '(goods) to arrive' contracts became active. Speculation spread to all kinds of activities, with generalised, with his own words, 'gambles on everything'. And then they evolved into futures[3] and, in sequence, to 'premium transactions' similar to options.

In Antwerp, during the sixteenth century, with capitalism on the rise, it was allowed for merchants to settle forward contracts with money, representing the difference between spot price and delivery price. These were known as contracts for differences, considered anticipations of futures contracts and widely employed during the Tulipmania of 1636–37 (Weber, 2009). This is due to the fact that, given the speculative fever, tulip bulbs were quite expensive as an underlying asset for physical delivery and specific arrangements could facilitate speculation. Kindleberger (1993) mentions the Tulipmania, also under capitalist logic. He cites puts and calls, highlighting that they were known at the time as 'trade in air', and future trading in commodities, which is commerce.

In Amsterdam, the maritime trade demanded forward contracts and other securities. Stocks and commodities were traded on term, that is, for future delivery, as has always been the case for merchant activity and with no necessity of *derivatives*. Also, there was cash settlement like contracts for differences. Short-selling was equally common, even after they were banned in 1610. In this kind of account, the legal aspects are the dominant institutional feature of *derivatives* (condition iii). Since at some point contracts became unenforceable, only OTC dealings based solely on reputation were feasible. And the crash of tulip prices did not lead to a full-blown crisis. Default, Weber (2009) seems to argue, is good for the economy under such circumstances.

Poitras (2009b. pp. 494–495) discusses the development of a *derivative,* actually options and forwards, market in Amsterdam after the opening of the bourse in 1611. According to him, this was the first time that those types of contracts were formally traded on a regular basis. Books written, with almost a century of interval, by Josef de la Vega and Isaac De Pinto, provided detailed accounts of speculative transactions in the Amsterdam exchange, mainly involving options on stocks and government securities. The trading system, Poitras argues, was enhanced by a new formal settlement scheme, the quarterly *rescontre,* which concentrated liquidity and allowed the carry-over of expiring securities. Speculation, he continues, sometimes required borrowing to keep paying the premiums and settling positions without cash, adjusting like a margin call.

Poitras (2009b) claims that there are primary sources for trading in financial options for joint stocks and government debt taking place in Amsterdam. However, there is no such information regarding commodities. He lists a few reasons, some of them mutually exclusive: price stability, forward contracts with terms fixed in years or just a few days and lack of access to physical trade and delivery. These justifications should be further discussed. When there is price stability, there would be no speculation causing it or profiting from it, and as a consequence no *derivative* transaction and no recorded evidence (condition ii). Yet, this would require some proof about well-defined and measured price stability in Amsterdam, since it was claimed that in the previous century prices were volatile in Antwerp. More important, there is no role whatsoever for *derivatives* when prices are stable. He argues, however, (2009b, pp. 492–3) that for some commodities, including grain, whale oil, salt and herring, prices were volatile and speculation was pervasive. Regarding the fixed terms, it is not clear why it would prevent documentation and recording at all. Finally, considering the lack of access, if contracts for differences can be traded, and options allow one to withdraw from the transaction by paying a premium, why would speculators not get involved with *derivatives* commodity trading, only with securities?

In the next three centuries, similar instruments were also negotiated in England, France, Germany and Central Europe. The British financial institutions were underdeveloped until the eighteenth century. Yet, by the end of the seventeenth century, an organised market for options was functioning in London, although it is not clear how important they were (condition iv). Anyway, call and put options played an important role in the South Sea bubble. Weber (2009) argues that the South Sea company issued partially paid shares. Buyers could buy the stocks in instalments. When a payment was made, it gave the option to pay the next instalment, continuing until the share was fully bought. It is argued that it was a compound option. Actually, it was only a payment in instalments, with a condition provision for continuity. Option is just a synonym for conditional purchase here. If the share price fell, the buyer could give up the right and avoid the next payment. Unlike the Tulipmania, however, the collapse of the stock price led to a severe downturn. This was, so it is argued, because contracts were enforceable in England. Default was not an option.

In 1734, the Sir John Barnard's Act was passed that nullified the future delivery of securities, but not of commodities, and short-selling operations. Yet, it is believed that it was not effective, shifting transactions to different markets, like restaurants' tables and cafés or bucket shops. Something along those lines also took place in France after the Mississippi bubble, with restrictions on speculative instruments such as short-selling and contracts for differences. Nonetheless, at the beginning of the nineteenth century, with capitalism fully developed, there was, it is argued, a *derivative* market for government bonds in France. The securities for future delivery were divided into forwards (*marches fermè*) and options (*marches à prime*). Arrangements became lawful within certain time limits, like future delivery in less than two months (Weber, 2009)

A similar pattern occurred in the German states, with a rapid growth in the number of securities traded, like bills of exchange, bonds and shares, not *derivatives*. Yet, by the end of the nineteenth century, whereas France enforced supposedly *derivatives* contracts, the German states had outlawed them. Weber (2009) claims that an incipient knowledge of *derivatives* prevented the full development of the markets. For instance, the possibility of combinations of contracts was ignored by the publications on the subject. Thought, or its lack thereof, it seems, shapes reality.

Weber (2009) affirms that in nineteenth-century Germany, contracts for future delivery were labelled '*Zeitgeschäfte*', or 'time-contracts'. These arrangements were split into forwards (*Fixgeschäfte*) and options (*Prämiengeschäfte*) or premium business. These contracts allowed one of the parties, by paying a fee, to retreat from the cash settlement within a specific date. It is similar to an option, but also to a penalty for early withdrawal from fixed-date deals typical of banking. Since delivery of the underlying in the case of stocks was out of reach for most agents, forward contracts were settled like contracts for differences, that is, with the losing parties paying the price difference. The risk of forward contracts is high, given the potential difference between spot price and delivery price. A safer alternative is an option, because it sets a maximum loss, measured by the premium.

What about the non-specialised literature? Consulting a random selection and some classic works on general financial history, it is possible to assess the existence of references to *derivatives* or specific arrangements. In the second edition of his *A Financial History of Western Europe* (the first appeared in 1984), Kindleberger (1993) does not acknowledge any financial role for *derivatives* in that subcontinent for the initial centuries. He covers a period, regarding monetary and banking matters, from the twelfth century onwards. A period that includes the long transition to capitalism. The entire interval of seven to eight centuries would be enough to identify *derivatives* if they existed as such, unless Kindleberger got it totally wrong.

The author mentions swaps, the arrangement that is missing in all accounts of ancient and middle-age '*derivatives*', but mainly connected to Central Banks' lender-of-last-resort measures in the nineteenth and twentieth centuries, that is, under modern capitalism, with the creation of a currency and metal swap network.[4] He also provides a graph of the forward exchange rate between the German mark and the British pound for 1922, and the associated estimated swap rate, not swap arrangement, with private premiums and discount rates associated with mark futures (actually forward) and the corresponding covered interest parity rates in London and Berlin. Kindleberger, however, emphasises that the data from smaller banking institutions, collected by Keynes and other authors, are not good, and stresses that markets in Berlin were chaotic in 1922. If *derivatives* were relevant (condition iv), such data would be promptly available, at least for part of the time.

Anyway, it is interesting to notice that the activities are about arbitrage and speculation, not hedging (condition ii).

The categorical denial is not limited to *derivatives* as a collective noun in the case of Europe. Specific arrangements with particular references are also creations of contemporary capitalism for some spaces of accumulation. Thus, as the Futures Industry Association (FIA) puts it in its official page (emphasis added): "FIA Europe was founded in 1993 in London as the Futures and Options Association, *just over a decade after the birth of financial futures* in Europe."[5] And two decades after the birth of financial futures in the United States, understood as specialised arrangements, in contrast to non-financial futures (commodities and so on).

It is not only in Europe. In underdeveloped countries, the arrangements were introduced much later. For instance, Somanathan et al. (2017) argues in the preface to the first edition of the book, published in 1998, that around 1985 futures trading was virtually unknown in India, by bankers, financial journalists and professors of finance and economics. Who did the trading, then? In the preface to the second edition, and connected to condition (iv), they affirm that 13 years later, *derivatives* were still insignificant in India. It seems that only historians did know about their mental existence. And the Marwaris.

Allen (2001), covering only the history of modern and contemporary global capitalist finance, does not mention *derivatives* either. He identifies swaps, but swaps of stocks in the case of government debt traded for company shares, which is, if not contrary, certainly at odds with most definitions of *derivatives*. He acknowledges commodities futures and forward exchange rates and mentions puts and calls. The absence of *derivatives* is also true in Chancellor (1999). The author mentions forwards, futures, options and swaps, but not *derivatives*. More important, they are connected to contemporary capitalism, not to previous economic systems. Ferguson (2008, p. 5) affirms that before the 1980s *derivatives* were virtually unknown, although he places the origins of futures in the nineteenth century.

Yet, the absence is not only in financial history works or institutional presentations. For instance, Helleiner (1994), when discussing the emergence of global finance after the demise of Bretton Woods, that is, the rise of contemporary financialised capitalism, mentions interest rate futures, options and swaps, but not *derivatives*, in the context of innovations defended as market-driven sources of globalisation. Weber (2009) and Swan (2000) mention that the word *derivatives* was introduced in the 1980s, probably, one assumes, because historians did not know that what they were researching was, after all, *derivatives*.

Poitras (2002, 2016), to defend an earlier existence of *derivatives*, refers to a renaissance, not appearance, that characterised the last quarter of the twentieth century. If this is correct, then there must be homologous arrangements in history with an interval of reduced or inexistent *derivative* activity after a period of identifiable existence. If historical research focuses on this time of idleness, then of course any conclusion would be biased in not finding *derivatives*. But the eternal *derivatives* view could not provide such evidence, mainly for swaps.

Saber (1999a) identifies the origins of what he calls 'speculative capital', *derivatives* being the best representative form, in the contemporary period, mainly with currency risks for multinational corporations on the one hand and risk appetite by speculators on the other. This is also the view of Panitch and Gindin (2012). By the same token, to highlight the contemporary nature of so-called *derivatives*, Magdoff and Sweezy (1987, p. 18) quotes a 1985 report by the Federal Reserve Bank of New York, in which the vice-president and assistant director of research, Edward Frydl, acknowledged that: (1) the volatility of financial assets prices had grown considerably in the previous years, with the *consequent* flourishing of instruments to transfer those risks, like futures, options and swaps, whose transactions had burgeoned; (2) more tellingly, the increased competition had squeezed financial earnings, and innovation was a way of escaping that.

Indeed, contemporary arrangements known as *derivatives* are underlined in the context of financial turmoil, as reflected in floating exchange rates with the repercussions on interest rates, assets or liabilities and soaring commodity prices. In Steinherr (2000)'s account, the end of Bretton Woods allowed foreign exchange rates to change by more and for longer periods than what was permitted before. More important, financial capital flows, based on varying expectations, would determine the direction of short-run changes.[6] In his view, since floating exchange rates created room for autonomous domestic monetary policies, interest rates would become equally volatile.[7] That is, a major watershed in the history of the arrangements is the end of Bretton Woods and the ensuing industrial manufacturing of risks. Lowenstein (2001) compares the new financial world with the old, based on mostly fixed nominal macro-financial prices or interest rates and foreign exchange rates. These movements retrieved the role of specific modern arrangements for contemporary needs of finance capital and introduced new ones that would cause the enormous growth shown in the previous chapter.

This brief excursion provides only indirect and partial support to the main claim of this book. If important works about the financial history of Western Europe, where capitalism originated and developed, do not recognise a role for *derivatives* before capitalism, and only a trivial role for specific arrangements thereafter, this suggests either that they did not exist or were not important for most of the long period covered in those accounts, not satisfying condition (i), neither condition (iv). Or that historians unduly neglected them, if one accepts the current teleological views. But since these works' upper temporal limit is the middle of the 1980s, when particular arrangements fused as *derivatives* were beginning to explode under financialised capitalism, it is rather the first interpretation that seems more appropriate.

On the other hand, modern and contemporary capitalism have three, not one, territorial loci of development for these arrangements: the northern part of the Americas, the western part of Europe and Northeast Asia. If *derivatives* are indeed historically identifiable, but important historians and researchers of global finance could not recognise them in their research for the modern period, they must be investigated in the most important national capitalist country, the United States. Thus, in his account, Markham (2002) names 'the age of *derivatives*' the period starting in the 1970s, again providing additional support to this book's argument. Lowenstein (2010) uses the same expression for an even more recent period. Henwood (1998) also affirms that in the mid-1970s, specific arrangements like options were relatively unbeknown. In his 11th edition, Hull (2021) claims that *derivatives* had become important in the past 40 years. This goes back to the 1980s, which is consistent with the available evidence. Partnoy (2009b) mentions that, even during the 1990s *derivatives* were virtually unknown.[8] *Derivatives* can, at most, be related to contemporary capitalism, and their component parts or arrangements are related to modern capitalism.

Thus, regarding modern arrangements in the U.S. capitalist space, Santos (2008) discusses the origins of commodity futures, not *derivatives*, trading, during the slavery time. He points out that, in the early nineteenth century, agriculture was not and could not be commercial, with grain production mobilised for subsistence and the surplus traded at local or at most at regional markets. With prices and price changes playing a minor role, there is no room for *derivatives*. And without *derivatives*, there are no price changes. Arbitrage (condition ii) would make sense only in physical regional markets. So, in a pre-capitalist economy, *derivatives* or the arrangements are worthless. This implies rejecting the eternal *derivatives* thesis for a long historical interval.

Technology seems a relevant key to the development of capitalism in the United States. Santos (2008) explains that transportation systems depended on the rivers, and New Orleans was the most important hub, being replaced later on by Chicago, although it is not clear that arrangements were developed in the former. Bulk grain shipping was too expensive, and the production was transformed into high value-added commodities before it was transported. The development of canals and ports changed that configuration, allowing long-distance shipping to larger urban areas and to foreign markets. Later, banks discounting notes, dealers, merchants providing credit lines, millers and commission houses turned grain trade into a very complex network of economic transactions. And this all took place, at that point of the transition to capitalism, without *derivatives* or arrangements, not imported from Europe, even though the time intervals, the necessity of financing unsold grains, price volatility, speculation and many different types of risks were present. Hence, *derivatives* did not exist (condition i) and were not relevant (condition iv).

According to Santos (2008), another major infrastructural change was the development of grain elevators, railroads and communication through the telegraph, enabling storage and cheaper transportation, further integrating the local and regional markets into national and international ones, which opened up the room for speculation. With increased volume of fungible commodities produced, stored and shipped, there was a growing demand for financing. The argument that introduces specific arrangements in the economy is that loans could be made at lower interest rates if producers could guarantee price and volume from buyers. So, they started trading forward-like claims.[9] Haug (2009) additionally argues that the telegraph allowed international arbitrage between Europe and the United States. Scholes (1998) also identifies the role of technology and communications for innovations and, in the specific case of *derivatives*, securitisation. However, arrangements were introduced long before securitisation. And long after capitalism was born.

So, many different works and representations could not spot *derivatives* as a singular financial phenomenon before the 1970s, not due to a supposed ignorance (Weber, 2009), but to a factual reason. Hence, there are discussions about *derivatives* that acknowledge that the relevant period for identification is the one inaugurated in the wake of the Bretton Woods unmaking. Therefore, the question of why arrangements were not introduced during the long time of transition to capitalism in the United States, given their eternity and earlier uses in Europe and Japan, cannot be avoided. And not only for agricultural commodities' prices and quantities, but also for the underlying related to financing major investment in canals, ports and other infrastructure. Were they all state-led? Are not the interest rates behind these operations risky? Why not unbundle the risks and sell them in the market? Thus, the existing facts point to the interpretation proposed in this book: there are stages of development, in which socioeconomic differentiation occurs over time, with fractions and classes being able to set the parameters for the growth and distribution of production, incomes and wealth that are specific to each period and cannot be fully anticipated.

Condition (ii): Specialised Agents, Functions and Uses of Arrangements

About condition (ii), attached logically to condition (i) since usage demands existence, are there recorded employment of arrangements, which are wrongly considered *derivatives*, by speculators, hedgers and arbitrageurs, that is, are there uses of *derivatives* before the transitions to capitalism? Is it instead possible to identify specific functions and the corresponding agents using *derivatives* in capitalist history? Can one pinpoint well-defined, specialised and economically significant (condition iv) groups of hedgers, arbitrageurs and speculators along the history and before the contemporary period?

A random selection of studies and commentaries of economic and financial history suggests that hedging was not a goal of economic agents for most of the time, regardless of arrangements, given that endogenous economic risks were not massively manufactured in pre-capitalist societies, by the very fact that condition (iv) cannot be satisfied, as argued below. For example, Steinherr (2000) provides indirect evidence against the existence of hedging in pre-capitalist societies. Without a chronology, he considers four stages in the seemingly historical or entrepreneurial evolution of risk management, and *derivatives* are considered the superior or latest one. This means they cannot be ancient or medieval, as pre-capitalist societies had a different nature and realisation of risks and the social necessity and ways to 'manage' them. But he does not identify the specific historical origins of innovations, since his narrative is not based explicitly on historiographical research, without approximate dates or documented evidence. So, it makes for a historical narrative of capitalist corporate finance, not a historical investigation.

What are the features that characterise the four phases proposed by Steinherr? Diversification and collateral; limited liability, bankruptcy laws, seniority rules and balance sheet structure; tradeable standardised instruments and liquidity by means of convertible securities traded in organised markets; finally, *derivatives* and risk management. This interpretation could be seen as teleological, since it points to a linear development of risk management techniques that has *derivatives* as a crowning achievement. Without research and literature, it is very difficult, if not impossible, to judge the articulation. For sure, these arrangements could be developed without a rigid historical or chronological sequence. They might have been developed simultaneously, but only in a capitalist society. It is mostly about default or credit risk, a feature that defines *derivatives* in some historical studies above.

Moreover, it is specifically about rules by a consolidated national state, and capitalist financial products and stocks, not flows of capitalist income that could be adversely affected by the functioning of markets. A given stock of funds may be loaned out to many small borrowers or to a few large debtors. Offering collateral is only feasible for the latter. So, these decisions are intertwined. And this is related to banks not being able to receive part of the loans disbursed. Could credit *derivatives* be an alternative? It is worth mentioning that the clause on Hammurabi Code discussed above is not a *derivative* and a collateral would have made it a modern risk management device. The reference to balance sheet structure makes it clear that hedging in capitalism can be done managing the composition of stocks.

Steinherr (2000) distinguishes between on balance sheet instruments, requiring capitalist accounting, and *derivatives*, back then still off-balance sheet. The supposed revolution of *derivatives* lies in the fact that no assets and liabilities need to be transferred, only net cash flows based on the former's referential values compared to values off-balance sheet (contract for differences). However, this arrangement can be used both for hedging and speculation depending on the existence of open on-balance sheet positions, but he makes no reference whatsoever to the need for waging bets. Of course, there must be an accounting reference value for the transaction to take place and this is a crucial issue for identifying the existence of specific arrangements and not to confuse them with delayed trade. Finally, he does not account for swaps.

Also, limited liability is merely a cap for losing the equity invested. Regulation by a capitalist state in the form of bankruptcy laws sets limits to the power of creditors over the income and assets of debtors. This is the clause in the Hammurabi Code. It cannot be an example of both *derivatives* and non-*derivatives*. Seniority rules just establishes the flows of payments associated with the quality or nature of stocks in the liability structure. Matching assets and liabilities requires capitalist accounting rules that overpowers the coercion of profitability. And since they usually involve different markets, except perhaps for financial firms, it is unlikely that the corresponding flows of expenses and revenues would balance.

Concerning the trade of standardised securities, Steinherr (2000) uses as an illustration of merchant shipping with uncertain results from international commerce by sea. Money anticipated for the venture is equity capital. Stocks are risk-sharing devices, that is, the risk of future losses. It is supposedly like an option, since they can be sold, just like not exercising a put. The analogy here, however, is an illusion. The amount of capital required by navigation is a technical and social necessity. The evolution of the capital goods industries will determine the specific form of machines, equipment, parts, and use of raw materials. Yet, under capitalism, crises could cause a devaluation of capital existing in excess regardless of the commercial outcomes. The risk is the same, it does not matter how it is shared by capital owners or shifted to speculators. And, of course, with the tendency of concentration and centralisation of capital, the two issues, share of capital and share of capital-loss risks, tend to conflate. Keynes used to say that individual risks can be shifted, but not the social risks. Moreover, standardised instruments for the transfer of capitalist property in organised markets have never been able to prevent major crises and bankruptcies and thus have a limited impact on hedging. Finally, liquidity is just the ability to convert assets into cash, changing the composition of stocks, in organised and moneyed markets that did not exist for most of economic history.

So, if his interpretation is valid, *derivatives* were not required even at the beginning of capitalism. Hedge became important under modern capitalism, but this function has become less relevant under contemporary financialised capitalism. For example, Haug (2009) claims that practices like hedging with options and delta hedging were all known at the beginning of twentieth century, identifying analogous functions. Also, focusing on a period that marks a long transition from late modern to contemporary capitalism, Panitch and Gindin (2012, p. 14) recognise *derivatives* as contemporary hedging devices. They remark that currency *derivatives* were developed after Bretton Woods to prevent instability and provide insurance against risks. And also to facilitate mobility of capital, similar to Saber (1999a). Thus, they claim that international trade and foreign direct investments would be restricted without such developments. Yet, they do not offer any evidence whatsoever that this was indeed the case, for example how much exporting and importing firms use currency *derivatives* and how much multinational corporations hedge with these instruments.

The existing evidence shows that merchants and multinational corporations are not the most important users of *derivatives* (see Chapter 4). More important, currency futures were introduced, long after forwards, to profit from instability, since destabilising speculation is the remit of those instruments. Furthermore, they argue that European capitals depended partially on the U.S. leadership. But after Bretton Woods Europe embarked on its old project of regional integration, including monetary unification, that is, abolishing intra-Euro Zone exchange rates. This makes currency *derivatives* completely useless for hedging and speculating purposes regarding the intra-Euro zone cross-border commercial, productive, monetary and financial flows.

Also, they contradictorily assume (2012, p. 17) that the continuous crises that were caused by a volatile global financial system were tamed by U.S.-provided liquidity, that is, the Treasury and the Federal Reserve, not Wall Street. To the extent that *derivatives* markets are part of the crisis-prone global financial system (see Chapter 8), there is a paradox in the defence of hedging offered by finance capital and pointing to the same capital and its mobility as source of instability. They also claim that neo-liberal legal rules could not end crises and that competition and hyper-mobility of capital contributed to destabilise the global economy (2012, p. 18).

If hedging is a modern and contemporary feature, speculation has also gained impetus with capitalism. The speculative fever of Tulipmania started when naïve buyers unconnected to the business of growing tulips entered the market. Purchase agreements did not require immediate cash payment, since the bulbs were usually delivered in the future. Thus, there was a huge pile of short-sale trades carried out without the delivery of bulbs (Poitras, 2009b). This is compatible with the greater fool theory of speculative behaviour as displayed in Malkiel (1999, p. 32).

Were these arrangements options or forwards? Poitras (2009b) discusses options market participants after the birth of capitalism during the Tulipmania in the seventeenth-century Low Countries. Tulip growers had no interest in collecting options' premiums. They wanted to sell bulbs for future delivery, which, of course, is not enough to be equated to forwards. Speculating with commodities was more attractive. Options would rather be issued by financial institutions, just like today, interested in collecting such premiums. Who would buy then? However, he argues that, despite the suitableness of option contracts for merchants involved in the Tulip bubble, given the uncertainty about the growth of bulbs and forward delivery, they were not used. But he does not explain why options were not used, except probably as rare gambles. So, gamblers would buy from finance.

What he identifies as forwards were used by Tulip traders instead, and the author describes the types of contracts available. When the bubble burst, a swarm of forwards went into default. Most of them were voided, since the anti-speculation legislation allowed the repudiation of contracts if the commodity for sale was not possessed by the seller when the contract was signed. Yet, some courts ruled that the difference payment had to be made, and the sellers had to pay a sum equivalent to customary merchant practice in case of refusal of delivery. These refusal premiums turned the proclaimed forward contracts into implicit option contracts. So, they are actually not forwards or even futures, that require exchanges. In fact, it was either speculation withcommodities or postponed delivery, a regular feature of trade under the stress of orders that cannot be fulfilled immediately, given that production takes time. Delivery also takes time in a context of less developed transportation networks or infrastructure, as discussed above in the case of the United States.

Speculation, Poitras (2009b) asserts, moved from Amsterdam to London, advancing with innovations, although the precise date of the beginning of the three-month *rescontre* clearing system is unknown. The same is true for stock options, including their speculative role in the price collapse of 1696 and the South Sea bubble crash. In the United States, Santos (2008) remarks that in the second half of the nineteenth century, speculation had already found in futures at CBOT and forwards a valuable channel for short-term gains. This suggests that the logic of capital as self-expanding value, with value accrual as the main purpose, was competing with the slave labour logic by that time. The author mentions that speculators were involved in the purchases and sales of forward-like contracts before delivery took place in a secondary market, since offsetting was not known at that time. General historians point to the same use. Allen (2001) discusses speculation, not hedging, with commodities futures. Thus, futures, but also forwards, are not seen as parts of a bigger set containing risk management tools, since risks were mostly assumed in this case. Chancellor (1999) mentions the four basic types of *derivatives* in the context of the history of financial speculation.

Speculation can, therefore, be identified, but as isolated activities without the capacity to produce relevant macroeconomic crises. Old instruments mentally identified with current practices were the tools of speculation. Arbitrage also played a role later on. Haug (2009) shows that relationships like put-call parity, necessary for arbitrage, were employed at the beginning of the twentieth century. He reports that the literature identifies important, without explaining how to gauge the importance, markets for equity options at the end of the nineteenth century, with published material from practitioners about trading techniques and profit charts. Yet, hedging call options with put options entailed by the put-call parity principle illustrates the financial logic of these arrangements, since they were supposed to, among other functions, to hedge income flows or underlying assets and liabilities. Risk is transferred from option to option and the real underlying loses its importance.

Another indirect and less rigorous evidence in favour of not only the hypothesis of *derivatives* as contemporary creation, that is, after modern capitalism, is to consider the reminiscences of contemporary *derivatives* users. Of course, the functions and uses could exist long before the contemporary period. And only unbiased historiographical research can precisely answer the question. The practitioners are usually not interested in historiographical research and their recollections may not be completely accurate. Moreover, they could stretch only to the beginning of their own or experienced mates' professional paths. But their perspective allows the rejection of the eternal *derivatives* thesis, converging to the condition (i).

From an operational point of view, Haug (2009) agrees that *derivatives* are used today like the instruments were used at the end of the nineteenth century and at the beginning of the twentieth century, except swaps. This relatively short interval prevents any homology in history. However, he mentions that many present-day pricing practices were developed gradually over time. If this is correct, then it is acceptable to claim that contemporary traders and practitioners are cleaver and more sophisticated than the previous generations, given the accumulated knowledge. Yet, by focusing on a specific arrangement, Robert Rubin argues that when he started trading stock options at Goldman Sachs, probably by the late 1960s or early 1970s, this kind of arbitrage was 'primitive'. They were old, but little known and illiquid. The firm had prohibited traders from negotiating options since the Great Depression, when it lost money with them (Rubin and Weisberg 2003). Das (2006) mentions that when he entered the *derivatives* industry by the end of the 1970s, "no qualifications were required". Bernstein (2005) affirms that his investment counselling firm started using equity options by the mid-1960s.[10]

The historical evidence is overwhelming in favour of speculative uses of arrangements, most likely protoforms, after, for an ontological reason, not before, capitalism was born. Thus, it is not surprising that speculation has been a function provided by them since their modern origins in Amsterdam in the seventeenth century (Gelderblom and Jonker, 2005). Poitras (2009b, p. 495) states that the majority of the agents in options markets at that period, for example, were formed by speculators driven primarily by the impulse to gamble. During this period, Japan was also developing speculative instruments with forwards and futures (West, 2000). There is a clear homology in the use: speculation then, speculation now. So, condition (ii) cannot be satisfied since risk management in the form of hedge is not a relevant concern prior to capitalism and even many decades before it was born. Arbitrage does not seem to be relevant as well.

Condition (iii): Institutional Setting and Economic Environment in the Introduction of Specific Arrangements

Unlike pre-capitalist societies, modern capitalism creates specific risks for production and circulation, not only finance, that require particular institutions, and contemporary capitalism manufactures risks on a large scale, requiring a transformation of older instruments and creation of new ones, mainly financial, with their corresponding functional institutions. But is there any evidence that there were pre-capitalist institutions supporting the workings of the *derivatives* found in their advocates' historical narratives or even of specific arrangements?

Following Swan (2000), Weber (2009) affirms that *derivatives*, probably meaning a couple of arrangements or options, existed in the Christian Canon Law. Similar to Swan (2000), who also focuses on juridical institutions and considers various definitions, he defines *derivatives* as a promise for the future but with an option of default. Yet, this definition seems *ad hoc* and is so broad as to include everything that involves any action happening over a given time interval and a chance of an outcome at the ending period not happening by will. History matters in his view because differences in legal institutions and customs (the sub-system) over time and across space created a broad variety of non-performance or default costs at different places and times (2009, p. 434). This would imply the appearance of options in some places and times but not in others. However, Weber and Swan seem to confuse pre-capitalist delayed or postponed commerce with *derivatives*.

How specifically does the Canon Law support *derivatives*? Why a religious institution, like the Catholic Church, would be associated with *derivatives*? Anyway, every law requires an object of regulation, like transactions or uses. But were there markets for *derivatives* before capitalism to be legislated over? Or even a modern state to legislate based on religion after all? Considering organised markets like exchanges, there is no evidence whatsoever. This prevents the trading of futures or standardised options, and, as a consequence, the very existence of *derivatives* (condition i).

Whereas Weber (2009) emphasises institutional changes based on laws and habits, Poitras (2009a) argues that regulatory oversight could not cope with changes in markets caused by the revolution in communication technologies, shifting the focus away from institutions. Of course, this is debatable. Helleiner (1994) argues that financial deregulation and international opening are political in nature, not technology-led. Even if technology plays a role, its secure use depends on regulation.

Virtually, all trades can occur in bilateral settings as an institutional decentralised environment. But the history of two arrangements that came to be considered part of *derivatives* is closely related to the formation of exchanges as a further step in the development of organised markets for centralising trades under modern capitalism. Another issue equally important is the possibility of institutional recording and publishing of organisational rules, prices, volumes and so on that would offer historical documents. On a bilateral trading basis, it is up to the parties the recording and maintenance of accounts. Of course, the fact that futures exchanges are modern institutions implies that condition (iii) could not be satisfied before the late seventeenth century, rejecting the eternal *derivatives* thesis.

When did futures exchanges start, then? Considering only futures and of course not *derivatives*, Moss and Kintgen (2010)[11] affirms that, in Japan, merchants working in warehouses traded auction bills backed by the harvested and stored rice, a staple, since the end of the seventeenth century. A market for these securities, in the island of Dojima[12] in Osaka, the rice capital, was officially authorised only in 1715, after almost two decades of informal functioning. At that time, Japan was in the middle of a long transition from feudalism to capitalism, with the exchanges accelerating the development of the latter by monetising commodities like rice. The required shogunate's imprimatur basically means giving legal status to an already existing informal economic transactions in informal institutions.

In 1721, however, the Dojima market was closed because the shogun assumed that rising rice prices were the result of illegal futures trading, known as book trading activity (Schaede, 1989). That is, trading on not-auctioned bills representing prepaid future rice harvests to be settled in cash or converted into auctioned bills. It was assumed that these unbacked bills stimulated hoarding of rice and higher prices. Moss and Kintgen (2010) comment that a crude future rice trading named '*tsumekaeshi*' developed among Osaka merchants by the end of the seventeenth century, but it was shortly associated with gambling and banned, although this prohibition was not effective.

Therefore, merchants kept trading futures, and the market evolved to the point of being considered the first organised futures market in history, although Gelderblom and Jonker (2005) claim that it was the exchange in Amsterdam and Poitras (2009b) that it was the one in Antwerp. The Japanese trade had standardised quantities, maturities, quality grades for rice and even a centralised record-keeping, margin adjustments, marking to market and settlement at a clearing house, around 1716. So, regulations and prohibitions were not binding and probably did not foster innovation, which had already happened. Some limited future trading was allowed again in 1722. A new Dojima exchange was reauthorised in 1725, but futures continued to be prohibited. The decades-old ban was lifted only in 1728, without a sizeable impact on transactions. The reason for granting legal status to the futures trading was the depressed level of rice prices, since this type of financial activity was associated with artificially higher prices, besides merchant gambling, opposing Confucian norms (Moss and Kintgen, 2010).

The authors explicitly state that the original exchange in Dojima was created mostly without regulation or support from government. By the same token, West (2000) and Schaede (1989) argue that the development of practices that culminated in the creation of the Dojima Rice Exchange, in still not completely capitalist Japan, happened initially without the shogunate intervention. Schaede (1989), in a usual description of early exchanges, affirms that the Dojima exchange was an autonomous association, seeking to supervise trading, regulate brokers and auctions, settle conflicts, register official closing prices and implement other administrative functions. She stresses (1989, p. 496) that the development and formalisation of business practices followed a private or market dynamics, not a process led by the shogunate.

The rice exchange was an autonomous, voluntary, self-regulated and non-profit initiative of the members (West, 2000). West contends that "Although participants operated in the shadow of latent state regulation, the government remained largely hands-off by, most importantly, denying legal enforceability of futures contracts" (p. 2574). And the rice exchange, in its turn, did not invent trade in rice since this commerce is probably quite old.

But there are also arguments about OTC arrangements in Japan during the same period that fits conditions (i) and (ii) more than (iii). Anecdotal evidence, probably apocryphal, since there are two different versions, indicates that a seventeenth-century Nagoya merchant, like Thales millennia before, anticipating a good harvest in a region and a bad harvest in another one, speculated with forwards. This was done by buying rice forward, or prolonged trading, according to Schaede (1989), but by paying an upfront sum and writing non-tradeable drafts. He, alone, then stored all the harvest and sold it at a profit after transporting it.

Yet, it seems like a traditional commercial speculative or arbitrage operation, not anticipations of *derivatives*. The risk for the speculator was a bad harvest in the first region and a good one in the second. And default is always a risk for sellers. Feudal Japan was dominated by landlords (*daimyo*) and *samurai*, with capitalism advancing though merchants introducing social differentiation as they accumulated wealth as warehouse superintendents and financial agents. They also ran credit houses or pay-and-convert money changers, according to Schaede (1989), and financed margin transactions for prepayment bills and action bill receipts, allowing gearing for traders.

Santos (2008) found the same initial features of the Dojima in the origins of the CBOT and other exchanges in the nineteenth century in the United States. They came initially into existence not to trade futures, but as "associations for dealing with local issues such as harbour infrastructure and commercial arbitration." So, condition (iii) could not be satisfied. Actually, exchanges performed other functions, such as grading, classifying, establishing standards, weighting and inspecting. Thus, the author informs that at the beginning of its operations, the CBOT seemed to be dedicated not to trade but to a voluntary meeting place where merchants could resolve disputes and discuss shared commercial concerns. It became a chartered corporate institution by the state of Illinois in 1859.

The first exchange mentioned along the line of voluntary associations was inaugurated in Detroit in 1847. The Chicago exchange, or Board of Trade of the

City of Chicago, was not the only one created in 1848. The exchanges at Buffalo and Cleveland were also inaugurated in that year, and Milwaukee in the next. So, spot and forward[13] trading was facilitated, but among many other activities associated with production and circulation (Santos, 2008). The website of the CFTC provides a useful synthesis of the historical developments of commodities exchanges in the United States under modern and contemporary capitalism.

Trading rules in the CBOT were enacted only in 1863 and the transition from forwards to futures, with regulations about membership, standardisation, margins and settlement started in 1865. This is also the year when slavery was abolished and capitalist development accelerated. The major problem back then, according to Santos, was settlement, with lack of counterparties willing to assume the other side. Clearing houses did not exist. They would develop gradually from the end of the nineteenth century, starting with the Minneapolis Grain Exchange in 1891,[14] to the beginning of the twentieth. Brokers performed most clearing functions by means of the so-called ring, a meeting with all the brokers that had connected positions, or transfer settlement, by shifting open interest among them.

Regardless of that, the exact beginning of formal, specifically organised capitalist futures trading in the United States is not consensual, given that the instruments were formally known as 'to arrive', not forwards or futures, let alone *derivatives*. The year 1874 has been suggested as a likely year (Santos, 2008). Somanathan et al. (2017), again, not a history work, however, states that in 1870, the New York Cotton Exchange (NYCE) was founded for trading cotton futures. In Europe, the London Metal Exchange was established in 1877. The CFTC (n.d.a., n.d.b. and n.d.c) points to the following exchanges or warehouses and dates: CBOT (1848), Kansas City Board of Trade (1856), NYCE (1870), Butter and Cheese Exchange of New York by dairy producers (1872), turned Butter, Cheese and Egg Exchange (1880), later NY Mercantile Exchange or NYMEX (1882) and Minneapolis Chamber of Commerce (1881).

The rapid development of capitalism in agriculture led to the opening of many exchanges in the United States, including former slave labour-based states. Thus, futures trading on the New Orleans Cotton Exchange began around 1882. But they remained concentrated in the agricultural Midwest and Northeast states that relied on wage labour, reinforcing the link with capitalism. The New York Futures Exchange was opened in 1890. Other exchanges appeared later, such as New York Produce Exchange, the Milwaukee Chamber of Commerce, the Merchant's Exchange of St. Louis, the Chicago Open Board of Trade, the Duluth Board of Trade and Chicago Butter and Egg Board (1898), later Chicago Mercantile Exchange (CME) (Santos, 2008, CFTC n.d.a).

As further evidence that futures exchanges could not have been fully developed in a pre-capitalist environment, given the regional dynamics and the plethora of commodities traded, typical features of capitalism like concentration and centralisation of capitals took place in the case of bourses very early on. Many exchanges have been formed by mergers and acquisitions. According to CFTC (n.d.a., n.d.b. and n.d.c), quite old MidAmerica Commodity Exchange (1868), which incorporated

Chicago Open Board of Trade and was acquired by the Chicago Board of Trade in 2004, the Coffee Exchange of NY (1882), renamed the NY Coffee and Sugar exchange in 1914, merged with NY Cocoa Exchange, founded in 1925, to form Coffee Sugar and Cocoa Exchange in 1979. In 1998, it merged with NY Cotton Exchange under the NY Board of Trade, or ICE (Intercontinental Exchange) futures after 2007.

Commodity Exchange (COMEX) of 1933 resulted from the merger of four exchanges: National Metal Exchange, Rubber Exchange of New York, National Raw Silk Exchange, and New York Hide Exchange. Four decades later, COMEX became an exchange specialised in gold, silver and copper futures. In 1994, it became part of NYMEX, which in turn has been a subsidiary or designated contract maker (DCM) of the CME Group since 2008. The latter had been formed in 2007 through a merger with CBOT. Also, CME, CBOT and CBOE created in 2002 the joint-venture OneChicago, an all-electronic exchange for single-stock futures as the result of the CFMA of 2000 (see Chapter 9) but closed in 2020. Besides the mergers and acquisitions, in the 2000s, many U.S. futures exchanges have become for-profit corporations rather than mutually owned non-profit organisations. In Europe, Euronext.Liffe created Nasdaq-Liffe Markets (NQLX) in a joint-venture with NASDAQ in 2000, but it was closed two years later.

The exchanges reflect the necessities of modern capitalism and the growth of production and circulation of agricultural commodities, raw materials and energy for consumption and industrial activity in urban centres. Commodities traded included metals and energy, and, in the NYMEX division, coal, crude oil, electricity, gasoline, heating oil, natural gas, palladium, platinum, propane and uranium. In the COMEX division, aluminium, copper, gold, silver, weather, CRB index, gas oil, corn, oats, soybeans, soybean meal, soybean oil, wheat, barley, flaxseed, canola, rye, cattle, hogs, pork bellies, cocoa, coffee, cotton, milk, orange juice, sugar, lumber and rice. It was the reign of agricultural commodities under modern capitalism, something unthinkable in a pre-capitalist setting and also in a contemporary setting with interest rates, foreign exchange, equity, and credit. There were only identical commodities, traded at different spaces and times. The organisation of capitalist institutions is not simultaneous nor homogeneous, but it clearly differs from previous economic systems.

Another important U.S. institution for arrangements to have a government imprimatur, a regulated nature, also sheds light on the issue of the true birth of so-called *derivatives*. The CFTC was created in 1974. It is interesting to observe that a regulatory body was created in the 1970s, more than a century after CBOT was inaugurated, the bourse itself tracking behind the initial coordination activities of traders. The government organisation not only did not refer to *derivatives*, but to futures alone, and moreover considered only commodities. Of course, regulation usually trails behind capitalist innovations and practices. It may thus appear completely anachronic. However, bringing back condition (i), the so-called financial *derivatives*, that is, arrangements designed to cope with financial prices and quantities in a specialised circuit, were introduced in the United States only two years before CFTC was created.

So, in the United States, the International Money Market (IMM) at the CME created foreign currency futures, not *derivatives*, in 1972. It was followed, ten years later, by the Philadelphia Stock Exchange. Dowd (2002) mentions that in 1973 the Chicago Board Options Exchange (CBOE) started trading equity call options, in line with Bernstein (2005). Interest rate futures, not *derivatives*, were then introduced by the CBOT between 1975 and 1977, having as reference Government National Mortgage Association (Ginnie Mae) securities and Treasury bonds. The IMM followed suit in 1976.

Steinherr (2000) considers that the Eurodollar *derivatives* created in 1981 were a watershed, with cash-settled contracts, a practice very old. So, if financial instruments traded in regulated exchanges were introduced in the 1970s and 1980s and could come to life due to the exchanges that introduced them, they belong to the contemporary capitalist period. They could not exist in the antiquity or in the Middle Ages, not even as very specific and independent arrangements that do not form a basket of risk management or speculative possibilities (condition ii) for most of modern capitalism. Condition (iii) cannot be satisfied.

Still regarding this condition, there is a contrasting view on the role of institutions like laws and regulations. Unlike Weber and Swan, Steinherr (2000), following Miller (1997), assumes that innovations in general, not only *derivatives*, can be explained by the existence of constraints like taxes and regulations, that is, modern institutions like state apparatuses. And also, the need of risk-sharing for completing markets or defending firms against take-overs in the specific context of the 1980s. But these are features of modern and contemporary capitalism, not of ancient history.

Contradictorily, Miller (1997) argues that low returns on existing assets led to the creation of *derivatives* by financial firms in order to diversify. Responding to the needs of finance capital, innovation, which by itself rejects the eternal *derivatives* view, was indeed an answer to falling profit margins and not to regulations or taxes, given that the latter did not change significantly since the CFTC Act of 1974. On the contrary, the deregulation of finance started, in the United States, in the early 1980s, with the Depository Institutions Deregulation and Monetary Control Act of 1980 (DIDMCA) and the Garn-St Germain Depository Institutions Act of 1982 (Garn-St Germain), both introduced to liberalise the Savings & Loans institutions (FDIC, 1997). It was not the result of religious institutions either.

Moreover, the longer history of specific arrangements in the United States, Europe and Japan defies this interpretation of an intervention-driven market formation. In the United States, the transactions in grains and the corresponding arrangements came into existence before the starting of taxes and regulations (see Chapter 9). Also, to the best of known available evidence, there are no discussions of public regulation, by pre-capitalist proto-states, of pre-capitalist protoforms of present-day arrangements. Of course, it does not back the eternal *derivatives* view either.

Santos (2008, italics in the original), discussing specifically futures, reinforces the finance-led view and the role of capitalist institutions like exchanges and discharges the regulation-led assumption:

> Futures exchanges *create* futures contracts. And, because futures exchanges compete for traders, they must create contracts that appeal to the financial community. For example, the New York Mercantile Exchange created its light sweet crude oil contract in order to fill an unexploited niche in the financial marketplace.

However, light sweet crude oil had then been in use for decades, with potential price volatility affecting crude oil companies, refineries and end-users of fuel. And they all could need hedging contracts or arrangements and probably found them in schemes not related to *derivatives*. But contemporary financial innovation is profit-driven and geared to speculators. Oil is a particular commodity like any other that becomes a mere support for the universal commodity: money as the difference of prices in two different periods. The analogy of modern and contemporary capitalist arrangements is possible because instruments, institutions and technology are moulded up by the accumulation drive. Analogy becomes homology. But this thrust is missing in pre-capitalist societies as an essential element.

Condition (iv): The Relative Economic and Financial Importance of Arrangements

This condition is a no-brainer and therefore its verification is short. It is important to differentiate between existence (condition i), albeit suggested and under-documented, and economic and financial importance. An arrangement may exist, at least in analogy, and be unimportant. Condition (iv) would not be satisfied. The literature discussed in the previous sections suggests that there is no evidence that the arrangements today identified with *derivatives*, when they existed, were economically and financially relevant before contemporary capitalism. There are simply no historical records demonstrating their significance. The functions performed today were not a fundamental tenet of the ancient, medieval and even modern economies. Specific arrangements similar or analogous to the contemporary ones could well be identified as sporadic, appearing in certain periods and places and thus not continuously necessary. So, even under financialised capitalism, specific arrangements experienced a boom, compared to other flows and stocks, only in recent decades, noticed by practitioners and measured by statistics because they became relevant.

Weber (2009) criticises some contemporary authors like Hull and Mishkin for showing that *derivatives* were financial innovations of the 1970s, due to financial volatility, and became truly important only after that initial period. He ironises the interpretation that financial markets were not volatile before the end of Bretton Woods and thus that *derivatives* had no significant hedging role to play. But it would be necessary to ask: what is the point of creating, for instance, a currency *derivative* in an institutional setting of fixed, albeit adjustable, rates? Even if the rates, except for the U.S. dollar, were adjusted, this was a decision to be made by central banks and the IMF, not speculators or arbitrageurs. Currency *derivatives* were unnecessary and of course they could not satisfy conditions (i), (ii) and (iii).

But how is it possible that instruments as old as money, as the eternal *derivatives* advocates have been arguing, could not be a significant part of the economic and financial world in the 1970s or before? Despite the protest, this is the empirical evidence for the period with data, regardless of how *derivatives* are understood and praised. As a consequence, regarding market size and volume of transactions, notwithstanding the fact that, unlike history, data collection and statistical science are modern creations, it is clear that *derivatives* provided a new trend in financial markets and the economy only after the 1970s, mainly in terms of growth and regarding the notional amounts and gross market value or replacement costs in terms of GDP or even wealth. Of course, the reported number of preserved contracts in clay tablets for Mesopotamia and in papyri for Egypt suggest that the specific arrangements could have been used by a few agents at certain periods and regions. The point here, however, is to uncover, beyond the potential functions, the relative economic or financial importance of these transactions since the socio-economic organisation was altogether different.

Concerning ancient economies, Poitras (2009b) argues that before the sixteenth century, good contracts with forward-like features were important to commerce, without explaining how to gauge the importance: "Some method of contracting for forward delivery has been an *essential* feature of commerce since antiquity" and "forward contracting became *essential* to urban merchants contracting with agricultural producers for crops prior to harvest or with fisherman for catches prior to arrival in port" (2009b, p. 491, italics added). If it was essential and it is known today that it was, the significance must be recorded and gauged somehow, with direct and/or indirect evidence. Yet, what are the sources? Where are the documents or similar records? And regardless of importance, it is clear that it is about deferred trade, not *derivatives*.

Weber (2009) emphasises historical sources like 'law and regulation, courts decisions, surviving contracts' for condition (i), but they can be extrapolated for condition (iv). For instance, surviving contracts, even if the analogy is accurate for a completely different society, may not represent the whole bulk of economic contracts. It could bias the interpretation about their importance. Law and regulation and court decisions, by the same token, can reflect the fact that a few merchants were influential and able to have their interests legislated and imposed by a proto-state, which should not be seen as similar to today' states. These transactions may not account for a large fraction of economic activity in a pre-capitalist society.

About modern capitalism, options and forwards were supposedly common in the bourse of Amsterdam in the sixteenth century. But the economic importance of the exchange is not discussed. Yet, Poitras (2009b, p. 487) remarks that this is probable, not certain. The imprecise nature of the claim suggests that financial and economic history so far has not provided clear-cut evidence that it was a common or regular market economically important indeed. He claims that by the mid-seventeenth century, the contracts were *actively* exchange-traded, with an advanced clearing system. Contradictorily, he affirms that *active* trade in options did not take place until the nineteenth century. Contradictions are pervasive. The indirect evidence of practitioners like Cox and Rubinstein (1985) rejects the latter argument, at least for the United States. They claim that options were obscure and trifling in finance in the 1960s. Markets were fragmented and deals were costly and hard to arrange. The turning point was the inauguration of the Chicago Board Options Exchange in 1973, that is, with a centralising institution supporting the trades. Condition (iv) cannot be satisfied.

The Historical Economic and Financial Ontology of *Derivatives* Denied Once More

With so many different interpretative proposals, it is necessary to classify them and organise a timetable in order to establish historical delimiters that make it clear that *derivatives* are recent intellectual, not real, creations. Regarding the history of transactions involving arrangements mirroring what only recently were added together as *derivatives*, discussed above, there are at least four major strands, each one existing for a different time span. By organising them from the longest to the shortest, the following periodisations can be identified. The first interpretation dates *derivatives* transactions, with commodities and loans, without swaps and futures, back to millennia (Swan 2000, Weber 2009), encompassing the antiquity and Middle Ages. The interpretation advanced in this book is that these deals are pre-capitalist, mostly scattered operations with merchant or commercial capital, not finance or *derivatives*.

A second approach considers *derivatives* markets more generally, without swaps, as appearing during the transition to capitalism during the sixteenth century in the Low Countries, now for both commodity and securities (Weber 2009; Haug 2009; Poitras 2009b). A third perspective locates the origin of modern *derivatives*, still without swaps, at the end of the nineteenth century, in the United States (Santos, 2008), emphasising commodities as underlying, or at the seventeenth or eighteenth century in Japan in the Osaka rice market (Moss and Kintgen 2010). Thus, this innovation also took place under the transition to modern capitalist conditions. Finally, a fourth view frames the literal rise, not origin, of arrangements named *derivatives* in the 1970s, after the demise of the Bretton Woods agreements, although swaps appeared in the 1980s, already under contemporary financialised capitalism.

Therefore, the four views might reflect stages of unequal appearance of supposedly similar arrangements in economic and financial history. There is a difference in terms of the underlying between the first and third and the second and fourth views that is fundamental. Before the 1970s, the bulk of *derivatives* transactions was mainly associated with commodities, not financial, transactions, except for the speculative frenzy in the Low Countries under the second interpretation. This long trend was reversed after Bretton Woods. Thus, one can propose the following classification for these histories of transactions considered to be *derivatives* or *derivatives*-like: pre-capitalist, including antiquity and Middle Ages, and capitalist, both modern and contemporary.

But regarding the economic and financial history itself, *derivatives* or analogous arrangements are connected to it in at least two different ways. Assuming the proposed periodisation based on the development of capitalism, the projected ancient arrangements, pseudo-*derivatives*, may have appeared in pre-capitalist, commercial or merchant societies that characterise ancient history (Breisach, 2007). It can be considered that, as mentioned, in the transition from medieval to modern, capitalist history, other arrangements appeared, but it was a specific event without scale and scope, preventing analogies and homologies. During the modern period, analogous arrangements can be spotted, mostly connected to agriculture. And then, in the contemporary history, the instruments gained scope and momentum under financialisation.

None of these four readings could satisfy all the four conditions. Pre-capitalist societies have no role (condition ii) for such arrangements or their supporting institutions (condition iii) as economically relevant tools (condition iv). So, condition (i) could never be satisfied. Also, the introduction of swaps under contemporary capitalism invalidates them all. *Derivatives* do not and did not exist ontologically. But there are and there were, except swaps and to some extent futures, specific analogous instruments in history that could be confounders. These past arrangements, claimed to be *derivatives*, are not identical, similar, analogous or homologous to contemporary ones. Contemporary transactions are not a necessary functional development of ancient deals, there being no homology. That is, they do not fit an evolutionary line, like Steinherr's (2000) treatment of hedging in modern capitalism. They are a projection of a current vision on past phenomena that bear some, at most distant, analogy. That is, it is rather a feature of modern or contemporary *derivatives* markets projected retroactively to a previous and different socioeconomic context, that is, an example of presentism.

So, a problem with most the of historical accounts of *derivatives*, not necessarily research, consulted, is a matter of teleology. In these narratives, a linguistic or formal issue related to the appropriate use of similar terms or identical words is confused with substantive economic issues, implying appropriation of past phenomena by present-day traces because, despite linguistic terms not being identical, the situations have formal similarities regarding time, with the treatment usually imposed by rhetoric. Trade is the common thing, given the symmetry where, in societies with commerce, the starting point is C, a commodity, and the ending point, in the *future*, is a different commodity, or C′. The fundamental issue is that between them there must be money M. Cash settlement based on the inverted logic of M–C–M′ would be irrelevant in pre-capitalist societies. These historical accounts mix etymology, ontology and taxonomy. Not to mention the ideological implication that some transactions should be considered natural because they have always existed. It is about true meaning, as Foucault would have (*les mots et les choses*). The things cannot be created by words.

In most ancient societies, there are not relevant long-distance trade and therefore organised foreign exchange markets, except for intermittent fairs. There were not banks and the temple played a role in many pre-capitalist societies (Hudson, 2024), but it is a different institutional setting. *Derivatives* are about money. Yet, Weber (2009) argues the historical role of banks in the spreading of *derivatives* is not very known by scholars. He claims that informal trading based on reputation is likely to have been supported by banking houses, like the Rothschild Bank, created already under capitalism. But since clients valued privacy, banks had to keep *derivatives* secret. And for some unknown reason, the records for these fundamental arrangements were never released or disclosed.

Money and therefore markets could not fully develop in ancient societies, because they require a set of conditions that these environments could not provide. Only under financialised capitalism, the instruments that are called *derivatives* can flourish and the collective arrangements can fully blossom in the imaginary, although the composition is never homogeneous. The nature of risk under capitalism is completely different. And it cannot be reproduced without risks. So, financialised capitalism started manufacturing risks and profitable instruments to deal with them, but this is definitively not the case for ancient societies.

Thus, at least for supposed ancient arrangements, there were no securities and no regular and organised markets. Most of supposed *derivatives* transactions are actually deferred payments with commodities or commodities delivered with a lag. It is a merchant arrangement for payment of real goods or assets. More than *derivatives*, they seem more like inverted commercial credit arrangements, with loans from the buyer to the seller for the right to the future good. Is it necessary to widen the scope of *derivatives* for the narratives to fit? Antonio and the flesh in his back in Shakespeare was a *derivative*-like transaction using human collateral in case of default? An example of collateralised debt obligation? Arranged marriage is a promise to deliver a bride in the future. And since there is no way to guarantee that it will happen, there is a risk of non-performance. Is this a *derivative*? What is a loan from the point of view of a borrower? A promise to repay with interest. But the borrower can default on it. Is it a *derivative*? It is a false analogy. A loan can be securitised. The corresponding securities are derived from the borrowing/lending. But are they *derivatives*?

The eternal *derivatives* thesis is, hence, teleological, although it might well be just attempts at interpreting only apparently analogous phenomenon in completely different societies. As Saber (1999b) argues, when options are transacted by managers of large dollar hedge funds, they cannot be compared to the same the use of a similar instrument by a Japanese farmer in the seventeenth century. Pre-capitalist societies could not have full *derivatives* with swaps for instance, but only fragments of similar arrangements with some vague similarity due to the passage of time, reinforced by rhetoric, to options and forwards. In the anecdotes about Thales, for example, the supposed trade is just a commercial intermediation to corner the olives or presses market. The fact that it looks like speculation over the future is immaterial; since it could not happen simultaneously, as that would be arbitrage.

When discussing ancient transactions as anticipations of contemporary *derivatives*, there is usually no detailed information about the content of the contracts, except for clay tablets showing loan conditions or deferred trade. What happens then is to assume rhetorically that they were *derivative*-like instruments and hope that no one would question it. It is a baseless interpretation. Even in commercial transactions, the time lapse is not enough to characterise a *derivative*, as mentioned by the IMF (see Chapter 1). Therefore, it is probably wishful thinking.

Free markets are good and eternal, and options are mostly about freedom of buying or selling.

Actually, it would be more accurate, following Marx, to state that arrangements that came to be called *derivatives* were not ripe before contemporary, financialised capitalism, although some specific transactions resembling current ones were part of modern capitalism. And even after the birth of capitalism, it could not fully mature until the former had geared to financial accumulation. Only when finance capitalism started, arrangements lumped together as *derivatives*, with swaps being introduced, exploded and the they could be statistically noticed and identified.

The missing records required by proper historical research cannot be replaced by anecdotes. Plenty of anecdotes can be invented. Another example can be offered regarding the ancient ontological inexistence of *derivatives*. In the cultural tradition of Egypt, pharaohs were embalmed. Sarcophagi were thus procured by the pharaohs before the uncertain time of their death. Since most people can die only after they are born, except stillborns, it must necessarily entail a time lapse and therefore past, present and future. They are not *derivatives*, and not even a homologous or analogous arrangement. That is, purchasing coffins before dying is not a forward. It is more like an insurance, probably because their heirs or religious organisations would not provide one. This is not necessarily an economic transaction. The motivation is religious, not to generate a gain or to avoid a monetary loss. They are not buying a good or service from a coffin maker who produces it for sale at a profit but just following the tradition in which a craftsman could be expected to manufacture the sarcophagus by a religious request.

So, a timeline that is not teleological would have it the following way: there were no *derivatives* before the 1980s, but there were analogous specific arrangements scattered over the long rise of capitalism, with different names, but with a pronounced speculative function. Thus, there were no analogous or homologous specific arrangements before the sixteenth century, only spurious attempts at projecting the present onto commercial and speculative activity in the antiquity. So, the arrangements are not very old. They were gradually introduced and transformed with the advent of capitalism and its changes, needs and spread. The first arrangements were related to agriculture and mainly trade, but equity and bills seemed also identifiable references. However, it is hard to measure their importance. Condition (iv) cannot be satisfied without further solid quantitative historical research. This modern setting remained the same for a long time. In the 1970s, the agriculture and trade became less relevant as references for the arrangements, being slowly transformed as sources of financial profits. With financialisation and the introduction of private swaps in the 1980s, the idea of *derivatives* could be introduced, a concept without an ontology.

Summing Up

This chapter shows that the problem for the eternal *derivatives* thesis is the fact that economic and financial history is made up of different economic systems.

Economic and financial functions of different arrangements cannot be the same for longer time spans. Commerce and the circulation of commodities share general or universal features, but different instruments and institutions. Pre-capitalist institutions make condition (iii) impossible. Cash is not central to pre-capitalist societies and therefore cash settlement is irrelevant. So, since the appearance of the first analogous arrangement up to the introduction of swaps, it took a couple of centuries, but within the capitalist era. Certainly, the time scale is not measured in millennia. *Derivatives* in Mesopotamia, Byzantium or Egypt would be a false dawn.

Arrangements started under modern capitalism, with speculative transactions based on agriculture and commerce, and finance being a residual. These were independent arrangements not distinguishable as a single collective entity. Contemporary capitalism changed all that, with finance requiring arrangements for accumulation when profits fell, and agriculture became a residual with feeble links to production. They are still independent instruments but lumped together as *derivatives*.

As a consequence, the four conditions presented at the beginning, of course, cannot be satisfied when the long history is considered. They form an ensemble that requires all of them to be satisfied co-jointly. But this can happen, historically, at most, only at a specific juncture. Condition (iv) makes sense only in capitalism. Conditions (i), (ii) and (iii) can only work together and are logically and historically connected. *Derivatives* are ideational creatures of financialised capitalism. Specific modern arrangements can be apparently analogous or even homologous to contemporary innovations, but they do not conform to *derivatives* as such. Only under contemporary, financialised and, the literature suggests, globalised, capitalism, they can fully flourish as a concept, although ontologically they cannot exist, with specific arrangements performing speculative functions in circuits belonging to different financial sub-systems, along with other instruments.

The ontological non-existence of *derivatives* as a whole shows that condition (i) cannot be satisfied and is related to the fact that the specific arrangements cobbled together do not share many characteristics, as argued in Chapters 1–3. There is no possible historical homology or analogy. So, before the sixteenth century, there were no arrangements and therefore no *derivatives*. In the ancient period, there were only contracts for postponed payments in trade and conditions for loans' defaults. And many false comparisons with tales and situations completely distant to contemporary economic negotiations.

In the Middle Ages, there were nothing, since the Church does not need *derivatives*, even if the afterlife implies a future time. In the transition from feudalism to capitalism, merchant activity introduced specific arrangements for specific need of fractions of commercial and money capital. This opened up the period of arrangements for commodities like cereals or grains. This development was very long and took to the twentieth century. In this first phase, the arrangements were basically tied to commodities, mainly to agriculture. Raw materials for industry were not important. With the rise of finance, the old arrangements were transformed, and new ones like swaps were introduced to support financial accumulation and valorisation.

The history of institutions like exchanges supports this claim, as they were introduced in the sixteenth century in the Low Countries or in the seventeenth century in Japan. The existence of laws or codes dealing with the arrangements considered *derivatives* despite the fact that swaps could not have been introduced, is spurious, as they point to commerce, not finance. Since the 1970s, financialisation changed capitalism. Financial accumulation needed new sources of profits. And as a consequence, the missing arrangements that make up what today are considered *derivatives*, and could not exist under preterite modes of production, were introduced.

Notes

1 It is telling that Chance (2008. p. 7) recommends: "(…) I would suggest that you do not spend a lot of time on the details of *derivatives* history. It's not that important." But Landes (1999, p. 347) would insist: "You do not solve a major problem by pretending that it does not exist and telling people to look elsewhere."

2 It is important to understand who was the counterparty speculating with the transferred risks if they could be transferred. If it is a large financial institution, opening up positions from several hedgers than *derivatives* could be allowing a significant systemic risk. In the ideal world, *derivatives* could represent a minor threat only if the situation were inverted. A large number of speculators assuming parts of a larger risk such that, if a loss occurs, it is not individually sizeable enough compared to relevant revenue flows and stocks of liabilities and net worth. But, again, this is basically transferring capitalist operations to pre-capitalist societies.

3 Poitras (2009b, p. 492) conflates 'futures' (his quotation marks) and forwards into 'time bargains'. The omnipresence of time again.

4 In this transaction, a central bank can use the currency of another country during a given period of time, or exchange one metal for another. The goal is not to hedge against or speculate with exchange rate or price risk (condition ii), but to access currencies or metals not otherwise available due to illiquid positions and therefore preventing against liquidity or insolvency risks. It is not about price movements, but flows of currency or metals, that is, about provisory transfers of stocks and provision of quantities of currency or metals to restore liquidity.

5 Available at: www.fia.org/fia/about-fia?utm_source=FIAWeb&utm_medium=Top. Retrieved December 2023.

6 Unlike most orthodox textbooks, Steinherr (2000) defines the short run as several years in chronological (calendar) time. Taylor (2010) measures the short term in one to two years. The OCC (1996) considers, intuitively more reasonable, the short run to be less than one year.

7 It is interesting to notice that in his account capital flows can affect exchange rates but not interest rates. The latter are exclusively policy variables. But international capital flows, in the host country, after entering the foreign exchange market, necessarily affect the money market before it is transformed in a different kind of capital. And since the money market is essentially about liquidity, interest rates can be and are affected as well. If not in countries in which the money market is deep and thick, certainly in most money markets in the world.

8 He informs that in the classic book on finance for the 1980s, *Barbarians at the Gate*, *derivatives* are not even listed in the index, and stock options appear once, in a footnote.

9 Santos (2008) quotes a study conducted in the 1970s, claiming that the first forward (literally 'time') contract was negotiated in the Great Lakes on "March 13, 1851. It specified that 3,000 bushels of corn were to be delivered to Chicago in June at a price of one cent below the March 13th cash market price." Nevertheless, he mentions more recent research providing evidence that forwards and futures were already traded consistently in the eighteenth century in New York Stock & Exchange Board under the name of 'time bargains' and later 'margin trading', emulating London and Amsterdam. These older transactions, of course, were not *derivatives*. He mentions another study naming forwards 'grain marketing'. Notwithstanding that, it is clear the emphasis upon time. Regarding older studies, Scott H. Irwin, from the Farmdoc project at University of Illinois, has a treasury of historical material on agricultural markets, including futures and forwards (https://scotthirwin.com/commodity-classics/). It is clear that in the United States, *derivatives* could be introduced only after the seventeenth century, despite the importation of capitalist institutions from Europe. But it took decades for specific arrangements only to be identified.

10 Bernstein (2005, pp. 331–333) argues that his firm, a small speculative mutual fund, started using OTC options on big stocks in the mid-1960s. The fund owned stocks and the firm sold calls on them to overoptimistic and unsophisticated speculators willing to pay a high premium on them. Of course, since it does not make any sense for corporations to hedge price fluctuations of their own issued and outstanding stocks in exchanges, equity options are all about speculation.

11 The authors also identify transactions in rice futures as financial rather than non-financial.

12 West (2000) remarks that the clan Yodoya's estate is usually pointed as the first futures trading locus, but it could be only one among many other sites.

13 As discussed before, forwards are OTC contracts, traded off-exchange. Santos himself is ambiguous when discussing the existence of forward markets (italics added): "Of course, forward markets could and *indeed did exist* in the absence of both grading standards and formal exchanges, though *to what extent they existed is unclear*."

14 This part of the text, or the reference cited, is not accurate, at least considering what the pre-CFTC history of futures regulation reports (CFTC, n.d.a). The commission shows that in 1947 the Minneapolis Chamber of Commerce was renamed the Minneapolis Grain Exchange. In 1881, according to the same governmental source, the Minneapolis Chamber of Commerce had established an exchange that was designed to promote trade in grains and to prevent abuses.

References

Allen, Larry. *The Global Financial System 1750–2000*. London: Reaktion Books, 2001.

Bernstein, Peter. *Capital Ideas: The Improbable Origins of Modern Wall Street*. New York: Wiley, 2005.

Breisach, Ernst. *Historiography: Ancient, Medieval and Modern*. Chicago: Chicago University Press, 2007.

CFTC. *History of the CFTC: US Futures Trading and Regulation Before the Creation of the CFTC*, n.d.a Available at: www.cftc.gov/About/HistoryoftheCFTC/history_precftc.html Retrieved April, 2024.

CFTC. *History of the CFTC: CFTC History in the 1970s*, n.d.b. Available at: www.cftc.gov/About/HistoryoftheCFTC/history_1970s.html Retrieved April 2024.

CFTC. *History of the CFTC: CFTC History in the 1980s*, n.d.c. Available at: www.cftc.gov/About/HistoryoftheCFTC/history_1980s.html Retrieved April 2024.

Chance, Don. "A Chronology of Derivatives." *Derivatives Quarterly* 2, (1995): 53–60.

Chance, Don. *Essays in Derivatives: Risk-Transfer Tools and Topics Made Easy*. 2nd ed. Hoboken: Wiley, 2008.

Chancellor, Edward. *Devil Take the Hindmost – A History of Financial Speculation*. New York: Farrar, Straus and Giroux, 1999.

Cox, John, and Mark Rubinstein. *Options Markets*. New Jersey: Prentice Hall, 1985.

Das, Satyajit. *Traders, Guns and Money: Knowns and Unknowns in the Dazzling World of Derivatives*. London: FT Press/Prentice Hall, 2006.

Dowd, Kevin. *Measuring Market Risk*. Chichester/West Sussex: Wiley, 2002.

Federal Deposit Insurance Corporation (FDIC). *History of the Eighties: Lessons for the Future. Vol. 1, An Examination of the Banking Crises of the 1980s and Early 1990s*. Washington, DC: FDIC, 1997.

Ferguson, Niall. *The Ascent of Money: A Financial History of the World*. New York: Penguin, 2008.

Gelderblom, Oscar, and Joost Jonker. "Amsterdam as the Cradle of Modern Futures Trading and Options Trading, 1550–1650." In: William N. Goetzmann and K. Geert Rouwenhorst (eds.) *The Origins of Value: The Financial Innovations that Created Modern Capital Markets*. Oxford: Oxford University Press, 2005.

Harvey, David. *Spaces of Capital: Towards a Critical Geography*. New York: Routledge, 2001.

Haug, Espen G. "The History of Option Pricing and Hedging." In: Wolfgang Hafner and Heinz Zimmermann (eds.) *Vinzenz Bronzin's Option Pricing Models*. Berlin/Heidelberg: Springer-Verlag, 2009: 471–486.

Helleiner, Eric. *States and the Reemergence of Global Finance: From Bretton Woods to the 1990s*. Cornell: Cornell University Press, 1994.

Henwood, Doug. *Wall Street: How it Works and for Whom?* London: Verso, 1998.

Hudson, Michael. *Temples of Enterprise: Creating Economic Order in the Bronze Age Near East*. Glashütte: ISLET-Verlag, 2024.

Hull, John. *Options, Futures, and Other Derivatives*. 11th ed. London: Pearson, 2021.

Kindleberger, Charles P. *A Financial History of Western Europe*. 2nd ed. New York: Oxford University Press, 1993.

Kummer, Steve, and Christian Pauletto. *The History of Derivatives: A Few Milestones*. Zurich: EFTA Seminar on Regulation of Derivatives Markets, 2012.

Landes, David. *The Wealth and Poverty of Nations*. London: Abacus, 1999.

Lowenstein, Roger. *The End of Wall Street*. New York: The Penguin Press, 2010.

Lowenstein, Roger. *When Genius Failed: The Rise and Fall of Long-Term Capital Management*. New York: Random House, 2001.

Magdoff, Harry, and Paul Sweezy. *Estagnation and Financial Explosion*. New York: Monthly Review Press, 1987.

Malkiel, Burton G. *A Random Walk Down the Street*. New York: W. W. Norton & Company, 1999.

Markham, Jerry W. *A Financial History of the United States. Vol. 3. From the Age of Derivatives into the New Millennium (1970–2001)*. Armonk, NY: M. E. Sharpe, 2002.

Miller, Merton. *Merton Miller on Derivatives*. New York: Wiley, 1997.

Moss, David A., and Eugene Kintgen. "The Dojima Rice Market and the Origins of Futures Trading." *Harvard Business School Case* 709-044, 2010.

Panitch, Leo, and Sam Gindin. *The Making of Global Capitalism: The Political Economy of American Empire*. London: Verso, 2012.

Partnoy, Frank. *Infectious Greed: How Deceit and Risk Corrupted the Financial Markets*. Revised edition. New York: Public Affairs, 2009b.

Poitras, Geoffrey. "The Early History of Option Contracts." In: Wolfgang Hafner and Heinz Zimmermann (eds.) *Vinzenz Bronzin's Option Pricing Models*. Berlin/ Heidelberg: Springer-Verlag2009b: 487–518.

Poitras, Geoffrey. *Equity Capital: From Ancient Partnerships to Modern Exchange Traded Funds*. New York: Routledge, 2016.

Poitras, Geoffrey. "From Antwerp to Chicago: The History of Exchange Traded Derivative Security Contracts." *Revue d'Histoire des Sciences Humaines* 20, (2009a): 11–50.

Poitras, Geoffrey. *Risk Management, Speculation and Derivative Securities*. New York: Academic Press, 2002.

Rubin, Robert, and Jacob Weisberg. *In an Uncertain World: Though Choices from Wall Street to Washington*. New York: Random House, 2003.

Saber, Nasser. *Speculative Capital & Derivatives: The Nature of Risk in Capital Markets*. Vol. 2. London: Financial Times/Prentice Hall, 1999b.

Saber, Nasser. *Speculative Capital: The Invisible Hand of Global Finance*. Vol. 1. London: Financial Times/Prentice Hall, 1999a.

Santos, Joseph. "A History of Futures Trading in the United States." *EH.Net Encyclopedia*, 2008. Available at https://eh.net/encyclopedia/a-history-of-futures-trading-in-the-united-states/ Retrieved April 2024.

Schaede, Ulrike. "Forwards and Futures in Tokugawa-era Japan: A New Perspective on the Dojima Rice Market." *Journal of Banking and Finance* 13, no. 4–5 (1989): 487–513.

Schinasi, Garry J., R. Sean Craig, Burkhard Drees, and Charles F. Kramer. *Modern Banking and OTC Derivatives Markets: The Transformation of Global Finance and its Implications for Systemic Risk*. Washington, DC: The IMF, 2000.

Scholes, Myron. "Derivatives in a Dynamic Environment." *The American Economic Review* 88, no. 3 (1998): 350–370.

Somanathan, T. V., Venkatramanan A. Nageswaran, and Harsh Gupta. *Derivatives*, 2nd ed. Cambridge: Cambridge University Press, 2017.

Steinherr, Alfred. *Derivatives – The Wild Beast of Finance: A Path to Effective Globalisation?* New York: Wiley, 2000.

Swan, Edward. *Building the Global Market: A 4000 Year History of Derivatives*. The Hague: Kluwer Law International, 2000.

Taylor, Francesca. *Mastering Derivatives Markets*. 2nd ed. London: FT/Prentice Hall, 2010.

Weber, Ernst J. "A Short History of Derivative Security Markets." In: Wolfgang Hafner and Heinz Zimmermann (eds.) *Vinzenz Bronzin's Option Pricing Models*. Berlin/ Heidelberg: Springer-Verlag, 2009: 431–466.

West, Mark D. "Private Ordering at the World's First Futures Exchange." *Michigan Law Review* 98, no. 8 (2000): 2574–2615.

6 The Phenomenology of It

The Intellectual Reflections Upon Modern Arrangements and Contemporary *Derivatives*

Introduction

The historical studies of so-called *derivatives* mentioned in Chapter 5 could not be convincingly found in pre-capitalist societies. Nor could the systematic reflections, ideas and thoughts on the arrangements be uncovered long before the nineteenth century, that is, their existence as a contemporaneous and historical phenomenon. Not a single reference researched shows archaic and medieval phenomenological treatments of any arrangement. Hence, the fifth condition for validating the pre-historical existence of *derivatives* cannot be satisfied either, if for nothing else, because all the other four could not be obtained.

Given their creation to satisfy capital needs over the centuries, the arrangements could not be designed mentally before capital itself and its instruments came into existence. Lest one considers that scholars could concoct or imagine something that did not exist because it was not needed, an invention, they could only try to figure out what was happening with arrangements in different circuits of capital after the fact, as history, albeit short. It does not matter whether or not circuits were old, new, sophisticated, thick or deep. The point is about whether or not specifics circuits or isolated transactions existed and if contemporaneous writers or historians were able to identify their workings and provide explanations or reflections.

Thus, *derivatives* have been summoned *ex post* to justify their fulfilment of capital needs, in terms of management of risks created by capitalism and other advantages (see Chapter 7). The fundamental issue, however, is that modern commentators, and modern historians later, did not think in terms of *derivatives* as a unified set of different arrangements and could discuss only fragments without a totality, based on the immediate appearance. Under capitalism, the most important apparent aspects are related to production, circulation, valorisation and reproduction of very particular capitals, with the consequent importance of time and space, money over time and space, and monetary price differences over times and spaces. Alienation and monetary fetishism impeded a complete view until finance took the helm in the 1970s.

It is therefore important to emphasise the difference between the recorded appearances of the things, or arrangements material archaeology, that in the case of *derivatives* is ontologically empty, and the thoughts about the things, interpreting

DOI: 10.4324/9781003137092-7

the records or the previous reflections on the subject, or arrangements cognitive archaeology. Both can deal with themes like the time when and the place where the things happened, the institutions that provided the settings for the things to happen and work, their socioeconomic importance, and the agents engaged materially and/or intellectually with the things, as practitioners may translate their operational practices into reflections and publish them (Bernstein, 2005, Das, 2006, Haug, 2009). But in the case of *derivatives*, only ideas subsist in the more recent past and only cognitive archaeology matters. Anyway, the former is a constraint to the latter. For example, OTC swaps were introduced under contemporary capitalism and could not exist before. If a thing does not exist, it is unlikely to think about it.

Arrangements defined by their trading in exchanges, like futures and options, are equally modern, not ancient. As mentioned in Chapter 5, organised markets for futures existed already since the nineteenth century, in London Metal Exchange (1877) or Chicago Board of Trade (1848),[1] and even earlier, in Osaka in eighteenth century (1715) or in Amsterdam in the seventeenth century (1611).[2] But there were no relevant contemporary discussions about them or the arrangements traded in there. This has been the subject of material archaeology.

As a consequence, ancient and medieval scholars could not discuss the arrangements. Besides, pre-illuminist thought was mostly philosophical and religious, scantly scientific. Only contemporary or future researchers, both under modern capitalism, could have the means for appropriate reflections after the seventeenth century. Hence, the evidence suggests that arrangements started being discussed seriously by the end of nineteenth century and mainly over the twentieth century, when they became important. Moreover, they were collapsed into *derivatives* only in the past 40 years or so, with swaps, right after the rise of financialised capitalism in the 1970s.

This chapter discusses the ideas that contributed to the description or interpretation of socioeconomic roles, pricing of options and functioning of modern arrangements, and, more recently, the first conceptualisations of contemporary *derivatives*. It is organised chronologically, starting with modern capitalism. A selected group of scholars writing about arrangements from the end of nineteenth century to the beginning of twentieth century are discussed. The chapter closes with some approaches that took place during the transition to contemporary financialised capitalism and finally the probable first use of the word *derivative* in its present meaning by the early 1980s.

Before Contemporaneous *Derivatives*: Reflections on Specific Arrangements Under Modern Capitalism

As mentioned, since *derivatives* did not exist in pre-capitalist societies, publications with dedicated thoughts about them could never be recorded. On the other hand, particular arrangements and some functions performed by them after the transition and birth of capitalism could only be discussed by modern and contemporary scholars looking back to a variable time horizon measuring the past, as history. Or, more recently, by contemporaneous observers and practitioners as present phenomena. Thus, a few scholars and practitioners had contemporary experiences under modern capitalism with specific arrangements, writing about some of their particular features as a narrative of their time, not a study of history, given that they were identified later by historians.

Thoughts about options at the end of the nineteenth century and beginning of the twentieth century

It seems that options, not *derivatives*, were the first arrangements to receive intellectual interest. Formulas for option pricing and optimal hedging were developed in a gradual manner, not by means of full discoveries. Weber (2009) mixes transactions with their interpretations, and this is inevitable in a single chapter dealing with writings of practitioners who publish their experiences. Reflections about these arrangements started in the nineteenth century. Weber (2009, p. 431) claims that, in the final decades of that century, practitioners like James Moser, not scholars, introduced graphical tools designed to mimic *derivative*, actually options, contracts, improving knowledge and attracting scholars to finance. "Profit charts made *derivatives* accessible to young scientists, including Louis Bachelier and Vinzenz Bronzin, who had the mathematical knowledge for the rigorous analysis of derivative pricing." This understanding allowed a better cognition of contracts and enabled innovations in the form of new combinations, like the straddle, a put combined with a call.

Thus, Bachelier and Bronzin, who had studied mathematics and physics, could learn about finance and give their contribution at the beginning of twentieth century. Bachelier published in French in 1900, and Bronzin published in German in 1908. They seem to be pioneers on option pricing. Haug (2009) argues that Bachelier considered a specific transaction, like the purchase of a futures contract, against a short call and then drew a profit and loss diagram at maturity. Since the payoff is the same as for a put, a put–call parity is obtained. He does the same for many other combinations, including options against options, known as bull spreads and call-back spreads. These combinations can therefore affect the risk–reward profile of options. Thus, the parity principle was known at the beginning of the twentieth century, earlier than most academic texts acknowledge as the pioneers. Similarly, Bronzin independently developed the put–call parity and other pricing schemes.

Yet, the reflections on options started earlier. Weber (2009) also affirms that Proudhon, the famous anarchist founder of the first communist international, published a commissioned manual on speculation through *derivative* trading in 1857. Haug (2009) identifies other authors developing the put–call parity in the Anglo-Saxon world before Bachelier, like Lefèvre in 1874, Castelli in 1877, when the London futures exchange was founded, and Emory in 1896, and before Bronzin, like Higgins in 1902, the arbitrageur Nelson in 1904 and Deutsch in the same year and Holz in 1905. So, these earlier studies focused on speculative and hedging strategies and profits.

Reflections on the Functions of Futures for Capital in the 1910s: Hilferding

From a critical perspective not concerned with how to augment profits, Hilferding did not consider hedge or arbitrage. According to Sotiropoulos (2012) only in the German-speaking world, *derivatives* were seriously discussed at the turn of the twentieth century, by, among others, Hilferding, with Max Weber contributing a few lustrums before. This excludes Bachelier and many others working in the Anglo-Saxon spaces, as mentioned before. Yet, Hilferding (1981) never mentioned *derivatives* in his works. Nor did Max Weber (2000). It is a projection of developments of the last half century onto the overlong past (presentism). The Austrian Marxist discusses solely futures, for both commodities and stocks, with a focus on the former.[3] Sotiropoulos (2012) also affirms that Hilferding's arguments can be generalised, but he does not show why this is indeed the case for options. Only money can provide general features in capitalism. Thus, futures, like any other value, are measured using money, and money represents the value of all commodities, including those not traded on futures exchanges, and capital.

The discussion of commodity futures with contracts held to maturity, on the other hand, makes perfect sense in the context of modern capitalism. Industrial capitals may need a hedge to cope with market instability caused by their very movements. And although it may sound like a futures contract provided the appropriate instrument for the hedge, as suggested by Bryan and Rafferty (2006) in their dollar example, it could be equally achieved by a long-term contract in spot markets. In the futures markets, delivery is unlikely, and cash settlement is the goal of speculators, with M–M′ as the essence of capital.[4]

On the other hand, Sotiropoulos is not clear about how capitalists can know with foresight future spot prices of commodities when they hedge, a point criticised by Keynes in the next subsection. One thing is the fact that futures prices of commodities are known today because there are quotations in the exchanges, reflecting speculative expectations. So, these are futures expected prices. Another completely different thing is to assume that futures prices quoted today will be equal to actual future spot prices, even on average. Hilferding defends that they are speculative and therefore hard to anticipate. So, for producers, hedging is not against any future spot price fluctuation, but against lower future spot prices. If prices go up, futures contracts do not provide hedge but become a hindrance to higher profits. No real capitalist may wish for that, as Sotiropoulos recognises in another passage.

Sotiropoulos also argues that Hilferding understood exchange-traded futures as tools for releasing reserves of balance sheet capital for non-financial firms, to which an average rate of profit accrues. This amount can be accumulated as commodities, not as hedge against price fluctuations, plying a focus on the production and realisation of value.[5] Hilferding thus anticipated an argument mobilised nowadays by *derivatives* advocates (see next chapter).

It is assumed that futures accomplish hedging by transferring all market risks to speculators. Hilferding argues that there are always short and long positions, that is, exposed and hedged values. If speculators are exposed along the entire chain of futures trades related to the original spot transaction, then Hilferding is correct. From the perspective of industrial and commercial capitalists, they are insured as speculators assume the risks. How the risks are further traded does not affect productive capitalists, as long as there are not financial disasters causing credit crunches. If the workers bear the cost of losses by socialisation, on the other hand, sales and profits could be affected.

However, as Sotiropoulos correctly argues, hedging many times entails costs that will divert capital from production to risk management. On the other hand, he does not seem to accredit the huge gearing provided by *derivatives*, minimising the displacement of surplus producing capital from productive circuits into speculative ones. Hilferding places emphasis on risks in the circulation process, on conditions for realisation, not on risks related to the entire valorisation cycle. Yet, considering the circulating capital and its relation to production, there are many production risks, such as foreign exchange risk for producers buying imported parts of circulating capital or exporting commodities, and mainly commodity price risk for domestic inputs and sales. Considering the circuit as a whole, the quantity of money starting as capital may be borrowed, creating interest rate and credit risk under certain conditions.

Thus, Hilferding considered only the risks in the last metamorphosis of commodity into money. Sotiropoulos (2012) equally exposes some important mistakes in Hilferding's discussion of risk premiums. Moreover, many times Hilferding conflates speculation with arbitrage. Sotiropoulos shows that, for Hilferding, positions in futures markets are held by seeking marginal gains by means of price differences that lead to marginal losses of equal magnitude on the other side of the transaction, in a zero-sum game. Losses are borne by outsiders, that is, traders who are not professional speculators. Speculation is seen as a means for stabilising market fluctuations. This is similar to Keynes' views on futures markets.

Commodity Futures and Currency Forwards in the 1920s: Keynes

Keynes, a scholar, policymaker and speculator or practitioner (Accominotti and Chambers, 2016) emphasised the functions of arrangements like forwards for currencies and, like Hilferding, futures for commodities and stocks, not *derivatives*. He made important theoretical contributions in the first half of the twentieth century. The first is about the uncovered interest parity condition and the role of currency forwards in the 1920s, connecting interest rates to expected spot future exchange rates (Keynes, 1923). He argued that deviations from the covered interest rate parity condition, that is, when foreign exchange risks are hedged with forwards, would not cause arbitrage unless the foreign exchange rates differentials and therefore profits associated with capital movements were large enough. He therefore connected two fundamental macro-financial prices, exchange (space) and interest (time) rates, through forward markets, without worrying about how forwards would be priced.[6] Thus, small differences in interest rates between two national circuits of money capital equals the expected change in the value of the national currencies as capital moves between them to valorise and accumulate, plus a small difference.

Fantacci et al. (2010) shows that, in the *Tract* and later in his *Treatise on Money*, in a reflection about transactions that pertain to modern capitalism, since real production is the most important source of valorisation, Keynes anticipated today's textbook treatments of specific arrangements. This scholarly work pictures Keynes thinking before financialised capitalism. He considered, for instance, warehousing, depreciation and other carrying costs. This is the world of real commodities. Speculators do want cash and do not want to assume costs associated with physical commodities.

Keynes assumed that, for food producers, the risk of undesired falling future spot prices requires hedging. And this hedge can be provided by futures contracts in organised exchanges. These arrangements fix the price and avoid reductions but also price hikes that would generate windfall gains. One would guess that speculators like Keynes sell the contracts assuming that spot prices will be higher when the contract expires, so they can buy food at a lower fixed forward price contracted and sell at a higher spot price in the future. The expected windfall gain of risk premiums goes to the speculators.

Yet, most speculators do not want future delivery of physical goods. They want a return settled in cash. Nonetheless, Keynes rejects the general explanation, since it implies that speculators are 'prophets' who can better predict future spot prices. He argues instead that they are risk-bearers, bidding insurance for an asked spread, that is, they earn the risk premium. The producer is willing to accept an expected lower but certain price rather than run the risk of receiving an uncertain but even lower price. This is the ambiguity or uncertainty aversion expressed by the Ellsberg paradox.[7] Thus, the difference between the expected future spot price and the accepted lower than expected price, fixed by futures contracts, is the expected gain of the speculator.

So, Keynes discussed forwards and futures without any reference to *derivatives* or even any attempt at exploiting the differences between them. Commodity options were also employed by him in his speculative activities (Marcuzzo and Sanfilippo, 2016). But swaps could not be conceived. In Fantacci et al. (2010), it is clear that Keynes sometimes conflated forwards with futures. This apparently minor point provides additional evidence that *derivatives* is a recent concept and that for modern thinkers and practitioners, like Keynes, the specific term employed to represent the movements of money is not very important.

Keynes also discussed the parameters for pricing. For him, future expected spot prices have a normal distribution of probability, with an average around the actual future spot price. At maturity, future spot prices are expected to be larger than currently quoted forward prices, on average (Fantacci et al., 2010). In this realm, he also anticipated another current question. For instance, Santos (2008) engages with the issue of prophecy. He considers that quoted future or forward prices at any date are the best rationally expected predictors of future spot prices, unless there are unpredictable forecast errors. Speculators are not clairvoyants, only rational. He also mentions the role of a risk premium. That is, current futures prices might be systematically below the expected future spot price if speculators demand a premium to be the counterparty. So, Keynes suggested a relation without the legerdemain of rational expectations.

Another fundamental theoretical contribution by Keynes and also Hicks is the relationship between quoted forward and expected future spot prices over the time interval from the signing of the contract to the maturity date when spot prices are binding. They may differ to the extent that this theory assumes normal backwardation, that is, the future spot price is always above the forward price, regardless of their individual levels and movements over time (Kawai, 1987). Hence, it is not necessary that future spot prices drop or are expected to drop. As mentioned, this difference is the risk premium, an upper limit to the growth of future spot prices in excess of expected forward prices given producers' acceptance of lower future spot prices. As a consequence, the expected future spot price is equal to the current forward price plus the variable risk premium. Since the risk premium is assumed to be, on average, diminishing but positive, then the future spot price is above the forward price fixed in anticipation. By the same token, backwardation requires that there are more sellers of forwards than buyers.

Backwardation is considered a normal situation by Keynes only when supply and demand are balanced and therefore prices tend to be stable. This assumes uncertainty away and forces the conclusion to be true and speculation always profitable. Hence, the so-called Keynes–Hicks theory of normal backwardation is not Keynesian at all, considering his other works. If there is an excess supply, on the other hand, the current forward price will always be above the lower future spot price, and rather than backwardation, there is a contango. The latter does not make the cost of hedging equal to zero, since the quoted forward price must fall below the anticipated spot price.

Thus, the expected future spot price fluctuates, making predictions more difficult, with increased risks even under conditions of organised futures markets. The current spot price initially falls, given the excess supply, creating room for the forward price to cover carrying costs by the amount of the contango. This makes the forward contracts more expensive, pressing for higher or rising spot prices lest speculators suffer not-yet-socialised losses. Thus, the future spot price must go above the forward price to allow a positive risk premium.

It is interesting to notice that when markets are not balanced, prices fluctuate and forward and futures contracts would be more necessary, but negotiating forwards or futures in this environment is more costly and riskier. As Fantacci et al. (2010) argues, the uncertainty void the strategy of keeping a constant long position in the forward market. The evidence points to profits of long speculators with expected spot price above forward price, even though their books are not usually available to the public. In the case of futures, profits exist for a few commodities.

Yet, backwardation seems difficult to prove empirically. A study cited by Fantacci et al. (2010) found net aggregate losses, but for the period 1925–1932, which includes the beginning of the Great Depression. A different research found, for a longer period, positive risk premiums for long speculators, but only for larger ones. Another test is to assess the trends in future spot prices. If normal backwardation theory is valid, then one should expect rising forward prices as contracts near maturity, since the time interval would become shorter, the probability of large price movements would diminish and therefore the risk premium should fall.

It is also intriguing to consider how the non-ergodicity[8] property could affect this old Keynesian proposition. Keynes assumed that, on average, future spot prices would be equal to average expected prices reflected on present forward prices. This is simply the difference between expected single price today and effective mean price tomorrow, just like adaptative expectations. So, under fundamental uncertainty developed by Keynes in other works, it is not possible to know if forward prices fixed today will be less than expected spot prices based on past averages. Otherwise, expectations converge to future spot price and market opinion can anticipate the future with foresight, not a self-fulfilling prophecy, but a predetermined path, notwithstanding the appeals to stochastic features. This makes forecasting irrelevant.[9]

It is clear that all the past and present intellectual treatments of the arrangements assume uncertainty away and imposes ergodic measurable risks as an intrinsic feature. Arrangements have monetary value because they somehow allow risks to be transferred with a price tag. Yet, there is no market mechanism to put a price on fundamental uncertainty, and many decisions regarding the future still need to be made under situations with no clear knowledge about the economic consequences.

These contributions could be influenced by Keynes' experience with real speculation. Considering specific commodities typical of modern capitalism, many contemporary empirical or historical studies reviewed by Fantacci et al. (2010) show an upward trend for wheat, for instance. In this market, in the years around the Great Depression, there was an excess production and prices fell. Fantacci et al. (2010) declare that wheat markets were organised in the first half of the twentieth century and therefore suitable for futures' standardised contracts. They spotted speculative activities with wheat in the second half of 1937 and speculation theorising based on the former. The authors argue that commodities were very important in Keynes' portfolio. He speculated with shares, currencies of developed countries and commodities, both agricultural, like cotton oil, lard, rubber, wheat, maize and sugar, and minerals like lead, copper and tin. This is not surprising, given that commodities were the single most important reference in futures markets under modern capitalism.

When in charge of King's College investment fund, the Chest Fund, Keynes adopted a more speculative stance, that is, not only conservative investing or hedging. In the decade before the publishing of *The General Theory*, Keynes ran Tilton Company, a financial investment company. In his portfolio, one-third was made up of commodities, mainly wheat forward, in addition to stocks, other securities and currency forwards (Fantacci et al., 2010; Accominotti and Chambers, 2016). In 1936, Keynes purchased forward wheat in values equal to one month of the entire England's consumption. And measured the capacity of the King's College Chapel to have physical delivery and store it (Fantacci et al., 2010). Keynes used limit orders in his speculations, that is, dealt only when prices reached a given value. So, his reflections had both theoretical and empirical foundations.

The Transition from Modern to Contemporary Capitalism: Options Pricing Again

Insomuch as arrangements were not economically and socially important before the 1970s, they could receive only sporadic mentions throughout most of history. Thus, there seems to be a significant gap in the 1940s concerning reflections on the arrangements. The phenomenological picture changed gradually during the transition from modern to contemporary capitalism, as more studies were developed. Santos (2008) provides many references about discussions of futures, not *derivatives*, in the first half of the twentieth century. For instance, he presents historical discussions about the efficiency of futures grain markets in the United States during the nineteenth century. One approach, developed and analysed empirically by Holbrook Working in the 1950s and 1960s, considered the price of storage or what is nowadays called cost of carry. This price reflected physical costs of storage with warehousing and insurance, the financial costs with interest payments, and the convenience yield given by the value of grain inventory.[10] The differential current price of contracts for different future maturities would be explained by the price of storage. If the differential was not equal to that price, then arbitrage in the underlying spot grain market and the futures grain market would cause the difference to disappear.

A study was carried out in the mid-century by Kruizenga, who rediscovered the put–call parity in 1956, and another by arbitrageur Reinach in 1961. Stoll, publishing in 1969, is usually and wrongly acknowledged by contemporary scholars as the first to formulate the put–call parity principle for options. Yet, Haug (2009) argues that the principle was already mentioned, notwithstanding the lack of clarity of ancient texts, to the beginning of the common era 2,000 years ago. And more recently by the beginning of the twentieth century. Nonetheless, looking back at the 1970s, Scholes (1998) ignores completely all the intellectual history of arrangements and declares that financial *derivatives* 'research', not advocacy, was initiated in 1973 by Black, himself and Merton (BSM), but without the label. Financialised capitalism naturalises finance, its circuits and vessels, but, it seems, also colonises its thinking.

So, why is primacy given to BSM in the a-historical literature? Haug (2009) claims that their goal was not to derive the formula, which existed already, but to propose a new derivation of it, starting with dynamic delta hedging or the capital asset pricing model (CAPM). In this new approach, the expected rate of return was no longer a constraint in their risk-neutral valuation. In equilibrium, Black and Scholes argue, the return on a hedged position, being long in an asset and short on another, must be the same as the yield on a riskless asset like treasuries. Haug contends that the continuous dynamic hedging extension relies on unrealistic assumptions, like normal distribution, no price jumping and constant volatility. Furthermore, it is not robust to breaks in these assumptions. It represented a regression.

Saber (1999a) equally criticises the Black–Scholes approach to valuation of *derivatives* (options, actually). He also considers the six assumptions adopted by the model hard to accept. For example, he mentions the absence of a bid–ask spread. How are financial intermediaries supposed to profit if they can only buy and sell at the same price? That is, how a market is supposed to work without transaction costs? He also rejects the traditional assumption of arbitrage implicit in these models.

By the same token, BSM assumed in 1973 that one could replicate an option by delta hedging continuously.[11] Haug (2009) criticises this approach, arguing that continuous static market-neutral delta hedging, in the real world, does not remove all risks by means of risk-free 'manufacturing' options. That is, it is not totally neutral, even if one assumes that no large jumps characterise asset prices. Effective risk reduction requires, according to him, dynamic hedging, to adjust the portfolio by transforming options types in the opposite instrument or puts into calls and calls into puts and so on. Anyway, static delta hedging and its limits were known to traders and authors at the end of the nineteenth century/beginning of the twentieth century but forgotten in the new 'original' formulations.

Also, just like Weber (2009), Haug contends that equations for option pricing were previously developed by authors like Sprenkel in 1961, Boness in 1964, McKean in 1965 and Thorp in 1969. Haug (2009) states that Thorp may have developed it years before he published. So, he may had kept it secret to heap monopolistic profits. Sprenkel stressed an important feature; that stock prices followed a Brownian motion and that before Paul Samuelson assumed it did, based on the work of Bachelier. He also inserted a market risk-aversion in his pricing formula. Boness equally derived a formula anticipating BSM. Additionally, the BSM option pricing formula demands a normal distribution of returns, whereas earlier equations, like the one devised by the mathematician Bronzin, was flexible enough to incorporate different probability distributions, while, at the same time, maintaining the put–call parity.

Usually, the option pricing formulas found in the literature include the following: the difference between the option' strike price and the spot price, a cumulative probability distribution of the previous price difference, weighted in a non-linear way by the time to expiration multiplied by the volatility of the underlying reference price (adjusted difference) and a second term including the volatility, the time to expiration and the normal density function of the previous difference (Haug, 2009, p. 479). Taylor (2010) presents a simpler approach to option pricing, suggesting five inputs and one output, such that the output is defined as a residual. Thus, if the goal is to calculate the premium (output), then the model requires a benchmark rate, the strike price, the expiry date, the volatility and the interest rate related to cost of carry (inputs). If the premium is known, it is possible to calculate the implied volatility and so on.

Considering the reflection about pricing from a practical point of view, or ideas from the capital perspective, Bernstein (2005, p. 331–332) reflects about the initial use of OTC options and futures by its investment firm in the mid-1960s. His discussion about these financial innovations came much later after his experience, as a historian of ideas in favour of capital. He affirms that practitioners did not think systematically about valuing options back then. Rules of thumb were enough. Prices were set intuitively in negotiations. Agents had not theoretical basis for explaining the prices. The only two parameters were time and interest rates. The change came with BSM. He equally stresses that Samuelson had published an article in 1965 about the pricing of warrants. Futures and forwards were thus ignored by that time.

Contemporary, Financialised Capitalism: The Origin of the Concept of *Derivatives*

So, different arrangements persisted as independent tools for most of the twentieth century. The proposal of naming them *derivatives* is a feature of contemporary, financialised capitalism. But this name was not coined right at the start of this new period, happening after a couple of years. Consider, for instance, some works from the end of the 1980s, with swaps already developed. Smith Jr., Smithson and Wilford (1989), for example, address the issue about differentiating the arrangements that make up *derivatives*, but without using this concept. In their discussion (Smith Jr. et al., 1989, p. 14), forwards, futures, swaps and options appear initially to be contrasting instruments. This is reinforced by industry publications and traders transacting in the four separated and specialised subcircuits.

However, for them, the differences are only apparent. The instruments share common properties and there are potential combinations of linkable things, or what they call off-balance sheet 'financial building blocks'. So, they consider the four arrangements together to be not a unique or monolithic construction, but rather independent building blocks that can be linked and combined into complex structures but not yet named *derivatives*. Of course, this seems valid for many other transactions that are not considered *derivatives*. Why limit the eligible blocks? Koppenhaver (2009) adopts a similar view, but with the concept in full use. Anyway, none of those or other perspectives provide a strong demonstration that there is indeed a unifying aspect that could validate the label. It is also important to differentiate between securities and transactions, since they point to fundamental differences. Securities are contracts negotiated in organised and probably liquid markets. Transactions with *derivatives* may not involve securities, for example when forwards are negotiated.

The issue is that they look so different because they are different indeed. It is not just appearance, but reality of specialised use values in specific circuits of finance capital. They can be linked and combined, like many other types of assets or liabilities, since they are measured in money and there is always time and space and variation over time and space. It is not exclusive of these four arrangements. Convertible bonds are combinations of tradeable loans and equity. Furthermore, there is no discussion about the sources of the increased risks that need to be managed and therefore about the necessity of developing specific combinations to cope with them. Different risks existed before and they had to be managed as well, possibly using on-balance sheet combinations. And to the extent that they, although not pervasive as in today's financialised capitalism, were managed, it was not by means of *derivatives*.

More relevant, different *derivatives* supposedly manage risks in specific ways. If an advantage of *derivatives* is flexible risk management at low costs, as argued in Chapter 7, then it is necessary to consider that flexibility lies in the differences. The costs are also different in terms of values and date of payments, since there are premiums paid upfront for options, including the need of reducing cost by zero-cost collars, for example (Saber, 1999b), and futures require margin deposits. Also, it is not clear why complexity should be a valuable attribute, since it creates opacity and pricing difficulties, opening up room for frauds on the one hand (discussed in Chapter 9) and crises on the other (Chapter 8). This means that there are no building blocks in reality, only an imaginary entity that has been dubbed *derivatives*.

Another important issue is that *derivatives* are not geared only to manage risks. They perform different functions, purportedly beneficial for capital also in different ways, as discussed in next chapter. The additional functions performed jeopardise any claim about a unifying role in contemporary financial transactions. Anyway, the argument of Smith Jr., Smithson and Wilford (1989) has important consequences for the historical discussion of the concept. As argued in the previous chapter, the history of these arrangements suggests that they are not overlapping in chronological terms. They came into existence at different points of economic history. The suggestion of combination came after the isolated parts worked independently for decades. The division of operational labour belongs to practitioners. What seems to be common, managing financial risks for capital, is only one among many other functions, some of which are exclusive of single arrangements.

In this regard, the intellectual origin of the particular *derivatives* concept in the English-speaking world, the only language considered in this research, is hard to be located. The *Journal of Derivatives* was created only in 1993. Regarding published books in economics and finance, given that they likely reach a wider audience and can diffuse ideas more effectively, the specific concept seems to have been used only in the early 1990s. Thus, Kolb (1992) is probably one of the oldest books in economics or finance to contain the world *derivatives* in the title. Yet, a brisk analysis of the 44 chapters in the book, made up of previously published works from the preceding years, shows that only one has *derivative* in the title, the piece written by Rubinstein. His chapter is a reproduction of an article published in the *Journal of Economic Perspectives* in the fall of 1987.

Rubinstein's own references are classical works in finance from a neoclassical perspective, but without any work displaying *derivatives* in the title. Of course, this does not mean the concept is not mentioned inside those publications, only that they were still not important to the point of making it to title. The appendix at the end of the chapter refers to "examples of applications of derivative assets analysis". It lists 70 works. However, no one of them has *derivative*(s) in the title. Concerning the use of the concept, he explains that "This paper uses the term 'derivative assets' in place of the common term 'contingent claims' used with some variation in meaning in the academic literature[12]" (Rubinstein, 1992, p.45, marks in the original). This suggests that 'contingent claim' was employed to refer to what today are known as *derivative*(s). As mentioned before, in the third edition of his textbook, Hull (1997) also explains that the two terms were substitutes.

As a consequence, at least by 1987, the terms *derivative*(s), *derivative*(s) securities or *derivative*(s) assets were known to a few scholars specialising in economics and finance, but probably not to the general readership interested in those very topics, besides the practitioners, of course. So, it is necessary to search the occurrence of the concept in previously published material. Following up with Rubinstein, to track a possible continuity, in the index of Cox and Rubinstein (1985), there is no reference to *derivative*(s). In the preface to the book, the authors mention the all-embracing nature of the option's valuation formula of Black and Scholes, deemed able to price different instruments, like warrants and convertible bonds. Yet, they do not lump these pieces of financial wealth together under the label of *derivatives*, if for nothing else because these are option-like securities.

Therefore, it is necessary to search through other general works and also the more specialised literature, even though financial arrangements can be considered technical and specialised in itself. Stoll and Whaley (1985) employs the term *derivative*(s) securities two years before Rubinstein. Thus, it was used in its current meaning back then. Were there previous uses? In 1981, the expression *derivative* market, in the singular, was employed by Moriarty et al., in an outlet with an applied focus. The understanding is that this market, not the instruments traded therein, was derived or induced as a necessary development of another existing markets. Thus, this was probably the oldest published article with *derivative* employed in the body of the text that could be found for this research. But the few references do not have *derivative*(s) in the title.

If the criterion is the publication date, then Moriarty et al. (1981) can be provisorily identified with the pioneer academic use of *derivative*(s) in its contemporary sense. On the other hand, it is worth mentioning that Bick (1982) has *derivatives* assets, pluralised and with a target on the objects traded, in the title. The paper was submitted to the journal in June 1981. And none of the references listed in this article, then again, has *derivative*(s) in the title. But this could be similar to Moriarty et al. In the same year, Dybvig and Ingersoll (1982) made reference to *derivative* (in the singular) assets along the text, contra-posed to primary assets, but the term is not present in the title of any of their references. Since the date of the initial submission was not informed, and probably there were drafts circulating, it could fall on the same class as Bick. Archival research would be necessary to provide exact dates regardless of their quality of being published in academic journals or not.

Finally, and providing additional support to our 'history of *derivatives* thought' hypothesis, that this concept first occurred in the early 1980s, Brennan (1979) came close to using the term *derivatives* in its economic contemporary meaning. However, he referred to its mathematical nature when discussing contingent claims. And his definition of the latter is almost identical to the current definitions of *derivatives* that emphasise the determinants of their value. At any rate, the author probably facilitated the transition from individual, scattered instruments traded in specialised circuits, to an all-embracing, collective name:

> THE ESSENTIAL FEATURE OF modern option pricing theory is the derivation of risk neutral valuation relationships (RNVRs) for contingent claims. A contingent claim is an asset whose payoff depends upon the value of another 'underlying' asset, the value of which is exogenously determined: a valuation

> relationship is a formula relating the value of the contingent claim, or its [mathematical] *derivatives*, to the value of the underlying asset and other exogenous parameter.
>
> (Brennan, 1979, p. 53, caps in the original, italics added)

This further suggests that the term *derivative*(s) was formally introduced in the specialised academic literature after 1979, probably in 1980–1981 if one considers the evidence gathered. So, it is clear that *derivatives* as a concept seem to have started gaining traction among the general educated population of the English-speaking world in 1990s. It is less clear, however, whether non-academic publications, like newspaper and magazines devoted to economics, finance and business, mentioned them in its full-fledged current meaning. It is something that needs more investigation. Notwithstanding this possibility, it seems correct to assess that, despite the rapid growth in the 1980s, it did not draw much ample intellectual attention as a concept. It remained limited and extremely circumscribed to the confines of specialised researchers in economics and finance.

To the extent that economic ideas usually follow material or real developments, it is not reasonable to assume that it took hundreds of years or millennia for scholars to identify and define an ontological phenomenon. The thing was not there, and therefore could be only, at most, suggested as a distant invention or innovation. It seems more intelligible to assume that it took only a few years for researchers to formulate a synthesis, since *derivatives* are not part of contemporary financialised capitalism as a reality, even though particular instruments can be considered at most part of modern capitalism since its beginnings.

Summing Up

This chapter exploited the intellectual treatment of *derivatives*, available only since the mid-nineteenth century and thus invalidating the fifth condition for the existence of pre-capitalist arrangements. Most discussions, and there were not many given the reduced socioeconomic importance of arrangements before the 1970s, were concentrated in the United States and Europe, loci of advanced capitalist development, considering option and futures pricing and the socioeconomic functions of specific arrangements, like futures and forwards.

So, arrangements were discussed, but with different emphasis depending upon the intellectual and professional interests and phenomenological lenses employed. First, the stress was on put–call parity and option pricing around the turn of the twentieth century. Next, the socioeconomic functions and roles of commodities futures gained importance, bearing the imprint of modern capitalism. In the 1920s, the time dimension was emphasised, in the form of arrangements like futures and forwards linking the present and the future. In the next decades, the call–put parity condition regained centrality, with new, but not necessarily better, approaches to pricing.

Then, under contemporary capitalism, the time dimension was subsumed by a hierarchical relationship, with the connection given by the derivation of arrangements after values were increasingly at risks manufactured by the movements of capital. There is time in the sequencing, but, after the circuits for arrangements are formed in an uninterrupted manner, they work simultaneously with spot values and time is only related to cash.

And just like material history, mental history can have a timeline. Under modern capitalism, there are scattered mentions during the Tulipmania. But the first focused thoughts about the arrangements took place at the end of the nineteenth century, with a discussion of options in Europe and United States. It continued with Hilferding and Keynes during the first decades of the twentieth century. More research is needed to identify the most important discussions during the 1930s, with Einzig, and mainly the 1940s, as there is, it seems, a major gap. In the 1960s, there was a renewed interest in option pricing and the put–call parity, culminating in the 1970s with BSM. It finally achieved the zenith under contemporary, financialised capitalism, with the invention of the concept of *derivatives*, a bloc formed by linked arrangements, in the early 1980s. But it is a concept without content.

Notes

1 Schaede (1989) informs that although the CBOT was created in 1848, the records were burned by the Great Chicago Fire (October 1871) and it is not possible to identify the kind of futures transactions carried out before 1871.

2 Once more, it is necessary to correct the claim that the CBOT and the CME were the first futures exchanges, as mistakenly assumed (Taylor, 2010, p. 77)

3 Hilferding (1981) tangled with stock futures in Chapter 8.

4 Sotiropoulos does not criticise the speculators' or finance capital's stance when he agrees that delivery is costly. Production and circulation are costly by definition because direct and indirect labour are not free. Yet, for producers, wholesalers and retailers delivery from suppliers and to customers is obligatory, and they will have to receive and deliver commodities anyway, with or without futures commodities exchanges. The labour used in production and circulation cannot be destroyed or reverted by cash settlement of contracts. So, most *derivatives* contracts (considering notional values) are fictitious in the sense that their paper claims on other previous paper claims exceed the total value created outside of financial circuits. This is equivalent to Marx's analysis of stock exchange swindles. *Derivatives* do not have real underlying as collateral (despite IMF (2009) claims on the contrary), only contractual reference to them. It is also fictitious because it is unconnected to production of values.

5 Milan (2014) argues, contrarily, based on U.S. firm-level data, that *derivatives* do not substitute liquid assets as insurance against market instability.

6 The work of Paul Einzig in the 1930s is also important for modern reflections on foreign exchange forwards.

7 Ellsberg demonstrates the paradox in his paper "Risk, Ambiguity, and the Savage Axioms". He claims that real-world decisions are inconsistent with the subjective expected utility theory exposed by Leonard Savage, a statistician who also came across the works of Bachelier and pointed it to Samuelson. For Ellsberg, decisions are better characterised by an ambiguity aversion, in which choices with quantifiable risks are preferred over those with uncertain or incalculable odds.

8 An ergodic regime is one in which a sample average equals the time or historical average, thus removing uncertainty. This environment is assumed in orthodox theories of market

equilibrium with certainty. However, if the world is non-ergodic, this type of reasoning is not relevant to understand it. The future is not simply an out-of-sample projection of past mean values (Davidson, 1972).

9 Saber (1999a) mentions how Citibank considered the importance of attempting to anticipate the future by means of forecasting. Risk management would thus be only a passive reaction. It is interesting to see a bank that apparently did not trust futures or forwards. Along the same line, he argues that on a given circumstance Deutsche Bank undid all its hedges.

10 See Marthinsen (2018) for a different definition.

11 Static market-neutral delta hedging of a portfolio of options and an underlying asset involves hedging a delta, or the variation in the value of the options when the price of the underlying asset changes. That is, the goal is to neutralise the impact of the variation in an option's price given a movement in the underlying price (see Chapter 3). Haug (2009) discusses works where the same neutral delta hedging can be obtained by means of warrants, another type of option, issued by the company instead of contracts traded on exchanges.

12 He continues: "The term 'contingent claims' is reserved to mean a class of assets (which includes derivative assets) whose payoffs are completely determined by a predefined set of underlying variables." Again, this suggests that financialised capitalism brings into force, within the financial system, a sub-system that includes contingent claims, futures, forwards, options, swaps, CDOs, CLOs and so on.

References

Accominotti, Olivier, and Chambers, David. "If You're So Smart: John Maynard Keynes and Currency Speculation in the Interwar Years." *The Journal of Economic History* 76, no. 2 (2016): 342–386.

Bernstein, Peter. *Capital Ideas: The Improbable Origins of Modern Wall Street*. New York: Wiley, 2005.

Bick, Avi. "Comments on the Valuation of Derivatives Assets." *Journal of Financial Economics* 10, no. 3 (1982): 331–345.

Brennan, Michael J. "The Pricing of Contingent Claims in Discrete Time Models." *The Journal of Finance* 34, no. 1 (1979): 53–68.

Bryan, Dick, and Michael Rafferty. *Capitalism with Derivatives: A Political Economy of Financial Derivatives, Capital and Class*. New York: Palgrave Macmillan, 2006.

Cox, John, and Mark Rubinstein. *Options Markets*. New Jersey: Prentice Hall, 1985.

Das, Satyajit. *Traders, Guns and Money: Knowns and Unknowns in the Dazzling World of Derivatives*. London: FT Press/Prentice Hall, 2006.

Davidson, Paul. *Money and Real World*. London: MacMillan, 1972.

Dybvig, Philip H., and Jonathan E. Ingersoll. "Mean-Variance Theory in Complete Markets." *Journal of Business* 55, no. 2 (1982): 233–251.

Fantacci, Luca, Maria C. Marcuzzo, and Eleonora Sanfilippo. "Speculation in Commodities: Keynes' 'Practical Acquaintance' with Futures Markets." *Journal of the History of Economic Thought* 32, no. 03 (2010): 397–418.

Haug, Espen G. "The History of Option Pricing and Hedging." In: Wolfgang Hafner and Heinz Zimmermann (eds.) *Vinzenz Bronzin's Option Pricing Models*. Berlin/Heidelberg: Springer-Verlag, 2009: 471–486.

Hilferding, Rudolf. *Finance Capital: A Study in the Latest Phase of Capitalist Development*. London: Routledge/Kegan Paul, 1981.

Hull, John. *Options, Futures, and Other Derivatives*. 3rd ed. Upper Sadder River: Prentice Hall, 1997.

International Monetary Fund (IMF). *Balance of Payments and International Investment Position Manual*. Washington, DC: IMF, 2009.

Kawai, Masahiro. "Backwardation." In: John Eatwell, Murray Milgate, and Peter Newman (eds.) *The New Palgrave: A Dictionary of Economics*. London/Basingstoke: The Macmillan Press Limited, 1987.

Keynes, John M. *A Tract on Monetary Reform*. London: MacMillan, 1923.

Kolb, Robert W. (ed.). *The Financial Derivatives Reader*. Miami: Kolb Publishing Company, 1992.

Koppenhaver, Gary. "Derivative Instruments: Forwards, Futures, Options, Swaps, and Structured Products." In: Robert W. Kolb and James A. Overdahl (eds.) *Financial Derivatives: Pricing and Risk Management*. New York: Wiley, 2009.

Marcuzzo, Maria C., and Eleonora Sanfilippo. "Keynes and the Interwar Commodity Option Markets." *Cambridge Journal of Economics* 40, no.1 (2016): 327–348.

Marthinsen, John E. *Risk Takers: Uses and Abuses of Financial Derivatives*. 3rd ed. Berlin: De|G Press, 2018.

Milan, Marcelo. "Macrofinancial Risks and Liquidity Preference." *International Journal of Political Economy* 43, no. 1 (2014): 43–64.

Moriarty, Eugene, Susan Phillips, and Paula Tosini. "A Comparison of Options and Futures in the Management of Portfolio Risk." *Financial Analysts Journal* 37, no. 1 (1981): 61–67.

Rubinstein, Mark. "Derivative Asset Analysis." In: Robert W. Kolb (ed.) *The Financial Derivatives Reader*. Miami: Kolb Publishing Company, 1992.

Saber, Nasser. *Speculative Capital & Derivatives: The Nature of Risk in Capital Markets*. Vol. 2. London: Financial Times/Prentice Hall, 1999b.

Saber, Nasser. *Speculative Capital: The Invisible Hand of Global Finance*. Vol. 1. London: Financial Times/Prentice Hall, 1999a.

Santos, Joseph. "A History of Futures Trading in the United States." *EH.Net Encyclopedia*, 2008. Available at https://eh.net/encyclopedia/a-history-of-futures-trading-in-the-united-states/ Retrieved April 2024.

Schaede, Ulrike. "Forwards and Futures in Tokugawa-era Japan: A New Perspective on the Dojima Rice Market." *Journal of Banking and Finance* 13, no. 4-5 (1989): 487–513.

Scholes, Myron. "Derivatives in a Dynamic Environment." *The American Economic Review* 88, no. 3 (1998): 350–370.

Smith, Jr. Clifford W., Charles Smithson, and D. Sykes Wilford. *Managing Financial Risk*. New York: HarperBusiness, 1989.

Sotiropoulos, Dimitris P. "Hilferding on Derivatives." *The European Journal of the History of Economic Thought* 22, no. 1 (2012): 77–96.

Stoll, Hans R., and Robert E. Whaley. "The New Option Markets." In: Anne E. Peck (ed.) *Futures Markets: Their Economic Role*. Washington, DC: American Enterprise Institute for Public Policy Research, 1985.

Taylor, Francesca. *Mastering Derivatives Markets*. 2nd ed. London: FT/Prentice Hall, 2010.

Weber, Ernst J. "A Short History of Derivative Security Markets." In: Wolfgang Hafner and Heinz Zimmermann (eds.) *Vinzenz Bronzin's Option Pricing Models*. Berlin/Heidelberg: Springer-Verlag, 2009: 431–466.

Weber, Max. "Stock and Commodity Exchange (Die Börse)." *Theory and Society* 29, (2000): 305–338.

7 In Defence of Contemporary *Derivatives*

The Advocacy of Risk Management for Capital and Beyond

Introduction

This chapter provides a brief, critical and non-exhaustive overview of recent, direct and indirect, arguments found in the literature, or deducted logically, favouring the economic and financial benefits for capital provided by *derivatives* and justifying their enormous growth. The assertions are sometimes complements or elaborations and other times additions to the three traditional functions of the arrangements, especially the first one: hedging, arbitrage and speculation. Although the latter represents the most important usage, it is usually not stressed as an advantage. The chapter thus presents new advantages beyond the frequently emphasised claim that, in an environment characterised by heightened volatility not caused by *derivatives*, they play a central role in insuring or hedging against risks, reducing potential losses and thus allowing economic growth, which benefits not only capital. This is deemed the first fundamental function of *derivatives* (Santos, 2008). So, *derivatives* can accomplish many other positive roles for capital, not only managing risks, widening their operational scope.

Indeed, Taylor (2010), for example, agrees that *derivatives* complement traditional transactions. However, the huge notional amounts or gross market values are too large to represent mere complements. They pertain mostly to the core function of *derivatives*: speculation under financialised capitalism. Anyway, some of the new functions are just presented or assumed, not demonstrated. By listing them, on the other hand, at least a preliminary mapping of non-traditional attributes found in the literature can be offered. Other purposes require more operational details, creating a heterogeneous presentation that reflects a sundry treatment received by these "complementary" roles in the literature. Furthermore, in many approaches, a set of benefits is listed, without tracing the connections in a detailed manner and thus considering the functions independent attributes. For example, Culp (2009) lists many supposed social benefits of *derivatives*. He first deals with hedging or risk transfer, the traditional functions. Next, he points to price discovery, also an often-cited role, adding new but not exclusive functions like inter-temporal resource allocation, financing assets, facilitating lending and inventory management and synthetic asset allocation. Are these functions interdependent? Are they derived from one another? Are they mutually reinforcing? It

DOI: 10.4324/9781003137092-8

is not clear. They may be "complements" to non-*derivatives* transactions, but not among themselves.

Regarding the methodology of this chapter, the discussion is based on textbooks and general studies. In this kind of approach, it is possible to emphasise different works and present their arguments in favour of *derivatives*, or to focus on the functions themselves, pointing one or a few works where they can be found. This is the perspective chosen despite the fact that the properties identified are varied among the works selected, but not always deep. So, each section below represents a single or a couple of favourable functions, made explicitly or deducted from the treatments given to *derivatives*. The review tries to assemble similar arguments and functions, but this was not always possible, because the new functions point to different roles, adding to the heterogeneity. Finally, it is worth mentioning that the statements are sometimes made in terms of the collective name, but other times considering the specific arrangements, which may suggest that not all arrangements may perform some of the functions identified. This points to a specialisation that could jeopardise the agglomerative treatment and support the ontological denial of *derivatives* as such.

The chapter starts with a synthesis of traditional arguments in favour of *derivatives*, which points to a revolution in risk management. The second section just warns about the necessity of considering the phenomena, not the names given to the roles. And then the next sections bring forth the other positive functions not related to risks performed by *derivatives* for capital.

The Revolutionary Role of *Derivatives* and Its Advocacy: Risk Management for Economic Growth

The common features of the exegetical *derivatives* literature include, by default, a lack of critical engagement and also one or two complementary defences. One is a justification proper, to circumvent the criticisms or deny their validity. Another one has arguments in favour of their existence due to beneficial functions performed for capital. Some of them were presented in the previous chapters regarding risk management, mainly hedging. A good way to synthesise the literature on these favourable functions is to highlight the most eulogistic ones. The competition to praise *derivatives* is hard, however. The President's Working Group on Financial Markets, a gathering of policymakers working at key monetary and financial governamental U.S. organisations like the Treasury, FED (partially private), CFTC and SEC, provides a good example. In a letter to the speaker of the House of Representatives, they write (PWGFM, 1999, italics added)[1]:

> One of the most *dramatic* changes in the world of finance during the past fifteen years has been the *extraordinary* development of the markets for financial derivatives. Over-the-counter derivatives have *transformed* the world of finance, increasing the range of financial products available to corporations and investors and fostering more precise ways of understanding, quantifying, and managing risk.

Steinherr (2000) compares the revolution in financial risk management brought about by *derivatives* to the industrial revolution. In his view, globalisation is driven by U.S. innovations in risk management and institutions promoting *derivatives* that boost economic efficiency. He asseverates that "The revolutionary *significance of derivatives* lies in the *extended scope*, *greater efficiency* and *lower cost* they provide for risk management, which, in turn, *opens up new activities* considered too risky without these tools" (Steinherr, 2000, p. 8, italics in the original).

Similarly, Dowd (2002) and Miller (1997), among others, defend the existence of a revolution in risk management in the context of increased volatility in financial markets. The lack of critical treatments is clear in Miller (1997). It seems like a financial institution-sponsored book. His exegesis of *derivatives* in the relevant chapters, as the book is mostly a compilation of previously published works and keynote addresses, completely minimises situations in which they could create significative financial dislocations and cause 'disasters' (his ironic marks). This may be named the stability neutrality feature.

The foreword to the book could not be more explicit in terms of the interlocked financial capitalist interests present in orthodox financial market theory.[2] It was written by Thomas Dittmer, co-founder of the commodities and futures brokerage house Refco in New York City.[3] He explains that Miller believed that there were no significative threats of collapse induced by *derivatives* at that time (1997, p. 68). Probably because collapses are always caused by governments, never by 'free' markets. Bernstein (2005), more realistically, argues that financial innovations allow speculators to take risks, not to avoid them, but also without causing financial collapses, reinforcing the stability neutrality.

Miller (1997) therefore downplays the systemic risks of geared *derivatives* positions, assuming that individual risks were well and creatively managed, just like Greenspan believed the same during the subprime collapse. Miller affirms that it is difficult not be get bewitched by the way that swap dealers dealt 'creatively' and 'ingeniously' with credit risks, combining credit management used in the interbank forward markets and clearing houses of futures exchanges (Miller, 1997, p. 36). The role of IAG in the CDS subprime collapse comes to mind. Dittmer reveals the defensive tactics (1997, p. vii, italics added):

> When derivatives are assailed, as they routinely are, especially by regulators and the media, *he* [Miller] *can always be counted on* to point out their value in managing financial risk, in tailoring a risk-return profile, and in price discovery. In all this, he is guided by his appreciation of the marketplace as the final decision maker. This is a key reason *his work has so much value for the financial community*. (…) A more skilled or more *enthusiastic supporter of the derivative industry*, particularly exchange-traded futures, would be hard to imagine.

As mentioned in Chapter 5, Panitch and Gindin (2012), converging with Steinherr (2000), assume that *derivatives*, by managing different types of risks, increase investment opportunities in the global capitalism, deepening the phenomenon. So, it is expected that investment would be relatively larger today than it was before the rise of *derivatives* in the 1970s. Steinherr (2000, p. xvii) equally claims that the economic gains of managing financial risks in particular may not be obvious, although they may be very large. How something that large cannot be apparent is not clear. However, he continues, hedging risks avoids income instability and reductions in consumption. According to him, another advantage of hedging, which should not be equated with *derivatives*, is to reduce the probability of costly bankruptcies. Steinherr makes the strong argument that historically the rhythm of development and progress depend on the capacity of entrepreneurs to manage risks.

In his view, large enough losses could cause insolvency and hence reducing investment and growth. The latter is driven by activities like discovery, innovation, exploring new spaces for resources, establishing trade routes with distant partners, introduce new methods of production and construct infrastructure to support industries. These capital investments require financing and are plagued by financial risks. Managing them means realising the investment plans and causing growth and development.

The six immutable or permanent functions of finance are, according to Steinherr (2000), providing payment services, mobilising resources to fund investment plans, transferring resources between agents, managing risks, offering price information for decision-making and changing incentives to boost efficiency. And, according to the discussion in the sections below, *derivatives* are related to all but the first one, although the arrangements are not permanent (Chapter 5). Yet, the change brought about by *derivatives* regarding managing risks are: identify, isolate, commoditise, price and trade. But it seems overrated. Identifying risks *ex ante,* if it is not only a list of probable risks, assumes a more or less stable environment in terms of previous patterns of volatility and business transactions. Yet, the very nature of volatility under uncertainty makes it a hard task. Exposure can be potential, not effective. And *derivatives* add to the uncertainty. Also, is it possible to completely isolate risks, including basis risk? The very nature of financialised capitalism, with different risks manufactured in large scale, suggests otherwise. What is really new is the commodification of future changes in prices that are named risks just because they cannot be forecast with precision and therefore jeopardises the ability to effectively price and transfer them.

The Novelty of the New Functions Is Not in the Name

The supposed revolution in risk management is associated with hedging. It provides functions like protection or insurance against the effects of market functioning on profits. This can be illustrated by the case of interest rate insurance. A synthetic forward or forward rate agreement (FRA) allows banks to calculate the implicit forward interest rate or the future, and therefore unknown, price of money. It is an example of price discovery, although the interest rate is not necessarily a market rate, but a percentage set by any individual bank or broker for a specific underlying transaction. So, there could potentially exist as many forward rates or attempts at anticipating the future rates as there are loans outstanding, including different rates for the same company depending on the existing credit arrangements in terms of amounts and lengths. In order to reduce the quantity of possible rates, the periods available for forward rates are standardised, making them mass marketable. This allows comparisons for different financial institutions offering FRAs. Non-standard periods typical of other OTC contracts would come at a higher price for money at longer periods.

In an FRA, there is commitment to off-balance sheet notional borrowing and lending, since interest rates must always impinge on real or imagined sums of money. Of course, contrary to cash, it is impossible to delivery interest rates, and the settlement must be made in currency, equal to the difference between the implied forward rate and the benchmark interest rate. The latter used to be the LIBOR, now it is the Secured Overnight Financing Rate (SOFR), which includes a profit margin dependent on the maturity, and then multiplied by the notional amount agreed upon and the proportional period of time.

However, Taylor (2010) recalls that it is impossible to know at the outset who will pay net, that is, the loser, and therefore who will receive net or be the winner, since the future spot benchmark rate is unknown and motivated the creation of an FRA in the first place. The buyer will have an insurance equal to the difference between the two rates. The goal of a FRA should be to avoid the volatile benchmark caused by financialisation, but it is contracted out already. If the benchmark enters the equation again, it is because it is the rate that accrues on the underlying. What is lost/gained on the underlying is gained/lost in the FRA, assuming no changes in basis and in the two positions, that is, in the *derivative* and in the cash market, requiring that all are perfectly matched. That is the meaning of interest rate insurance: it prevents increases in interest expenditures for the borrower in the cash market and therefore increases in interest revenues by lenders in the same market. It fixes the final net interest payment to the existing amounts at the start. Calling it insurance instead of hedging makes no difference. The real novelty must be in the functions performed.

Beyond Risk Management: Alternative Functions of *Derivatives*

Stability Neutrality Restated, Completing Markets and Shielding Firms against Takeovers

The stability neutrality mentioned before is an indirect argument, a reaction to criticisms in face of major *derivatives* failures (see Chapter 8) and thus not a reference to a positive function. According to advocates, instability and financial collapses caused by, or at least with a contribution from, *derivatives*, should not be attributed to the instruments themselves, but to rogue traders and unsupervised transactions. The problem is lack of effective hierarchy. Stulz (2008, p. 48), for example, blames the low-level managers for the disasters. In this case, it would be necessary to explain how such well-paid professionals could get it so wrong so many times. The conclusion that corporations are irrational cannot be avoided.

Stulz argues that, besides choosing inadequate gauges of risk that cause mismeasurement, managers may not communicate their calculations appropriately to superiors. When they do, the top echelons use them to fix the willingness to take risks, but without information they cannot succeed to monitor them and sustain the targeted positions. Of course, if the measures are wrong, not communicating them should be a positive action. Why not pay them with stock options to improve performance, as discussed below?

On the other hand, Steinherr (2000) emphasises risk-sharing, not in terms of hedging, but for completing markets when there are missing risk exposures for non-existing underlying or defending firms against hostile takeovers with stock options or poison pills for current capitalists that dilute control if other capitalists want to force the purchase by following stock- market freedom. The nature of risk changes here: the risk of forced transfer of the ownership over assets and equity.

General, Assumed Benefits: Innovation, Competition, Efficiency, Liquidity, Transparency and More

The PWGFM assembled in 1999 to provide advice regarding financial matters, mainly regulation, in its eulogistic or exegetical role, defended that OTC *derivatives* provide innovations both in products and in settlement and trading and thus should not be regulated (see Chapter 9). The group's appeal to innovation is based on the belief that regulation strangles it. Steinherr (2000) equally emphasises the innovative nature of *derivatives*, but assuming that regulation provides incentives for innovations. Both these points have been dismissed historically (see Chapter 5). Anyway, innovation should be considered only in terms of comparisons with previous periods. It is not *per se* positive, since it must be diffused and adopted.

Like the PWGFM, Stulz (2003) claims that *derivatives* allow firms to innovate and change what they do, to think of new profitable strategies. Financial innovation breeds industrial innovation. He discusses the case of Bombardier. Besides airplanes, the company has a line of snowmobile products. With weather *derivatives*, it can adopt a marketing campaign based on the probability of snowfall. It is not clear if weather *derivatives* can hedge business affected by excess or shortage of snow, however.

It is not only about innovation. When proposing changes to the Commodities Exchange Act to free OTC *derivatives* from any regulation (Chapter 9), the PWGFM report believes that they would promote not only innovation, but also competition, efficiency, liquidity and transparency to OTC markets, while reducing systemic risk, protecting consumers and maintaining U.S. leadership.

General Benefits Suggested: Price Discovery, Financial Growth, Information and Productivity Enhancing

Culp (2009) lists among *derivatives* functions the frequently referred function of price discovery in spot markets. Given the higher liquidity in *derivatives* markets necessary for speculation and gearing necessary to boosting speculative transactions in those settings, it reaches mean values for the arrangements that, to avoid continuous arbitrage, requires corresponding or consistent prices in the spot markets.

This means that prices are discovered in the *derivatives* markets and transmitted to spot markets for the underlying, even if the volume of transactions is relatively reduced in the latter. The prices are actually imposed on the spot or underlying markets by speculation. This is not discovery, since the future is unknown and the expected prices are guesstimates.

On the other hand, Scholes (1998) claims that *derivatives* add net value to customers of financial firms. The benefit is explained indirectly by using as evidence the rapid growth of their markets. They could not grow if they were not useful. By this reasoning, financial bubbles are good as long as they never pop, which is impossible. By its turn, Santos (2008) argues that futures are seen as an efficient collateral because the required margins cost less than the inventory value in the case of commodities and assets (see also Culp 2009). Are *derivatives* definitively needed to hedge? They may not, but when they are used, they are supposedly the cheapest alternative, which could explain the efficiency feature. He underlines another function, the third fundamental one: provide information about market's expectations of future economic events. Gelderblom and Jonker (2005) claim that *derivatives* increase productivity, an argument also defended by Steinherr (2000), although the causal mechanisms are not clear. It has to go through increases in non-financial capital accumulation.

International Reserves, Capital Raising, Releasing and Replacing

The IMF (2009) allows *derivatives* to be kept as international reserves. This supposedly provides protection against international volatility and boils down to hedging. Yet, it may not be a substitute for foreign exchanges if central banks have huge exposures to multiple currencies. Moreover, they can be used for speculative reasons, contributing to international instability, as the sub-prime collapse shows.

Derivatives allow capital raising, as investor are more willingly to sponsor business whose financial exposures are hedged with *derivatives* (Culp 2009; Santos 2008; Scholes 1998). This implies that speculators hardly get sponsored by any means. Santos (2008) argues that another important purpose of commodity futures markets, equating them with *derivatives*, or the second fundamental function, is to allow firms to acquire operating capital, that is, short-term loans for financing the acquisition of intermediate goods like grains or oil, including whole inventories. In line with Scholes, he argues that lenders are more inclined to finance, at lower rates that implies efficiency, inventories insured against risks.

Circumventing regulation and releasing tied up capital are two functions welcome by *derivatives* advocates. This is the argument in Miller (1997) and Steinherr (2000) presented in Chapter 5, which proves the PWGFM wrong. Operationally, Taylor (2010) discusses how, in order to anticipate a future interest rate and hence avoid uncertainty, a bank could create a synthetic forward on balance sheet. This is done by borrowing long in the wholesale cash market and depositing the proceeds in the same market for a short period before the settlement date, which implies pre-lending. That is, the deposits are made when the benchmark interest rate is fixed and the discounted payout can be made. The bank could lend it short to debtors in retail markets for the remaining of its contract, that is, in usually three, six or 12 months or for the near future, never today, until maturity. She shows how this strategy, despite the fact that it allows the bank to 'discover' (actually offer) the price of money or the implied forward interest rate, immobilises credit lines and implies extra capital for adequacy requirements. Thus, to avoid costly regulations and increase profits, banks invented the FRA, or OTC forward, to fix the forward interest rate without on balance sheet commitments.[4] This is in line with Steinherr's (2000) and Miller's (1997) argument that regulation fosters innovations and Hilferding's view that exchange-traded futures can release productive capital (see Sotiropoulos 2012 in Chapter 6).

Therefore, on top of bringing new capital to the circuit of accumulation and valorisation, by tearing risks apart, *derivatives* can also, according to its defenders, free up capital. Stulz (1996) goes as far as to claim that proper risk management can replace equity capital. This is because hedging financial exposures obviates the necessity of equity for supporting the business activities. This necessarily has a secondary effect on the gearing space for capitalist units, in addition to the intrinsic *derivatives*' capacity of increasing exposures with reduced amounts of capital. In Chapter 9, other possible consequences of releasing capital by changes in *derivatives* regulation are discussed.

Yet, Bernstein (2005, p. 332) offers a different view for writers of American call options. He affirms that, since the call could be exercised at any time before maturity, his investment counselling firm had to guarantee delivery of shares to option buyers. So, this tied up the firm's capital and cost it interest income lost. At the same time, the buyers could earn interest until the time to decide to exercise or not the option. *Derivatives* do not favour all capitals the same way.

Thus, some *derivatives* could also be used to increase capital and therefore enlarge investment or speculative opportunities. Firms may not engage in investment if it is not, or less, profitable. Since profits are the difference between revenue and costs, *derivatives* could increase the former or reduce the latter. But since they are zero-sum games, the losses could bring investments down in a proportional way to gains boosting investments. An important issue here is about concentration of revenues in large financial institutions (shown in Chapter 4), whose investments cannot compensate for less intense capital accumulation in the non-financial sector. Another relevant issue is that losses could be distributed among many financial capitalist firms, such that they could be considered individually immaterial. This is the supposed advantage of sharing risks.

This function of making sums of money available does not discriminate between the different types of capital that may be attracted and the functions that it will perform. Instead of enticing capital that can be applied to activities as a way to boost effective innovation, productivity and welfare, as it replaces less productive capital, *derivatives* may facilitate the operation of speculative capital, as argued by Saber (1999), but destroying all different types of wealth during crises.

Scholes (1996) mentions that *derivatives* also facilitate investing in securities. That is, finance capital boosts fictitious capital. Since securities have many different types and levels of risks, this means that *derivatives* are, contradictorily, risk management tools and risk-taking instruments as they allow hedging and speculation in the same transaction. Of course, this contradiction is entirely about contemporary, financialised capitalism.

Eliminating Maturity and Flow Mismatches, Flexibility and Market Integration

Eliminating mismatches between assets and liabilities is another supposed advantage of *derivatives*. Goodman and Fabozzi (2002, p. 1) discuss the constitution of a collateralised debt obligation (CDO) as an illustration. This derived security is 'backed' by a diversified pool of underlying or assets, including bonds, other asset-backed securities, like mortgages, real estate investment trusts and bank debt.[5] The underlying assets serve as collateral to the debt obligations issued by the sponsor to finance the acquisition of the former. Past the non-call period, the assets can be liquidated to pay down debt tranches, since the debt obligations are structured in hierarchical layers, and unwind the embedded *derivatives* positions.

In an arbitrage transaction, the sponsor earns the spread between assets and structured liabilities. That is, interest and principal in the case of cash flow transaction or the total return from active management of the collateralised assets in the case of market value transactions. *Derivatives*, actually interest rate swaps, enter the picture as embedded instruments because the collateral assets may be long-term coupon bonds, yielding a fixed rate, whereas the senior tranche, usually the largest share of the debt structure, may depend on floating rates like the SOFR. Then the CDO pays a fixed long rate and receives the short floating one, configuring a mismatch. The swap eliminates the differences in expenses and income, using the value of the senior tranche debt as the reference for the notional value and payouts.

It is important to notice that exposures to credit risks always exist, despite the fact that credit *derivatives* are available. Risks are present even when the backing assets are not purchased. Resuming the discussion about the different types of risks (Chapters 2 and 3), Goodman and Fabozzi (2002) brings new aspects, dividing credit risk into default, or the risk that the issuer fails to make timely payment of interest and amortisation of the principal, credit spread or the risk of a devaluation in the issuer's debt due to an increase in the credit spread, and downgrade, or the risk that the issuer is downgraded by a rating agency. Thus, another function performed by *derivatives*, in line with Culp (2009), and credit default swaps in particular, is to allow the institutions to synthesise a CDO when the pool of collateral assets are not owned, but the security has the credit risk exposure of those assets transferred to it. In both cases, the *derivatives* have the legal priority over the other liabilities in the structure, showing the political power of the large issuers of *derivatives*, or banks.

It is also worth remembering that pledging collateral was considered a step in the evolution of risk management by Steinherr (2000) (Chapter 5). This requires a qualification of *derivatives* as the last step in this historical development of capitalist risk management. Collateral has not, perhaps, lost relative importance, but it may have become more difficult to evaluate its role under financialised capitalism. In CDOs *derivatives* are complements to collateral. This means that there are many transactions for which they cannot provide stand-alone hedging services. And, finally, it goes without considering the fact that *derivatives* can be used for speculative purposes.

On that same thread, Steinherr (2000) shows how natural hedges could occur in banking with the support of *derivatives*. Banks have a mismatch between long-term, fixed interest rate assets and short-run, floating rates liabilities, with the latter rates generally exceeding the former. This can create a negative interest rate exposure. Asset and liability management would need increasing the long-term assets, with government bond purchases for example, or decreasing the quantity of floating rate liabilities. *Derivatives* provide an alternative way to hedge the liability risks at a lower cost without changing the balance sheet composition. However, Saber (1999) argues that even when assets and liabilities are perfectly matched, their prices can change differently and lead to substantial losses, as in the case of Bank One in 1994. And when this happens, basis risk becomes an insoluble problem.

Although a blunt critic of *derivatives*, Saber understands that they have an important attribute: flexibility. Actually, this could be the synthesis of all different benefits listed in this chapter. *Derivatives* have many different uses for capital that cannot be captured by the three traditional functions. For example, by facilitating capital flows, a result of capital raising or releasing, they allow the linking of different markets around the world, melting them into a large space for valorisation and accumulation of capital. The new functions are interrelated.

Elastic Volume of Transactions

In the foreword to Peck (1985a), the then President of the American Enterprise Institute, William J. Baroody Jr., highlights specifically the introduction of trading in financial futures and their extraordinary growth.[6] He argues that, between 1970 and 1984, the volume of futures trading increased more than tenfold. And that by the end of 1984 financial futures accounted for 50% of total trading. Magdoff and Sweezy (1987, p. 22) present a chart showing an index for the industrial production in the United States slopping upwards between 1960 and the mid-1980s, from about 50 to around 120. Over the same period, the volume of futures trading, measured by the Futures Trading Association, skyrocketed from an index close to 10 to one reaching 370.

Notwithstanding the affirmation of Scholes (1998), what economic benefits this futures growth had provided indeed? An increase in industrial output? So, an indirect and somehow inverted argument, is that an elastic volume of *derivatives* transactions, which are easy to achieve given their low costs, could potentially enhance a large growth of industrial activity, by raising, releasing or replacing capital or with the introduction of new industrial products. Or just hedging different types of risks. Again, the new roles are somehow intertwined. It is not clear what would happen in the absence of *derivatives*. This is another theme for historians. On the other hand, the Golden Age happened before the explosion of *derivatives*. And industrial output could be higher without transfers of profits to the financial sector typical of financialisation.

Regarding this comparison, it is important to keep in mind that total industrial output flows may not be the proper gauge to compare to futures performance, and the latter may not be the best gauge of financialised capitalism in general and *derivatives* in particular in the United States. Considering risk management only, it worth noticing first that not all industrial production is exposed to commodity, equity, credit, interest rate or exchange rate risks. The fractions of industrial capital with some exposure would be more appropriate to compare at first. Second, however, even the capital portion with risk exposures may not use futures to hedge. Third, exchange-traded futures are only a small part of the new financial arrangements developed since the 1970s that explain the financial explosion.[7] Fourth, a fraction of the agricultural production and mainly financial services may also be affected by volatility. Fifth, notional underlying values are not transferred or transacted, being only used as reference for calculating payments at settlement. But it is a good approximation of *derivative* activity nonetheless.

Yet, rather than an elastic supply of effective arrangements, the difference could suggest a lack of compass between the production of goods and financial flows and stocks under a sub-system of the financialised capitalism. At any rate, this quantitative growth has as a consequence a qualitative change in the nature of capitalism, that is financialised, driven by very short-term gains and returns and crisis-prone, not stability neutral as claimed above. Thus, the growth of industrial production and even faster futures trading could be a spurious correlation. It seems more like speculation outpacing production. That is, if economic growth is missing, *derivatives* growth is not. The revolution has faded away.

Besides the rapid growth of *derivatives* in the 1980s, it is also interesting to point out that Magdoff and Sweezy (1987) show a strong growth of debt for all different institutional sectors (households, financial and non-financial corporations and government) over the same period. In Minsky's view, since income has not grown at the same rate, then the agents are assuming more speculative and Ponzi positions (Minsky, 1975, 1982, 1986). This means that more agents were potentially exposed to interest rate risks, foreign exchange risks or credit risks. Has the economy become more resilient to these risks due to *derivatives*? Actually, the economy developed a fragility and an intensified propensity to crises. The U.S. stock market crashed in 1987. According to the FDIC (1997), the number of banking failures skyrocketed in the 1980s and early 1990s. Also, the number of household/consumer bankruptcies accelerated in the mid-1980s. Were they all not hedged?[8] No, since hedging is for capital and may not work.

Reduced Transaction Costs, Specialisation and Economies of Scale

It has been argued that transaction costs are reduced by *derivatives*, which is also related to efficiency. But it is not clear whether this decrease is absolute or relative. The reduction could be valid if one transaction only were necessary to hedge during a long period. Since this cannot be true under financialised capitalism with volatility created continuously, including also the contribution of *derivatives*, the relevant cost cannot be per one transaction, since they are mostly for the very short run. Hence, transaction costs are entailed by a frequent necessity of managing risks. So, as important as the notional value or the gross market value, it is the turnover of the number of transactions or contracts (adjusted for duplicities).

If hedging requires additional hedges to match positions and avoid exposures, every subsequent transaction entail transaction costs (fees). The frequency of transactions requires continuous hedging and continuous flows of expenses. And the frequency is also explained by the fact that *derivatives* cause increased volatility in the first place. By the same token, there are cost differences in terms of specific arrangements. Moriarty et al. (1981, p. 61) synthesises both issues, comparing the case of futures to options and how more costly hedging is with the latter. Of course, a single futures transaction may not be enough if contracts are short and have to be rolled over:

> a single futures position can neutralize exposure in the underlying asset. Accomplishing the same hedge with options requires either simultaneous put and call transactions in three separate markets (assuming put-call-futures parity), or so-called 'delta' hedging (which entails continuous adjustments, hence significant transactions costs).

And other costs are reflected in the time value of contracts, the difference between the premium and the intrinsic value of options, which accounts for cost of carry, for example. Here the issue of scale in the performance of traditional functions mentioned by Taylor (2010) in Chapter 2 becomes clear and connects with the elastic volume of transactions. Banks and other financial institutions have dedicated personnel with advanced technology taking care of risk management and, mainly, speculation and arbitrage. On its 2006 first quarter report on bank *derivatives* activities,[9] with the sub-prime on the making, the Office of the Comptroller of the Currency (OCC, 2006) declares (p.1, italics added):

> Bank supervisors normally have concerns about when a market or product sector is so heavily concentrated. In the case of derivatives activities, however, the OCC has fewer concerns about the concentration in activity and exposures, because the business of structuring, trading, and managing the full array of risks in a portfolio of derivatives transactions is *highly specialized. Very few institutions have the resources, both in personnel and technology, to support the requisite risk management infrastructure.* As a result, derivatives activity is appropriately concentrated in those few institutions that have made the resource commitment to be able to operate the business.

So, a banking oligopoly in *derivatives* is not a problem for captured regulators. The volume of transactions justifies the huge notional values due to economies of scale. Banking concentration causes an increased value of transactions and also of notional values, reducing costs per unit or transaction. But it creates an enormous amount of fees along the chain. In the macro scale, this is the social cost of market volatility. Who pays for it?

Alignment of Incentives by Executive Compensation

Another important function identified for specific arrangements within *derivatives* is to complement business executives pay-checks (Supanvanij and Strauss 2010). Corporations can offer compensation packages that include call options to supposedly align interests between top managers or agents and capitalists or principals. Thus, if a corporation has an expected fat return, its stocks will have a higher price, and so will the corresponding call options with lower strike prices. The executives will exercise their right to buy and purchase the stocks, becoming capitalists along the way. On this issue, The IMF (2009, p. 96) distinguishes between conventional options as *derivatives* to 'trade risks' and options as pay:

> Employee stock options are options to buy the equity of a company, offered to employees of the company as a form of remuneration. (...) Employee stock options have similar pricing behavior to financial derivatives, but they have a different nature – including arrangements for the granting and vesting dates – and purpose (i.e., to motivate employees to contribute to increasing the value of the company, rather than to trade risk). If a stock option granted to employees can be traded on financial markets without restriction, it is classified as a financial derivative.

Would it be different if the stocks themselves were given out instead of options? Why would executives want their received stocks to lose value but not their call options on the same stocks? Anyway, who collects the premium in the case of call options? Besides the questions raised by the instrument, the point is that arrangements can play different roles, not always related to risks.

Summing Up

Based on this chapter analysis, one might wonder: what *derivatives* cannot accomplish? Given all the supposed advantages and benefits identified, and they are not exhaustive at all, and possibly reflected in their market size, considered by Scholes to be evidence of their prowess, just like the growth of slave trade demonstrates that slavery can only be a terrific enterprise, it is hard to believe that the arrangements have not promoted higher investments and growth in the global capitalist economy since the 1970s. Thus, investment is lower today. Of course, it could be still lower without the marvels of *derivatives*. The secular stagnation would be a secular recession. *Derivatives* are the saviours of capitalism.

Since the survey in this chapter is not ample, it is possible that many benefits could still have not been spotted, just like financial and economic history could not identify *derivatives* (Chapter 5). New research is necessary to exhaust all the positive adjectives found in the dictionaries. Hence, not pretending to be complete, we could list 41, besides the traditional three, that require many other specialised functions and that could be qualified in terms of ingenuity or creativity: providing inter-temporal resource allocation, financing assets of all types, facilitating lending and inventory management, synthesising assets or other stocks, understanding, structuring and quantifying risks, extending the scope or range of financial products, increasing efficiency, lowering costs, including transaction costs, opening new risky activities, managing credit, offering stability neutrality, tailoring risk-return profiles, discovering prices, globalising U.S. capitalism by opening new investment opportunities, smoothing out income and consumption, avoiding costly bankruptcies, risk-sharing for completing markets or avoiding takeovers, supplying competition, liquidity, and transparency, reducing systemic risk, protecting consumers, maintaining U.S. leadership, allowing innovation in products and in settlement and trade, productivity enhancing, pledging efficient collateral, informing about market expectations, increasing international reserves, circumventing regulation, capital raising, releasing immobilised capital, replacing equity, eliminating maturity and flows mismatches, flexibility and market integration, providing elastic transactions, providing specialised services with economies of scale and aligning incentives of agents and principals. As a consequence of all these advantages, *derivatives* have grown fast.

Thus, despite the existence of redundancies and overlays, there are more than 40 reasons to support *derivatives*. However, this would be a biased conclusion, since the private and social costs, to use the lingo of orthodox economics, related to them and with only a few scratched in this chapter, are either dismissed, downplayed or ignored. To make a fair judgement, the problems caused by *derivatives* must be considered. That is the task of next chapter.

Notes

1 The reference to the interval 1984–1999, along with the remark about 'the development of the markets' is another indirect evidence against the eternal *derivatives* view (see Chapter 5). And the reference to corporations and investors makes it clear that *derivatives* are instruments for capital.

2 Scholes (1998) also mentions conducting 'research' (my ironic marks), paid by Wells Fargo Bank.

3 That author must be taken with great care on moral grounds. According to MarketsWiki (www.marketswiki.com/wiki/Thomas_H._Dittmer, accessed on May 25, 2024), Dittmer had important political connections in Washington, D.C. The website reports that he won a pardon for his stepfather Ray E. Friedman, also a founder of Refco, a large futures commission merchant, when the latter was convicted for fraudulent sales of chickens to the U. S. Army in the 1950s. It also informs that "Refco was one of the most fined firms in the history of the futures industry. In 1979, it was fined a then-record $250,000 by the Chicago Mercantile Exchange, and Dittmer received a six-month trading suspension". And that in 1999 "(…) the firm paid a $8 million fine to the CFTC for accusations it helped manipulate customer accounts." In that same year, "(…) Refco also suffered from customer defaults and Dittmer supposedly made a deal with Edwin L. Cox, a Texas businessman who was convicted of bank fraud and pardoned by U.S. President George H. W. Bush, to help restore the business." Finally, MarketsWiki states that "Dittmer was one of several Refco insiders who were sued by the Refco Litigation Trust for $400 million." Dittmer retired from Refco in 1999. The firm went bankrupt in 2005 after an accounting

fraud. It is important noticing that Refco is not an exception. See also Frunza (2016a; 2016b), CFTC (n.d.e) and Chapter 9 of this book.

4 Actually, Goodman and Fabozzi (2002) shows that a collateralised debt obligation (CDO), a structured *derivative* not emphasised in this book, motivated by the goal of removing debt from balance sheet, could accomplish the same goal and reduce the capital adequacy requirements.

5 The IMF (2009, p. 87) explains that CDOs and other similar asset-backed securities or structured finance represent a securitisation of illiquid assets and thus provides liquidity necessary for tradability. They basically repackage existing assets "into new instruments that are structured to meet the liquidity, creditworthiness, and return preferences" of investors. So, they are not part of the plain vanilla arrangements, adding layers of financial capital that become the underlying. *Derivatives* are no longer derived (see Chapter 6).

6 Again, this reinforces the argument against the eternal *derivatives* view discussed in Chapter 5.

7 As shown in Chapter 4, the collection of *derivatives* data by the BIS started around that time. The OCC has information about banks' use of *derivatives* starting in 1990. Futures have been a less important instrument in *derivatives* markets, much less than swaps.

8 One would expect an increased amount of credit *derivatives* under such circumstances, since bankruptcy is the nullification of the capacity to pay back. However, these instruments were introduced only in 1993, for commercial loans motivations. Was regulation not stiff enough to promote innovation in the 1980? As mentioned, deregulation started right in the 1980s.

9 The OCC repeats some conclusions verbatim in many reports.

References

Bernstein, Peter. *Capital Ideas: The Improbable Origins of Modern Wall Street*. New York: Wiley, 2005.

CFTC. *History of the CFTC: CFTC History in the 2000s*, n.d.e. Available at: www.cftc.gov/About/HistoryoftheCFTC/history_2000s.html Retrieved August 2024.

Culp, Christopher. "The Social Functions of Financial Derivatives." In: Robert W. Kolb and James A. Overdahl (eds.) *Financial Derivatives: Pricing and Risk Management*. New York: Wiley, 2009.

Dowd, Kevin. *Measuring Market Risk*. Chichester/West Sussex: Wiley, 2002.

Federal Deposit Insurance Corporation (FDIC). *History of the Eighties: Lessons for the Future. Vol. 1, An Examination of the Banking Crises of the 1980s and Early 1990s*. Washington, DC: FDIC, 1997.

Frunza, Marius-Christian (ed.) *Introduction to Theories and Varieties of Modern Crime in Financial Markets*. Oxford: Academic Press/Elsevier, 2016b.

Frunza, Marius-Christian (ed.) *Solving Modern Crime in Financial Markets: Analytics and Case Studies*. Oxford: Academic Press/Elsevier, 2016a.

Gelderblom, Oscar, and Joost Jonker. "Amsterdam as the Cradle of Modern Futures Trading and Options Trading, 1550–1650." In: William N. Goetzmann and K. Geert Rouwenhorst (eds.) *The Origins of Value: The Financial Innovations that Created Modern Capital Markets*. Oxford: Oxford University Press, 2005.

Goodman, Laurie S., and Frank J. Fabozzi. *Collateralized Debt Obligations: Structures and Analysis*. New York: Wiley, 2002.

International Monetary Fund (IMF). *Balance of Payments and International Investment Position Manual*. Washington, DC: IMF, 2009.

Magdoff, Harry, and Paul Sweezy. *Estagnation and Financial Explosion*. New York: Monthly Review Press, 1987.

Miller, Merton. *Merton Miller on Derivatives*. New York: Wiley, 1997.

Minsky, Hyman. P. *Can It Happen Again? Essays on Instability and Finance*. Nova York: M. E. Sharp, 1982.

Minsky, Hyman. P. *John Maynard Keynes*. Nova York: Columbia University Press, 1975.

Minsky, Hyman. P. *Stabilizing an Unstable Economy*. New Haven, CT: Yale University Press, 1986.

Moriarty, Eugene, Susan Phillips, and Paula Tosini. "A Comparison of Options and Futures in the Management of Portfolio Risk." *Financial Analysts Journal* 37, no. 1 (1981): 61–67.

Office of the Comptroller of the Currency (OCC). "Quarterly Report on Bank Trading and Derivatives Activities, First Quarter." 2006. Available at: www.occ.gov/publications-and-resources/publications/quarterly-report-on-bank-trading-and-derivatives-activities/files/pub-derivatives-quarterly-qtr1-2006.pdf Retrieved June 2024.

Panitch, Leo, and Sam Gindin. *The Making of Global Capitalism: The Political Economy of American Empire*. London: Verso, 2012.

Peck, Anne E. (ed.) *Futures Markets: Their Economic Role*. Washington, DC: American Enterprise Institute for Public Policy Research, 1985.

President's Working Group on Financial Markets (PWGFM). "Over-the-Counter Derivatives Markets and the Commodity Exchange Act." 1999. Available at: https://home.treasury.gov/system/files/236/Over-the-Counter-Derivatives-Market-Commodity-Exchange-Act.pdf Retrieved June 2024.

Saber, Nasser. *Speculative Capital: The Invisible Hand of Global Finance*. Vol. 1. London: Financial Times/Prentice Hall, 1999.

Santos, Joseph. "A History of Futures Trading in the United States." *EH.Net Encyclopedia*, 2008. Available at https://eh.net/encyclopedia/a-history-of-futures-trading-in-the-united-states/ Retrieved April 2024.

Scholes, Myron. "Derivatives in a Dynamic Environment." *The American Economic Review* 88, no. 3 (1998): 350–370.

Scholes, Myron. "Global Financial Markets, Derivative Securities, and Systemic Risks." *Journal of Risk and Uncertainty* 12, (1996): 271–286.

Sotiropoulos, Dimitris P. "Hilferding on Derivatives." *The European Journal of the History of Economic Thought* 22, no. 1 (2012): 77–96.

Steinherr, Alfred. *Derivatives – The Wild Beast of Finance: A Path to Effective Globalisation?* New York: Wiley, 2000.

Stulz, René M. "Rethinking Risk Management." *Journal of Applied Corporate Finance* 9, no. 3 (1996): 8–24.

Stulz, René M. *Risk Management and Derivatives*. Mason, OH: South-Western/Cengage Learning, 2003.

Stulz, René M. "Risk Management Failures: What Are They and When Do They Happen?" *Journal of Applied Corporate Finance* 20, no. 4 (2008): 39–48.

Supanvanij, Janikan, and Jack Strauss. "Corporate Derivative Use and the Composition of CEO Compensation." *Global Finance Journal* 21, no. 2 (2010): 170–185.

Taylor, Francesca. *Mastering Derivatives Markets*. 2nd ed. London: FT/Prentice Hall, 2010.

8 Trial by Its Financialised Essence

Derivatives Guilty of Speculation, Instability and Debacles

Introduction

As shown in Chapter 7, many accounts of *derivatives* found in the conventional literature are overly laudatory. Thus, their apologists were on the defensive following the financial crash of 2007–2008, a major indictment of *derivatives*. Although this was not the first nor the last crisis associated with the arrangements and their speculative drive, they were astonished anew by the assault that *derivatives* received for the collapse, fearing responses like Dodd–Frank (discussed in Chapter 9). And then they rushed to defend *derivatives* and the economic interests behind them, as they usually get paid to do, appealing to false explanations: the problem was not *derivatives* themselves, but those who misused them.

In this second line of defence, which does not ignore collapses, *derivatives* are stability-neutral. So, the criticisms to the instruments, and not to the agents, are misguided. The problem is conjunctural and behavioural, not endemic or systemic. Nonetheless, *derivatives* seem to be able to accomplish many things, but not to hedge against mismanagement, even with stock options. Also, it is assumed that rogue traders would find other means to be harmful if the arrangements known as *derivatives* did not exist. This seems correct. Follies, and financial follies in particular, have been a hardy perennial of capitalism. So, the portfolio of crash-the-economy arrangements was enlarged.

But speculation is inevitable within the *derivatives* sub-system, since the exclusive occurrence of natural hedges is unlikely most of the time and perhaps all the time. Absent natural hedges, speculation is necessary. So, hedge may need speculation, but speculation does not need a corresponding hedge. The point, therefore, is to consider how problems created many times with the fundamental contribution of *derivatives*, can be solved by *derivatives* themselves, as they add destructive power to the arsenal of crisis-inducing tools and magnify intrinsic trends. To answer this question, it is necessary to acknowledge that *derivatives* create new difficulties that did not exist before. They perform socially negative functions that are not considered in the cost calculations of efficiency.

Hence, unlike the previous chapter, in which some favourable arguments for *derivatives* were put in doubt, this one briefly surveys a non-exhaustive sample of arguments against *derivatives*, including the hedging function as compared to

DOI: 10.4324/9781003137092-9

pervasive speculative roles. As mentioned, these assessments are either ignored or dismissed as wrong-headed. The chapter also presents situations of *derivatives* failures and financial crises or losses associated with them. It provides evidence that, despite their volume, or because of it, the usage of *derivatives* cannot prevent major financial collapses, or at least to distribute the existing risks to a large number of capitals in such a way as to make on-balance sheet devaluations or corresponding losses systemically irrelevant, and that it can contribute to substantial economic and financial losses. This is expected if one considers the intrinsic instability of capitalism and how *derivatives* enhance it.

Derivatives add a net and significant layer of instability on top of other speculative tools, which affects uncertainty and cannot be quantified and reduced to risk. And they could create additional disorder by fabricating an unstable environment or a sub-system that could not exist without them, including the promise of solutions. The magnitude of total notional amounts is intrinsically and systemically risky and destabilising. That is, even if *derivatives* could be mobilised a priori entirely to risk management functions, the recognition that part of the risks to be managed may only exist due to them nullifies the assumption. That is, *derivatives* are not passive arrangements that, in a context of exogenous instability in a given institutional setting, provide tools to cope with risks created by other market mechanisms. Even in the absence of frauds, the combination of large-scale gearing, speculation and capital interconnectedness within and between different circuits is always the key to fragility, instability and crises.

Systemic, sectoral, conglomerate and individual risks are, in part, derived from the lack of correspondence between underlying and *derivatives* positions. Notional values or gross market values do not match the underlying exposures. Even after adjusting for offsetting positions, the values in the *derivatives* circuits are still much larger than other financial and economic stocks and flows in other circuits or even all circuits. Therefore, it cannot be about hedge. It is purely fictitious capital seeking valorisation. Scholes (1998) for instance argues that financial firms need (do they?) to hedge only a residual risk, far smaller than the gross amounts contracted out with clients. Thus, since the amount of *derivatives* is netted out of counterparts offsetting positions, much larger than the total value of wealth or income flows at risk, financial firms are trading and earning speculative profits with the arrangements, not hedging.

Moreover, the forecasting industry has not faded with the growth of *derivatives*. If they were effective instruments, the market pricing of the future, or discovery, would make forecasting irrelevant. As consequence, the main contribution of *derivatives* seems to be the strengthening of financialisation that caused the occurrence of severe macro-risks in the first place. It changes the return structure of assets, reinforcing the rapid accumulation of financial wealth to earn financial incomes in detriment of real capital accumulation. It also boosts gearing, with corresponding financial expenses, making otherwise smaller absolute falling values into larger declines, causing illiquidity and insolvency, possibly in chains.

This chapter deals mainly with failures, crises, collapses and losses directly or indirectly related to legitimate uses of *derivatives*, not focusing on frauds. The latter are discussed in Chapter 9. It also complements some of the criticisms raised in Chapter 7 about the shortcomings of supposed beneficial functions. It has two sections only, apart from this introduction and the conclusion. The next section deals with the multiple failures of *derivatives*, emphasising the first fundamental function. And the third section tackles some debacles caused by *derivatives*.

The Multiple Failures of *Derivatives*

Derivatives possibly fail along the four tens beneficial functions presented in Chapter 7. But for lack of space, only a few are considered in detail below. Others are just mentioned or overlooked. The failures can be direct or indirect in terms of their participation. Starting with the former, regarding price discovery, for example, Poitras (2016, p. 470) explains that antiquated settlement and margin, not trading, activities in the *derivatives* circuits for equity, with significant delays, have contributed to creating systemically destabilising risks that jeopardises price discovery in the spot market for stocks. Moreover, he states that these risks are magnified by the possibility of speculating via new short sales with stocks already sold but not yet settled and sometimes not even located, with failure to deliver. These short trades in equity *derivatives* markets, Poitras continues, generate further inter-market arbitrage negotiations that are transmitted to the cash market. He mentions a short trade done in 2010 using 75,000 S&P 500 contracts valued $4.1 billion in the underlying index. The inter-market arbitrage crashed the ETF market on the Archipelago exchange (ARCA) and distorted the pricing of some big stocks.

On the other hand, Section 730 of Dodd–Frank Act, about large swap trade reporting, prohibits large agents from entering a swap contract that plays a price discovery function. The price is 'distorted', in this case, when it is fixed by large traders. So, absent regulation, *derivatives* can distort rather than discover prices if markets are free. In exchanges, futures and options contracts are standardised. This means that at any time contracts are available at an objective price. Fixed by whom? The market makers. Usually a bunch of large financial institutions. Dodd–Frank is off the mark. But how could large banks anticipate the future and know the right price? They cannot. It might be argued that these prices are normal, regular or usual. But if this is the case, why should anyone hedge? Hedge would be needed only if prices are not normal, regular or usual.

What about individual risk reduction or sharing? Steinherr (2000) many times presents a benign view on the role of risk management for economic growth. And, as discussed in Chapter 5 and in this chapter, economic and financial history provides a more negative view. Pillage, colonialism, imperialism, to mention just a few, have perhaps performed a more important role. Yet, unlike the staunch advocates, other times he is aware that the issue is more complex. For instance, he argues that the history of finance provides evidence that risk reduction not only creates new risks, an innovation hardly mentioned, but neglects spillover effects, when, for example, large market participants follow the same strategy, like program trading, and allows excessive-risk taking, leading to 'disasters'.

But it is worth asking: are *derivatives* indeed risk-reducing by hedging, as the first fundamental function predicts (Santos, 2008)? Or, do the values hedged surpass destabilising speculative positions? There are two issues here regarding the flaws of *derivatives*. One is that hedging is not effective. And another is that it is, but nonetheless cannot compensate for speculation-caused risks. For example, Poitras (2016) remarks that delta hedging and portfolio insurance played a key role in the 1987 stock market crash in the United States after investors started using options for implementing the former, supposedly continuously hedged, to achieve the latter, supposedly insured – an evidence of ineffectiveness.

On the other hand, effectiveness is a valid assumption for social risks only if there is a large number of speculators assuming parts of any individual hedged exposition, since a hedger transfers its individual risk, that is then divided up, not multiplied, by the number of speculators as counterparties. Yet, the social original risk has not disappeared. It is split, not necessarily evenly, among speculators. If there is only one big speculator, then the initial social risk is only transferred, not individually reduced by many individual accounts. If a single speculator assumes a larger risk and has a fragile financial position, social risks are increased above the original, not reduced. And even if there is a large number of speculators, but they are all geared, and *derivatives* have embedded gearing, the division does not reduce individual risks in the same proportion. The whole is greater than the sum of its parts. There is also the question of speculators opening positions or assuming exposures without a matching hedging necessity. Pure speculation and magnified individual and social risks.

As mentioned in Chapter 3, Friedman (1969) defends that stabilising speculation is beneficial and destabilising speculation is not harmful. If this is the case, speculation in spot markets would be a social replacement for individual *derivatives*, even though he uses futures markets as examples of neutral destabilising speculation.[1] So, risks would be cancelled out by an increased amounts of speculators, since they would either destabilise prices without harm, or stabilise them, making *derivatives* redundant in both cases. In the case of stabilising gambling, speculators sell when the price is high as they have perfect foresight and know that prices will not keep going up, and buy when the price is low as they have perfect foresight and know that prices are close to bottom and cannot fall any further. This view assumes the greater fool away, postulating long-run rationality among professional speculators and rejecting any behavioural economics insights. But the conclusion that *derivatives* are irrelevant is unavoidable.

There are other issues with this view. Just to highlight another one: what does it mean high or low prices? There must be a parameter to be compared to. Conventional economists believe that the parameter is a supposed market equilibrium price or mean, normal, regular or usual price. Actually, the perfectly competitive market equilibrium price. But how the price reached higher levels, for example, if one wishes to go beyond flat earth arguments in terms of growing demand or falling supply in perfectly competitive spot markets? The theory of a greater fool being assumed away is a possible guess. Speculators buy assuming that they can sell at a higher price to fools in the near future, because they have short horizons. For example, day traders are quintessential speculators by their very nature. As the name tells it all, they have the goal of buying and selling quickly at a profit. Thus, the price is high because speculators are willing to pay a high price now to sell at an expected higher price later. There is no way to know when the flow of fools will get short, only that it will. Uncertainty prevails even in the short term in financial markets. *Derivatives*, given their liquidity, accelerates the process. And given their quick turnovers, are the best fit to speculators.

So, if speculators depend on price changes, they will buy and sell in markets with volatility. Are *derivatives* traders they just noise traders, that is, they do not add to the long-term volatility? It does not seem so. Consider the speculative attacks against the British pound in 1992 using also futures and options. A single big speculator like George Soros played an important role. And how many other episodes happened since then? Speculators are not passive, selfish-less market price regulators or stabilisers, but active players, with vested interests in price changes, that is, in markets that do not have a gravitational equilibrium price, either competitive, cornered or oligopolist, and do not have a stable and slow-changing, predictable equilibrium price. That is exactly what speculators are not wishing for.

The problem with speculation, which is usually destabilising, is that the bubbles they help blowing up must always pop up. In this case, the high prices crash, not because they must quickly adjust to imagined equilibrium levels, but because they have played the role of transfering income from newer fools to previous buyers. The latest fools have a huge loss in wealth that cannot be hedged by *derivatives*. Since they are usually geared, the losses outspread to other balance sheets.

It is assumed that losses would be lower if prices could drop slowly and risks re-transferred, which denies the bubble. But which level they would fall to? A normal, historical trend? It does not matter, because, if prices are changing in quick short-term movements or in slow medium and long-term movements, they do not have to experience a reversal to a variable mean (a la Markowitz's portfolio), since the mean depends on the period of time used to calculate it. The mean is not a static statistical measure. Deviation is the issue. Thus, if the standard deviation is high and variable, the mean does not shed any light on the long-term behaviour of prices for the horizon of speculators. The point is that, for them, long-run trends are irrelevant, since they work on a different, shorter time span. That is, if prices follow a random walk, what is the importance of *derivatives*? They would be needed in theory, since prices would be unpredictable. Yet, if *derivatives* cause random walks in the first place, they could only, in the best scenario, compensate the volatility created by them. But at a net social cost. Destabilising speculation cannot be neutral.

Credit default swaps can also fail regarding risk transfers. If banks are assumed to be specialised information-processing machines about the prospective capacity of borrowers to pay back money borrowed and therefore the most apt institution to lend money, why would they transfer the risk of potential non-performing loans to perhaps less skilled agents, like AIG over the sub-prime collapse? Only if they know that the loans are toxic assets. *Derivatives* then facilitate not the transfer of risks, but the transfer of assured losses to too big to fail organisations. And the counterparty speculates with the concentrated risks that are not indeed risks but guaranteed huge defaults. And they know it, but it does not matter for speculation. This transaction is not transparent, efficient nor competitive.

Systemic problems are pervasive under *derivatives*. Lowenstein (2001) details all the relevant systemic problems with LTCM. *Derivatives* were considered relatively new, blowing the eternal *derivatives* view presented in Chapter 5. He argues that the New York Federal Reserve Bank (FED) was worried about the fund and the interconnected balance sheets, a point also raised by Steinherr (2000) and Saber (1999a). A relevant issue here is the fact that *derivatives* used to be off-balance sheet, with implicit gearing (Breuer, 2002) and lack of transparency. Breuer mentions that LTCM's on-balance-sheet gearing was not a reliable measure of exposure, although the ratio moved from a factor of 25 to an astonishing 167. He mentions that the off-balance-sheet gearing ratio increased from 270 to 2,100.[2] The hedge fund engaged in arbitrage, exploiting price differences between spot and futures markets for treasury securities. But arbitrage is supposed to be riskless. At first the gains were on average bigger than losses, relying on economists with PhDs in Rocket Science and a Swedish Central Bank Prize winner, erroneously associated with the Nobel Prize, that is, economic geniuses. Anyway, the fund was too big to fail when it collapsed. So, LTCM was about conventional speculators and therefore as irrational in their beliefs as their historical and contemporaneous mad crowds, but with interconnected balance sheets.

Regarding the sub-prime collapse of 2007–2008, Lowenstein (2010) mentions a speech by Gary Gorton, titled 'The Panic of 2007', presented at a Federal Reserve Bank of Kansas City Jackson Hole conference, in 2008. For Gorton, the banking system was metamorphosing into a shadow one, characterised by off-balance sheet and *derivatives*.[3] The very crisis contributed to the enactment of new legislation regulating, to a certain extent, OTC *derivatives*, and requiring a transfer to the balance sheet (see Chapter 9). *Derivatives*' growth also started showing a different trajectory over time, stopping the continuous growth displayed since the 1990s and 2000s (see chapter 5). But in a situation of crisis, volatility and losses, *derivatives* hedging transactions should have grown, not diminished. And the banking sub-system turned out to be what it had always essentially been under capitalism: an organisational form of money capital seeking to self-expand, be it by interest rates on loans or speculative capital gains on different assets, including *derivatives*, or other types of arrangements.

Steinherr (2000) argues that the systemic risk brought about by *derivatives* is not necessarily related to the gigantic notional or open interest outstanding amounts. What is crucial in his view is the global interconnectedness of balance sheets in a context of unregulated and highly geared *derivatives* positions. Saber (1999a) argues along similar lines. He focuses on the linkages between markets or flows of transactions, not balance sheets, provided by the presence of speculative capital in the form of *derivatives* carrying out arbitrage operations around the world. Flexibility and market integration are actually means to overspill and spread out instability and collapses.

Gearing is another source of instability within the *derivatives* sub-system. Blinder (2013) criticises the CFMA enacted in 2000 for keeping OTC *derivatives* unregulated (see Chapter 9). He blames 'disgraceful' mortgages, but mainly 'wild and woolly' customised *derivatives* that turned the sub-prime crisis into a 'catastrophe'. Blinder claims that *derivatives* based on mortgages promoted reckless gearing and imposed widespread losses. This assessment is compatible with the position that *derivatives* are not intrinsically crisis-inducing. Unregulated *derivatives* are the problem. Markham (2002) states that *derivatives* entered a period of crisis, meaning market contraction, after some OTC disasters, just when they were supposedly more needed. But they also took part in the feast when finance rebounded. So, advocates pay attention only to the recovery phase.

The economic dynamics of the underlyings points to other shortcomings of so-called *derivatives* regarding hedging. They may be unnecessary, as recognised by Hull (1997). A futures contract has no collateral, only a margin account. Its price is based on fictitious projections. In the case of commodities, on the other hand, spot market prices are for sale prices, derived from prices of tangible production. Money represents the right to buy them at a known or spot price today, but not known for the future, which means risk of higher prices. Does a call option with a known strike price prevents this risk? For the commodity seller, it does not make sense. A put option would not either with higher future spot prices. Premiums are wastage.

Consider a call option to buy corn by a food-processing company. If the future spot price goes down below the strike price, it may not exercise the option and forfeit the premium. And this does not obviate the need to buy corn. It could buy corn futures instead, without a premium. Again, future prices could be expected to go up, and futures contracts could reflect that. So, a corn-processing firm could enter a futures contract with a known price. In the future, the spot prices could be lower again, and the firm would not pay the prices set by the contract. So, they could be paying less than would be the case without *derivatives* if prices fell substantially. And corn producers would be worse off selling at the spot prices, not the prices they agreed to sell at in the past. The gain of the processing firm is the loss of the corn producer, in a zero-sum game. Thus, *derivatives* affect distribution in a given economic context.

The interesting point is that *derivatives* can change the economic context and add another layer of uncertainty into the picture. This happens when speculators have to negotiate in physical markets with storage. So, for the corn processing firm, corn is necessary, but *derivatives* are not. They might be helpful for the company if future spot prices or costs are higher than they are today, and the difference is larger than the costs of entering the *derivatives* contract, considered low. But it is impossible to know in the present if *derivatives* are needed or not in the future.

Das (2006) provides several reasons for not trusting *derivatives*. They are deemed a cheaper alternative to hedge risks. But risks in this case cannot be considered something exogenous. Risks are affected by the market behaviour of participants, including the frauds he witnessed. There is always the basis or price risk, since this is the monetary parameter set to establish cash settlements based on the strike price. It is an expectation. If one looks into the future, there is uncertainty and doubt. If onelooks into the past, it may not be replicable. Again, are options a solution? It provides a floor to losses, but it does not completely eliminate them. If it provides unlimited gains, it turns out to be an instrument for speculation, not hedge. It is an option to insure on the downside and to profit on the upside. The latter will entice speculators and market dynamics that will bring losses even to those without *derivatives* positions as in the collapses discussed above and below.

The cash settlements for price differences suggest that *derivatives* do not eliminate the need to hold idle cash in case of unfavourable price movements. If *derivatives* do not obviate the need of liquidity holdings, including for margin calls, it may be redundant. Even if it provides a low-cost solution, it is still a cost. Holding liquid short-term securities, on the other hand, provides increased safety and small gains. Of course, during a crisis that could have been generated by *derivatives* themselves, the capital losses produced indicates the need of replenishing cash. It all boils down to keeping liquidity as a reasonable answer to uncertainty and also to risks (Milan, 2014).

One of the advertised advantages of exchanges for *derivatives*, actually futures and exchange-traded options, not listed as the 42nd in Chapter 7, is the reduced credit or counterparty risk brought about by the existence of centralised clearing houses. Yet, clearing houses may also face liquidity and solvency troubles. Baker (2019) informs that in 2018 the Norwegian power trader Einar Aas defaulted on his obligations to NASDAQ Clearing AB, the private company responsible for clearing transactions at that exchange. The organisation is considered a systemically important clearing house by the Financial Stability Board created after the 2007–2008 sub-prime collapse. Although assuming this type of risk is what justifies the existence of such companies, the author affirms that the clearing-house losses exhausted about 66% of the default reserve fund, shattering financial markets and regulators.[4]

Baker (2019) mentions examples of clearing-house failures over contemporary history, not listed in table 8.1 in the next section, like the *Caisse de Liquidation* in France in 1974, the Kuala Lumpur Commodity Clearing House in Malaysia in 1983 and the Hong Kong Futures Exchange Clearing Corporation in Hong Kong in 1987. He quotes a study claiming that the clearing houses of the Chicago Mercantile Exchange (CME), Options Clearing Corporation and the Chicago Board of Trade (CBOT), were close to failure and a catastrophe was only averted by the intervention, as it is usually the case, of the Federal Reserve. Baker states that even the U.S. Treasury recognises that clearing houses are an important source of systemic risk. In his view, this potential generalised disruption is caused by the existence of global interdependencies among systemically significant clearing houses, banks and financial institutions. The finance capital system is a complex of fragile arrangements and institutions.

Another direct failure of *derivatives* (or *derivatives*-like arrangements) is related to executive compensation with stock options. Managers can buyback the company' stocks, boosting their prices in the underlying market after the vesting period. This will have the same effect as a higher profit on the stock options given to the executives. It is not about efficiency, but power. Thus, Bebchuck and Fried (2004) argues that executive compensation using incentives, like for example run-of-the-mill, long-term (10-year) American options, do not align firms' goals with those of their managers. In this case, executives have everything to gain and nothing to lose, except the cost of time, since they do not pay the premium. As a consequence, in this case, they have an incentive to assume risks the firm might otherwise not take to boost stock prices. So, arrangements increase values at risk. And an important issue not considered by this line of research, for obvious reasons, is that executives may generate higher profits by intensified exploitation of workers and suppliers, not to mention accounting shenanigans. Hence, if all employees are dependent on the continuous success of the firm for their pay and/or employment, why not grant options to all workers, not only the ones at the top of the hierarchy?

Besides the above major direct problems with *derivatives*, there is a myriad of other minor issues. For instance, manipulation is also normal in *derivatives* markets, as discussed in Chapter 9. It suffices here to draw attention to some schemes. Frunza (2016b, p.144) quotes a study of Gallmeyer and Seppi with a model to analyse the behaviour of agents willing to manipulate the value of their *derivative* portfolio by means of artificial market orders in the underlying market. These calls alter the price transitorily. The proposed framework can be extended when the manipulators place an order on another *derivative*, obliging the sellers to place orders in the underlying market to avoid losses.

Also, Santos (2008) cites a study conducted in the 1980s stating that only 32% of all contracts introduced by exchanges between 1960 and 1977 were actively traded in 1980. Innovation is not panacea. This waste of resources is probably due to the creation of contracts that are too complex and irrelevant, although probably highly profitable when first launched. Saber (1999b, p. 3) lists 32 *derivatives* 'products' in a brochure prepared by a single bank. Even though some of the products are standard, and most of them are options, there are clearly contracts developed to lure fool traders and speculators.[5] This is confirmed by Das (2006). The same can also be true of exchanges themselves. Santos mentions the shutdown of the New Orleans Exchange in 1983. As argued in Chapter 5, there is a concentration and centralisation movement of capitals accumulated in exchanges. Since large banks dominate the *derivatives* business, there has been forming a behemoth fragile financial capitalist economy.

Regarding a single indirect problem with *derivatives*, Collins (2020) reports that, in April 2020, amidst the COVID-19 pandemic, the future contracts for the May 2020 West Texas Intermediate (WTI) oil prices plunged by more than 40%. The culprit, in his view, was the U.S. Oil (USO), a large exchange-traded fund based on commodities futures. It rolled over the future May contract, of whose total outstanding volume it owns 25% and opened new positions in the June and July contracts. This is not about competition. Anyway, the fund can do that by accepting oil delivery in May or selling futures oil contracts. Since *derivatives* are not about hedging and physical delivery, the decision is always to sell, bringing prices down. Of course, this also fits in the discussion on price discovery. And with falling prices come reductions in the U.S. oil rig count and employment in the oil and supplying sectors, at the same time that oil storage by speculators reaps enormous windfall profits.

Collins affirms that ETFs cause distortions in the commodities futures curve, that is, the curve relating future spot prices to maturities. Guedj et al. (2011) argues that, if the storage is not expensive, speculators can seat on the physical commodity. But if it is, then a way to gain exposure to commodities, that is, to speculate, is by means of futures.[6] Thus, unlike other ETFs, commodity funds cannot always have the underlying in the portfolio, which implies involuntary gearing and therefore increased risks and spillovers of risks. Not risk reduction by any means.

Poitras (2016) evaluates ETFs in terms of an overarching history of equity and equity-like capital ownership, but these funds have other underlying and types. Regarding ETFs in general, he shows that, in 2014, there were $2 trillion invested in those funds, from $7 billion in 1997, excluding fictitious investments of ETFs in other ETFs. Saber (2017, p. 144) mentions $3 trillion, what suggests lack of transparency in the data. Poitras mentions that ETFs, like hedge funds and *derivatives*, were introduced in the context of a declining managed mutual funds industry. ETFs are non-geared, fixed type of assets and open-ended managed funds, although some of them are geared. The Toronto Index Participation Shares (TIPS) started trading in 1990, being the first continuously traded fund. There are specifically *derivatives*-based ETFs as a subclass of ETFs.[7] Synthetic ETFs account for 45% of the market in Europe, according to Saber (2017). This illustrates the point that *derivatives* are not the only speculative weapons of mass destruction, although it is probably the cheapest. If they get replaced in the near future as prime speculative vehicles, it is by ETFs or OTCTFs.

From *Derivatives* Failures to Debacles

The selected failures discussed above are not abstract themes. They have concrete consequences for capital, labour and the state. So, Jacque (2015) organises the debacles by all four basic *derivatives* instruments. If structured products were considered, the list would be much longer. In the table 8.1 a few selected fiascos, to use Partnoy (2009a) word,[8] are organised by the corporations or organisations affected and by *derivatives* type. A longer list can be found in Grima and Thalassinos (2020), whereas Lleo and Ziemba (2014) provide the most common reasons for losing money with *derivatives* in banks and hedge funds, with a special focus on LTCM.

Of course, *derivatives* are a zero-sum game, and the money lost by a player is gained by another. If the losses cause further reductions in transactions and accumulation later, larger than the increased volumes enticed by gains, then it becomes a negative-sum game. There is a process of redistribution of income internal to the financial system, since the non-financial sector is made up of mostly, not always, passive players. But socialised losses can reach all sectors and agents.

The ocurrence of losses and panics caused by *derivatives* span many decades, one of them even before the age of contemporary *derivatives*, and many instruments, underlying and institutions, not only banks or financial firms. The fact that there is a relatively ample number of non-financial companies in the remarkable large losses list, including a Central Bank and a municipality, is revealing about losers and winners in this market. This goes against Scholes' (1998) opinion that financial infrastructure and understanding lag behind financial innovation. It is hard to see the net value added by *derivatives* to non-financial firms.

To avoid redundancies, only a couple of cases from table 8.1 are detailed. An interesting starting point is the Metallgesellschaft AG' subsidiary, MG Refining and Marketing. The firm could not hedge long-term forward positions for lack of counterparties. This should not be a surprise, since *derivatives* are mostly arrangements for short-term financial gains, not to hedge physical storage, better served by buying oil in the spot market and holding it until delivery. Marthinsen (2018) argues that this would be a natural choice, but it was considered too expensive in a volatile environment where falling prices could not be assured. The other hedging alternative was buying short-term energy futures contracts and OTC swaps, or stack-and-roll, if prices and basis increased. The loss caused the company to get close to bankruptcy (Kuprianov, 1995).

Marthinsen (2018) mentions that the Procter & Gamble losses with swaps in 1993–1994 were the largest related to those instruments in the U.S. manufacturing industry. The $157 million non-cash charges to pre-tax earnings, despite small, were above the after-tax earnings of $152 million for that same period. Interestingly, the counterpart in the swaps, Bankers Trust, earned $144 million from its financial risk management division during the first quarter of 1994.

Jacque (2015) describes the case of Shell's Japanese oil refiner subsidiary, Showa Shell Sekiyu K.K. In 1993, it lost five times the company's pre-tax profits and 82% of shareholders' equity in foreign exchange deals. The losses started in 1989, with dollar positions of crude oil imports hedged with 90-day forwards, but speculation drove the company's treasury into much larger exposures continuously rolled over, avoiding settlement as the yen kept depreciating. The exchange rate risk was inevitable even if the company decided to purchase oil from Shell with long-term fixed prices contracts. And the exchange rate remained unfavourable for more than four years starting in 1990.

Another famous case is the Gibson Greetings Cards (GGC). The firm entered swaps contracts to reduce funding costs and, at first, it ended the deals at a profit. And then started new geared swaps. After it lost money this time, it doubled the bet, making 29 amendments in the new contract, becoming more and more geared and complex. GGC lost between $20 million, the total profit of the previous year, and $27.5 billion in 1994, depending on the source. Bankers Trust, according to Jacque (2015), lied and manipulated the transaction – an example of dishonesty risk (see Chapter 2).

Considering financial firms, Citibank also faced losses of $8 million in 1965 associated with currency forwards when exchange rates were quasi-fixed before contemporary capitalism. But they were mild compared to non-financial firms' losses. They represented only 1% of the estimated underlying value, less than 9% of the bank's profit at that year and less than 20% of the bank's daily gyrations in foreign exchange markets. In the deal, a trader speculated against the British

Pound, at the time exchanging at the rate of \$2.80=£ 1.00. Jacque (2015) explains that the par value was slightly flexible, in this case with a ceiling of \$2.82 and a floor of \$2.78. The new labour cabinet was pressured to devalue the pound, given the persistent balance of payment deficits, and the Citi's trader bet that the exchange rate would not change in the next 12–18 months. Jacque painstakingly shows why forwards make currency speculation much easier, since it escapes proper internal supervision and control, supporting the view of Stulz. It is not only because it is cheaper than speculation in the spot market.

The speculative strategy involved buying Sterling Pound forward at rates below the floor, like \$2.69=£1 for maturities ranging from 9 to 18 months, as the Bank of England increased interest rates to shore up the currency, causing a discount in the forward exchange rate imposed by the covered interest rate parity. And also sold pounds for shorter maturities that would be rolled over, with cumulative short-term losses until the long-run forwards would be settled. As the trades were off Citi's limits, the bank discovered the deal and unwound the positions before the long-term profits could be cashed in.

In another case, the Bank Negara Malaysia started, according to Jacque (2015), speculating in currency markets in 1988. The Central Bank acted as macro hedge fund. The Malaysian Ringgit had a pegged exchange rate with the U.S. dollar and the Yen. It was set at M\$2.60=\$1, with a fluctuation band of 2.25%. In 1992, the bank speculated against the British Pound, betting against Soros that the Bank of England would not devalue and stay in the European Exchange Rate Mechanism (ERM). It purchased sterling pound forward for delivery in three or six months. Forwards were at a discount with the higher interest rates set by the Bank of England. The Negara bank lost \$3.2 billion when the pound was expelled of the ERM under the speculative attack coordinated by Soros, and lost 30% of its value overnight.

As shown in Chapter 4, JP Morgan Chase is among the top four *derivatives* trader in the United States. Yet, the bank lost more than \$6 billion in 2012. Marthinsen (2018) rejects the view that the problems were caused by the famous London Whale, named after the bank leading trader due to its enormous trading volume. The Synthetic Credit Portfolio, created in 2008 to hedge tail-end risks and kept secret for four years, had tripled in three months before the collapse, reaching a notional value of \$157 billion. The losses were the result of speculation, including the use of funds from federally insured customer deposits, violating the 'Volcker Rule' in the CFTC implementation of the Dodd–Frank Act. Thus, the large losses occurred after Dodd–Frank was enacted and despite it, suggesting an important ineffectiveness in the form of loopholes or exceptions granted by U.S. state agencies.

Saber (1999a, p. 235) mentions the case of Investors Equity Life Insurance Co. in Hawaii. The company had, in 1993, \$16 million in net worth. But it had assets equivalent to \$186.8 million, a gearing ratio, unweighted by assets' size, of almost 12.[9] The notional value of futures contracts in Treasury bonds reached almost \$1 billion, with geared purchases. It is clear that there is no financially sound way the company could have such exposure. Another less obvious issue, but perhaps more important to the understanding of *derivatives*, is that the Treasury issues fixed-rate bonds. It has no interest rate risk if held to maturity. Buyers of treasuries in this case would have no risk. *Derivatives* have no role to play in this financial transaction. Yet, speculation is what drives these sub-systems. Since it is not about interest rate risk, as there is none, it is about capital gain or losses in secondary markets, with volatility in the price of bonds. Of course, this implies changes in interest rates for new buyers as a consequence, but it is not the aim of *derivatives* transactions.

Finally, it is not clear whether or not Lehman Brothers should be on the list. Wiggins and Metrick (2019) mentions the existence of interpretative disputes regarding the role of *derivatives* in its collapse. One view states that the bank caused losses only after the bankruptcy, and therefore the form that the latter assumed was the responsible. Also, the *derivatives* trading arm, Lehman Brothers Specialty Financing (LBSF), added value to the estate.

The other view claims that Lehman huge involvement with *derivatives* is the direct cause of massive loss of value, between $35 billion and $75 billion, and therefore it should be held responsible for the gigantic losses. The authors inform that, although the figures cannot be known for sure, when Lehman filed for bankruptcy protection, it had 906,000 *derivative* transactions booked, largely OTC, with an estimated notional value of $35 trillion. The U.S. GDP in that year was $14.8 trillion – but, again, notional values are just a measure of fictitious capital commitments. This represented 5% of the global *derivatives* notional value.

The bankruptcy caused the automatic termination of 733,000 contracts, including decisions of counterparts. The settlement process of this huge amount of trades, according to Wiggins and Metrick, was lengthy and carried out under special treatment. Other trades were bulk-sold by CME, for example. CDS were auctioned. The discussion about the systemic consequences should not be downplayed. *Derivatives* transmitted shocks and exacerbated the crisis.

Therefore, *derivatives* have an extensive list of corporate losses that are either dismissed or justified by its advocates. But they cannot explain why they occur other than blaming reckless individuals, never the arrangements. They do not acknowledge that these events are not isolated, but pervasive. They are embedded in the very nature of the arrangements and the financialised regime that created them. And the significant crashes are never fully developed in a systemic maelstrom because of government regulation and massive interventions.

Summing Up

This chapter argues that *derivatives* may fail in performing the functions listed in the previous chapter, including price discovery, innovation, transparency, liquidity, competition, efficiency and executive compensation, to mention a few. Even the most important one, hedging, can be irrelevant and, when necessary, fail, both in general or in terms of specific arrangements. Mismanagement cannot be hedged either. Negative spillover effects of *derivatives* and herd behaviour are inevitable. Gearing in intrinsically speculative operations with many chained balance sheets creates systemic or at least large enough risks, increasing rather than reducing them.

Table 8.1 Selected major *derivatives*-related losses

Capitalist group	*General and specific* derivatives *used*	*Losses (year)*
Metallgesellschaft AG	Forward energy *derivatives* (oil) with embedded options, oil futures and oil swaps	$1.33 billion (2003)
Procter & Gamble	Interest rate swaps	$157 million (1993–1994)
Showa Shell Sekiyu K.K.	Currency forwards	$1.07 billion (1993)
Gibson Greeting Card	Interest rate swap	$20 million (1994) (Marthinsen) or $27.5 million (1994) (Jacque)
Citibank	Currency forwards	$8 million (1965)
Long-Term Capital Management	Swaps	$4.5 billion (1998)
Barings Bank PLC	Stock index futures	$1.3 billion (1995)
Bank Negara Malaysia (Central Bank)	Forwards	$2.1 billion (1994); $3.3 billion (1992)
Amaranth Advisors LLC	Futures (spreads)	$6.4 billion or $6 billion (2006)
Sumitomo	Commodity futures	$2.6 billion (1996)
Allied Lyons	Currency options (straddles and strangles)	$91 million (1991)
Allied Irish Banks	Currency options	$691 million (2002)
Société Générale	Equity call options	$7.2 billion (2008)
Orange County	Interest rate swap	$1.65 billion (1994)
AIG Financial Products	Credit default swap	$25.7 billion (2008)
JP Morgan Chase	Credit *derivatives* (synthetic credit portfolio).	$6.2 billion (2012)

Source: Elaborated by the author based on Marthinsen (2018), CFTC (n.d.e) and Jacque (2015)

But even ordinary risks do not seem to be well-managed with *derivatives*. There is basis risk, not to mention dishonesty risks, with frauds and manipulation. Many *derivatives* products are useless and obsolete, representing waste. Excess liquid assets may be a consequence of all that. Clearing houses may also fail, pointing to the maintenance of counterparty risks. *Derivatives* cause risks to grow.

Thus, this is not about misuse, but about using it according to its ultimate function: accumulation of fictitious capital under conditions of financialised capitalism. And this is accomplished by means of pervasive geared speculation that exceeds hedging, as contracted values exceed values at risk. Moreover, the failures can also be indirect, as *derivatives* became part of other complex speculative arrangements like ETFs. Permanent instability, heightened volatility and frequent crises and losses are the most important outcomes of *derivatives*.

The consequences show up in the form of debacles, crises and losses. The social costs are not factored in in the cost calculations of the efficiency of *derivatives*. There are many recorded concrete cases of *derivatives*-induced losses. And sometimes they are concentrated in non-financial firms, showing that *derivatives* are not only instruments of financial accumulation, but also of valorisation of finance capital by means of inter-capitalist redistributions, but also intra-capitalist conflicts within the non-financial sector with natural hedges. When losses get chained and cause economic crises, *derivatives* show their systemic potential and even financial institutions are partially punished. Can regulation prevent that?

Notes

1 Milan (2014) argues that national regulations were temporarily stabilising during the Golden Age of capitalism regarding macro-financial prices, given their capacity to curb destabilising speculation.

2 Breuer (2002, p. 237) shows the top 25 commercial banks gearing for the period 1995–2000. While the on-balance sheet gearing is stable, the gross gearing, including off-balance sheet, fluctuates, but it is always above the on-balance sheet measure. For the other banks, both measures are close and falling over the period.

3 Lowenstein (2010) informs that Gorton run swap risk models to AIG's hothouse *derivatives* unit, Financial Products, based in London and financed in very advantageous terms by the 'perfect' AAA credit rating that AIG had gained from its experience in insurance.

4 Baker quotes Paul Tucker, former deputy governor of the Bank of England in the epigraph of the article. Tucker alerts that when a central clearing house goes bust, there is mayhem. And bigger than would be the case for the largest banks or dealers failures. Capitalism breeds and needs centralisation but cannot withstand concentrated losses.

5 Examples include roll up put and roll down call options, guaranteed exchange rate option; outperformance options, alternative (either-or) option, lookback currency option and LIBOR in-arrears swap agreement.

6 It shows that, at that time, the returns on commodity ETFs were not correlated with commodity prices, not being able to diversity a portfolio for hedging purposes.

7 The dedicated page on ETFs, ETF.com, states that there are 34 *derivatives* ETFs funds in the United States, under the category of currency, and with more than $5 billion in assets. Most of them are based on crypto-currencies and the largest one has $1.9 billion in assets. Source: www.etf.com/topics/derivative, Retrieved May 2024.

8 Meaning 'Fixed Income Annual Sporting Clays Outing', a *derivatives* gathering of the Derivatives Products Group at Morgan Stanley.

9 This was the maximum gearing ratio allowed in the United States under the old net capital rule for investment banks, changed in 2004 to allow more freedom to finance capital (see Chapter 9). But the company in question is an insurance one, and this type of capital is usually associated with conservative strategies, considering the long run, not the short run gains. But under financialised capitalism short-termism is a pervasive feature of most business strategies.

References

Baker, Colleen M. "Incomplete Clearinghouse Mandates." *American Business Law Journal* 56, no. 3 (2019): 507–581.

Bebchuck, Lucian, and Jeff Fried. P*ay Without Performance: The Unfulfilled Promise of Executive Compensation.* Cambridge: Harvard University Press, 2004.

Blinder, Alan. "Five Years Later, Financial Lessons Not Learned: A Good-Though-Weak Law Sinks Under the Weight of Special-Interest Lobbies." *The Wall Street Journal*, (Sept. 10, 2013): A15.

Breuer, Peter. "Measuring Off-Balance-Sheet Leverage." *Journal of Banking & Finance* 26, (2002): 223–242.

CFTC. *History of the CFTC: CFTC History in the 2000s*, n.d.e. Available at: www.cftc.gov/About/HistoryoftheCFTC/history_2000s.html Retrieved August 2024.

Collins, Jim. "The U.S. Oil ETF, USO, Is the Culprit Behind Oil's Massive Plunge." *Forbes*, April 21, 2020. Available at: www.forbes.com/sites/jimcollins/2020/04/20/the-us-oil-etf-uso-is-the-culprit-behind-oils-massive-plunge/?sh=579259aa24e8 Retrieved May 2022.

Das, Satyajit. *Traders, Guns and Money: Knowns and Unknowns in the Dazzling World of Derivatives*. London: FT Press/Prentice Hall, 2006.

Friedman, Milton. "In Defense of Destabilizing Speculation." In: Milton Friedman (ed.) *The Optimum Quantity of Money and Other Essays.* Chicago: Aldine, 1969.

Frunza, Marius-Christian (ed.) *Introduction to Theories and Varieties of Modern Crime in Financial Markets*. Oxford: Academic Press/Elsevier, 2016b.

Grima, Simon, and Eleftherios Thalassinos. *Financial Derivatives: A Blessing or a Curse?* Rebecca D. Gonzi and Ioannis E. Thalassinos (eds). Bingley: Emerald Publishing Limited, 2020.

Guedj, Ilan, Guohua Li, and Craig McCann. "Futures-Based Commodity ETFs." *The Journal of Index Investing* 2, no. 1 (2011): 14–24.

Hull, John. *Options, Futures, and Other Derivatives*. 3rd ed. Upper Sadder River: Prentice Hall, 1997.

Jacque, Laurent. *Global Derivative Debacles: From Theory to Malpractice*. Singapore: World Scientific Publishing Co. Pte. Ltd., 2015.

Kuprianov, Anatoli. "Derivatives Debacles: Case Studies of Large Losses in Derivatives Markets." *Federal Reserve Bank of Richmond Economic Quarterly* 81, no. 4 (1995): 1–39.

Lleo, Sebastien and William Ziemba. "How to Lose Money in Derivatives: Examples from Hedge Funds and Bank Trading Departments." *The London School of Economics and Political Science*, Systemic Risk Centre, Special Paper no. 2, 2014.

Lowenstein, Roger. *The End of Wall Street*. New York: The Penguin Press, 2010.

Lowenstein, Roger. *When Genius Failed: The Rise and Fall of Long-Term Capital Management.* New York: Random House, 2001.

Markham, Jerry W. *A Financial History of the United States. Vol. 3. From the Age of Derivatives into the New Millennium (1970–2001)*. Armonk, NY: M. E. Sharpe, 2002.

Marthinsen, John E. *Risk Takers: Uses and Abuses of Financial Derivatives*. 3rd ed. Berlin: De|G Press, 2018.

Milan, Marcelo. "Macrofinancial Risks and Liquidity Preference". *International Journal of Political Economy* 43, no. 1 (2014): 43–64.

Partnoy, Frank. *F.I.A.S.C.O. – Blood in the Water in Wall Street*. New York: W. W. Norton & Company, 2009a.

Poitras, Geoffrey. *Equity Capital: From Ancient Partnerships to Modern Exchange Traded Funds*. New York: Routledge, 2016.

Saber, Nasser. "The Challenges of Regulation of Derivatives." In: Raphaël Douady, Clément Goulet, and Pierre-Charles Pradier (eds.) *Financial Regulation in the EU: From Resilience to Growth.* Cham: Palgrave MacMillan/Springer International Publishing, 2017.

Saber, Nasser. *Speculative Capital & Derivatives: The Nature of Risk in Capital Markets*. Vol. 2. London: Financial Times/Prentice Hall, 1999b.

Saber, Nasser. *Speculative Capital: The Invisible Hand of Global Finance*. Vol. 1. London: Financial Times/Prentice Hall, 1999a.

Santos, Joseph. "A History of Futures Trading in the United States." *EH.Net Encyclopedia*, 2008. Available at https://eh.net/encyclopedia/a-history-of-futures-trading-in-the-united-states/ Retrieved April 2024.

Scholes, Myron. "Derivatives in a Dynamic Environment." *The American Economic Review* 88, no. 3 (1998): 350–370.

Steinherr, Alfred. *Derivatives – The Wild Beast of Finance: A Path to Effective Globalisation?* New York: Wiley, 2000.

Wiggins, Rosalind Z., and Andrew Metrick. "The Lehman Brothers Bankruptcy G: The Special Case of Derivatives." *Journal of Financial Crises* 1, no. 1 (2019): 151–171.

9 Financialised Capitalism and the State

Deregulating Finance, Regulating *Derivatives*?

Introduction

The views expressed in Chapters 7 and 8 may lead to completely different conclusions regarding the necessity of regulating *derivatives* by the state, considering that for the most part of the contemporary period, nearly all important financial instruments and market practices have not been largely constrained by governments. That is, the laissez-faire approach prevailed for a large part of the sub-system for a long time. This means either that they performed the assumed functions attributed by its advocates in Chapter 7, or that the latter's excuses when the instruments clearly failed were taken seriously, and nothing else was considered. Non-regulation should be considered the right policy and regulation should never be suggested. The deregulation and liberalisation trend inaugurated in the 1970s and 1980s by neo-liberal reforms should had been kept unchecked and OTC *derivatives* markets should have remained forever untouched by the state.

But if the criticisms raised in chapter 8 are at least partially valid, mainly the ones concerned with the frequent eruption of crises in which *derivatives* are an important trigger or ferment, not to mention frauds and manipulations, then their regulation should have been an obvious, yet maybe not completely or even somewhat effective, measure sought after by national or regional states and multilateral organisations. From this perspective, the problem assumed in the aftermath of every single crisis, scandals, frauds or significant individual losses, like the ones presented in the Chapter 8, has been a lack of, or a very loose, regulation of these fractions of finance capital. It assumes that regulation is always the only possible answer to crises and frauds.

Historically, however, this pro-financial regulation view has prevailed, in a strongly political sense of the word, only after the 2008 sub-prime financial collapse, but never questioning the problems associated with the concept of *derivatives* and the specific circuits this broad term refers to. On the contrary, this chapter proposes that, from a historical perspective, present-day partial regulations in advanced capitalist countries, and having the United States as a model, can be seen as another piece of evidence in favour of the inexistence of *derivatives* as a unified financial phenomenon and or as a permanent or trans-historical feature of the economy,

DOI: 10.4324/9781003137092-10

pertaining instead to the contemporary dynamics of finance capital, that is, a recent development of financialised capitalism and its crises.

This chapter is organised as follows. After the introduction that proposes a new interpretation for the dynamic relationship between state and finance capital in general, the particular historical evolution of non-regulation, soft or ineffective regulation, deregulation and re-regulation is discussed considering the U.S. experience, starting with commodities futures during modern capitalism and then presenting the evolution of this type of regulation under contemporary financialised capitalism and finally the regulation of OTC financial swaps, with only a brief reference to the European regulation. The final section concludes with a synthesis and evaluation of the proposed interpretation.

The Spiral of Changing Regulatory and Deregulatory Regimes

Abstract financial regulation as a generic concept is a universal feature of all modern capitalist societies with a complex state apparatus, developed commodity production and circulation, and therefore evolved monetary and financial circuits, with sophisticated institutions, practices and instruments. In those socioeconomic settings, the state provides, at a certain time following a legislative vacuum filled by self-regulation, the legal mechanisms to decide what is allowed and what is not to finance capital. This is due to the latter's frequent capacity to damage itself, or some of its fractions, and the non-financial and non-commoditised parts of the economy that are nonetheless fully dependent on money and finance, and therefore jeopardising the regular social and political reproduction of capitalism. Yet, since the dynamics of socioeconomic class conflicts is itself regulated by specific norms and rules, projecting singular restrictions in each national or regional space, and with trends varying over time, abstract regulation must always assume particular forms in terms of peculiar territorial and historical ordinances.

That is, concrete financial regulation is specifically national or regional and historical, even though one can speak of rule-making as an abstract activity of the state curbing the movements and positions of finance capital in general and its ancillary instruments in specific circuits of valorisation, like the *derivatives* subsystem, in particular. Regulation must be directed objectively to actual practices or movements of value, that is, forms of commodities and capital. Thus, many concrete regulations of finance capital and its fractions, especially banking capital, were introduced under modern capitalism, after the crises generated under classical, less regulated or self-regulated capitalism. This lack of state regulation of finance capital in general was a common feature of many capitalist countries during the nineteenth century (Drach and Cassis, 2021). After major financial disruptions, national governments autonomously or through international coordination erected a sturdy regulatory system in the 1930s and 1940s, following the breakdown caused by the Great Depression of the twentieth century, contributing as a consequence to the Golden Age after World War II.

On the other hand, the temporary absence of major crises in the post-World War II period, probably allowed by regulation, however feeble, may have created excessive surplus capital and as a consequence increased capitalists' political sway over state branches, that is, over politicians, magistrates and bureaucrats. This is valid for capital in general and also for more economically and politically powerful fractions of capital, in particular. In other words, different groups of capitalists, and even financial capitalists as a whole, have variable degrees of influence over specific state divisions, generating all kinds of asymmetries and privileges regarding non-regulation, light regulation and deregulation. The net outcome is complex and hard to grasp.

But then, lobbying the state branches is not the only weapon of capital. Finance capital, starting with the creation of Eurodollar market in the 1950s, with Midland Bank in London operating in the circuit of forward foreign exchange market (Schenk, 1998), had the ability to circumvent national regulations, but worked concomitantly also for deregulation. The contemporary period that started in the 1970s, with the end of the Golden Age, was marked by a clear pattern of financial deregulation and liberalisation carried out by national states, with differing scopes and rhythms across space and time (Helleiner, 1994)[1]. Repealing regulations, in a neo-liberal context of overall political pressure from capitalists to delegitimise the government, is actually an important goal for the more dynamic or most profitable fractions of financialised capital. In this regard, from a more generic historical perspective, financial deregulation and liberalisation that characterises neo-liberalism took place in monetary and financial markets over the second half of the twentieth century, mainly after the end of Bretton Woods (Drach and Cassis, 2021). As a consequence, frequent crises were inevitably resumed under deregulation (Allen and Gale, 2007).

The primary mode of political regulation of the tendency towards financial crises, that is, legislative constraints on finance capitalist practices of distributing capital over spaces and sectors as a mechanism of managing accumulation geared to unstoppable short-term valorisation, was gradually demobilised by neo-liberalism. This is because, as Saber (1999) correctly argues, speculative capital abhors regulation. Thus, the ultimate mode of political regulation of crises in contemporary capitalist societies, viz., socialising losses by the very state who could not sustain the circuits of capital regulated, but uses fiscal and monetary policies for bailing out capitalists, was the available option. However, the frequency of financial crises and the threat of lower growth of potentially redistributable incomes to feed excess surplus capital, with the corresponding income and wealth concentration, and also the potential destruction of large chunks of finance capital itself, created challenges for finance. The general financial deregulation trend had to be, at that point, if not backtracked, at least partially moderated in its pace, and the primary mode of regulation at least partially resumed, with weak specific re-regulation, when compared to the modern capitalism era, in face of the crises that financial markets, *derivatives* included, have continuously enticed or contributed to from the 1990s on (UNCTAD, 2011).

Regardless of the specific national evolutions and configurations of the above trends, the abstract interconnections between state and finance, from a regulatory perspective, or deregulatory for that matter, which of course does not exhaust all state–capital links, can be thought as assuming a historical sequence typical of a spiral. It starts with the earliest accumulation of capital and a lack of, or loose, formal regulation, prevailing self-regulation at most. It leads to crises, exacerbated conflicts or frauds, regulated by politically unstable socialisation of losses, which pushes for the first mode of regulation. This stage is characterised by temporary stability and resumed rapid accumulation, with new leading surplus capitals entering either the old circuits transformed by the very crises or the new ones formed afterwards. It is not a return to the initial phase, but a different one, sharing only general complexions. Innovations are introduced. And then there is a gradual movement towards deregulation, followed by renewed types of crises, frauds and crashes, identical socialised losses, and then re-regulation, with new types of constraints, and so on.

Present-day financialisation, albeit a consequence of liberalisation and deregulation since the 1980s, does not seem to have qualitatively changed that overall mechanism but has rather intensified the rhythm of the movements, speeding up the gyrations over the spiral during the inter-crises stage, because finance capital is more prone to generate crises than other fractions of capital (Mader et al., 2020). Since the phases of the spiral have different durations, it is not a regular cycle. Still, considering the relationship between the state as regulator and the private realm of financialised capitalism to which the *derivatives* sub-system belongs, in the case of the latter instruments, especially those traded in OTC markets linked to finance, that part of the spiralling sequence where deregulation fits in is mostly missing. So, different fractions of finance capital are in different phases of the spiral, although specific developments may cause them to converge fast to similar stages, given the universality of money and mainly when large sums of money are rapidly destroyed.

That is, until recently, there was simply a sustained non-regulation or loose regulation of OTC *derivatives* for most part, characteristic of the primitive stage typical of accumulation under classical capitalism, obviating the need of repealing previous restrictive acts, that is, of deregulating, and therefore also of circumventing the rules. Considering the sub-system as a whole, Markham (1987, p. xiii) argues that, observing the U.S. experience, before the 1970s and 1980s, the attempts at regulating futures were not successful. Only by that time regulatory actions became pervasive and an integral part of the futures industry, "which has for years styled itself as the last true bastion of free enterprise, unrestrained by burdensome federal regulations." But OTC instruments remained out of oversight. As neo-liberalism deregulated finance and entered a new phase of the spiral, OTC *derivatives* could be seen as a model.

This is because the most important contemporary arrangements lumped under the concept of *derivatives* are new, whereas the older modern instruments such as futures and options were transformed by financialisation, with a relative replacement of the references, finance substituting for commodities as the main money accumulating device. Lack of regulation of the OTC-specific arrangements introduced in the 1980s, as a consequence, fits this interpretation for most of the period until the subprime crisis jump-started the Dodd–Frank Act three decades later in the United States, accelerating the pace of contradictions and creating a cleavage between finance and its *derivatives* sub-system. The spiral was twisted and crooked. These deals associated with the new stage of capitalism were introduced during a period of stark opposition, by finance capital in particular and capital in general, to state primary constraints on capitalist practices to the extent that frauds were isolated and crises and private losses were not severe enough, or were ultimately socialised.

Thus, in that particular historical phase, capital's political movements have not been about moderating the degree of deregulation, slowing down the motion up the spiral, since the most important OTC *derivatives* instruments were not regulated at all, but instead regulating them for the very first time, forced by the transformations that finance capital promoted in the accumulation, valorisation and mainly devalorisation of capital through crises. As a consequence, legislators could not trust the *derivatives* advocates' view, in face of a harsh reality for the majority of the non-wealthy voting population socialising losses via bailouts, quantitative easing and growing government debt. The regulation of *derivatives*, mainly OTC contracts, could no longer be avoided after the sub-prime crisis, reverting partially the neo-liberal offence against the state bashfully reining in finance capital. Naturally, this quasi-reversal movement is an oscillating phenomenon, with long twists and turns, and it is necessary to pinpoint that regulation of OTC financial *derivatives* contracts represented a watershed in a wave of overall financial deregulation.

OTC *derivatives*' inaugural regulation has actually been targeted at specific arrangements like swaps because, by definition, it cannot cover all types of transactions coalesced under this generic concept, lest it aims at boosting crises' levers even more, or creating undesirable circumventing routes that lead to the same outcome, viz. financial collapse. Thus, state regulation for the first time as a consequence of crises made possible by new instruments, set them apart from the other fractions of finance capital under neo-liberalism, highlighting their *differentia specifica* as an innovation under contemporary financialised capitalism, a new mechanism of valorisation and accumulation of fictitious capital that was almost exempt from constraints for almost three decades.

This singularity has necessarily a counterpart in the state apparatus when more concrete measures have to be addressed. For example, in the United States, taking into account only so-called *derivatives* and the executive branch of the state, there have been disputes within the sub-system between the Securities and Exchange Commission (SEC) and the Commodity Futures Trading Commission (CFTC) that reflect the ontological difference between the instruments that are collapsed onto this broad definition. That is, the new stage of capitalism intensifies intra-state agencies' conflicts brought about by financialisation and securitisation, with specific CFTC's functions overlapping with those of the SEC as finance replaces commodities as the more important reference for contracts. And there is certainly more room for other intra-capitalist class conflicts with so many money-centred bodies with regulatory capacity within the financial system, like the Government Accountability Office (GAO), Financial Stability Oversight Council (FSOC), Office of the Comptroller of the Currency (OCC), Fed, Treasury and so on. The general capitalist interests represented in the state apparatus are not always convergent to particular capitalist interests represented in the agencies when crises and losses escalate and the primary mode of regulation is called upon, for instance.

On top of that, the issues presented in the next sections raise additional doubts about the ability of even targeted regulation of singular instruments to tame their negative properties as sources of instability and destruction of surplus capital, financialised or not, for longer periods. That is, as indicated before, even comprehensive regulations can still be eventually circumvented, as was the case with the Eurodollar market during the Golden Age, suggesting that it cannot be effective for a long time span as the conflicts and struggles change the direction and level of the spiral.[2] This purposeful deviation does not seem a financial innovation in the sense of an improvement or cheapening of financial services or products for end users, as argued by their defenders, but rather a source of extra profits for the capitalist units implementing them, besides an extra layer of systemic risk. It hence appears only a way to embellish geared strategies concocted to escape the primary mode of regulation of financial crises tendencies.

This strategy allows a few organisations, mainly financial institutions, to earn handsome speculative profits at first. Yet, when the circumvention turns out to be misguided, as is usually the case, and crises materialise because regulation expires and ceases to function, however partial, the ultimate mode of regulation of crises in contemporary capitalist societies comes into force. Dodging norms accelerates the spiralling movement towards the next crisis, transformed by the previous accumulation trends. Outwitting regulation, however, is necessary only when the latter is somewhat effective, that is, during the initial years of restrictions, which may create pressure for deregulation. As a consequence, deregulation is not, historically, the only possibility for profit-thirst capital. Both can be complementary tools for the continuous search of unconstrained accumulation, valorisation and socialisation if devaluation and losses happen, with deregulation being superjacent or subjacent on circumvention during the initial restrictive periods.

The existence of a spiral, with different intervals with variable duration, and the fact that there are innovations superimposed on a particular stage only, imply that one cannot discuss specifically the regulation of *derivatives* and its evolution in more concrete or historical terms for longer periods, like the longue dureé of the French Annales School of History (Tally Jr., 2010; Quinn et al., 2025). Moreover, innovations in this sub-system are staggered, and controls or attempts at controlling have different time lapses and discontinuities. Thus, the regulation of OTC *derivatives* can be found only in contemporary national legislations, with only some sporadic bans seen in modern history.

Summing up, in order to grasp specific historical regulatory or laissez-faire issues about *derivatives* as an illustration of the spiral, a few international experiences should be presented, but space constraints prevent a wide coverage. Nonetheless, two important recent regulations of national or regional OTC *derivatives* markets can be considered remarkably similar to the extent that one is a mirror image of another: those rules in the United States and the equivalents in Europe, with a delay. These two national and regional spaces cover most *derivatives* activities in the world, as mentioned in Chapter 4, at the same time that a comparative perspective would be somewhat redundant if this imitative regulatory feature is accepted.[3] In this regard, it is important to study the chronological evolution of concrete movement involving lack of regulation and then regulatory and deregulatory aspects involving forwards, futures and options under modern capitalism, with swaps added under contemporary accumulation in the United States, as an average representative of developed nations. This highlights the historical differences between the modern and the contemporary periods of U.S. capitalism, a feature more important than spatial contemporary national experiences of that latest phase.

Commodities Futures Regulation under Modern Capitalism in the United States

Lending support to the claims above, Santos (2008) affirms that commodity futures trading, not *derivatives*, was unregulated until after World War I, despite the strong social and political opposition to this business, associated with speculation and manipulation that lowered the prices of commodities.[4] Markham (1987) explains that farmers opposed, in particular, the short selling of contracts, assuming a downward pressure on prices exerted by them. Santos (2008) reasons that this lack of regulation can be explained by the fact that the proposed legislations tried to outlaw futures, rather than regulate them, and that grain prices experienced a strong growth between the end of the nineteenth century and beginning of the twentieth. One can add that the resulting profits made over the period turned commercial and speculative capital politically much stronger, probably avoiding legislative controls. The CFTC (n.d.a) affirms that bills were proposed for the first time in Congress only in the 1880s, three decades after CBOT creation, to regulate, ban or tax futures. The first tax was enacted in 1898, half century after CBOT, and lasted for only four years. In 1914, the Cotton Futures Act imposed another specific tax on cotton futures trading. In the same year, a new levy on all futures was enacted just to be repealed in 1916, when a new tax on cotton futures was introduced to fix constitutional problems with the previous law.

Notwithstanding the inexistence of specific federal or state regulation other than taxation during this first phase of the spiral, the CFTC informs that exchanges like CBOT were self-regulated (CFTC, n.d.a.). That is, markets cannot subsist without rules made with a directly non-commercial, non-individually profitable objective. Buying and selling require legitimacy that can only be granted by rules enacted by the state. However, this is only acceptable if one assumes that corruption, buying and selling laws, is non-existent. The moral restrains buying and selling to the marketplace.There are no monetary deals in a complete institutional vacuum, since manipulation such as 'cornering the market' is intrinsic to profit-seeking, but it harms capital by means of 'unfair' competition if it is not generalised. The power of capital cannot be mobilised at daylight.

Considering the period after World War I, the CFTC (n.d.a.) mentions the Future (sic) Trading Act (FTA), of 1921, regulating futures trading in grains and imposing a tax on futures and options trading outside the exchanges indicated as contract markets by the Secretary of Agriculture of the Federal Government. Hence, systematic regulation properly started almost three quarters of a century after CBOT formally organised existing grain trades. Saber (2017) argues that the FTA was an earlier attempt to differentiate between trade for hedging purposes, conducted in licensed exchanges, and speculation and manipulation, like pump and dump, taking place in the bucket shops, also borrowed from Amsterdam. As a consequence, contracts for future delivery of commodities should be negotiated only in exchanges, and OTC forwards were banned. The FTA, however, was judged unconstitutional in 1922.

Saber (2017) also claims that no further legislative measures were taken until the end of Bretton Woods. But regulation of futures, not *derivatives*, continued to be part of modern U.S. capitalism, although it is not clear whether or not they were effective (Markham, 1987). More important, this first attempt at regulation, more than three quarters of a century after the first organised market appeared, was a response to fraud and market manipulation (Markham, 1987). Self-regulation, which does not disappear when formal, state regulations are enacted – there being an overlapping – was not enough without police power monopolised by the state. Capitalists could not do it on their own without the Leviathan.

As grain prices started falling in the early 1920s, the U.S. Congress enacted the Grains Futures Act (GFA) in 1922 to regulate the exchanges, that is, the marketplace. The GFA was similar to the FTA but prohibited off-contract-market (exchange) futures trading rather than taxing it. The GFA created new bureaucratic bodies as projections of interests of capitalists associated with concrete commodities production and circulation, not necessarily farmers, on the state apparatus, like the Grain Futures Administration (GFA) under the Department of Agriculture and the Grain Futures Commission (GFC), with a reporting system for monitoring and supervising. Santos (2008) argues that since the GFA targeted exchanges, it could not be enforced on traders, as agents, making it less effective to achieve certain goals as a consequence.

A crucial new legislation was passed in 1936, with the Commodity Exchange Act (CEA) replacing the GFA and encompassing a larger number of regulated commodities, not only grains, whose list was enlarged over the years as the legislation was amended. Actually, according to the CFTC (n.d.a), all references to grains in the GFA were switched to commodities, adjusting to modern capitalism still not ruled by finance capital. That is, it was less specific regarding farm production and more encompassing in terms of concrete agricultural use values. The GFC was replaced by the Commodity Exchange Commission (CEC). It also created the Commodity Exchange Administration (CEAd), subsequently merged and consolidated with other agencies, subordinated to U.S. Department of Agriculture, not to the SEC created two years earlier, to supervise trading and prosecute manipulation, such as wash sales and accommodation trades, a perennial feature of finance and speculative capital. A Commodity Exchange Authority (CEAu) assumed the CEAd roles later.

Santos (2008) shows how the CEA had many impacts on trading. These include fixing limits on speculative activity and position sizes, regulating the role of futures commission merchants, segregating customers' funds by function, banning options trading of agricultural commodities and imposing restrictions on futures trading by determining which commodities could be traded on which exchange. It was the heyday of modern capitalism. The options ban was effective until 1981, when the neo-liberal repeals abolished it andanother segment of the spiral was reached. The CEA also set the statutory framework under which the CFTC, created in 1974, nowadays operates, having authority to establish regulations as part of title 17 of the Code of Federal Regulations (CFR). Saber (1999) mentions the Commodity Exchange Act (CEA) as an example of legislation to prevent the CFTC from interfering with OTC transactions.[5] It is important to remember here that the CEA was enacted in the context of the Great Depression of the twentieth century, with falling commodity prices, and crises are regulation feeders in the spiral model, even though the relationship between futures, forwards and options and reduced prices is not always clear.

It took more than two decades for new regulations to be introduced after the CEA, mainly related to persistent fraudulent cases. In 1958, the Onion Futures Act banned the futures trading of onions after manipulations that took place in 1956. And in 1963 there happened another scandal, the Great Salad Oil Swindle. The existing regulations were insufficient, showing their limits (CFTC n.d.a.; Markham, 1987). The CEA was amended in 1968, in an attempt to boost the regulation capacity of the authority. However, Santos (2008) evaluates that legislation was lagging behind the rapid growth in futures trading in the 1960s and 1970s. Indeed, Sackheim (1982) mentions a 400% increase in the volume of trading between 1964 and 1974. Thus, in 1974, 126 years after CBOT was created, another fundamental state decision regarding futures was made. The Commodity Futures Trading Commission Act (CFTA) was passed, creating comprehensive government oversight of all futures trading. The CFTA also created the Commodity Futures Trading Commission (CFTC), with ample potential regulatory powers over futures transactions and exchanges, overseeing and authorising changes in the existing contracts, an exhaustive list of commodities and other instruments used as references and also the introduction of new contracts (Markham, 1987). Yet, the commission was created with a sunset provision of four years (Sackheim, 1982). This interval gave finance capital, then on the rise as contemporary capitalism began, sufficient time to concoct efforts to lobby and making the Act void, without the necessity of a reauthorisation in 1978. But this only if the extra powers of the latter potentially menaced to damage speculative profits at these initial years of effective regulation. This inverted opt-out provision for speculative capital has been a permanent complexion of CFTC.

Most of the traditional production-related subjects dealt with by the CFTC, however, were anachronic, to the extent that modern capitalism, which they belonged to, was being superseded by contemporary financialised capitalism. That is, the CFTA was enacted during the transition from modern to contemporary capitalism, but assuming the immutable economic structure of the former. It therefore suggests that futures were still considered the principal instrument or type of contract, when OTC options and mainly swaps related to the rise of finance capital were becoming more and more important and reflected in the very activities of the commission. For instance, the legislation focuses on exchanges as the main *loci* for trading, when unregulated OTC markets were poised to become much larger a few years later. And it assumes that commodities were still a relevant underlying, when financial elements were surmounting physical-referenced contracts (Jickling, 2003).

For sure, this does not mean that commodities could not be financialised, and that *derivatives* did not play a role in this process. Wellum (2020) argues, for example, that oil futures, in the context of major price shocks and energy crisis, gave an important contribution to the financialisation of the U.S. economy. Another equally telling occurrence is worth discussing. A figure with five stacked pie charts showing the composition of the number of contracts in futures trading from 1970 to 2004 has circulated over the internet to highlight the financialisation of the U.S. futures trading. In 1970, agriculture was dominant, with metals being the other minor slice. In 1980, currencies and financial instruments appeared for the first time, with two small shares. In 1990, financial instruments represented about half of the pie, and energy contracts entered the chart, in line with what Wellum (2020) found. Financial instruments kept increasing their share until the last available year. Currencies and metals shrank in relative terms.

The point here, however, is not how financialisation changed the composition of futures trading. First, the number of contracts may not be a good indicator of financialisation. Notional values or open interest are more revealing. But what is relevant is the fact that financialisation did not only change the composition, but the very meaning of futures trading. It is not about futures (and options) anymore, but about swaps, as it shown below. Finance capital overhauled all these previous arrangements in a way that single instruments and specific references that used to be important under modern capitalism, on their own, were becoming increasingly irrelevant from a financial point of view. If the CFTC were to be a contemporary, updated institution, connected to the then really existing capitalism, it should have been called FIFUOPTC (Financial Futures and Options Trading Commission), a difficult acronym. An initial D for *derivatives* would be out of question, of course. This anachronism, in the context of a financialised capitalism, created a regulatory overlap with the Securities and Exchange Commission (SEC), initially concerning stock index futures and single-stock futures. The phenomenon promotes a regulatory farrago between both underlying (stocks) and type of contract, to the extent that financial futures, experiencing rapid growth, belonged to the same contract category of fictitious capital, but to a differing underlying class of finance capital and source of profits.

These tensions and anomalies led to the Futures Trading Act of 1982–1983. It revised the Act of 1974, allowing options trading on agricultural commodities, representing a feature of financialised and speculative capital. Commodities contracts no longer pertained to the M–C–M′ Marxian circuit, but to the M–M′ circuit, since no physical delivery was needed and settlement had been in terms of money for a long time. Nowadays the Commission oversees and regulates all futures contracts in the United States, and thus its name is outmoded. Adding complexity to the mettle, most of the present amendments are passed to include new commodities and new contracts under the law. The latest one were cryptocurrencies, as the CME Group launched a bitcoin futures contract in late 2017.

Actually, the CFTC recognised the introduction of financial futures in the industry earlier in the 1970s but could not realise what it portended. Equally interesting is the fact that some innovations were unregulated, nailing the prejudice that regulation fosters innovations as escape routes. And many innovations were actually introduced after the CFTC Act under the approval of the latter. That is, it is clear that regulation sometimes is only a legal endorsement of industry particular interests, or approval of new legal recipients for the creation and circulation of fictitious capital. Thus, the views contrary to regulation do not make sense in this regard. The defenders of *derivatives*' deregulation or non-regulation for the sake of innovation assume what Saber (1999, p.4) identifies as presuming "the incompatibility of derivatives and regulation, as if the notion of innovation per se was antithetical to regulation." As already mentioned, the CBOT was founded in 1848 and the Kansas City Board of Trade was created only eight years later, suggesting an insufficient territorial or sectoral reach of the CBOT, with spatially fragmented agricultural, commercial and financial capital from an institutional point of view. These institutional changes are about the centralisation of the trading of grains and show the inadequacy of contraposing regulation and innovation, since the latter usually appears first and only when it malfunctions the former enters the scene.

The CFTC confirms Saber's assessment (CFTC, n.d.b, italics added):

> Previous histories have cited September 11, 1975 as a significant date in the CFTC's history because of the Commission's approval of the *first futures contract on a financial instrument* – the Chicago Board of Trade Government National Mortgage Association certificates futures contract. However, the *first futures contract on a financial instrument approved by the Commission* – relating to foreign currencies – was actually introduced by the Chicago Mercantile Exchange three years earlier in 1972. The Commission authorized this contract on July 18, 1975 when *it authorized exchanges to continue trading futures contracts previously unregulated* by the Commodity Exchange Act.

The timelines witness the transition from modern production- and circulation-based capitalism to contemporary financialised capitalism, with Chicago bourses best representing the changeover (CFTC n.d.b, bold in the original): "November 26, 1975 – The CFTC approves the first futures contract on U.S. government debt – the Chicago Mercantile Exchange 90-Day U.S. Treasury bill futures contract." And also "August 2, 1977 – The CFTC approves the first futures contract on long-term U.S. government debt – the Chicago Board of Trade U.S. Treasury bond futures contract."

Nonetheless, since continuous frauds and manipulations characterised the industry, they justified the maintenance of both regulations and the commission. In 1976, there was deceit over the Maine potato march contracts. In 1977, excessive speculative positions in soybeans and several declared emergencies in coffee futures. In 1978, the commission suspended contracts for foreign commodity options in the United States due to the London options sales fraud,[6] a circumvention of the options ban of 1936 associated with dealer options on physical commodities. Wheat futures contracts were prohibited on March 1979 (CFTC n.d.b). And it never stopped.[7]

Despite criticisms from finance capital and its cheerleaders, unreasonable in the context of an agency surrendering to their interests most of the time, the continuous frauds and manipulations may have contributed to the fact that the CFTC was reauthorised for four more years by President Carter in 1978, under the Futures Trading Act (FTA), and again, surprisingly in a burgeoning neo-liberal environment, by President Reagan, but only in 1982–1983 with a newer FTA, under the Shad–Johnson accords between the SEC and the CFTC upon banning single-stock futures (Jickling, 2003), with the agency functioning for a few months without authorisation. Reagan reauthorised it again in 1986 with a newest FTA. It has been reauthorised since then, but with some mandate lapses in between and sometimes only for shorter periods.

Neo-liberalism has created an environment hostile to regulation since the 1980s, but not to state actions aimed at boosting cut-throat competition between capitals of different sizes, or at socialising losses. As mentioned, this is a period of financial deregulation in the United States. Business concerns about regulation of exchange-traded futures, not *derivatives*, which again suggests the existence of fundamental historical misrepresentations, attracted the attention of market advocates in the middle of the 1980s. The work organised by Peck (1985) focus on specific themes such as margins, competition, capital formation, tax treatment, trading floor practices, funds, cash settlement and liquidation methods and livestock futures markets – issues important to the futures community, but completely distant from the reality of the financial futures and other instruments on the rise.

CFTC (n.d.c, bold in the original), presenting the history of the commission in the neo-liberal 1980s, shows the effects of the growing financialisation of the economy. Cash settlement represents the quintessential nature of contemporary financialised capitalism, connecting with the circumvention promoted by the Eurodollar markets in the 1950s. And options on futures the quintessential complexion of unfettered speculation under such phase. Equally revealing are the transactions involving a stock index and of Treasury bonds in the original commodity exchanges, as Kansas could not lag behind Chicago, highlighting the transition. Hybridisation of commodity and finance in 1989, a necessary feature, the rise of swaps, and exemption clauses demonstrate, if one additional demonstration was needed, the financialisation of U.S. capitalism and the decline of anachronic futures commodity trading:

> "**December 8, 1981** – The CFTC approves the first futures contract settled in cash at expiration, the Eurodollar contract on the Chicago Mercantile Exchange."

> "**February 16, 1982** – The CFTC approves the first futures contract based on a stock index, the Value Line Index Average traded on the Kansas City Board of Trade."

"**August 31, 1982** – The CFTC approves the first options on futures contracts (...). The contracts include options on sugar futures (...); options on gold futures (...); and options on Treasury bond futures on the Chicago Board of Trade."

"**January 6, 1983** – The CFTC approves the first options based on stock index futures contracts: an option for the New York Stock Exchange Composite Index futures contract on the New York Futures Exchange, Inc. and an option on the Standard & Poor's 500 (S&P 500) Index futures contract on the Chicago Mercantile Exchange."

"**July 17, 1989** – The CFTC approves final rules addressing the regulation of hybrid instruments that combine characteristics of commodity options with debt, preferred equity, or depository interests and, at the same time, approves a policy statement concerning swap transactions and rules establishing an exemptive framework for certain hybrid instruments with limited commodity option components."

Before the presentation about regulation reaches the 1990s and encroaches to the new millennium, it is important to briefly return to an issue raised earlier in this section and in other parts of this book – that lack of government regulation in the first phase of the spiral does not mean a regulatory void in the sense of complete dearth of rules that cannot be bought and sold. At least directly. This is because there is 'self-regulation' enforced by organisations or institutions within the industry since the beginning, that is, in the period previous to the CFTC, CEA and CFA, and continuing to this day. As a consequence, many overlapping directives are introduced: some of them administrative and some other technical. Considering specifically accounting requirements, for example, the Statements of Financial Accounting Standard 133 and 157 were issued by the Financial Accounting Standards Board (FASB) in the United States. The equivalent in Europe is International Accounting Standard (IAS) 39, replaced by International Financial Reporting Standards (IFRS) 9, and IFRS 7 in the UK. Taylor (2010) informs that, after these rules, there are no more off-balance sheet recordings in Europe. On another issue, if *derivatives* are so old, why the accounting standards were issued only recently?

More interesting, the self-regulatory associations are registered with the state regulatory agencies. And many times, as it is clear from the historical record in the 1980s, the state outsources functions to the self-regulating bodies, like the Financial Industry Regulatory Authority, Inc. (FINRA). Another contemporary example in this direction, suggesting an overlap of state and capital's regulation in the new phase of controls, is the ISDA Master Plan (Charles, 2012). Of course, it is impossible to list and discuss all the relevant self-regulatory rules. The same is true for state legislation. It is up to law specialists to provide a complete and exhaustive inventory of all *derivatives* legislation and to accountants to shed light on reporting requirements. A final issue, given the role of exchanges in formulating rules for their members, is related to the recent movement of mergers and acquisitions among exchanges, discussed in Chapter 5, which is an example of centralisation and concentration of capital, making operational self-regulation more comprehensive territorially and putting pressure on the state to surrender. Yet, since this type of rule-making cannot go beyond the industry interests and geared speculation with systemic implications is considered normal, from time to time, state regulation is necessary, mainly to preserve capital itself. Or saving capitalism from financial capitalists.

Consolidating Contemporary Capitalism, Changing Modern Regulations: Neo-liberalism and the Commodity Futures Modernization Act (CFMA)

The neo-liberal counter-revolution that started in the late 1970s and early 1980s gained momentum in the 1990s. The only part of the *derivatives* sub-system that was regulated, the exchange-traded contracts, were an obvious exception in an environment of financial deregulation. But this misfit would not endure for much longer. CFTC was reauthorised by President Bush under the Futures Trading Practices Act (FTPA), and the legislation was crystal clear about the power of the CFTC in exempting OTC contracts from regulation (CFTC, n.d.d, bolds in the original, italics added):

> **October 28, 1992** – President Bush signs the CFTC's reauthorization legislation, the Futures Trading Practices Act of 1992 (FTPA), expanding the CFTC's regulatory authority and reauthorizing the agency until October 1994. The Futures Trading Practices Act, among other things, *granted the Commission the authority to exempt over-the-counter (OTC) derivative and other transactions from CFTC regulation* and provided for registration of local traders.

In less than three months, the commission shows the neo-liberal zeal in exempting part of the *derivatives* sub-system from regulation and boosting the financialisation (CFTC, n.d.d): "January 22, 1993 – Using new exemptive authority granted in the Futures Trading Practices Act, the CFTC exempts certain swap agreements and hybrid instruments from regulation under the Commodity Exchange Act." The 1993 staff report titled "OTC Derivative Markets and Their Regulation" concluded that no regulatory change of OTC *derivatives* was needed at the time, that is, no regulation should be introduced. Since for capital time is money, the speed is not surprising. Actually, time is one important reason for regulatory phobia from capital. For instance, the introduction of new contracts, that is, new sources of profits, under typical regulation, could take months for approval. As a consequence, in 1997, the neo-liberal CFTC passed fast-track rules for reducing capital anxiety and approving new contracts in ten days (against 365 days before) or contract amendments (45 days against 180 days before) (CFTC, n.d.d). Besides velocity measures, the liberty of finance capital remained strong in the commission: "March 23, 1999 – The CFTC approves for the first time an order exempting certain cleared swap agreements from most provisions of the Commodity Exchange Act and Commission regulations." (CFTC, n.d.d).

At the same time, in the exchange-traded monetary circuit, manipulations, not surprisingly, continued. In 1994, two CBOT members, Anthony Catalfo and Darrell Zimmerman, manipulated Treasury bond futures and put options on the exchange. In the same year, BT (Bankers Trust) securities was fined for frauds in OTC transactions with Gibson Greetings Cards, as already mentioned in Chapter 8. The CFTC was reauthorised under President Clinton in 1995, since manipulations had no end. In 1996, Fenchurch Capital Management Inc. of Chicago was slapped a monetary civil penalty due to market manipulation and cornering the CBOT ten-year Treasury note futures contract. The CFTC entered into a settlement with Sumitomo Corporation in 1998 for manipulating the copper market in 1995 and 1996, imposing a tiny civil monetary penalty (CFTC, n.d.d).

But the softness of the CFTC in relation to capital was not unchallenged. Lowenstein (2010) asserts that under the leadership of Brooksley Born, between 1996 and 1999, the CFCT changed course and attempted regulating OTC *derivatives* tightly, but the effort was squelched by more powerful players with ties to financial institutions and thus favouring deregulation that ended in the form of a new neo-liberal legislation in the year 2000 to avoid future similar attempts. Yet, in 1997, the CFTC approved futures and futures options contracts on stock market indices at the CBOT that the SEC had vetoed for considering their base narrow (CFTC, n.d.d). Of course, CFTC can regulate futures, not *derivatives*.

The old anachronism, mainly regarding the physical reference, commodities, reasserts itself, and was used as an excuse to keep financial deals with different forms of money exempt from regulation. Anyway, a significant issue here is indeed the defeat of a first serious initiative in favour of a tighter regulatory perspective, a little more than two decades after the creation of the CFTC, notwithstanding the fact the commission was not adversarial to finance most of the time, except for the most extreme fractions of manipulators and fraudsters, including the exemptions of OTC contracts.

In a major example of the neo-liberal revolt, despite the legal illusion of regulation, in 2000 the U.S. Congress passed the Commodity Futures Modernization Act (CMFA). The legislation reauthorised the CFTC for five more years, overhauled the Commodity Exchange Act of 1936, putting definitively an end to modern capitalism regulation, provided more legal certainty of no regulation whatsoever for the biggest part of the sub-system, in particular the still unregulated OTC circuit, and introduced other measures. Among the latter, there were new organisations, such as *derivatives* clearing organisations and new exchange types like designated contract markets, *derivatives* transaction execution facilities, exempt boards of trade and exempt commercial markets. Former Treasury undersecretary for domestic finance Gary Gensler[8] remarked clearly to the bond market association in New York on September 19, 2020, the new world of financialised capitalism[9] (italics added):

> *As the markets turn increasingly to swaps* to take on some of the functions played by Treasury securities, it is ever more important to provide legal certainty

> for these OTC derivatives. We have worked vigorously to pass legislation providing legal certainty for *swaps under the Commodity Exchange Act*. I am very pleased to announce that we reached agreement late last night with Congress on such legislation, the Commodity Futures Modernization Act of 2000. This legislation, if enacted, will provide legal certainty, *promote innovation, and enhance the competitiveness of U.S. financial markets*.

This interpretation goes against the superficial views exposed by Miller, Steinherr and other advocates of *derivatives*. Yet, although the CFMA maintained the OTC market unregulated, due to powerful organised financial interests, the existence of regulation of other circuits within the sub-system suggests that *derivatives* are not about mechanisms for dealing with volatility in prices or risks only. As argued, there is an institutional setting. Furthermore, in this particular bifurcation in the spiral, it would be necessary to show why all the agents with exchange-traded contracts did not move to OTC circuit of the sub-system, since exchanges continued to be regulated, albeit softly. The prerogatives of finance capital include a relatively unregulated OTC market and privileges when the end-buyers go bankrupt. The CFMA sustained parts of the Futures Trading Practices Act of 1992, which prohibits state-level legislations to treat OTC *derivatives* and security-based *derivatives* for what they really are many times: gambling. It also bans legislating them illegal. It thus centralises regulation at the federal level, concentrating power and facilitating the bargaining of finance capital over politicians and the state bureaucracy.

Financialisation many times requires unmediated channels between capital and the state, since democracy can be dangerous to the former, including legislating effective regulation. Thus, in 1988 President Reagan, with an executive order, an instrument that cannot be repealed by Congress, created the Presidential Working Group on Financial Markets (PWGFM).[10] This group had an important role in the neo-liberal maintenance of unregulated OTC *derivatives*. The PWGFM in November 1999 was composed of Lawrence Summers (Treasury Department), Alan Greenspan[11] (Federal Reserve), Arthur Levitt (SEC) and William Rainer (CFTC). The PWGFM believed consensually and unanimously that the CFMA would allow the United States to maintain a competitive position in the global OTC derivative markets. That is their main preoccupation. PWGFM (1999, letter to the speaker of the House of Representatives) asserts:

> A cloud of legal uncertainty has hung over the OTC derivatives markets in the United States in recent years, which, if not addressed, could discourage innovation and growth of these important markets and damage U.S. leadership in these arenas by driving transactions off-shore.

And (PWGFM, 1999, p.1), repeating arguments used a year before by Alan Greenspan, that: "The Working Group has concluded that under many circumstances, the trading of financial derivatives by eligible swap participants (...) should be excluded from the CEA." As a consequence, the CFMA explicitly prohibited the

SEC and CFTC from regulating OTC swaps. The CFMA enacted by President Clinton did not blindly follow the recommendations of the pro-finance PWGFM's report, however. He was far more favourable to financial interests, having enacted, before the CFMA, the Gramm–Leach–Bliley Act of 1999, revoking Glass–Steagall and being the single most important neo-liberal measure in terms of financial deregulation. For instance, the largest investment bank holding companies were left untouched by regulation – big banks, big profits, huge political influence over the legislative and executive branches. All that less than a decade before the subprime mortgage collapse.

Clinton argued that the CFMA was fiercely defended by Greenspan, that he and Summers could not change his mind, and the Act was passed with a veto-proof supermajority, showing that Congress was fully swayed by finance capital. It seems that Clinton, Summers and Robert Rubin, the latter not in the PWGFM but defending the same interests, supported the pro-OTC *derivatives* legislation, opposing any regulation (Ferguson, 2013), in agreement with the neo-liberal zeitgeist. Indeed, in a 1998 hearing before the Committee on Banking and Financial Services, U.S. House of Representatives, Greenspan, well attuned to financialised capitalism, was contrary to giving the same treatment to commodity and non-commodity contracts.[12] Actually, these efforts led to a 1998 moratorium on CFTC willingness to change the regulatory status of OTC *derivatives* and currency trading, showing the strength of the pro-finance capital coalition.[13]

The new legislation, however, did not prevent old practices (CFTC, n.d.e). In 2001, the CFTC, with the new authority of CFMA, filed many complaints against fraud and illegal futures contracts on foreign currency to retail investors. In the same year, it fined Avista Energy, Inc. and a NYMEX floor broker for manipulating electricity futures. In the next year, Dynegy Marketing and Trade and West Coast Power LLC paid a fine to settle charges of manipulation and false reporting of gas natural prices and volumes. Actually, frauds using *derivatives* were so pervasive that in 2002 a Corporate Fraud Task Force was created by the government. An undercover operation, called Wooden Nickel, tried to prosecute agents stealing millions of dollars through sales of illegal foreign currency futures in 2003. In that same year, the CFTC and the National Futures Association (NFA) announced new rules to avoid fraud in the retail off-exchange foreign currency market (CFTC, n.d.e). The problems with natural gas contracts continued in 2003 and 2004. For instance, even bankrupt Enron kept manipulating prices, operating an illegal futures exchange and selling fraudulent lumber futures contracts.

The Task Force was not able to end the manipulations and frauds. In 2006, charges against Shell Trading U.S. Company and Shell International Trading and Shipping Co., subsidiaries of Royal Dutch Shell, for prearranged trades were settled. In the same year, an enforcement action was filed against BP Products North America, Inc. (BP), a subsidiary of BP plc (formerly British Petroleum) for manipulating the price of propane and cornering the market. In 2007, the hedge fund Amaranth manipulated the price of futures contracts for natural gas.

Actually, new legislation could have contributed to some of the frauds related to energy contracts. Thus, if there were any regulatory doubts raised against the

CFMA for its neo-liberal approach to *derivatives*, they turned out to be relevant by 2001, over the collapse of Enron, since the Act had a completely unregulated treatment of OTC energy *derivatives*. It became known as the 'Enron loophole' (Jickling, 2008). Another Act, the Farm Bill, was passed in 2008, at the height of the sub-prime collapse, to regulate energy *derivatives*.

After the Federal Reserve supplied loans to rescue the American International Group (AIG) in September 2008, the CFMA came into spotlight again. This time the criticism was due to its treatment of CDS and other OTC *derivatives*. As a consequence, after all these problems, on August 11, 2009, the Treasury Department, changing its instance of a decade before, sent to Congress a draft legislation to implement its proposal to amend the CFMA and other laws to provide comprehensive regulation of all OTC *derivatives*. This proposal was revised in the House and passed on December 11, 2009, as part of the Dodd–Frank Wall Street Reform and Consumer Protection Act, discussed below. This lent support to the critics of CFMA, and that the CFTC was, surprisingly right in, for the very first time, facing the financial industry in a serious manner by the end of the 1990s.

Financialised Capital on the Lead: Gearing, Net Capital Rules and the 2004 Pro-OTC *Derivatives* SEC Changes

The Office of the Comptroller of the Currency (OCC) report for the second quarter of 1996 mentions new risk-based capital guidelines that provide banks with an option in terms of calculating their netted potential future credit exposures, that is, notional amounts outstanding adjusted for positions that are offset against other counterparties. The institutions can report the net exposure by disclosing netting arrangements on a detailed counterparty basis or then estimating their netted credit exposures on an aggregate basis. Of course, the former is a more informative and accurate measure of credit risks. But banks were not obliged to disclose the method chosen, suggesting another important freedom for an important fraction of finance capital. This approach used to include brokers and dealers that were part of the financial institutions under the SEC's voluntary Consolidated Supervised Entity (CSE) programme for the five largest conglomerate of investment banks.

Brokers and dealers have their own specific regulation regarding gearing, the SEC Rule 15c3-1 (CFR, 2024). Their unified net capital rule was a mandate created by the SEC in 1975 to regulate their capacity in terms of liquid assets to honour their obligations to customers and creditors in case of adverse market conditions, that is, to limit gearing. Jamroz (2020–2021) argues that, until 1992, *derivatives* were not covered by this rule neither. Again, different fractions of finance capital have different political powers reflected in their favourable regulatory treatments. And given those instruments' built-in magnified gearing capacity, this exemption from the primary mode of conflict regulation amounted to the effect of Buffett's famous financial weapons of mass (wealth) destruction metaphor, with the government left to rely only on the ultimate mode of socialisation. It was a matter of time before it would blow.

The SEC amended the rule in 2004 to implement the voluntary CSE program, introducing different capital requirements for brokers-dealers engaged exclusively in OTC *derivatives* securities activities that could opt out of the then existing net capital rules. This alternative method was silty. The goal was to encourage those agents not to engage in similar deals outside the United States or outside the broker-dealer structure (in the case of non-securities). This is accomplished by permitting the use of internal value-at-risk (VaR) computations in estimating their net capital. Basically, the change in legislation allowed a different private calculation for estimating the tentative net capital for the broker-dealers that were exempt from fulfilling the extant rule. The calculation included the balance sheet value of *derivatives* and of securities without an existing market once the SEC had approved the use of mathematical models to determine additional funding like subordinate liabilities, deductions like illiquid assets and haircuts (discounts) from equity for calculating net capital for those securities.

Of course, by reducing their haircut and holding only a minimum capital, broker-dealers could increase their positions and become still more geared, despite SEC's assessment that haircuts were less important than customer margin loans, repurchase agreements and stock lending (GAO, 2009). GAO found out preliminarily that by 2008, when the CSE programme was aborted, gearing had increased by all CSE institutions. The SEC justification was that the exemption from net capital rule would release the funds held in reserve as a cushion against losses on their investments. Those sums could then be directed to investment in other markets, but one may conjecture that it was mainly additional speculation and risk of losses.

Hence, unlike what is claimed by Taylor (2010), the ability of *derivatives* to release capital for more profitable uses, to the extent that the release is effective, under financialised capitalism, this additional capital, besides reducing the ability to cushion losses, increases the prospects of losses, individual and social, by redirecting capital to speculative circuits. The net capital rule amendment of 2004 has been identified as possibly contributing to the financial collapse of 2007–2008 (Kwak, 2012). When the CSE programme was discontinued at the deepest moment of the sub-prime crisis, the then chairman of SEC Christopher Cox recognised that voluntary regulation does not work. It is not clear if he would have the same assessment for self-regulation. Anyway, he also expressed concerns about the completely unregulated $60 trillion market for credit default swaps (SEC, 2008).

It is important to notice that net capital is only part of this fragile-by-design regulation. Despite, or perhaps because, the belief that *derivatives* are effective risk management tools, GAO (2009, p. 41) states that "SEC did not rate risk management systems or use a detailed risk assessment processes to determine areas of highest risk." In view of the 2007–2008 crisis, the agency concludes that the existing regulatory capital framework, whose goal should be the alignment of capital with risk, was not able to completely capture relevant risks and reinforced pro-cyclical gearing ratios, not addressing the issue of systemic risk. The GAO mentions the finding that regulators agree that systemically important financial institutions, and their soft regulators, underestimated capital needs for specific risk exposures. For instance, regarding credit risks, the evaluation is that the Basel I structure is not very risk-sensitive. This allows banks to increase their credit risk exposures without aligning their capital requirements, since socialising eventual losses is assumed.

Equally interesting, the agency adds a new risk to this book's list so far: the trading book risks, related to internal risk models of some large banks. The report affirms that these statistical models underestimated the market risks and capital requirements for illiquid trading assets. In terms of liquidity risks, finance capital underestimated the vulnerability to a prolonged dislocation or shortage of cash and cash equivalents. Or perhaps they were betting that the Federal Reserve would provide it on demand, given the Greenspan's put. Finally, the GAO mentions off-balance sheet exposures related to the lack of capital by some large banks against the risk that the assets held by their special purpose entity (SPE) could have to be brought back on the balance sheet if these entities failed.

The GAO tries to understand the failures of financial regulation, making circumvention irrelevant, and to identify the most important elements that caused such failing in terms of developments in financial markets and products associated with gearing. One of these determinants are the new and complex financial products that jeopardises financial stability and hinders even the partial understanding of risks. The report concludes, *ex post factum*, that "(…) less-regulated over-the-counter derivatives markets have created systemic risks and revealed market infrastructure weaknesses" (GAO, 2009, p. 60). *Derivatives*, mainly credit default swaps, had been used to increase gearing. The GAO proposes the regulation of OTC *derivatives*, which was finally carried out by the Dodd–Frank Act discussed below.

A Major Crisis Along the Spiral and the Dodd-Frank Regulation: Specific Arrangements, Broad Laws

The loose regulation of futures exchange trades, the deregulation of net capital rules and the lack of regulation of OTC transactions suggested that a major crisis was a matter of a short time. And then in 2007 and 2008, the sub-prime crisis erupted, with *derivatives*, especially their innovations, playing a significant role. This collapse is an expected result of the spiral dynamics, even though the precise date cannot be forecast. Yet, the spiral model of financial regulation is not the only interpretation of finance capital complex connections with the state in nurturing crises. Kane's (1977; 1981) idea of a dialects of regulation, equally valid for finance in general and not only for *derivatives*, seems very useful to understand the back and forth of state–capital legal relationships, albeit less interesting than the idea of a spiral, since there is no role for deregulation in it, as it does not have a state theory behind its explanations.[14] In his interpretation, financial abuses and collapses cause economic crises and then regulation is introduced to avoid repetition. But financial capitalists attempt to escape regulation by introducing innovations that change the original arrangements, increasing risks and fragility and causing new abuses and dislocations, until new regulation is enacted again. This loop seems to go on indefinitely.

The historically staggered launching of arrangements that came to be known as *derivatives* has certainly not changed the overall model, although it certainly adds complexity to it, multiplying the sources of instability at different points in time. On the other hand, *derivatives* advocates revert the cause–effect direction. For example, in the context of the Asian financial crisis in 1997, Alan Greenspan marshals the argument that *derivatives* could not be blamed, since they were not the cause, but a symptom of the collapse (they could not avoid it with risk management, nonetheless). Another issue is related to the fact that *derivatives* are supposed to unbundle, repackage and price risks and end the dialectics of regulation once for all. The use of *derivatives* for hedging purposes would automatically guarantee the correct risk measurement, as reflected in its price. Do not *derivatives* marketsdo that, after all? What is internalised in capitalist enterprises to be managed as residual risks after *derivatives* are employed? By the same token, what is left to the market to price if firms adopt internal practices that minimise risks? Why regulation has to 'correct' the market and internalised risk management tools when crises that were not supposed to happen due to the very existence of *derivatives* erupt?

Regardless of how this failure of systemic or aggregate risk management is explained, the so-called sub-prime mortgage crisis and massive socialisation it required enticed the urgent political need of regulation, typical of delayed responses, specially of OTC *derivatives*. And since regulation is conducted by the state, politics is flashed out in this scenario. As if another piece of evidence were needed to validate Kane's theory or the spiral approach for that matter, the global financial crisis after the sub-prime mortgage collapse led policymakers in the advanced and underdeveloped capitalist countries to propose a new framework for backing reforms of OTC *derivative* markets, without explaining why it was not done before, given that all that they recognise as leading to the collapse were very well known for a very long time. The explanation is the power of finance capital and its most profitable fractions.

The studies by Helleiner et al. (2018) highlight the challenges of regulation under globalisation. To the extent that capital is an international force, regulatory issues necessarily affect transborder or extraterritorial aspects, including the required institutional cooperation among nations. Although the focus of this chapter is the United States, it is important to point to discussions in the Group of 20 (G-20),[15] including a larger number of countries. The group Leaders' Statement, during the Pittsburgh Summit in 2009, defends that (G-20, 2009, pp. 2, 7 and 9, italics in the original):

> We committed to act together to raise capital standards, to implement strong international compensation standards aimed at ending practices that lead to excessive risk-taking, to improve the over-the-counter derivatives market and to create more powerful tools to hold large global firms to account for the risks they take.
>
> (…)
>
> Since the onset of the global crisis, we have developed and begun implementing sweeping reforms to tackle the root causes of the crisis and transform the system

> for global financial regulation (...) We have enhanced and expanded the scope of regulation and oversight, with tougher regulation of over-the-counter (OTC) derivatives, securitization markets, credit rating agencies, and hedge funds.
>
> (...)
>
> *Improving over-the-counter derivatives markets*: All standardized OTC derivative contracts should be traded on exchanges or electronic trading platforms, where appropriate, and cleared through central counterparties by end 2012 at the latest. OTC derivative contracts should be reported to trade repositories. Non-centrally cleared contracts should be subject to higher capital requirements. We ask the FSB [financial stability board] and its relevant members to assess regularly implementation and whether it is sufficient to improve transparency in the derivatives markets, mitigate systemic risk, and protect against market abuse.

Despite the international implications, it is possible to understand the intricacies of the capital–state relationships considering only the U.S. experience with regulation. As a consequence of the sub-prime explosion, OTC markets, at least the standardised deals, were regulated in a systematic way for the very first time in the U.S. financial history (West and Kerfoot, 2013). The question remains: What is the precise share of standardised contracts in the total and what should be done about them, since the raison d'étre of OTC markets is to avoid standardisation? Anyway, the Dodd–Frank Wall Street Reform and Consumer Protection Act of 2010 (U.S. Congress, 2010) enacted a regulation of OTC swaps, despite the essential opposition of finance capital, as pointed by Saber (1999), and the fierce resistance from the U.S. Treasury serving it, as it is clear from the 1999 Presidential Group's report and the attempts at preventing the CFTC from seriously engaging with the OTC circuits before the CFMA.

The specific regulation is in the Title VII of the Act, or the Wall Street Transparency and Accountability Act of 2010, from sections 711 to 754 and from sections 761 to 774. It aims at increasing transparency and reducing gearing to prevent systemic risk from building up (West and Kerfoot, 2013). It is presumed thus that Wall Street was not transparent nor accountable before, and this opacity prevented accurate evaluations of risk exposures. Decentralised transactions do not provide centralised information, unless regulation forces such diffusion. Dodd–Frank amends the Commodity Exchange Act and the Securities Exchange Act for definitions and designing regulators able to promulgate rules or orders, such as the CFTC for subtitle A and the SEC for subtitle B, besides generic prudential regulators, including the newly created Financial Stability Oversight Council (FSOC), a new projection of capitalist's interests in the state agencies. The firewall between CFTC and SEC or between anachronic modern capitalism and contemporary financialised capitalism under Dodd–Frank is clear, a distinction that reflects the power of different fractions of capital, but nonetheless becomes irrelevant under financialised capitalism with subsumed production and circulation under the necessity of convergence of all transactions to quick cash settlement.

The first subtitle, A, deals with the regulation of OTC swaps markets, and the subtitle B tackles the regulation of security-based swaps markets.[16] Thus the generic Act deals basically with swaps, specific instruments, with only marginal references to options, forwards or futures (West and Kerfoot, 2013)[17]. The definition of 'swaps' in Dodd–Frank is comprehensive, being, perhaps over-inclusive, to use Lynch (2011) term. It would be a good substitute for *derivatives*, creating circumventing rules by just changing denominations.

This over-inclusiveness may be functional for finance capital. For example, the Act allows the Secretary of the Treasury to exempt foreign exchange swaps and foreign exchange forwards from the definition of the term 'swap', which, it seems, was done very early on (West and Kerfoot, 2013). A swap is not a swap if specific fractions of capital want it so. This has an enormous importance for this work. Why not regulate OTC *derivatives* in general? Why encompass many different specific arrangements under 'swaps'? The source of concern of Dodd–Frank seems correct, since swaps are the single most important arrangement negotiated in the sub-system and were at the centre of the sub-prime mayhem. And they are very specific and could not be regulated by a broad, *derivatives* legislation. In this case, the Act would not be specific enough and would be completely circumvented.

Subsections 714 (1) (A)(B) and (2) (A) (B) consider as an abusive swap or security-based swap, according to the CFTC and SEC, any transaction detrimental to the stability of a financial market or to participants in a financial market. Of course, the threat cannot be considered at the individual transaction level and therefore abusive instruments could never be identified. But nonetheless the commissions must collect information and issue a report with respect to them. According to section 715, if an entity domiciled in a foreign country could undermine financial stability in the United States, the commissions and the Treasury have to power to prohibit it from participating in the American financial market. But if a similar American entity is identified, what should happen? In a context of continuous mergers and acquisitions, or concentration and centralisation of capital, virtually all U.S. financial entities can undermine stability in the United States.

Section 716 is particularly important, since it prevents government bailouts in the form of assistance like loans, credit facilities, asset purchases, guarantees and so on to entities in case of swaps-related failures, except insured depository institutions involved in *bona fide* hedging and traditional banking activities, including credit default swaps cleared by registered clearing organisations. That is, it prohibits specific tools pertaining to the ultimate mode of conflict resolution, assuming that the primary mode enacted would suffice. And there is also a ban on proprietary trading of *derivatives* by insured depository institutions regulated by the CFTC, known as Volcker Rule, or Section 619, specifically related to covered funds such as hedge funds and private equity funds, but also commodity pools (West and Kerfoot, 2013).

Approval of new *derivatives* products is regulated in Section 717, and the novel status of *derivatives* products in Section 718. These two aspects have a relevant element for the discussions carried out in this book. The advocates of *derivatives* argue that regulation fosters innovations as a way to escape or circumvent the former. Yet, legislation creates a framework to legally validate economic and financial innovation, granting a legitimacy that private institutions do not have. This is important for end users, such that they are not misled by the presence of dishonesty risk. Section 727 enforces the publication of swap transaction data using real-time reporting, and the swap data repository institutions are introduced in Section 728.

Another germane issue is related to central clearing of swaps transactions (Helleiner et al., 2018). Section 723 obliges the clearing of swaps and group, category, type or class of swaps in specialised, registered organisations (contract makers) defined in Section 725, at execution facilities defined in Section 733. The clearing organisation must measure its credit risk exposures every day, settle the transactions and adopt procedures to minimise default, such as margin requirements (regulated in Section 736). Thus, it creates a synthetic exchange in OTC markets and undermines completely the business model of decentralised bilateral transactions, requiring some third party to clear them, for a fee. This may cause costs to increase. However, the section 723 provides some escape routes. It admits exceptions, if one of the counterparties to the swap transaction is not a financial entity, or uses swaps to hedge or mitigate commercial risks and notifies the regulator how it "meets its financial obligations associated with entering into noncleared swaps." And also, at the discretion of the regulator, small banks, savings associations, farm credit system institutions and credit unions. Since regulation must have loopholes found by profit-thirst capital, not all swaps are required to be cleared.

An interesting aspect about Title VII is the mandatory nature of studies in Section 719. In clause (a) (1), it is stated that the CFTC "shall conduct a study of the effects (if any) of the position limits imposed (...) on excessive speculation and on the movement of transactions from exchanges in the United States to trading venues outside the United States." (U.S. Congress, 2010, p. 280). The imposition of limits (Section 737), a tool employed since modern capitalism, seems a very promising way to curb speculation in general, not only in *derivatives* markets, if the limits are binding and not too high. The same provision (ibidem) requires the chairman of the CFTC to prepare

> biennial reports on the growth or decline of the derivatives markets in the United States and abroad, which shall include assessments of the causes of any such growth or decline, the effectiveness of regulatory regimes in managing systemic risk, a comparison of the costs of compliance at the time of the report for market participants subject to regulation by the United States with the costs of compliance in December 2008 for the market participants, and the quality of the available data.

Although the Dodd–Frank legislation has as its target the large financial institutions able to disrupt the rest of the economic system from the monetary-financial circuits, mainly major swap participants and swap dealers defined by means of tests, it reaches all units and sizes of capital dealing with swaps. Hence, there were other fractions of finance capital discontent with it, generating interest group conflicts and coalitions (Helleiner et al., 2018). Thus, the growing use of supposedly low-risk or plain vanilla customised (OTC) swaps by community banks was one of the motivations for the title VII of Dodd–Frank Act (Federal Reserve Board, 2011). For instance, in a meeting between the Federal Reserve Board staff and a representative of the Independent Community Bankers of America (ICBA) on September 28, 2011, issues related to the proposed rule on margin and capital requirements for covered swap entities were discussed (FED, 2011). The smaller institutions argued against Dodd–Frank's prohibition of the re-pledging of initial margin or re-hypothecation committed from the community bank to mid-level swap dealers, and next from that swap dealers to the counterparties on the other side of the swap chain transaction. As a consequence, dealers would have to have capital and margin for every swap entered into with community banks, creating idle funds – a crime against capital.

The ICBA also complains that exempting the swaps that banks arrange in connection with origination of loans for their customers from causing banks to be considered as swap dealers is not enough, since the loans and the swaps may not necessarily be transacted in the same deal. However, it is clear that small banks may be exempt from many obligations under Dodd–Frank.

Regulation works in complex ways. Unregulated finance is so powerful in its capacity to disrupt the economy that even supposedly 'unfair' regulations, in its own view, can be able to avoid larger crises when *derivatives* are involved. Wiggins and Metrick (2019) show that even with Lehman Brothers under bankruptcy court protection in 2008, before Dodd–Frank, the *derivatives* were exempt from automatic stay provision,[18] and therefore had a favourable treatment. They argue that Dodd–Frank has not changed that clause. A possible justification is the likelihood of triggering a systemic crisis by forcing creditors to sell assets to compensate for the *derivatives* losses if they were not protected along with the rest of the estate. Yet, systemic failures have happened under the supposed protection of *derivatives* (hedge). Also, West and Kerfoot (2013) mention a series of postponements of the effective date of specific Dodd–Frank regulation by the CFTC, buying finance capital more time, that is, more money.

West and Kerfoot (2013) draw attention to the fact that Dodd–Frank was introduced during a period of crisis-induced re-risking process. The data presented in Chapter 4 show indeed a *shrinking derivatives* market after the financial meltdown. So, business was not disrupted by regulation any more than it was by its own speculative dynamics. But lack of appropriate regulation caused a systemic collapse and the consequent shrinkage. The authors highlight the importance of reducing counterparty risk and increasing transparency by disclosing information and price discovery.

The latter means that OTC markets, since they are highly decentralised, and information is private, cannot discover market prices, in the sense of efficiently aggregating information, and thus centralisation is needed to publicly inform market prices to all participants. West and Kerfoot (2013) also stress the importance of de-gearing by required capital and margin requirements and the denial of government financial assistance for *derivatives*-related losses. Regulation so far has been able, it seems, to prevent another financial turbulence. It is in initial, effective regulatory phase of the spiral.

How can one make sense of all that? The link between the state and capital is continuous and dialectical. Capital tries to escape regulations when they are effective, and regulators, always with a lag that depends on the eruption of crises or relevant losses, to catch up, but not too fast nor completely. For instance, regarding the more recent period, Johnson (2019) highlights the existence of proposals for regulating ETFs. This suggests that no legislation is comprehensive enough to prevent existing circuits of finance capital in every single sub-system to introduce a new form of risk, or even the creation of new circuits. That is, the state cannot come up with a universal rule that can capture the specific speculative arrangements that innovation brings to the market, twisting old circuits or opening up new ones. Not surprisingly, Baer and Kiernan (2020) report how the industry is fighting the proposed regulations of those arrangements, as anticipated by Saber (1999). Actually, as shown by Humphries (2010), the geared breed of these funds are simply a way to circumvent margin-rule restrictions imposed on them by regulators.

Before this chapter is concluded, it is important to briefly discuss *derivatives* regulation in Europe, bearing in mind that, since the United States functions as lighthouse for global capitalism and mainly global finance (Steinherr, 2000), when it changes norms and rules, either emulation or obedience follows. Panitch and Gindin (2012, p. 9) consider this imitative behaviour as fundamental to manage the informal U.S. empire built, among others, by unregulated finance, as it facilitates coordination necessary to internationalise the strategies of national states.

When discussing regulation in Europe, the integration of the space for capital circulation, valorisation and accumulation requires, to be coherent, integration of regulatory issues. So, Poitras (2016, p. 476) argues that, in Europe, harmonisation of norms allowed the building of a single rulebook governing trading on institutions like Euronext's equity security and *derivatives* markets. An important step in this process was the approval of the Markets in Financial Instruments Directive (MiFID) in 2007. However, Bertilorenzi (2022) claims that regulation in Europe is fragmented, as already mentioned by Drach and Cassis (2021). In the United Kingdom, for instance, prevails the self-regulated model of commodities future exchanges. The European Commission was swayed by large traders in the City of London not to regulate these transactions.

Considering the spiral adapted to a different space that makes identical rules impossible, right after Dodd–Frank, in 2012 the European Union adopted the European Market Infrastructure Regulation (EMIR) (European Union, 2012). The similarities with Dodd–Frank are alarming, but justifiable within the cooperation and coordination framework of global finance capital (Helleiner et al., 2018; U.S. Congress, 2010; G-20, 2009) or the emulation drive identified by Panitch and Gindin (2012). The aims of the EMIR include increasing transparency in the OTC *derivatives* markets. Again, this means that they were not transparent enough before, but this did not prevent the advocates to state that, since it is market-based, it is trans-lucid and also mitigates credit risk and reduces operational risk. A good crisis can bring light to the darkness. Or to forward blindness.

Transparency requires reporting requirements of detailed information on contracts to trading repositories and making them available to supervisory authorities like the European Securities and Markets Authority (ESMA). The repositories have to publish aggregate positions by class of *derivatives*. Mitigating credit risks or reducing counterparty credit risk of all standardised OTC *derivatives* contracts is achieved by means of central clearing through Central Clearing Counterparty (CCP). Finally, reducing operational risks requires market participants to monitor and mitigate fraud and human error by using electronic means to promptly confirm the terms of OTC *derivatives* contracts.

Summing Up

The historical evolution of the institutional aspects of *derivatives* sub-system in the United States seems to follow a clear pattern of a spiral: lack of legal regulation with self-regulation followed by frauds, manipulations and crises, which imposes state regulation, resumed accumulation and extra profits, pressure for deregulation, renewed crises and partial re-regulation. These movements provide an important tool for understanding the connections between the state, society at large and capitalist practices in terms of different fractions of capital, focusing on instruments that they introduce in specific circuits for valorisation, accumulation and devalorisation. The implementation and subsequent changes in legislations, after self-regulation by traders themselves, reflect the transformations in capital accumulation and its mechanisms and crises. In the nineteenth century, there were unregulated forwards and then standardisation created futures under modern capitalism based on production and circulation of commodities. Taxation of single commodity futures was the effective but short-lived measure by the state at that time. In the twentieth century, the first regulatory measures were introduced with the Grains Futures Act. That is, regulation proper was introduced only decades after the industry centralised and organised the deals in exchanges. An important landmark was the Commodity Exchange Act during the Great Depression, generalising the regulation to a larger number of commodities. The effectiveness of such measures, however, must be further researched. The fact that evasions were identified, such as the Eurodollar market in the 1950s, with forward foreign exchange contracts, suggests that controls were at least partially restrictive, as they should.

Later, with the transition to contemporary capitalism, agriculture, subject to commercial capital (traders) and speculation, gave room to financial transactions. Industrial capital is mostly absent from *derivatives* circuits, even though agricultural commodities and metals represent important inputs or circulating capital and therefore should have the volatility in their prices hedged. Finance capital became increasingly important but was not subject to regulation on the same ground as commodities since they were out-of-scope innovations. Regulation therefore lagged a lot behind, and the anachronic Commodity Futures Trading Commission Act was enacted in 1974, focusing on commodities and futures. Options were most of the time banned when they involved commodities, and swaps were poised to become the main traded contracts in new OTC financial circuits. The approach of the CFTC was to make unregulated financial innovations legal, usually bowing to finance capital interests. Nonetheless, the transition to financial hegemony created strains between the CFTC and the SEC.

Despite regulation, frauds and manipulations continued to characterise the financial system and the *derivatives* sub-system, with the CFTC at most impeding profits earned in illegal or abusive trades. But instead of tightening the rules and punishments, the opposite happened. Shortly after the passage of the CFTC Act, neo-liberalism started sweeping the advanced capitalist nations. And a wave of financial deregulation was unleashed, culminating, in the case of the *derivatives* sub-system, with the Commodity Futures Modernization Act in 2000, which was not modernisation, in fact, since it was incompatible with contemporary capitalism. This legislation represented a major protection or hedge against the proper ruling of OTC contracts. And this financial loophole was defended by the CFTC. Thus, regulation does not mean more controls. Sometimes, they represent less restrictions and only legitimise speculative circuits. A complementary measure took place in 2004 with the new net capital rule for *derivatives* brokers and dealers. Gearing reached levels similar to the end of the 1990s, when major financial problems occurred.

As the spiral model suggests, a crisis was in the making. The pseudo-modernisation of CFMA became crystal clear with Dodd–Frank, since the former was not able to prevent a systemic crisis and did not focus on OTC swaps, the main instrument responsible for the sub-prime collapse. Regulation in this case was only a response to the state's previous designed incapacity to effectively regulate OTC markets. Advanced capitalism entered a new stage, the re-regulation mode, and Europe simply copied the U.S. legislation, with specific targets that are not able to cover all the risks accumulating in the financial system. Thus, even Dodd–Frank does not seem to be completely effective, as major failures happened after it was enacted and implemented, notwithstanding the fact that it was delayed for many years. So, the spiral model of the relationship between state and finance capital suggests that the current phase is still one of continuous instability and ineffective regulation typical of a modified laissez-faire, with new sources of financial collapse, like the ETFs, waiting for the opportunity to reevaluate capitals down.

Notes

1 The Oxford English Dictionary informs that the word 'deregulation' was used for the first time in 1963.

2 In the Ph.D. dissertation that gave birth to this work, the interpretation of the post-Second World War trends suggested that the international regulation implemented under Bretton Woods lasted *de facto* for about two or two and a half decades, during the Golden Age of Capitalism. If one considers today the national regulations that followed the Great Depression of the twentieth century, like Glass-Steagall and its Regulation Q in the U.S., the *de jure* time span was longer, although the *de facto* interval may have been shorter. Russell (2007) shows how finance capital unravelled those New Deal banking reforms by circumventing restrictions, moving from *Pax Financus* to *Bellum Financus*. That is, circumvention took place before the legislation was repealed in the 1990s.

3 Drach and Cassis (2021) present important regulatory and deregulatory differences among advanced capitalist countries. But it is worth mentioning that *derivatives* do not receive an emphasis in their work. National cases in Europe show that *derivatives* dealing with financial circuits of capital were introduced only in the 1990s, with almost a two-decade difference compared to the U.S. Again, this is another evidence that these specific arrangements are creations of contemporary financialised capitalism, not of the entire financial and economic history of capitalism or other previous modes of production.

4 Considering the main thesis of this book, it is important to notice that the arrangements traded then were not futures, but, according to the CFTC (n.d.a.), forwards or "to-arrive" contracts, similar to the deals in Amsterdam (see chapter 5). Gradual standardisation led to the development of futures and their full trading by the 1870s, with future prices quotes and specialised contracts, and later to a clearing house.

5 It is worth mentioning that the CEA was enacted in 1936 and the CFTC was created only in 1974 by the Commodity Futures Trading Commission Act, having received a large number of amendments over time, as discussed in this chapter.

6 A fraud carried out by the convicted criminal for commodities scam Alan Abrahams. See *Time Magazine* (1978).

7 CFTC (n.d.c) shows actions taken against frauds, scandals and manipulation in the 1980s. One decision is related to the Cold War embargoes, suspending futures deals on wheat, corn, oats, soybean meal and soybean oil for geopolitical reasons. Manipulations in the silver futures market by the Hunt family spanned from the end of the seventies to the beginning of the eighties. An episode usually not discussed under the problems with *derivatives* is the case of Volume Investors, Inc., a clearing member of COMEX that defaulted on an option on gold futures deal in 1985. Soybean futures were again a source of concern regarding fraudulence by the end of the 1980s.

8 Gensler resigned as chair of the Securities and Exchange Commission (SEC) at the beginning of 2025. He was formerly chair of the Commodities Futures Trading Commission (CFTC). Before joining the government in 1997, Gensler worked, as it is almost always the case, at Goldman Sachs for 18 years (see biography at www.sec.gov/about/commissioners/gary-gensler and also at https://docs.house.gov/meetings/GO/GO00/20130910/101277/HHRG-113-GO00-Bio-GenslerG-20130910.pdf, both Retrieved March 2025).

9 The full text is available at: web.archive.org/web/20090831103536/http://www.treas.gov/press/releases/ls889.htm

10 The full text of the executive order of 1988 is available at: www.archives.gov/federal-register/codification/executive-order/12631.html

11 Greenspan is also related to *derivatives* through the Greenspan's put, the easing of monetary policy after large stock prices declines between 1987 and 2006, bailing out speculators (Mullin, 2023). The is one of the tools of the ultimate mode of crisis resolution under financialised capitalism, as argued before.

12 The 1998 full testimony of Alan Greenspan is available at: www.federalreserve.gov/boarddocs/testimony/1998/19980724.htm

13 The letter of the financial triumvirate, Rubin, Greenspan and Levitt, against the attempt of CFTC at regulating OTC derivatives is available at: home.treasury.gov/news/press-releases/cftcltr

14 Cassis, in Drach and Cassis (2021), equally offers a new interpretative tool. He compares the same sequence to a cycle, invoking the image of swinging pendulum. Regulation was enacted in the 1930s, deregulation took place in the 1980s and by 2010 regulation

became again necessary. He then rejects this cyclical perspective regarding the deregulation that took place in the 1980s, arguing that regulation is country- or region-specific, with relevant sectoral differences and allowing self-regulation, and thus deregulation cannot be seen as an abstract concept. As it is clear now, while the specificity argument seems undisputable, it implies only a difference in terms of timing, with delayed measures, but not of territorial scope, since capital tends to homogenise spaces over time. Anyway, the cycle or pendulum metaphor and the dialects of regulation are put aside in this chapter in favour of the spiral.

15 Not to be confused with the G20 of the largest international banks.

16 Considering another layer of complexity, there are also mixed swaps, a combination a pure swaps and security-based swaps. Hybrid instruments have been an important aspect of *derivatives* and a source of regulatory confusion, as discussed already in the 1980s by Markham (1987). Hence, with just a single arrangement is already hard to conflate them all under a universal umbrella, and differentiation is imposed by concrete reality of the specific circuits of capital. Only money is universal. This highlights the point raised throughout this book. There are no *derivatives*, only specific arrangements with unique features that are not enough for characterising them and label them using a generic term articulating two separate entities in time by an *ex post* derivation.

17 West and Kerfoof (2013) provides other examples of regulatory changes that impact futures and options, such as rules on investments of customer funds in futures and options accounts and speculative position limits.

18 The automatic stay is a 1978 provision in the U.S. bankruptcy law that temporarily prevents creditors from pursuing debtors for the money that they are owed (www.cacb.uscourts.gov/faq/automatic-stay-what-it-and-does-it-protect-debtor-all-creditors)

References

Allen, Frank, and Douglas Gale. *Understanding Financial Crises*. Oxford: Oxford University Press, 2007.

Baer, Justin, and Paul Kiernan. "Leveraged-ETF Seller Urges Investors to Fight Proposed Regulation." *The Wall Street Journal,* January 30, 2020. Available at: www.wsj.com/articles/leveraged-etf-seller-urges-investors-to-fight-proposed-regulation-11580390914?reflink=desktopwebshare_permalink Retrieved March 2023.

Bertilorenzi, Marco. "Futures of Europe: The City of London's Commodity Exchanges, the European Economic Community, and the Global Regulation of Futures Trading (1960s–1980s)." *Enterprise & Society* 24, no. 3 (2022): 731–758.

Charles, GuyLane. "The ISDA Master Agreement – Part I: Architecture, Risks and Compliance." *Practical Compliance & Risk Management for the Securities Industry,* (Jan./Feb. 2012): 25–32.

Code of Federal Regulations (CFR). "Title 17, Chapter II, Part § 240.15c3–1 Net Capital Requirements for Brokers or Dealers." (2024 [1975]) Available at: www.govinfo.gov/content/pkg/CFR-2024-title17-vol4/pdf/CFR-2024-title17-vol4-sec240-15c3-1.pdf Retrieved December 2024.

Commodity Futures Trading Commission (CFTC). "History of the CFTC: U.S. Futures Trading and Regulation Before the Creation of the CFTC." n.d.a. Available at: www.cftc.gov/About/HistoryoftheCFTC/history_precftc.html Retrieved August 2024.

Commodity Futures Trading Commission (CFTC). "History of the CFTC: CFTC History in the 1970s." n.d.b. Available at: www.cftc.gov/About/HistoryoftheCFTC/history_1970s.html Retrieved August 2024.

Commodity Futures Trading Commission (CFTC). "History of the CFTC: CFTC History in the 1980s." n.d.c. Available at: www.cftc.gov/About/HistoryoftheCFTC/history_1980s.html Retrieved August 2024.

Commodity Futures Trading Commission (CFTC). "History of the CFTC: CFTC History in the 1990s." n.d.d. Available at: www.cftc.gov/About/HistoryoftheCFTC/history_1990s.html Retrieved August 2024.

Commodity Futures Trading Commission (CFTC). "History of the CFTC: CFTC History in the 2000s." n.d.e. Available at: www.cftc.gov/About/HistoryoftheCFTC/history_2000s.html Retrieved August 2024.

Drach, Alexis, and Youssef Cassis. *Financial Deregulation: A Historical Perspective*. Oxford: Oxford University Press, 2021.

European Union (E.U). "Regulation no. 648/2012 of the European Parliament and of the Council of the European Union on OTC Derivatives, Central Counterparties and Trade Repositories." 2012. Available at: https://eur-lex.europa.eu/legal-content/EN/TXT/PDF/?uri=CELEX:32012R0648 Retrieved July 2024.

Federal Reserve Board (FRB). "Meeting between Federal Reserve Board Staff and Independent Community Bankers of America Representative." 2011. Available at: www.federalreserve.gov/newsevents/rr-commpublic/ICBA-meeting-20110928.pdf Retrieved October 2022.

Ferguson, Charles. "Why I Am Cancelling My Documentary on Hillary Clinton." *HuffPost,* September 30, 2013. Available at: www.huffpost.com/entry/hillary-clinton-documentary_b_4014792 Retrieved April 2024.

Government Accountability Office (GAO) *Financial Markets Regulation: Financial Crisis Highlights Need to Improve Oversight of Leverage at Financial Institutions and Across System*, GAO-09-739, July 2009.

Helleiner, Eric, Stefano Pagliari, and Irene Spagna. *Governing the World's Biggest Market: The Politics of Derivatives Regulation after the 2008 Crisis*. New York: Oxford University Press, 2018.

Helleiner, Eric. *States and the Reemergence of Global Finance: From Bretton Woods to the 1990s*. Cornell: Cornell University Press, 1994.

Humphries, William. "Leveraged ETFs: The Trojan Horse Has Passed the Margin-Rule Gates." *Seattle University Law Review* 34, (2010): 299–323.

Jamroz, Michael P. "The Treatment of Derivatives under the SEC's Net Capital Rule." *Business Lawyer* 76, no. 1 (2020):183–210.

Jickling, Mark. *The Commodity Futures Modernization Act of 2000: Derivatives Regulation Reconsidered*. Congressional Research Service Report for Congress. The Library of Congress, 2003. Available at: www.everycrsreport.com/files/20030129_RL30434_61567c1724974670e031eae57f457269ee3c8253.pdf Retrieved January 2024.

Jickling, Mark. *The Enron Loophole*. Congressional Research Service Report for Congress. The Library of Congress, 2008. Available at: www.everycrsreport.com/files/20080707_RS22912_526be317ec7cc2fc1ab5948ae4d3b69584d6fb2d.pdf Retrieved January 2024.

Johnson, Katanga. "U.S. Securities Regulator Proposes New Rules on Use of Derivatives in Exchange Traded Funds." *Reuters*, November 25, 2019. Available at: www.reuters.com/article/economy/us-securities-regulator-proposes-new-rules-on-use-of-derivatives-in-exchange-t-idUSKBN1XZ2I3/ Retrieved December 2023.

Kane, Edward J. "Accelerating Inflation, Technological Innovation, and the Decreasing Effectiveness of Banking Regulation." *The Journal of Finance* 36, no. 2 (1981): 355–367.

Kane, Edward J. "Good Intentions and Unintended Evil: The Case Against Selective Credit Allocation." *Journal of Money, Credit and Banking* 9, no.1 (1977): 55–69.
Kwak, James. "What Did the SEC Really Do in 2004?" *The Baseline Scenario*, 2012. Available at: https://baselinescenario.com/2012/01/30/what-did-the-sec-really-do-in-2004/ Retrieved October 2024.
Lowenstein, Roger. *The End of Wall Street*. New York: The Penguin Press, 2010.
Lynch, Timothy E. "Derivatives: A Twenty-First Century Understanding." *Loyola University Chicago Law Journal* 43, no. 1 (2011):1–51.
Mader, Philip, Daniel Mertens, and Natasha van der Zwan (eds.) *The Routledge International Handbook of Financialization*. London/New York: Routledge, 2020.
Markham, Jerry W. *The History of Commodity Futures Trading and its Regulation*. New York: Praeger Publishers, 1987.
Mullin, John. "The Fed, the Stock Market, and the "Greenspan Put": Does the Fed Ease Monetary Policy After Large Stock Market Declines? Should It?" Econ Focus, (first quarter, 2023): 10–13. Federal Reserve Bank of Richmond.
Panitch, Leo, and Sam Gindin. *The Making of Global Capitalism: The Political Economy of American Empire*. London: Verso, 2012.
Peck, Anne E (ed.) *Futures Markets: Regulatory Issues*. Washington, DC.: The American Enterprise Institute for Public Policy Research, 1985.
Poitras, Geoffrey. *Equity Capital: From Ancient Partnerships to Modern Exchange Traded Funds*. New York: Routledge, 2016.
Quinn, Sarah, Francisca G. Baeza, and Devin Collins. "The Longue Durée of Finance: New Research on Old Financial Markets." *Annual Review of Sociology* 51, (2025): 213–231. https://doi.org/10.1146/annurev-soc-031021-105657
Russell, Ellen. *New Deal Banking Reforms and Keynesian Welfare State Capitalism*. New York/London: Routledge, 2007.
Saber, Nasser. "The Challenges of Regulation of Derivatives." In: Douady Raphaël, Clément Goulet, and Pierre-Charles Pradier (eds.) *Financial Regulation in the EU: From Resilience to Growth*. Cham: Palgrave MacMillan/Springer International Publishing, 2017.
Saber, Nasser. *Speculative Capital: The Invisible Hand of Global Finance*. Vol. 1. London: Financial Times/Prentice Hall, 1999.
Sackheim, Michael S. "Administrative Enforcement of the Federal Commodities Laws by the Commodity Futures Trading Commission." *Seton Hall Law Review* 12, no. 3 (1982): 445–469.
Santos, Joseph. "A History of Futures Trading in the United States." *EH.Net Encyclopedia*, 2008. Available at https://eh.net/encyclopedia/a-history-of-futures-trading-in-the-united-states/ Retrieved April 2024.
Schenk, Catherine R. "The Origins of the Eurodollar Market in London: 1955–1963." *Explorations in Economic History* 35, (1998): 221–238.
Securities and Exchange Commission (SEC). "Chairman Cox Announces End of Consolidated Supervised Entities Program." 2008. Available at: www.sec.gov/news/press/2008/2008-230.htm#:~:text=Press%20Release:%20Chairman%20Cox%20Announces,the%20SEC%20and%20the%20Fed Retrieved April 2024.
Steinherr, Alfred. *Derivatives – The Wild Beast of Finance: A Path to Effective Globalisation?* New York: Wiley, 2000.
Tally Jr., Robert T. "Meta-capital: Culture and Financial Derivatives." *Cultural Logic: An Electronic Journal of Marxist Theory and Practice* 17, (2010): 1–21.
Taylor, Francesca. *Mastering Derivatives Markets*. 2nd ed. London: FT/Prentice Hall, 2010.

The President's Working Group on Financial Markets (TPWGFM). "Over-the-Counter Derivatives Markets and the Commodity Exchange Act." 1999. Available at: https://home.treasury.gov/system/files/236/Over-the-Counter-Derivatives-Market-Commodity-Exchange-Act.pdf Retrieved June 2024.

Time Magazine. "Business: Options Scam in Boston." January 20, 1978.

United States of America Congress (U.S. Congress). "Dodd-Frank Wall Street Reform and Consumer Protection Act." January 5, 2010. Available at: www.cftc.gov/sites/default/files/idc/groups/public/@swaps/documents/file/hr4173_enrolledbill.pdf Accessed June 2024.

UNCTAD. *Post-Crisis Policy Challenges in the World Economy. Trade and Development Report*. New York/Geneva: United Nations, 2011.

Wellum, Caleb. "Energizing Finance: The Energy Crisis, Oil Futures, and Neoliberal Narratives." *Enterprise & Society* 21, no. 1 (2020): 2–37.

West, M. Holland, and Matthew K. Kerfoot. "The Impact of Dodd-Frank on Derivatives." *Fordham Journal of Corporate & Financial Law* 18, no. 2 (2013): 268–325.

Wiggins, Rosalind Z., and Andrew Metrick. "The Lehman Brothers Bankruptcy G: The Special Case of Derivatives." *Journal of Financial Crises* 1, no. 1 (2019): 151–171.

10 The Radical Political Economics of *Derivatives*

A Heterodox Interpretation

Introduction

This chapter proposes a preliminary and partial interpretation of the arrangements embedded in the contemporary financial system and known as *derivatives*, mainly by mobilising a couple of different but complementary heterodox approaches, already discussed in the previous chapters, without such classification, or introduced here. It considers the arguments and evidences presented so far to provide a critical perspective on this subject, identifying the ways that arrangements have transformed financial circuits, increasing the velocity of circulation and accumulation of financial capital and, by cumulative pressures for profits, capitalism itself, reinforcing a financialised economic structure. And then capitalism laws and trends, like crises and Schumpeterian-like 'destructive creation', have transformed finance and its enlarged circuits, its dynamics and the *derivatives* sub-system. Individual circuits ebb and flow, with the structure being conflated with the conjuncture, as the former becomes liquid, to borrow a term from Zygmunt Bauman.

It is preliminary because the heterodox approaches that included direct or indirect references to risks belong to a vast tradition, but were developed, except for Minsky, under modern capitalism and before financialisation and swaps, for instance. That is, they considered risks on a different scale, and need updating. Financialisation has been scrutinised for the past decades (Chesnais 2016; Mader et al. 2020; Palley 2013), but the new risks and how finance capital fabricates them to accumulate and change the logic of capital valorisation do not seem to have been addressed in depth. The focus must be on how economic and financial risks are related to contemporary capitalism in a dialectical way. Thus, theoretical treatments of financialised capitalism and the manufacturing of risks on a large scale are an ongoing discovery that have entered the heterodox economic theory gradually. This chapter proposes another step in this direction.

Some theoretical inputs or building blocks that tackle with risks can be put together to try to assemble the puzzle of arrangements as they pertain to modern capitalism. And then the transformation of capitalism by finance capital and the new role of old and new risks must be addressed, also transforming the theory of contemporary capitalism. A radical political economics must explain *derivatives*' ontological inexistence, the nature and scale of risks under different capitalist

DOI: 10.4324/9781003137092-11

configurations, the historical and present evolution of concrete arrangements, their intellectual pedigree as ideology, their functions in modern and contemporary capitalist economies, their social criticism and their economic and financial consequences. This was partially developed in the previous chapters as an invitation to further research.

It is therefore partial because the task of reconciling so many different but interconnected dimensions and theories cannot be accomplished in a single chapter, and only a small part of this intellectual endeavour of synthesis is suggested below. Hence, this chapter searches mainly some heterodox thinkings about risks and how they are related to capitalism and the specific ways to cope with them.

As discussed in chapter 6, *derivatives* are a contemporary intellectual invention. Only more recent heterodox authors, like Minsky, could have dealt with the concept. The founding heterodox authors could not have included *derivatives*, at most only the uncategorised specific arrangements. Keynes alone got close to futures, forwards and options contracts, having speculated with them. On the Marxist side, Hilferding also discussed futures, not *derivatives*.

The chapter is a critical extension of Chapter 6 on the intellectual reflections, retrieving and assessing heterodox accounts and other treatments of arrangements. Since the heterodox research discussed is concentrated on the macro scale, except for Kalecki, who has an integrated macro–micro approach, other forms of risks identified cannot be properly treated. This is the case of operational risks, not discussed here, although it was mentioned by Magdoff and Sweezy (1987). It thus considers a macro-financial setting, but also capitalist decisions that reflect class conflicts and income and wealth distribution, in a context of permanent but changing endogenous instability. It is thus also an extension of criticisms carried out in Chapter 8. It is organised in the following way. The Marxist account is considered first, as the basic framework. And then it is complemented by post-Keynesian approaches, before a synthesis is provided.

Commodities, Money, Capital and Risks Under Capitalism: A Marxist View

There are three central issues revolving around contemporary capitalism, for capital: the modified role of risks, slow capital accumulation amidst technological revolutions and asymmetric relationship between finance and industrial capital (financialisation). Yet, heterodox approaches on the dynamics of modern capitalism focused, since the nineteenth century, mostly on the really real option of coerced capital accumulation, that is, accumulation of stocks of constant, mainly fixed, capital and technology. However, the accumulation of money capital in the form of cash, loans and other types of securities and liquid assets is also central to capitalism and mainly to financialised capitalism (Crotty 2017, Mader et al., 2020). It allows the circuits of capital to start but also to be interrupted, by means of crises, or slowed down by diversion of funds to speculation.[1] The new nature of risks, however, have not been treated explicitly.

Contemporary arrangements that are named *derivatives* are thus part of the first and third central issues, of a financial explosion or uncontrolled growth of finance capital that characterises financialised capitalism since the 1970s due to changes in the way that risks are created and 'managed'. But also related to the second, as capital accumulation became subsumed and somewhat disconnected from production. Magdoff and Sweezy (1987) was one of the first works to notice it, associating the phenomenon with stagnationist tendencies of mature monopoly capitalism. Lack of additional productive opportunities for accumulated profits directs corporations' uninvested surplus increasingly to financial circuits, assuming various forms, including *derivatives*.

Thus, the rapid growth of some arrangements (see Chapter 4) must be contrasted with the fact that real production of commodities and industrial capital has grown slowly. This is partially due to waste and parasitism in the form of forced rents extracted by banks and other financial institutions, including dealing with risks that they continuously fabricate. But mainly the financialisation of non-financial firms, which increased their participation in financial circuits (Stockhammer, 2004). Nonetheless, the new role of risks was not captured by Magdoff and Sweezy.

There are relatively more risks, or values at risk, today than in the past because risks are a source of huge profits. Considering the rate of capital accumulation, it has slowed down in the United States after the Golden Age. *Derivatives* is a big (private) bank or monopoly capital business. Are these organisations bloated? Less efficient? Magdoff and Sweezy (1987) show that the patterns of investments and finance are disproportionate. If more financial intermediate steps like risk management are necessary today to enhance investments, finance capital is probably less efficient nowadays. But perhaps the issue is not so much one of stagnation or reduced growth rates, as suggested by the authors. The relevant question is that industrial capital growth has not expanded in tandem with accumulation of finance capital in general and *derivatives* in particular.

If all the claimed benefits of *derivatives* are real, where is the empirical evidence about performance under contemporary capitalism? As discussed in Chapter 7, advocates of *derivatives* and even critics claim that their use is tied to additional investments that could not be carried out due to increased risks, without explaining why they have increased. Yet, investments have been lower under contemporary capitalism with the explosion of *derivatives*. The advocacy lacks a sound investment theory, an approach able to make sense of existing evidence.

In addition to slack of investment, the distribution of income has shifted from labour to capital, as shown by Piketty (2013). There is a wedge between the paths of compensation (wages and benefits) and productivity. But there is a redistribution between classes and within classes. Financial profits have been usually higher. Speculation is a zero-sum game, there being redistribution among capitalist firms. And here all the phenomena observed converge: redistribution not of a larger income, as would be expected if one believes the narrative of *derivatives* advocates, but of per capita income that grows slowly at the same time that financial profits expand continuously.

As shown in Chapter 4, *derivatives* today are mostly about OTC interest rates swaps negotiated by banks and thus to interest-bearing money capital. Then foreign exchange, for international circuits of money, capital and commodities. Then only come commodities, the foundation of modern capitalism, equity and credit, also the vital force of capitalism. Of course, these orderings depend on specific circuits and arrangements. More important, firms that accumulate industrial capital are usually not the ones using *derivatives* for hedging (Emm, 2019).

Besides the *Monthly Review* authors, what does Marxist theory have to offer for explaining these trends? How Marx (2004) dealt with some risks of modern capitalism in the circuit of industrial capital by mobilising categories like values, money, capital and in particular commodities? Why risks have been commodified only at this contemporary time, given the historical centrality of commodities, money and finance to capitalism?

Before this question is addressed, one may go back to Hegel, according to whom everything that is real is rational. Its method in terms of subjects (content/specific) and predicates (form/general) is useful to rationalise the arrangements, as Saber (1999) defends, emphasising contemporary historical changes in social relations and thus in other constraints to explain the commoditisation of risks. Arrangements today are both subjects and predicates. But they were presupposed for a couple of centuries. Their combined economic potential was assumed but could not blossom. Only when capitalist is qualitatively transformed by their cumulative and quantitative expansion along with the growth of other forms of finance capital, they become a subject, able to affect specific circuits of accumulation and distribution. Yet, they are also predicates of underlyings. The 'underlying' as subject is mostly related to the traditional capitalist circuits. Arrangements were subjects without predicates, except for labour exploitation. Financialisation turned them into predicates of finance capital. There is reciprocity.

In order to understand these changes, it is necessary to resort to historical comparisons. The relevant transition is the one from the centrality of commodities and money under modern capitalism to the overwhelming dominance of money and finance under contemporary capitalism. There were changes in forms but also changes in the velocity of changing from one form to another. Money has the capacity to transform itself almost instantaneously into commodities, capital and many other money-forms, except when crises interrupt its traditional circuits. Commodities in capitalism must be transformed into money. Capital must be put to valorise, accumulate and reproduce, but this requires moneyness. A problem happens when there is immovableness caused by liquidity risk, that is, incapacity to return to money-forms. It is a continuous return to and of money that guarantees that capital maintain its movement and, more important, that value self-expands at the highest and, today, quickest possible rate. It is not idle money in the circuit of productive industrial capital, as claimed by Hilferding (1981).

This suggests that the nature and mainly the scale of risks are different for a pre-capitalist economy characterised by the circuit C–M–C′. Nature constrains the capacity of producing agricultural C and C′ and transporting them. On the other hand, commercial transactions having loose formal similarities with current arrangements are ancient, since the movement between C and C′ involves time and different tools can be mobilised to cope with the future delivery and payments.

Yet, there is some overlapping between modern capitalism and pre-capitalist simple commodity production and circulation, with nature losing importance. Arrangements like futures or options were not recognised transactions in pre-capitalist societies with some degree of developed commodity trade. Under modern capitalism, with the circuit inverted to M–C–M′, risks are interspersed in every transmutation in the longer industrial capital cycle M–C =MP $\{C_k, V = M_w\}$ … P … C′–M′, with a potential hedging role for arrangements. The difference about capitalism is that the fundamental trade is the one between labour force $V = M_w$ and capital C_k and reflected in the production of surplus value M′ – M, distributed among different fractions of capital. And there is no arrangement for that fundamental exchange – well, not yet.[2] Also, workers in the circuit M_w – C′ cannot buy arrangements for hedging, although unhedged increases in the prices of consumption goods in their basket reduces real wages, and reductions in sales of commodities can cause increases in unemployment.

In the circuit, there are commodity risks in the passages of M to C_k and C′ to M′ and reflected in the difference M – M′. In Marx, these risks are present in the idea of commodity' *salto mortale* or realisation of surplus value produced by the transformation of commodities pregnant of value into money C′ – M′. This is also the somersault of capital and its forms. If C′ are inputs in other productive processes, then commodity *derivatives* would still be a potential hedge. If C′ are traded in overseas markets, then foreign exchange arrangements could be mobilised. If both were about hedging.

In the case of commodity producers, one risk in the production process is that changes in the price of circulating capital C_{kc} – never fixed capital C_{kf}, since stocks usually are not hedged, except for their fictitious representatives in the case of shares, or loans and inventories – affect negatively the movement M – C by increasing the relation C/M and thus reducing the amount of capital that enters the production phase and therefore the amount of value that can be self-expanded by labour exploitation or alienation.

Also, there is a risk that changes in the price of commodities to be sold falls, affecting the metamorphosis C′ – M′ by changing the relation C′/M′ and therefore the nominal profit contained in M′. Other risks may appear. But there is money capital to start the circuit and that depends on the *salto mortale* of commodities to earn interest out of profits, if the initial M was borrowed. If floating interest rates rise before C′ is transformed into M′, there will be less profits left to the industrial capitalist to accumulate. This could explain the rapid growth of interest rate instruments, mainly OTC swaps and the slowdown in accumulation. Since interest is a deduction from industrial profits, it reflects the disputes between industrial capital and financial capital or interest-bearing money capital, with the levels and volatility of rates affecting profits levels and calculations. These movements can also affect bank's prospects, creating credit risks.

However, arrangements focus on prices variations, not volumes. And risk of non-realisation of profits must consider the quantities of commodities. Exchange-traded futures and options contracts have fixed quantities standardised.[3] From the perspective of producers and sellers, if *derivatives* were about hedging against falling prices only, assuming that quantities would be completely sold at the contracted prices, then contracts would not need to set volumes. On the other hand, since futures are not specifically designed to hedge, physical delivery of commodities is not likely, even if it were desired, since there is cash settlement, and speculation by necessity generates over-trading, as mentioned below.[4]

Thus, there are two fundamental, but connected risks combined from the perspective of industrial capitalists for the circuit C′ – M′: lower prices and disappointing commodity sales in volumes, the latter affecting also commercial capital. Considering only prices, from an empirical perspective that embraces complexity, the entire chain of transactions could be affected by lower prices at the end of it. It would be necessary to investigate to what extent retail trade, wholesale and producers are all hedging. Of course, business bargains would be another tool to 'insure' against unfavourable price movements. Just like Hilferding argues, monopolies capable of guaranteeing prices compatible with expected profits would make *derivatives* redundant for them. Yet, they usually cannot control sales and *salto mortale* is a permanent threat. Inventories would continue to play a role in adjusting profit margins and prices along the chain. From the perspective of industrial capitalist buyers in the circuit M – C_k, hedging against price rises may be insufficient for the same reasons.

The presence of other fractions of capital in the circuit, like finance, explains why cash settlement has been a permanent feature of arrangements. It was introduced to facilitate the circulation of finance capital and allow speculative profits upon alienation. Cash settlement may hide a fundamental problem of *salto mortale*: the issue of assuring the delivery of quantities of goods. Industrial capitalists cannot give up delivery of C′ to wholesalers and purchases of the components of C_k, mainly circulating capital, from suppliers. Consumers do not have delivery contracts with retailers. They can buy only what is available at a given time and place. But retailers do have agreements with wholesalers within the circulation of commercial capital. And the latter with producers. If producers fail to deliver, all the chain is affected. It is not only that commercial capital will have to pay higher prices. It will have to acquire the expensive commodities. And even if they are willing to forfeit their right to a fixed contract price and pay a higher one, a more important problem is the lack of commodities. And for volumes without delivery, *derivatives* may provide no guarantee.

Returning to the commoditisation of risks under contemporary financialised capitalism, this happens as generation of pseudo-commodities, since they may have use value and apparent exchangeable value, but not value based on abstract labour. Use values are related to unpredictable changes in money prices, or apparent exchangeable values, over time and space caused by movements of capital within and between circuits. Sotiropoulos (2012, p. 16) emphasises the separation between underlying commodities and *derivatives*, the latter being an abstract reflection of the former, which duplicates their appearance without connections of their use values. Thus, speculators are fractions of the capitalist class not interested in producing use values but buying anything that may bear the form of exchangeable values, including pseudo-commodities. It must be essentially tradeable, including risks.

Thus, the circuit illustrates the fact that *derivatives* are traded by capitalists. It is about reproduction and expansion of capitalist wealth in the initial form of accumulated money, but with new arrangements that intra-capitalist, distributive class conflicts have enticed. However, industrial capitals do not seem to need *derivatives* as an intrinsic condition for their production and reproduction, whereas big money capital under financialised capitalism does need. The former may be in a position to need hedging only due to the financialisation of commodities, with price volatility for both purchases and sales. This includes agricultural commodities in capitalist farming, metals, minerals, oil and so on.[5] But a natural hedge could occur with negotiated long-term prices. And more research is needed to understand the patterns of transactions between big food companies, big farms and commodity trading firms, besides mining, oil and extractive industries, verifying the importance of continuously uses of *derivatives* to hedge.

For example, Saber (1999) discusses how, for hedged producers, ownership of commodities represents a protective cushion against price volatility and a cover for hiding the costs of hedging, since they own the deliverable goods. He claims that there is no risk of producers being ruined for slightly lower prices or changes in the basis. And that farmers limit potential profit by accepting upper and lower bounds for prices, an argument similar to Keynes' view (Chapter 6). Heavy losses can happen only if producers sell more futures than they can deliver. And over-trading has been indeed a feature of *derivatives*. Santos (2008) compares the gauges of different periods. For 1884–1888, the annual average of 23.6 billion bushels of grain futures was eight times the average annual production. For 1966–1970, the future trades of 25.8 billion bushels was four times the average annual crops. The ratio jumped to 11 in 2002. He also mentions similar numbers for cotton.

Yet, Saber's claims are a valid reasoning for a period of commodity dominance that is past, that is, for the period of modern capitalism and its arrangements. For example, he contrasts the position of commodity producers with that of contemporary arbitrageurs. He assumes that the latter do not need any ownership to enter a forward contract and even to guarantee a line of credit and therefore eventual losses are not backed by 'collateral'. This could bankrupt them. Of course, for futures, there are margin requirements along the way and the necessity of liquidity for margin deposits, contrary to what Hilferding claims, and therefore the nature of speculative capital imposes the norms. In their businesses, arbitrageurs must get it right, anticipating both the direction and size of the change in basis risk. If they do not, they must find the money to compensate the loss. To the extent that arbitrageurs are usually large financial institutions, ownership and their value over time is an issue for both parts.

Anyway, commodity *derivatives* are less important today than they were under modern capitalism. Are commodity circuits less risky? Or commodities have become less important tools for speculators? If commodities risks are less important in the *derivatives* circuits under financialised capitalism, finance capital and its macro-financial prices risks are more important. Financial deals in *derivatives* are much more important in terms of transactions and values, mainly for fractions of money capital. First, money capital or interest-bearing capital related to banks and capitalist borrowers. Again, indebted workers do not buy *derivatives* to hedge the risk of interest rates hikes or default. Second, money capital circulating in different national monetary spaces, with foreign exchange. This is also valid for commercial capital and industrial capital operating in international circuits. Third, capital in the form of equity.

The movement of money capital M – M′ has been accelerated by arrangements, with M – A – M′ and A being an arrangement, a mechanism and not a change in form of the same substance, with M – C – M′ being displaced. Hilferding captures the acceleration of forms in the circuit M – A – M′. This is usually a neglected point, except for Saber (1999) treatment of speculative capital. Hilferding (1981, p. 156, italics added) argues that

> he [the speculator] must be able to exploit *immediately* all price differences, including those which will occur in the future. He must therefore be able to buy or sell at *any moment*, for any future *moment of time*, and this is precisely the essential characteristic of futures trading.

This is only possible in the circuit M – M′, with cash settlement.

This phenomenon has led some Marxist scholars to wrongly identify *derivatives* with money. Thus, Sotiropoulos (2012, p. 16) claims that, unlike ordinary commodity spot markets in which M represents the value of C, in exchanges the futures contracts becomes representatives of money, not A. For him, futures exist as monetary forms M, given that they 'measure-reflect' the future value of the underlying commodities C. So, following Hilferding (1981), he assumes that *derivatives* are a new form of money.

A similar argument is proposed in Bryan and Rafferty (2006). This work provides an interpretation overemphasising the international dimension of *derivatives*. They claim that *derivatives* are a new form of global money, performing "a role that is parallel to that played by gold in the nineteenth century": the role of "anchor to the financial system". Yet, as shown in Chapter 4, foreign exchange arrangements are not the most important ones. The latter exist primarily because there is no longer any monetary anchor in the world, fixing exchange rates as an institutional restraint on the movements of finance capital.

Yet, futures contracts or other arrangements do not represent money nor measure-reflect values at every point of time and space. They cannot even take up the functions of money as standard of prices, hoarding and means of circulation and payment. They are not substitutes for money. Even the doubtful ability to provide a stable measure of prices *ex ante* must be questioned, since this could be achieved by other means, including standardised contracts for customised periods. Not all commodity spaces have futures exchanges. Spaces of accumulation are heterogeneous and cannot be homogenised by *derivatives*. Price instability is the lifeblood of speculative finance capital.

The point to be emphasised is that *derivatives* tackle with money price appearances and their changes over time, not value-essences. The two fundamental issues here are time and/or space and change. Since change can only occur over time and space, the first is necessary. But change may not occur. In financial markets, institutional settings may intentionally prevent changes when they are considered harmful to the agents involved. This is the role of circuit breakers in stock exchanges, for example. They allow negative changes in prices up to a limit. This is also how Bretton Woods Agreement allowed governments in advanced and modern capitalist countries to control macro-financial prices, with fixed but adjustable exchange rates and capital controls to prevent interest rate movements. Changes occurred only slowly, and therefore *derivatives* for financial transactions were not necessary.

Moreover, arrangements are not about stocks, like money or gold. They are about flows and directional or differential flows. The international circuits of capital and commodities do not need an anchor, only the profitable means to deal with the consequences of not having one. It creates a sub-system of arrangements, and money belongs to a different sub-system in the same financial system. So, *derivatives* are not money in substance or form. If cash settlements are needed to replace C by A, then, of course, arrangements and money cannot be conflated. If margins accounts are kept in liquid form, and not in terms of arrangements, they cannot be conflated.

Derivatives are not money. But are they capital? Yes and no. *Derivatives* cannot generate genuine surplus value, only fictitious valorisation. Capital requires time, and exploitation, in Marxian terms, is the quantitative relationship between necessary and surplus abstract labour time. And hedge provides, at most, conservation of values. But the duplication that generates the concept as something derived from a reference remits to fictitious capital as a very promising venue for future investigations. The doubling of pseudo-value typical of fictitious capital is present in the relationship between *derivatives* and underlying, as suggested by Sotiropoulos.

Are *derivatives* a commodity, like risks? Yes and no. When they are, it is apparent, since there are exchanges for some arrangements. But a *sui generis* commodity, with a fictitious exchangeable value. The use values are related to the functions (see Chapter 7). But they are not true commodities, since there is no value generated by abstract labour exploited as 'underlying', as profits are formed through expropriation and upon alienation. As a consequence, risks also are and are not a commodity. They have use value for speculators, but not for hedgers. And some arrangements imply an exchangeable value for risks to be traded. Risks here as pure, abstract measures, since they are related to changes in a given quantity of money. *Derivatives* are supports for money creating more money out of risks increased by the very movement of money in search for more money.

Money, Finance, Investments and Risks: A Post-Keynesian View

How have risks been treated in the post-Keynesian tradition? There are not many dedicated texts. One exception is Kalecki (1937). Writing under modern capitalism, he connects two difficulties of capitalism: individual investment and risks. Kalecki belongs to a context of modern arrangements, but never discusses futures, forwards or options. His focus is on the determinants of investment, and, just like the contemporary literature, he considered risks. In that piece, he emphasises the individual decision about the optimum size of an investment constrained by an optimum amount of capital, but using a neoclassical marginal analysis.[6] Kalecki assumes that capitalists know all relevant current prices and have a rather vague and subjective estimate as to the probable future change in those prices and costs. So, they do not need objective *derivatives* quotations.

He nonetheless assumes that, in the short run, these expectations are knowledge, on par with precisely known current economic variables, and upon which investment plans are made. This eliminates uncertainty. Given the amount of capital and the method of production that maximises the efficiency of investment, the combination of that stock of capital with labour and raw materials, whose current prices are known, the capitalist can estimate the future returns of new investments. By discounting the prospective yields using the rate of marginal efficiency of capital, a linear function of investment, it is possible to estimate the needed amount of capital expenditures. Of course, in this scenario, *derivatives* would not be needed, since the nature of risks are related to shutting off the firm if the investment fails, depleting the capitalist's wealth. Arrangements cannot hedge against insolvency.

The maximum prospective profit depends therefore on the amount of capital, which varies from firm to firm, regardless of their sizes. Kalecki rejects the orthodox idea that the amount of investment is limited by diseconomies of scale or imperfect competition. The prospective gain is equal to the maximum prospective profit adjusted for the financial cost represented by the interest rate and an undefined risk factor whose nature initially is not clear. The optimum size of investment is reached when its marginal efficiency is equal to the interest rate plus risk, both initially assumed to be constant, which again makes *derivatives* worthless. For him, the problem is raised when the assumption of a marginal risk independent of the size of investment is relaxed. For capitalists, mainly small ones, the larger their own investment is, the more endangered is their equity.

Also, the capital accumulated in this form is illiquid, and can be sold, if at all, in an emergency at a heavy loss, risking their reserves and increasing the probability of defaulting on eventual loans taken, having to pay higher interest rates. *Derivatives* cannot hedge liquidity risks. There is a role for hedge, not necessarily with *derivatives*, here. The principle of increasing risk is related to increasing marginal risk of increased capital accumulation with own funds, not increased interest rates nor lower equity prices. For him, foreign exchange risks were not relevant either.

The risk of a higher interest rate charged by lenders is not dependent on changes in money and credit circuits, but upon the portfolio composition of firms, given the increased share of fixed assets and reduced share of liquid ones. And with regard to liabilities management through increasing debt, although it is not clear what is the share of financing associated with external funds. There might be room for *derivatives*, certainly not on OTC markets if the firm's situation is known. And, for formal large business, banks can find ways to know. The Kaleckian firm could offset the higher rates with exchange-traded futures and options but not swaps.

Considering a reverse behaviour, if firms anticipate the above scenario, they will assume higher risks and invest more, because it would be possible to offset their expected higher interest rates with arrangements, like buying interest rate call options or interest rate forwards (FRAs). Although, as the firm grows, it may affect local credit markets, if there are some left, not engulfed by financial globalisation. So, they can avoid additionally high interest rates, but not the effects of increased gearing on higher spot rates. If this behaviour is followed by many other firms, options may become equally more expensive, for example. And the system becomes more fragile. Specific arrangements may induce taking more risks, fostering the belief that they can be managed and solvency and illiquidity avoided.

A problem here is that Kalecki assumes interest rates changing linearly with credit exposition, not exponentially. So, it is about levels, not changes. And he then drops out the interest rate to calculate marginal net profitability. He usually does not emphasise the role of interest rates on investment decisions. Also, an increase in the amount of capitalist saving out of retained profits can shift the restrain imposed by the marginal risk, since it is possible to invest more without reducing the liquidity or safety. Thus, investment increases. Again, the interplay of stocks and flows can be managed without *derivatives*. The problem is insufficient saving.

If one accepts the view advanced by Stulz (1996) that a capitalist unit using risk management with *derivatives* has a higher capacity to borrow, then Kalecki's principle of increasing risk must be qualified. But is Stulz's argument valid? Risk management in the absence of *derivatives* is the business of adjusting assets and liabilities and mainly contracts such that flows of revenues and expenditures are not significantly affected by changes in prices and rates. But this assumes a configuration of the ownership of the existing stocks. Equity capital is not only a cushion for changes in the value of assets and liabilities. It is also money with investment potential, accumulating assets and reducing the insolvency risks of gearing implied by Kalecki. Therefore, a practice like managing risks associated with flows caused by the composition of assets and liabilities cannot replace a stock like equity capital, just like managers cannot replace capitalists to the extent that control must be exercised on units of existing capitals.[7] Risk management, in this regard, is a fetish and should be added to commodity fetishism as a social illusion.

Considering another post-Keynesian author, Minsky, *derivatives* are compatible with his Wall Street paradigm (Minsky 1986). Many of Minsky's works are contemporaneous of the new phase, after the passage from modern (Amsterdam/Osaka/Chicago) to contemporary (New York/London) arrangements. But he did not pay enough attention to *derivatives*. Minsky (1975) missed an important link to the contemporary stage that was forming when he coined the term. Longer periods of stability assumed by him, however, have become less likely. Permanent instability and financial fragility were inaugurated by the hegemony of finance capital.

Besides an acute financial analysis of specific net flows associated with different ratios of assets to liabilities, his treatment of risks, following Keynes, includes borrower's (insufficient income) and lender's risks (default). For dealing with lender risks associated with debts under contemporary capitalism, credit default swaps could be mobilised. But they have not been relevant in arrangements' circuits, although they have caused instability and crises (Troncoso, 2019). Minsky (1982) shows the dynamics of debt and income, or of variations in stocks and flows, to identify the impact of sudden changes in interest rates on balance-sheet and solvency reversals. So, Minsky (1986) discusses the indirect risks of interest rate, not of future loss income by creditors or increased expenses by borrowers, but of present value reversals of borrowers' wealth that cause liabilities temporarily to exceed assets, and liquid liabilities to exceed liquid assets, causing bankruptcies and liquidity crunches. Insolvency risk again.

Positions in arrangements are about notional amounts with balance-sheet or income repercussions. Notional amounts do not change by definition after the contract is signed. But flows using them as references do. Hedging is about net positions in *derivatives* causing compensating changes in income flows when prices change. In Minsky, the prolonged stability of net income flows, named hedge only by coincidence, cause gradual increases in stocks like debt and gearing, moving to speculative, another coincidence, and Ponzi positions. Financial fragility increases, that is, changes in interest rates can cause net worth to become negative.

Yet, stability should reduce the need of insuring flows only in the short run, under hedge. Increases in gearing and also in speculation are self-reinforcing as open positions create more fragility or sensibility to changes, and also additional speculative deals that reinforces instability. Even small variations are threatening under Ponzi, like the LTCM debacle shows. But for the *derivatives* industry to thrive, instability is necessary. Continuous macro-financial instability is no longer a hypothesis, but a fact. As *derivatives* contribute to intensify it in a dynamic environment, then Minsky's argument is reverted. Continuous instability makes destabilising unlikely. However, this does not mean *derivatives* could play a positive role.

Minsky (1982) shows that after instability leads to crashes, big government steps in to replenish the capital destroyed and socialise losses, making private *derivatives* irrelevant for hedging. Recent episodes of big (central) bank and big (bail-out) government abound, like AIG over the sub-prime collapse. Policymakers, not *derivatives*, have avoided "It", that is, another Great Depression. There was only a Great Crisis in 2007–2008 after the Great Moderation or secular stagnation. The point is that *derivatives* like CDS alone could have triggered another profound depression by fabricating artificial creditors without any lender's risk.

It is not only that, for post-Keynesians, important risks like insolvency and liquidity cannot be hedged. It is essentially that fundamental uncertainty cannot be hedged and *derivatives* are irrelevant. Liquidity preference or holding sufficient cash in this case is a favourite form of hedge for capitalists, because there are both illiquid wealth as underlying and corresponding flows of net income at risk to be hedged against market follies (Milan, 2014). Money, not arrangements, allows capitalists to travel the turbulent waters of time, essence of *derivatives*. This is the universal representation of wealth in capitalism. It connects the past, the present and the future better than arrangements. Money is an insurance, just like short-time deposits earning interest. But banks may go bankrupt and FDIC can hedge demand deposits in the United States. However, whereas deposit insurance provides protection to working class households and small capitalists, they are irrelevant for capital as a whole.

For Keynes (1936), the risk of illiquidity must be detailed, like equity in the form of shares. There is a hierarchy, and individual liquidity does not converge to social liquidity. There are no *derivatives* for this second type of liquidity risk, that is, for insufficient aggregate capacity to transform assets and goods and services into money. That is why risk cannot replace uncertainty. In a certain manner, liquidity risk is another approach to *salto mortale*. Or *salto mortale* is just liquidity risk in a different coat.

As Davidson (1972) argues, an ergodic world makes *derivatives* unnecessary. Yet, a non-ergodic work has no role for *derivatives* either. That is, arrangements are impotent when uncertainty is considered, and ineffective when risks are the relevant issue. Both are part of capitalism. But since speculation is a means to short-term profits, and *derivatives* have to facilitate speculation, they are needed for financial capitalists, but not for hedging. In this regard, Keynes the speculator can be invoked to explain how *derivatives* could transform speculation by changing the proportions between bulls or pessimist sellers and bears or optimist buyers. Bear and bull markets can change liquidity conditions and cause interest rate risk.

Despite the reduced role of credit *derivatives* in the sub-system, credit crises remain central to contemporary capitalist dynamics. Moreover, banks that monopolise the *derivatives* contracts deal with all payments. This is another channel for systemic risk that needs further investigation. It is related to the centrality of money for capitalism. In a crisis, the threat is one of moving full speed to a world of neoclassical general equilibrium barter, where there is no money and circuits cease to function.

This hierarchy of money implies the prominence of interest income. This is the law of rentiers' capitalism. But rentiers earn fixed income, the safe type. And big (private) banks are there to make sure that unhedged interest incomes are hedged institutionally. So, is the liquidity trap that hurts rentiers and breeds bears still relevant in the presence of interest rate *derivatives* as downside interest rate risk is almost completely eliminated at the lower bound[8]? The sub-prime mortgage crisis suggests that it is. And *derivatives* are not designed to hedge interest rate risks, but to cause them instead, by transmitting volatility to cash markets. Unconventional monetary policy is mobilised to overcome the trap. Again, *derivatives* are unnecessary. Additional research about interest rate arrangements under conditions of liquidity trap is necessary, though.

Post-Keynesians, therefore, can argue that *derivatives* cannot avoid uncertainty. And even some risks may not be hedged. Others may be, but hedge may turn out to be unnecessary. For post-Keynesians *derivatives* are irrelevant on another dimension. Other regulatory mechanisms convergent to post-Keynesian arguments were historically mobilised to provide insurance against different types of risks, such as fixed exchange rates and capital controls for curbing foreign exchange volatility in international circuits, national regulation over interest rates or fixed long-term rates, national supervision of credit, national buffer stocks for commodity prices and so on. For example, Glass–Steagall separated deposits and long-run tradeable assets to insulate payment institutions in the United States. Research about how securitisation changed that is another gap.

By the same token, as discussed in Chapter 9, regulation has a dialectical relationship with capitalism. Under financialised capitalism, given the speculative essence of contemporary *derivatives*, all these mechanisms were dismantled by neo-liberalism and risks were enhanced and commodified, transferring additional income and wealth to banks and other financial institutions.

Summing Up, But Not Too Much: A Synthesis of Marxism and Post-Keynesians

It is now possible to synthesise the two complementary views: On the one hand, Marxism with an emphasis on commoditisation of risks, commodity risks or *salto mortale*, and the assumption that the new interest rate and foreign exchange risks and transformations of arrangements respond to the needs of contemporary finance capital in its fictitious nature to accelerate the movement from M to M′. Intra-capitalist class conflicts explain interest rate risks and the importance of OTC swaps. The parasitic nature of contemporary finance and the superstructural apologetic ideology of risk management fit *derivatives* nicely. On the other hand, Keynes–Kalecki–Minsky with an emphasis on risks that cannot be hedged, like liquidity and insolvency, and also on credit and systemic risks in the context of permanent instability and financial fragility. Arrangements are not necessary as risks could be treated by regulation or liquidity holdings. More important, fundamental uncertainty cannot be hedged or eliminated.

A heterodox synthesis must consider, besides the challenges identified in the introduction to this chapter, the basic mechanism behind *derivatives*: contracts with parameters for the future, references associated with capital fixing notional values, a time interval between present and future and differentials in terms of the price of the references and the parameters. The intra-capitalist redistribution focuses on the differentials. For example, interest income growth belongs to interest-bearing capital. It is connected to credit or banking capital, as part of the capital assumes the institutional form of banks, which surprisingly do not hedge using credit default swaps. The importance of profit upon alienation is clear: hedge funds, ETFs and other funds, as pools of money, under money manager capitalism, require *derivatives* as a source of profits via redistribution.

Credit crises and systemic risks occur because capitalism represents a totality. It is about all relevant circuits of capital, interconnected on a global scale, or even at the national or regionallevel. *Derivatives* amplify those risks to an unseen scale, since the stock of speculative capital grows faster than the ability to transfer the flows of money to its concentrated holders, given generalised over-trading. There is always a risk of a crisis. Financialised central banks and other regulators must avoid that, but at same time, avoiding preventing fictitious capital from valorising and accumulating. They prefer to wait and see and act afterwards, socialising losses and regulating softly (Chapter 9).

Both views take into account the centrality of money and time to understand the varieties of capitalism. An older term used to refer to forwards in the United States was 'to-arrive' contracts, since delivery, when it happened, took place a couple of months later, that is, after contracting. However, this lag is always a feature of capitalist production. The completion of the circuits of capital requires the mobilisation of different forms of capital and it implies necessarily the passage of time, from money to commodities, and then to production processes and finally to sales and money again. Saber (1999) provides a very good synthesis of the time involved in the different circuits of capital. So, commodities to-be-produced by human labour in a productive process are always 'to-arrive'. The passage of time, on the other hand, involves uncertainty and not only risks, requiring a post-Keynesian complementation.

Contemporary financialised capitalism changes the nature and scales of risk such that hedging may eventually become necessary. Speculation is pre-capitalist, but capitalism magnifies it. It is part of a process of creating new speculative vessels like *derivatives*. It is about capital, and hedging and speculating with *derivatives* must be seen as originating in a historical phase when financial profits were lacklustre. The arrangements answer to a need of creating the conditions for boosting profits expressed in variations in cash, but without capital, and therefore not related to exploitation of labour, and with an intrinsic gearing. The lack of initial capital is a different form of starting the circuit M – M′ without a dependency on previous own flows of profits or banking credit. It is pure and simple speculation, a hardy perennial, with attempts at valorising capitals by means of rapid transfers of money or what Marx calls profit upon alienation. *Derivatives* are cheaper to speculate with. Besides hedge and speculation, there is also arbitrage with *derivatives* (Saber 1999). It is commercial capital and finance capital combined, as an outcome of financialised capitalism.

What is missing in both views? The risks of changes in the value of equity and foreign exchange rates under conditions of a money manager capitalism or Wall Street paradigm. Hilferding discussed joint stock companies and promoter's profit as a starting point, just like Keynes discussed the role of forwards, not *derivatives*, in his interest covered parity model. As mentioned in Chapter 6, Keynes (1923) considered the international movements of capital and the interest rate covered parity, including the foreign exchange risk. But these are pre-Keynesian works. Keynes belongs to heterodox field due to his later works, since he wrote about forwards from his practical experience as speculator and thus embodying its ethos and worldview. Keynes (1936) mentions that it is hard to get rid of old ideas. It is also hard to get rid of naturalisation processes.

Concerning equity arrangements, they are quantitatively unimportant. In the secondary markets, or stock exchanges, the issue is about individual liquidity for the shareholders. The price of stocks in theses circuits does not strongly affect the decisions of promoting capital accumulation. Equity *derivatives* can serve the purpose, not from the perspective of joint stock companies, but of fictitious capital. Could Marxist's fictitious capital be relevant then?

Derivatives are all about duplicating synthetically and inversely the underlying in the form of notional values. Yet, the correspondence is not binding, and *derivatives* can arrange for larger notional amounts than there are references at risk. Hedging with *derivatives* requires Minskyian speculation and Ponzi schemes. Duplication turns into triplication, quadruplication of notional values and so on, increasing fragility and instability, just like stock markets overvalue stocks in relation to book value or replacement costs manifold. If shares are fictitious capital, then equity *derivatives* represent fictitious positions to the third degree.

Regarding foreign exchange arrangements, it is related to the international circulation of money, commodities and capitals. It is a compound of financialisation and globalisation. The latter brings another layer of uncertainty to capitals, since now real and fictitious surpluses are produced and mainly distributed in many parts of the world, and flows of money, commodities and capitals have to be converted into different currencies. The layers of risk are superimposed. The intra-capitalist class disputes include not only industrial capitalists, but also money and commercial capitalists, from different parts of the world. This exposes money-trading capital and finance capital to currency risks. Exchange rate volatility is related to the struggle between capitals in their movement, and the movement of their incomes, across borders.

The strength of U.S. capitalism on a global scale is partly due to the fact that there is a single currency ruling over the national space of accumulation, realisation and transfers of surplus (NRC 1995). European capitals longed for something similar with the Euro. Another source of risk is thus eliminated for most of intra-European capitals. But since capitalism has an inner trend of expansion that does not recognise economic or financial frontiers, the problem is put back on the picture. Can currency *derivatives* regulate the distributive struggle between commercial firms, multinational corporations and international finance capital?

More generally, considering the fundamental circuits of the *derivatives* subsystem, assuming post-Keynesianism is wrong and hedging is effective and relevant in *derivatives* circuits, one ferment of uncertainty is eliminated. But there remains the conflict about distribution that is based, internally in the national space with a national currency, or supranational in the Euro zone or in countries with foreign currency replacing the national one, on the level of interest rates and their changes over time. Hedging could smooth intra-capitalist class transfers or redistributions of income.

For Marx, the interest rate is not ruled by objective laws, unlike industrial profits. This adds to the uncertainty surrounding their levels and mainly the change in those very levels over time. Central banks can play a role, but they historically have sided with the banks and financial interests, in a very subtle way that imposes informal or formal rules on their influence over interest rates, reducing slightly the overall uncertainty about their levels and rhythm of change. When interest rates are stable and predictable, the division may be contested, but not too fiercely. Financialisation causes the interest rates to vary in a way that creates additional uncertainty not only about realising the surplus, but also its division between fractions of capital.

So, what has happened to gross revenues of banks with *derivatives*? The data in Chapter 4 show a completely disproportional share of interest rate instruments. Thus, *derivatives* are not only instruments to manage risks and provide hedge. They are instruments for boosting financialised incomes, including those of industrial capitals. That is, more than contributing to higher incomes through investment and growth, they bestow finance capital the tools to appropriate for itself a higher share of the national income, which is not growing as fast as during the modern phase of capitalism, probably because of financialisation and neo-liberalism reduced capital accumulation. And arrangements have been essential for that trend. LiPuma and Lee (2004) have a very good metaphor about financialised capitalism. *Derivatives* and risks are like a treadmill. Financialisation, with the support of neo-liberalism, magnify traditional risks and create additional new risks. And *derivatives* are sold as the solution. As the treadmill is the source of profits it cannot be stopped endogenously. Post-Keynesians believe that Big Government and Big Bank can slow it down. Marxists think that crises will crash the treadmill, before new ones are introduced.

Notes

1 Saber (1999b) emphasises *derivatives*' intrinsically speculative nature, proposing the concept of speculative capital. This characterisation is downplayed by Bryan and Rafferty (2006), for whom this issue is secondary. Hilferding (1981), on the other hand, discussed commodity futures as representing the basic capitalist spirit, that is, profit-seeking. So, speculation is not a distortion of capitalist virtues, but the averment of its inner trends. It is worth mentioning that any capitalist can speculate, as long as she has money available. Yet, with margins and premiums, generalised speculation with arrangements is unlikely without a huge chunk of money-capital. Collecting option premiums, mainly when options are not realised, can be also a source of income for finance capital.

2 It would not be difficult to conceive or design, or even claim any analogy as additional proof of the pervasiveness of *derivatives*, wage-indexed futures contracts similar to inflation-indexed instruments. Or bilateral forwards for wage adjustment rates having as 'underlying' companies' sales. Or productivity-wage swaps. Or call exit (or quit) options and put firing options. And suddenly, it is discovered that the labour contract for wages and benefits is actually a *derivative* having as the underlying the labour force performed (effort) reflected in the flow of commodities produced by it.

3 Santos (2008) exemplifies the difficulties associated with delivery when quantities are not centrally standardised by an exchange. Futures markets cannot work properly without centrally planned rules for contracts. In OTC markets, they are called Master Plans.

4 Saber (1999a) equally argues that speculative capital, by eliminating profitable arbitrage opportunities, has to rely increasingly in a higher volume of geared trades.

5 As mentioned before, Saber (1999a) quotes a study mentioning that, in the early days of the CME, futures trading in eggs and butter was about speculation, not hedging. Santos (2008) argues indeed that in the nineteenth century, producers, lay persons, legislators and courts distrusted futures, associating them with gambling and manipulation. He mentions the occurrence of many market corners of different grains, but it is not clear that futures were the tools employed to manipulate the trade. Nonetheless, many laws were passed to prohibit short sales and futures, only to be repealed soon after (Chapter 9). The

anti-option movement led to attempts of outlawing options along with futures. The anti-bucket shop controversy at that time also jeopardised the legitimacy (and local monopoly) of exchanges, like the CBOT. Saber (2017) considers the CBOT and CME to be bucket shops with enough capital.

6 Kalecki suffers here from the problem he identified about the confusion between stocks and flows, using capital and investment interchangeably.

7 Saber (1999a, p. 236) is harsh in his criticism of Stulz:

> The errors in this single paragraph – where credit capital, equity capital, derivatives, hedging and risk management are thrown into a confused mismatch – are industry standard when it comes to derivatives. In the context, the bizzare (sic) conclusion that follows is also natural. No other subject in economics and finance has generated so much incorrect theorizing and hypothesizing. (...) these errors in derivatives are the norm.

It is hard not to agree with Saber here. Yet, he contradictorily affirms that *derivatives*, by linking different markets via arbitrage, melts equity and debt.

8 In reality, liquidity trap and the zero interest rate lower bound must be revised after negative interest rates in Europe (see Mattos et al. 2019).

References

Bryan, Dick and Michael Rafferty. *Capitalism with Derivatives: A Political Economy of Financial Derivatives, Capital and Class*. New York: Palgrave Macmillan, 2006.

Chesnais, François. *Finance Capital Today*. Leiden: Brill, 2016.

Crotty, James. "The Centrality of Money, Credit and Financial Intermediation in Marx's Crisis Theory: An Interpretation of Marx's Methodology." In: James Crotty (ed.) *Capitalism, Macroeconomics and Reality*. Northampton: Edward Elgar, 2017: 72–106.

Davidson, Paul. *Money and Real World*. London: Macmillan, 1972.

Emm, Ekaterina E., Gerald D. Gay, and Honglin Ren. "Corporate Risk Exposures, Disclosure and Derivatives Use: A Longitudinal Study." *The Journal of Futures Markets* 39, no. 7 (2019): 838–864.

Hilferding, Rudolf. *Finance Capital: A Study in the Latest Phase of Capitalist Development*. London: Routledge and Kegan Paul, 1981.

Kalecki, Michal. "The Principle of Increasing Risk." *Economica,* New Series 4, no. 16 (1937): 440–447.

Keynes, John M. *The General Theory of Employment, Interest and Money*. London: Macmillan, 1936.

Keynes, John M. *A Tract on Monetary Reform*. London: Macmillan, 1923.

LiPuma, Edward; Benjamin Lee. *Financial Derivatives and the Globalisation of Risk*. Durham: Duke University Press, 2004.

Mader, Philip, Daniel Mertens, and Natasha van der Zwan (eds.) *The Routledge International Handbook of Financialization*. London/New York: Routledge, 2020.

Magdoff, Harry, and Paul Sweezy. *Estagnation and Financial Explosion*. New York: Monthly Review Press, 1987.

Marx, Karl. *Capital: A Critique of Political Economy*. Vol. 1. London: Penguin, 2004.

Mattos, Olivia B., Felipe D. Roz, Fernanda O. Ultremare, and Guilherme S. Mello. "Unconventional Monetary Policy and Negative Interest Rates: A Post-Keynesian Perspective on the Liquidity Trap and Euthanasia of the Rentier." *Review of Keynesian Economics* 7, no. 2 (2019): 185–200.

Milan, Marcelo. "Macrofinancial Risks and Liquidity Preference." *International Journal of Political Economy* 43, no. 1 (2014): 43–64.

Minsky, Hyman. *Can It Happen Again? Essays on Instability and Finance*. Nova York: M. E. Sharp, 1982.

Minsky, Hyman. *John Maynard Keynes*. Nova York: Columbia University Press, 1975.

Minsky, Hyman. *Stabilizing an Unstable Economy*. New Haven, CT: Yale University Press, 1986.

National Research Council (NRC). *Following the Money: U.S. Finance in the World Economy*. Washington, DC: The National Academies Press, 1995.

Palley, Thomas. *Financialization. The Economics of Finance Capital Domination*. New York/London: Palgrave Macmillan, 2013.

Picketty, Thomas. *Le Capital au XXIe Siècle*. Paris, Seuil, 2013.

Saber, Nasser. *Speculative Capital: The Invisible Hand of Global Finance*. Vol. 1. London: Financial Times/Prentice Hall, 1999.

Santos, Joseph. "A History of Futures Trading in the United States." *EH.Net Encyclopedia*, 2008. Available at https://eh.net/encyclopedia/a-history-of-futures-trading-in-the-united-states/ Retrieved April 2024.

Sotiropoulos, Dimitris P. "Hilferding on Derivatives." *The European Journal of the History of Economic Thought* 22, no. 1 (2012): 77–96.

Stockhammer, Engelbert. "Financialisation and the Slowdown of Accumulation." *Cambridge Journal of Economics* 28, no. 5 (2004): 719–741.

Stulz, René M. "Rethinking Risk Management." *Journal of Applied Corporate Finance* 9, no. 3 (1996): 8–24.

Troncoso, Joshua. "Time Traders: Derivatives, Minsky and a Reinterpretation of the Causes of the 2008 Global Financial Crisis." *Journal of Post Keynesian Economics* 42, no. 3 (2019): 469–486.

Conclusion

Derivatives, Finance Capital and the Transformation of Capitalism

It is now necessary to summarise the relationships between *derivatives*, finance capital and the transformation of mainly advanced, financialised capitalist economies. But before this summary is offered, it is important to highlight the gaps that need to be addressed in order for our understanding of *derivatives* to expand, on top of those already identified in Chapter 10. What is the missing research not considered here? It is immense. Without being exhaustive, it would be important to assess the differences in *derivatives* use by capitalist units located in different national spaces and the ones internationalised. And differences in national and regional regulations of *derivatives* and their impact on crises, accumulation strategies, income and wealth distribution and so on. This reflects the different national and regional velocities of financialisation.

From an empirical perspective, it is necessary to cross-exploit the existing databases. More archival research is needed to set firmer grounds about the real economic and financial history of specific arrangements to completely overcome the pseudo-pre-capitalist history of *derivatives*. The birth of *derivatives* as a concept also needs more investigation, mainly in the passage of the 1970s to the 1980s. And, of course, the history of economic and financial thought on the *derivatives* sub-system is much needed. It would also be necessary to widen the scope and extend the analysis to underdeveloped economies, assuming that they usually imitate the developed ones with a variable lag. Yet, since *derivatives* are mostly about U.S. financialised capitalism, it seems that additional research can shed light on the details, not on the overarching issues. There are also the perennial and fundamental gender aspects, as the authorship and agency related to *derivatives* research and practices have men at the centre. Finally, there is a gap concerning the concentration and centralisation of capital, as *derivatives* are a big bank game.

What are the conclusions implied by the research carried out? This book has three main conclusions based on the arguments, evidence and systematisation of research presented in the previous chapters. The first is, perhaps, the most ambitious. Contrary to many general works and even part of the specialised literature, it claims that *derivatives* as a collective concept should be considered a very recent *intellectual* development, with a short categorial history dating back to the beginning of the 1980s, but without an unfaltering ontological existence. Moreover, the

DOI: 10.4324/9781003137092-12

independent arrangements that came to be known as a single entity are actually stitched together by means of a myth, a dogma or at most a metaphor using other sciences or fields of knowledge in which there is a primary factor and an organically derived element whose existence, therefore, can only be imaginarily attributed to the former. But from an ontological point of view, *derivatives* as such do not exist as a real or material phenomenon in the sense that they could subsist independently of the mental exercises that postulate their existence, so it does not matter how many times the word has been repeated since the early 1980s. As the saying goes, if a falsity is only printed often enough, it becomes a quasi-truth, and if such a half-truth is repeated often enough, it becomes an article of faith. Thus, there are no effective transactions of buying and selling involving *derivatives* on par with those pertaining to specifically actual contracts like futures, forwards, options or swaps. But, according to Hegel, all that exists is rational. And the reason for the existence of *derivatives* as a concept is the ideological need of finance capital and financialised capitalism regarding risk management.

This mental category has been used, even by radical scholars, as an uncritical shortcut for simplifying a complex sub-system, characterised by a web of institutions and very different instruments. All related to economic and financial stocks and flows of profits and losses that redistribute incomes and wealth. But actually, the arrangements cannot share totally common features to the point of making them perfect substitutes that would justify the idealistic or metaphysical concept. Worse yet, many times the professionals use the collective term to refer to individual or specific kinds of contracts that have unique features.

The exercise of sorting them out by the literature into forward-type and option-type instruments is in itself evidence that there are different forms and that they should not be lumped together if a rigorous treatment is sought. Even when only the four plain vanilla instruments are considered, it is impossible to identify a common denominator without mischaracterising the parts of this pseudo-whole. Contingent claims, for example, one of the initial names mobilised to summarise these transactions, are broader in scope, representing more than arrangements lumped together as *derivatives*, but sharing the feature of being conditional and thus pertaining to the same financial sub-system.

The lack of a consensual and universally accepted definition of *derivatives* (Chapter 1) can be explained by this absence of a common attribute other than instruments for financial profits in a context of risks industrially manufactured under financialised capitalism. By the same token, risk transfers cannot be a shared attribute, since risks can be shifted by other mechanisms that are not *derivatives*, like insurance. As a consequence, even today, after more than a couple of centuries that the particular instruments have been used, there is an insufficient methodological development to classify, measure and synthesise the components of *derivatives*, even from an accounting perspective, at the private realm and at the national statistics. Nobody can know what *derivatives* are when the specific arrangements are considered jointly (Chapter 2).

When it comes to the history of the particular arrangements, on the other hand, the factual evidence or pieces of evidence are about either transactions or deeds that are, at best, similar to operations that centuries later came to be forcefully identified as *derivatives*, in a major teleological projection. In many unreflective historical accounts discussed in Chapter 5, anything that involves the postponement of delivery is identified by hurried interpretations as a *derivative*, in a clear confusion with typical delayed commercial transactions. And there are indeed historical records of transactions that involve proto-forms of arrangements that are part of what today is mistakenly called *derivatives*, but that, of course, did not exist as such back then. Another major problem with the '*derivatives* always existed' reading is the existence of long time intervals without the documented existence of such contracts or informal arrangements. The narrative is full of historical holes that jeopardises the pre-capitalist *derivatives* historical hypothesis. That is, *derivatives* started in ancient societies, disappeared during the Middle Ages and were resumed during the seventeenth century in Europe and a century later in Japan. When arrangements were last reintroduced under modern capitalism, the institutional environment followed, with the rise of the exchanges. This could not have happened in the previous appearances, since these instruments are part of modern and mainly contemporary capitalism and its financialisation trend.

This has a major ideological appeal that trade and profit motivation have been universal features of human beings. Adam Smith's natural "propensity to truck, barter, and exchange", since "nobody ever saw a dog make a fair and deliberate exchange of one bone for another with another dog" is retrieved as a *moto perpetuum*. This can only mean that dogs never fully realised the advantages of swapping long bones for shorter ones in multiple settlement moons. *Derivatives*, in these narratives, have been around for 4,000 years and are old. At the same time, there is the contradictory approval of innovation (new) and creativity (creation). Many advocates of *derivatives* share the view that they represent a revolution, a singular innovation. In Chapter 5, four conditions were considered for the existence of pre-capitalist *derivatives*: existence, uses, institutional backing and socio-economic importance. No one was satisfied.

In order to make sense of these confusing views based on inappropriate narratives and set the record straight, we proposed a division of the economic, rather than financial, history of these instruments. There were no *derivatives* in ancient or medieval societies, not even proto-forms. Isolated instruments and proto-forms appeared in the transition from mercantilism to capitalism with the rise of the merchant class, and so they are associated with commodities and commerce. As a consequence, there are specific arrangements associated with deferred delivery that comprise the modern 'pre-*derivatives* era'. The commodities' circuits developed contracts to increase the length of time to complete the transaction.

However, cash settlement has been an enduring feature of even commodity *derivatives*, showing actually a proto-financialised economy. As a consequence, the specific contracts that are today called *derivatives* are an offspring of contemporary capitalism, in particular during its financialised stage after the 1970s. They are therefore new, contemporary phenomena. And it occurred not often, but gradually. Swaps were not part of the instruments until the 1980s, even though they could be synthesised from forwards. Credit *derivatives* were introduced only in the 1990s. This is again reflected in the institutional setting, with the consolidation of OTC transactions. Of course, the ontological non-existence is reflected in the phenomenological realm discussed in Chapter 6. There are not and there could not be reflections about *derivatives* or their components for most of the recorded written history. The concept was probably coined at the beginning of the 1980s.

The second conclusion, and in accordance with the previous claim, *derivatives* are about finance capital, in the United States in particular, although, if one accepts the discussion carried out in the initial chapters, this is not enough to call them financial *derivatives*. Throughout most of history, financial instruments properly, that is, associated specifically with financial rather than economic in general transactions, associated with financing production and circulation, represented a small portion of the total transactions. Commodities were the most important reference for contracts until the 1970s but lost space in the circuits.

The deregulation and liberalisation trends intensified in the 1980s and 1990s (Chapter 9), but without touching the new arrangements, representing a major transformation in capitalism, with risks, whose nature and scale changed, being continuously manufactured, and, with it, a change in *derivatives*. First, in terms of instruments, with the creation or development of swaps that came to dominate the sub-system and, next, credit instruments. Second, in terms of the capitals involved in the transactions, with finance replacing productive and mainly merchant capital, including cross-border flows. Equity *derivatives*, on the other hand, have not been relevant and only stresses the speculative nature of these arrangements.

Hence, modern and contemporary arrangements are strongly associated with financial earnings, capital gains and speculation, not with hedge or any other advantageous function claimed by many advocates (Chapter 7). There is strong evidence in the literature that firms do not hedge with *derivatives*. And that even financial institutions do not seem to hedge using *derivatives* like swaps either. They engage in *derivatives* for trading and earning profits. The circuits are dominated by large U.S. banks (Chapter 4).

Do these financial institutions provide useful services to end-users of *derivatives*, as claimed by its advocates? If this is indeed the case, why capital accumulation in the United States has not recovered to the levels seen during the Golden Age under modern capitalism and has fallen as a share of GDP instead? As Chapter 4 shows, *derivatives* circuits show a growth pattern out of pace with real flows and other stocks even if they add to large financial incomes and the financial sector has gained more and more importance in GDP.

Thus, in the United States, most *derivatives* contracts are related to interest rates. It is about finance capital and it is about money over time. Interest is the typical income of rentiers. They are also part of bank revenues and gross expenses of non-financialised non-financial firms, households and governments. If the claim about *derivatives* allowing risk management and expansion of investment projects is valid, then one should be observing an enlarged circuit of capital accumulation since the 1970s, with more risk-averse capitalists entering it through capital expenditures , and the extant capitalists boosting the scale of their operations. In other words, GDP growth rates should be higher since then. But the 1970s marked the end of the Golden Age and modern capitalism in the West. And to the extent that Asia presents today a more dynamic economic outlook, mainly China and India, is by other means, like managed exchange rates and state-owned banks, an environment in which *derivatives* cannot thrive.

Risks are inherent in capitalism (Chapter 3). This is consensual. But the understanding of their meaning depends on the perspective mobilised and thus their consequences are not at all agreeable. In economics, the effects of such developments are better captured by heterodox approaches like those of the Monthly School, Marx, Hilferding, Kalecki, Keynes and Minsky, besides many critical scholars (Chapter 10). Cash settlement is an evidence that even commodity instruments are not related to the real production of tangible commodities or intangible non-financial commodities. This finalistic monetary settlement is best captured by the Marxist notion of a money nexus without commodity intermediation, with money turning into capital by the circuit with arrangements A: M – A – M′. And in many *derivatives* transactions, the full initial M is not required, adding a new layer of gearing but also of fictitiousness.

Heterodox views discuss risks in the context of a capitalist economy, not as ethereal categories. And understand finance and the role of *derivatives* in reinforcing the trend of income and wealth concentration towards finance capital. It is different to understand *derivatives* under a contemporary, financialised capitalist society, under a modern, real production capitalist society and under proto-forms in pre-capitalist societies characterised by the village fair or even during the transition to capitalism. This interpretation raises doubts about the views of advocates, which highlight the importance, necessity and advantages of *derivatives* to fractions of non-financial capital in capitalist societies (Chapter 7). And, of course, the heterodox view is based on a critical account of *derivatives* due to their failures in delivering net added value to non-financial capitalists.

The third conclusion is that the necessity of trying to save capitalism has changed the *derivatives* sub-system as well. So, regulation of *derivatives* has changed a lot if we consider the U.S. experience alone (Chapter 9). One consequence of the second proposed contribution described above is the necessity of better regulatory norms and laws, in line with post-Keynesians. Since the direct or indirect contribution of *derivatives* to the eruption of crises has become more frequent (Chapter 8), regulation or lack of appropriate constraints has been a recurrent concern.

However, there has been no major finance-originated systemic crisis since the sub-prime mortgage collapse in 2008. It is another research that must be carried out. This does not mean that financial problems associated with *derivatives* have disappeared at all, including banking losses and exchanges or clearing houses near bankruptcy. But most of the constraints imposed by recent legislation, like the Dodd–Frank Act, considers moving OTC transactions to exchanges to be the contract makers, or adopting clearing houses. Yet, the magnitude of the individual losses, not to mention systemic problems, can bring even the larger clearing houses close to collapse, summoning the big government to the rescue, with taxes and bailouts, and the big central bank's last resort liquidity operations, and so on.

Thus, *derivatives* or the arrangements that are identified under this false umbrella have indeed brought an important, slow transformation of capitalism in the transition from its modern, commodity-dominant, to its contemporary, financialised phase. Of course, no single fraction of capital, be it financial, commercial or industrial, and within it the distinct concrete forms assumed, can be a single causal factor in rapidly changing such a complex and comprehensive socioeconomic structure, increasingly transitioning into a conjuncture. But they can gradually affect the direction and rhythm of capital accumulation, surplus creation and redistribution, and also contributing to and magnifying crises that stimulate institutional change.

So, *derivatives* transform capitalism. Yet, *derivatives* have also been transformed by the changes in capitalism, including the changes brought about by them. For instance, the introduction of swaps in the 1980s and credit *derivatives* in the 1990s, to mention just two, are a consequence of changes brought about the new dynamics of capitalism, especially in the United States, in the preceding years, including the role of the other forms of *derivatives*. Finance capital increases the number of its concrete forms, inaugurating new circuits of valorisation of fictitious capitals and realisation of profits.

Under financialised capitalist conditions, risks are pervasive and created by the regular functioning or malfunctioning of financial valorisation, accumulation and reproduction. Therefore, hedging seems to become necessary on the aggregate, which does not mean it is effective, when rentiers and speculators change the rates of intra-capitalist transfers of income, increasing their own share in detriment of other forms and fractions of capital. A consequence is a defensive position entertained by other capitals.

But there is a clear historical sequence, starting with speculation reining free by deregulation and liberalisation. Volatility then increases, that is, geared speculation does not stabilise circuits. It rather brings additional instability. Capitals driven to longer-term profits lose organisational capacity, since their time horizon is plagued by uncertainty. Part of them turns to financial speculation for rapid profits, reinforcing financialisation. The other part has to protect the phases of its circuit regarding money, commodity, production, commodity bearing surplus and increased money, from magnified transfers to financial capitalists and rentiers. But the problem is that they might seek hedge, not always effective as such, in the very circuits and subsystem where they have a disadvantage. Not to mention frauds.

Thus, they face the 'free' choice of losing money in the spot or cash market associated with the volatile flows tied with their assets and liabilities, or try to limit them in the *derivatives* circuits. To the extent that instability is permanent under this configuration, and this is what is employed to justify *derivatives*, they would have to keep continuously transacting in *derivatives* circuits, with a stream of fees and net negative cash settlements to financial capital. If end-users leave the *derivatives* circuits, the struggle becomes internal to finance, with larger institutions concentrating and centralising the sub-system by fusions and acquisitions. *Derivatives* are about U.S. largest banks' financial needs.

How was capitalism transformed by *derivatives*? They reinforced the instability and mainly capital becoming more fictitious. Or was it that *derivatives* reflected a fundamental change in the competition for profits, enhancing a trend of bolstered financial accumulation, with financial capitalists taking the lead? The pervasive latent trend is the one described by M – A – M′. This implies cash settlement, overpassing commodities ownership, even during the heyday of commodity futures trading. Have *derivatives* been transformed by financialised capitalism? Yes, by regulation and innovation, with the introduction of swaps and credit *derivatives*, but the latter are small, even though they fundamentally contributed to the 2007–2008 sub-prime crisis.

The focus on money transfers is another way to approach distribution of income and wealth. *Derivatives* are about finance and fictitious capital. From finance capital, by finance capital to finance capital. Commercial and industrial capitals are negligible in this circuit of valorisation and transference. *Derivatives* and capitalism have a dialectical relationship. Capitalism actively transforms the remaining capitals not destroyed by impersonal forces of profit-seeking and crises. The latter are the result of reduced profits continuously searching for gearing through on and mainly off-balance sheet values. The transformation of surviving capitals is carried out by their dialectical relationship with the state,with regulation temporarily replacing capitalist freedom.

The state compensates the destruction of capital and at the same time deregulates finance, causing risks in general and financial risks in particular to skyrocket, pressing for re-regulation. The innovation in accumulation and valorisation is basically a specific arrangement to deal with those risks, which boost fictitious capitals. This creates counter forces in the form of crises by means of Schumpeterian-like 'destructive creation', which end up transforming passively the U.S. capitalism, with the introduction of innovations to solve the problems created by the previous innovations, but also by state regulation, deregulation and re-regulation. Thus, *derivatives* influence how surplus and fictitious profits are created and mainly distributed, creating fragility and frequent crises, but without destruction of capital or with destruction only in notional terms – paper losses alone, soon offset by central banks and governments.

So far, severe financial and economic crises, whose occurrence cannot any longer be separated from *derivatives*, to a greater or lesser extent absorbed by Minsky's big bank and big government paradigm (Chapter 10), have not been able to offer a strong motivation for gradually eliminating them. Regulation is always and dialectically lagging behind and not necessarily effective, notwithstanding the absence of major financial disruptions in the advanced capitalist nations since the sub-prime mortgage crisis.

The euthanasia of the rentier, which represents the collapse of *derivatives*, is still a distant chimera. And since hedging is definitely not the goal of those arrangements, reducing instability and volatility in the so-called underlying spot markets will not do the job. In the long run, by means of cumulative changes, capitalism has been profoundly transformed by *derivatives*, with a hefty thrust to financialisation and instability. And *derivatives* have been at best mildly modified by systemic capitalist crises, many of which they had contributed to. Perhaps, and only perhaps, a paradigmatic crisis or breakdown can partially overhaul the existing financialised capitalism, while the impending climate crises finish the rest, with weather *derivatives* gaining false momentum and perspectives of solution.

Index

Note: Endnotes are indicated by the page number followed by "n" and the note number e.g., 111n5 refers to note 5 on page 111.

For Product Safety Concerns and Information please contact our EU
representative GPSR@taylorandfrancis.com
Taylor & Francis Verlag GmbH, Kaufingerstraße 24, 80331 München, Germany

www.ingramcontent.com/pod-product-compliance
Lightning Source LLC
LaVergne TN
LVHW010650300926
849161LV00005B/1088
* 9 7 8 0 3 6 7 6 8 3 5 2 8 *